THE WAR IN MEXICO

by
ANTON ADAMS

COLOR PLATES BY
MIKE GILBERT

THE EMPEROR'S PRESS
Chicago, Illinois

Original Edition; Published in 1998

ISBN 1-883476-08-9

Printed and Bound in the United States of America
by Print Systems, Grand Rapids, Michigan

Color Plates by Mike Gilbert

Maps by Anton Adams, Anton J. Adams & R. E. Lee

Color Flags by Kim Sampin

Black & White Flags by David McElhannon

The Emperor's Press
5744 West Irving Park Road
Chicago, Illinois 60634 U.S.A.
Telephone 773-777-7307

TABLE OF CONTENTS

Dedication

to Meghan, Mariah, Michelle and Colleen, their mother

PREFACE

The military history of the Mexican-American War is not very well known today by students in either the United States or Mexico. This is true despite the fact that the men who fought in the war, especially the Americans, wrote quite a bit about their experiences at the time. The typical history class may touch on the political issues and causes of the conflict and most likely will end by showing how much territory was lost by Mexico and gained by the United States. The term 'Manifest Destiny' is usually brought up but includes much more than the story of the Mexican War.

The main reason given for the relative obscurity of the Mexican-American War is that it is overshadowed both by the Revolution that preceded it and the major war that came after. The Texas Revolution and the legend of the Alamo occurred only ten years before the war and can legitimately be claimed as the beginning of many of the problems between Mexico and the United States. The American Civil War began just thirteen years after the end of the Mexican conflict which, in retrospect, had served as a training ground for the generals of the much larger and longer war between the North and South.

The armies and the battles of the Texas Revolution harkened back to the days of the American Revolution itself some fifty odd years previously. A ragged militia of a newly formed Republic standing up to the regular army of a despotic state. Although the adventurers, outcasts and opportunists of Sam Houston's army may not compare well with the minutemen of Colonial America, fortunately for them the Mexicans were not British redcoats either. The story of the Alamo, along with Bowie, Crockett, Travis and Santa Anna is one of the most well known in American history.

The American Civil War has often been described as the first modern war that introduced the concept of "total war" the way that we understand it today. The Union and the Confederacy utilized all of the new technologies available for waging war and they mobilized their national economies to do so. The student of history today cannot help but learn the causes and effects of the War between the States. The Civil War is recognized today as one of the most important events in the history of the United States.

The Mexican-American War bridges the gap between these two events and has something in common with both of them. In 1846 the Americans would once again fight a larger Mexican Army, but this time it was with a well trained professional army of regular soldiers later supplemented by State volunteers. The junior officers, mostly graduates of the Military Academy at West Point, would acquire valuable experience during the course of the war that they would put to use throughout their careers. Many of these men would end up leading the soldiers of the Civil War as Generals in command of brigades, divisions, corps and armies.

The final results of the Mexican-American War are common knowledge among students of history. The United States would be successful in battle and gain control from Mexico over much of what is currently the American Southwest. The loss of the war by Mexico would result in the continued turmoil and instability in government that they had known since gaining independence from Spain. The story of how these events came to pass and what actually happened on the battlefields in Mexico is not as well known.

The purpose of this book is to explore some of the aspects of the military history of the Mexican-American War that are not dealt with in many other sources. In addition to describing where and when the battles took place, every effort has been made to accurately portray what the soldiers looked like and to explain how the armies actually fought. The data presented for the orders of battle includes the armies of both sides and is as complete as possible. While this information may be more extensive than can be found in any other single source, it does not claim to be an exhaustive study of the subject. Biographical sketch material has been included to give the reader a better idea of the cast of characters involved and how many of them went on to become major participants in the American Civil War that followed. This vast collection of names and dates does not purport to be the last word on the subject, but it should provide the serious student a solid foundation that can be built upon. The maps used here have all been based on the original battlefield surveys performed by the American engineers in Mexico. They include among their ranks Robert E. Lee, George B. McClellan, Joseph E. Johnston, George Meade, P. G. T. Beauregard and John C. Fremont among others. Many relevant photographs have also been included to further illuminate the subject materials. In the final analysis, this is the book that I would have liked to have had when I began my research into this war more than ten years ago.

The information gathered together here has been found in a myriad of different sources originating from both sides of the Rio Grande, although the barriers of distance, language and the scarcity of Mexican writing on the subject have resulted in an emphasis on the American point of view. Many of the source materials that were used, including several Spanish language editions, were made available through the Interlibrary Loan at the Addison Public Library whose staff was always very

helpful, for which I thank them. I must also thank Terry D. Hooker, the President and Founder of The South and Central American Military Historians Society and Editor of its newsletter "El Dorado". He generously provided me with copies of some of the original Mexican uniform decrees for references. I would also like to thank Ken Bunger for an inspection of source materials unavailable to me, Duane Warnecke for providing me with some difficult to obtain articles, and to Keith Cantine in Lexington, Kentucky, for researching the Sate flags. I would like to thank my father, Anton J. Adams for his help with the maps, and my mother, Jeannine for moral support. I would like to thank Mike Gilbert for his patience and willingness to work with me on the uniform plates for the book. Thank you also to Kim Sampin for her help with flags. I want to thank Todd Fisher of Emperor's Press for all his help, without which this book would not have seen print. Despite all of the help and encouragement I have received, clearly any errors or omissions are solely my responsibility as the author.

INTRODUCTION

The Mexican-American War, known in the United States simply as the Mexican War, and in Mexico as the War of North American Intervention, was a critical one for both the United States and Mexico. Hindsight suggests that the war could have been avoided, and indeed many people on both sides did attempt to avoid going to war. But, in the end, a serious lack of understanding of their neighbor by both countries made this conflict inevitable.

The *History of the Conquest of Mexico* by William H. Prescott was published in 1843 and it brought Mexico to the attention of the American public as nothing else at the time could have. Before this the southern neighbor of the United States was little known except as a strange and mysterious land where the customs were antiquated and the inhabitants poor. The American soldiers that marched into Mexico discovered a land of many contrasts and a culture completely different from the one to which they were accustomed. The Mexicans were seen as inferior by many Americans. Their old world heritage being from Spain and having, by association, Moorish attributes, was seen as contributing to a weakness of character and moral values. This attitude seemed to be confirmed by the firsthand experiences of the soldiers who pronounced Mexican customs inferior upon comparison with their own simply because they were different. Despite this initial prejudice, the soldiers did manage to learn to appreciate many facets of Mexican culture and their horizons were broadened by their experiences in a foreign land.

The soldiers wrote home about Mexico and the war was reported in the press more extensively than any other war had been up to that time. The people at home followed the course of events closely and used their copies of Prescott's book as a guide to the country, as did the soldiers on campaign. The Americans convinced themselves that what they were doing was for the good of the Mexican people. The Americans claimed that they were not making war on the people of Mexico, only their leaders. The corruption that was rampant in the Mexican government and the army confirmed the fact for the American soldiers that the Mexican people were oppressed and would be glad to be liberated from these dishonest institutions. The American people had no trouble at all undertaking this noble task as it was their "manifest destiny" to spread their civilization and culture throughout the continent from the Atlantic to the Pacific. They saw themselves as the hope of the future for all of mankind.

Mexicans admired some of the same ideals and principles upon which the United States had been founded. Many believed that American methods and institutions might work in Mexico as well. There was a 'peace' faction in the government that wished to maintain friendly relations between the two countries if at all possible. Unfortunately, since gaining independence from Spain, Mexico had been burdened with a government that was totally dependent upon the military. In times of crisis or political turmoil one or more new 'candidates' for the job of El Presidente would 'pronounce' for the office with the support of their local generals and accompanying regiments and march on the capital to seize the reins of power. That was not the way the system was supposed to work, but that is the way it had been for the past two decades. With this system a Mexican president could not even appear to be weak, especially when it came to dealing with a foreign power. Failure to uphold and further the interests of Mexican nationalism and patriotism could mean the end of a President's term. The corruption that infested every aspect of Mexican politics allowed almost any deal to be made as long as appearances were maintained and 'face' was saved by those involved so as not to be connected publicly to any distasteful acts or policies.

The attitude of Mexico towards the United States underwent a change during the Texas Revolution. The tacit approval given by the United States to the rebels in Texas, even though the government maintained official neutrality, was evidence enough for most Mexicans to distrust the motives of their northern neighbor. The proposed annexation of Texas by the United States eight years later removed any doubts that Mexico had of hostile intentions. The Mexicans began to fear the intrigues of the Americans and were wary of the application of force that was being brought to bear against them. The only recourse for the leaders of Mexico was to oppose any settlement of the issues that called for concessions to the Americans. Resistance to the United States was the only common ground among Mexican politicians. When the administration of President James K. Polk began to offer solutions to the Texas border problem and other claims against

Mexico that included the transfer of Mexican territory to the United States, it was a solution that was impossible for the Mexican leadership to accept. The hardliners in the government concluded that war with the United States was the only alternative.

President Polk had done everything possible up to this time to settle any disputes with Mexico peacefully. The Mexican government broke off diplomatic relations with the United States in March of 1845 when it became clear that the Americans had decided to annex Texas. To make matters worse, the Texans claimed their natural boundary as the Rio Grande River while the Mexicans always understood it to be the Nueces River. The summer months saw Mexico preparing for immediate war with state and federal troops being called out, money being borrowed for arms and ammunition and new guns being mounted in fortresses on the coast. Fortunately, by the fall Mexican tempers had cooled a bit and this allowed President Polk to try diplomacy to resolve the dispute.

The Texas question was not the only issue on the table with Mexico. Claims against her by United States citizens in amounts exceeding six million dollars had been filed with an international tribunal which had reduced the amount to some two million dollars to be paid with interest by Mexico. The initial payments had been made for the first year and then Mexico defaulted on them. In addition to these problems, the United States desired to extend its boundaries to the Pacific Ocean by acquiring California from Mexico. This was a goal for which the Americans were trying to negotiate a deal and were willing to pay good money when the Texas problem arose.

The Polk administration sent John Slidell as the new minister to Mexico to try to smooth over relations and make the Mexicans an offer that they would not refuse. The United States was ready to assume all claims by its own citizens against Mexico and pay them off in return for acceptance of the Rio Grande boundary for Texas. In addition an offer of graduated payments in excess of forty million dollars was authorized in return for territories, including western New Mexico and all of California north of Monterey, to be sold to the United States. Slidell was given the power to negotiate these terms and was to start out offering only about half of the total amount authorized, which many thought the Mexicans would feel was adequate payment.

The cash strapped government of President Jose Joaquin de Herrera was actually willing to negotiate. Herrera did not want a war with the United States but the war faction in the capital was very vocal and exerted a great deal of pressure. So Herrera made proclamations of hostility and preparations to fight while he sought for a way to end the dispute peacefully. Herrera realized that Texas was already

a lost cause to Mexico. Several attempts over the last ten years had kept the borders aflame with war and spilled the blood of hundreds on both sides but had failed to bring the rebellious state back into the fold. California was another Texas just waiting to happen. Mexican claims of ownership were in name only. The Mexican governor, General Manuel Micheltorena had been driven out in February of 1845 and the insurrectionist regime under Pio Pico was in control. The last thing that the *Californios* wanted was to be ruled by distant politicians in Mexico. To negotiate with the Americans over these issues would be to admit that Mexico's claims were not as valid as she originally made them out to be. When word of Slidell's mission leaked out cries of 'traitor' came from extremists and opponents of Herrera who wanted war with the United States.

Slidell's major misunderstanding resulted from a faulty translation of the desires expressed by the Mexican foreign minister Juan N. Almonte. The Mexicans would receive a commissioner to settle existing disputes but would not accept a new minister which would reopen official diplomatic relations and possibly invalidate Mexican claims to Texas. But if Slidell accepted a reduced role for his own mission his own powers to negotiate would be compromised. As it turned out, Slidell's arrival in Mexico City in December of 1845 could not have come at a worse time for the Herrera government. The Mexican Council rejected Slidell's credentials and refused to receive him. Slidell backed off to Jalapa and complained of the bad faith of the Mexicans and their unwillingness to cooperate. Meanwhile Herrera tried to win some public support for a peaceful policy of reconciliation but it was of no use. In mid-December General Mariano Paredes y Arrillaga issued a *pronunciamiento* from San Luis Potosi against the Herrera government and marched on Mexico City with the Army of the North to take over the reins of power. On December 29 Herrera left the capital with Paredes only twelve miles away. With Paredes in power chances of a peaceful settlement were now remote. He assured the Mexican people and the hardliners in the army and government that the integrity of their territory would remain intact. This resulted in a stalemate with neither government able to give ground without looking weak to their constituencies.

The Polk administration was alarmed and surprised when the news reached Washington but the President lost no time in ordering Taylor's army to the Rio Grande. His orders were to maintain America's claim to the disputed territory and to act as a deterrent to the use of force by the Mexican army but not to consider Mexico an enemy unless she committed the first overt act of war. Polk was criticized for this move by those who claimed that it was too aggressive and forced Mexico's hand, but if the American army had not occupied the area Texas would most likely have lost all claim to it. Diplomacy was given one more chance with Slidell submitting a new application for recognition in early March but it was already too late. The news of Taylor's army moving to the Rio Grande, which had been designed to push the Mexicans towards negotiations had instead committed them more than ever to war.

The U.S. Army on the march, by James Walker

THE WAR IN MEXICO

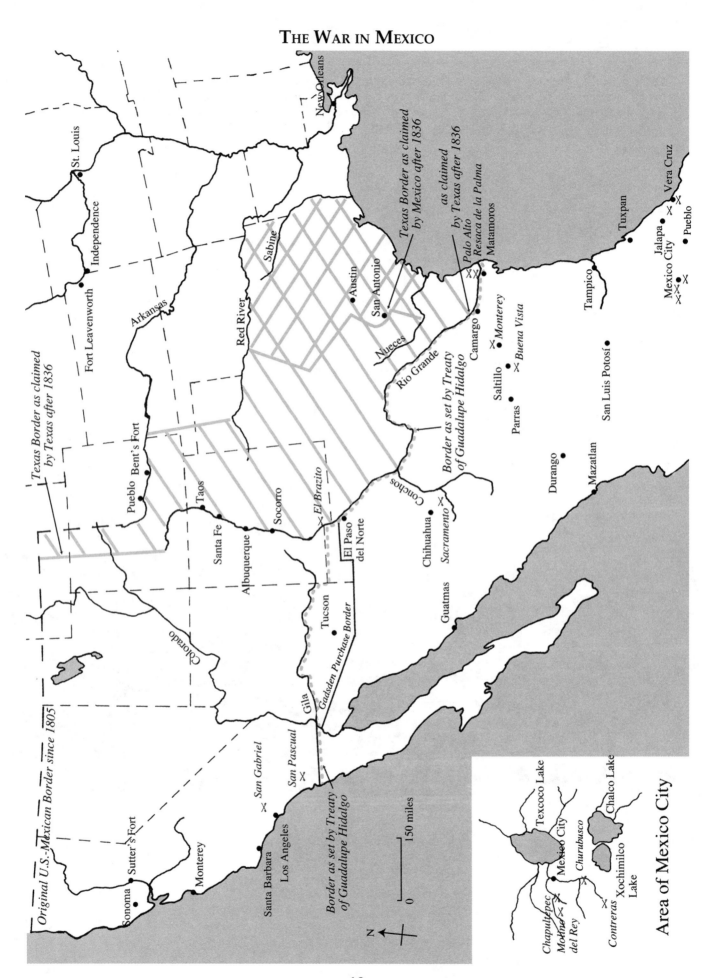

St. Louis

Independence

Fort Leavenworth

Arkansas

Red River

Sabine

New Orleans

Texas Border as claimed by Texas after 1836

Texas Border as claimed by Mexico after 1836

as claimed by Texas after 1836

Austin

San Antonio

Palo Alto
Resaca de la Palma
Matamoros

Nueces

Camargo

Monterey

Buena Vista

Rio Grande

Border as set by Treaty of Guadalupe Hidalgo

Saltillo

Parras

San Luis Potosí

Tuxpan

Tampico

Vera Cruz

Jalapa

Mexico City

Pueblo

Texas Border as claimed by Texas after 1836

Pueblo   Bent's Fort

Taos

Socorro

Santa Fe

Albuquerque

Colorado

El Brazito

Conchos

El Paso
del Norte

Chihuahua

Sacramento

Guatmas

Durango

Mazatlan

Tucson

Gadsden Purchase Border

Gila

Original U.S.-Mexican Border since 1805

San Gabriel

San Pascual

Sutter's Fort

Sonoma

Monterey

Santa Barbara

Los Angeles

Border as set by Treaty of Guadalupe Hidalgo

150 miles

0

N

Area of Mexico City

Texcoco Lake

Mexico City

Chalco Lake

Churubusco

Chapultepec

Molino
del Rey

Contreras

Xochimilco
Lake

10

CHRONOLOGY OF THE WAR

1835
June 30   Texas settlers revolt against Mexican rule

1836
February 23-
March 6   Siege and assault on the Alamo by the Mexican Army under General Antonio Lopez de Santa Anna.
April 21   Battle of San Jacinto; Sam Houston's victory over Santa Anna ends Texas Revolution.
July 4   United States recognizes the Republic of Texas

1842
October 19   Commodore Thomas ap C. Jones in the frigate *United States* seizes the port of Monterey, California while under the impression that the U.S. has gone to war with Mexico.

1844
November 2   James K. Polk elected tenth President of the United States
December 6   Antonio Lopez de Santa Anna deposed as President of Mexico

1845
March 4   President James K. Polk inaugurated
March 24   Commodore John D. Sloat takes over as commander of the U.S. Pacific Squadron
March 31   Mexico breaks diplomatic relations with the United States
June 15   General Zachary Taylor order to move his army into Texas
July 4   Texas accepts annexation to the United States
July 25   General Zachary Taylor arrives at St. Joseph's Island near Corpus Christi, TX with his Corps of Observation
September 14   Jose Joaquin de Herrera elected President of Mexico
September 16   John Slidell appointed as new minister to Mexico
December 9   Captain John C. Fremont arrives at Sutter's Fort, Alta California
December 29   Texas admitted as the 28th state of the United States
December 31   Herrera deposed as President of Mexico

1846
January 4   Mariano Paredes y Arrillaga becomes President of Mexico
January 13   Taylor's army ordered to the Rio Grande
March 8   Taylor's army leaves Corpus Christi, TX
March 28   Taylor's army arrives at the Rio Grande opposite Matamoros as the Army of Occupation
April 25   Captain Seth Thornton's patrol of the 2nd Dragoons ambushed and captured at Carricitos Ranch, TX
May 8   Battle of Palo Alto
May 9   Battle of Resaca de la Palma (Resaca de la Guerrero)
May 13   The United States declares war on Mexico
May 14   Blockade proclaimed against Mexican ports of Alvarado, Matamoros, Tampico and Vera Cruz
May 17-18   General Mariano Arista evacuates Matamoros
June 5   Colonel Stephen W. Kearney and the Army of the West begin to leave Fort Leavenworth, Kansas for Santa Fe
June 15   Oregon treaty signed between Britain and the U.S.
July 1   Mexico declares war on the United States
July 4   Bear Flag Republic declared at Sonoma, Alta California
July 7   Monterey, California occupied by Commodore Sloat with a naval landing party
July 9   Naval landing party occupies San Francisco, California
July 14   American army under Taylor occupies Camargo
July 19   Bear Flag Republic ends as Fremont is mustered into U.S. service at Monterey, California
July 29   Command of the Pacific Squadron transferred from Commodore Sloat to Commodore Robert F. Stockton; San Diego, California seized by a naval landing party and garrisoned by men under Fremont

THE WAR IN MEXICO

August 6	General Mariano Salas becomes acting President of Mexico after Paredes is deposed; Marine landing party seizes San Pedro, California
August 7	Unsuccessful attack on Alvarado by elements of the Home Squadron
August 13	Los Angeles occupied by Commodore Stockton with naval landing party
August 14	Mexican forces in Alta California surrender
August 16	Santa Anna arrives at Vera Cruz under order of safe passage from U.S.
August 17	Kearny occupies Santa Fe, New Mexico with the Army of the West
September 2	Landing party at San Blas spikes 24 cannon; blockade declared at San Blas
September 3	Commander Samuel F. Du Pont, the captain of the *Cyane* captures the Mexican sloop *Solita* and the brigantine *Susana* off San Blas
September 14	*Cyane* captures Mexican brigantines *Correo*, *La Paz*, and *Manuela*, schooners *Adelaide*, *Eliza*, *Julia*, *Mazolea* and *Victoria* and the sloop *San Jose* at La Paz, Baja California
September 20	Battle of Monterrey, Nuevo Leon
September 25	General Wool departs San Antonio with American Army of the Center for Chihuahua; Kearny departs Santa Fe, headed for California
September 30	Gillespie surrenders Los Angeles to Flores
October 1	*Cyane* captures Mexican schooners *Fortuna* and *Libertad* at Loreto, Baja California
October 2	*Cyane* captures the Mexican schooner *Rosita* at Loreto, Baja California
October 4	*Cyane* captures Mexican sloops *Alerto* and *Chapita* at Muleje, Baja California
October 6	Kearny and the Army of the West meet Kit Carson with news of the fall of California
October 7	*Cyane* launches a boat expedition at the harbor of Guaymas and burns the Mexican brig *Condor* and the gunboats *Anahuac* and *Sonorese*
October 15	Second assault on Alvarado made by Commodore Conner
October 23	Commodore Perry seizes Frontera, Mexico at the mouth of the Tabasco River
October 25	Commodore Perry captures Tabasco
November 14	Commodore Conner occupies Tampico with 300 man landing party
November 16	General Taylor occupies Saltillo
November 18	Major General Winfield Scott appointed to command expedition to Vera Cruz

November 23	Scott leaves Washington for Mexico; Kearny learns of the uprising in California
December 6	Battle of San Pascual, near San Diego, CA; Santa Anna elected President of Mexico
December 12	Kearny arrives at San Diego, CA
December 14	Doniphan leaves Santa Fe and heads for Chihuahua with the 1st Missouri Mounted Volunteers
December 21	Wool's army unites with Taylor at Saltillo
December 23	Santa Anna becomes the new President of Mexico, after Salas is ousted. Gomez Farias is his Vice-President
December 25	Battle at El Brazito
December 27	El Paso occupied by Doniphan; General Scott reaches Brazos Santiago

1847

January 3	Scott arrives at Camargo
January 8	Battle of San Gabriel near Los Angeles, CA
January 9	Battle of La Mesa, CA
January 10	Kearny and Stockton retake Los Angeles, CA
January 13	All ends in California with the signing of the Treaty of Cahuenga
January 14	Taylor's troops requisitioned by General Scott depart Victoria for Tampico
January 19	Insurrection and massacre at Taos, New Mexico
January 23	U.S. troops arrive at Tampico from Victoria
January 28	Mexican Army under Santa Anna leaves San Luis Potosi heading North to challenge Taylor
February 3-4	Colonel Sterling Price puts down revolt at battle of Puebla de Taos, New Mexico
February 11	Congress passes the "Ten Regiment" Bill
February 22-23	Battle of Buena Vista (La Angostura)
February 28	Battle of the Sacramento
March 1	Doniphan's men occupy Chihuahua
March 9	U.S. amphibious invasion of Mexico at Vera Cruz begins
March 21	Commodore Conner relieved by Commodore Matthew C. Perry
March 29	City of Vera Cruz surrenders to U.S. army
March 30	Naval landing party seizes San Jose del Cabo, Baja California
March 31	Alvarado captured
April 2	The American army begins the march inland to Mexico City

CHRONOLOGY

April 13 — Naval landing party seizes La Paz, Baja California

April 18 — General Scott defeats Santa Anna at the Battle of Cerro Gordo; Commodore Perry captures Tuxpan with a naval landing force of 1519 men

April 19 — American army occupies Jalapa

April 22 — General Worth's division occupies Perote

May 4 — Twelve months volunteers returned to Vera Cruz by General Scott for shipment home (more than 4,000 men)

May 15 — General Worth's army occupies Puebla

May 21 — Doniphan joins Wool at Buena Vista

June 3 — Scott's line of communications cut off from Vera Cruz

June 16 — Commodore Perry captures the port of Tabasco

July 14 — Brigadier General Franklin Pierce leads a force of 2,500 men from Vera Cruz to reinforce General Scott

July 19 — Americans evacuate Tabasco due to the outbreak of yellow fever in the area

August 6 — Pierce's column reaches the city of Puebla

August 7 — Scott's army advances from Puebla on Mexico City

August 12 — Action at the National Bridge

August 19-20 — Battle of Contreras (Padierna); Battle of Churubusco

August 24 — Santa Anna and General Scott agree to a truce at Tacubaya

September 6 — Tacubaya truce ends

September 8 — Battle of Molino del Rey

September 13 — Battle of Chapultepec

September 14 — U.S. army occupies Mexico City

September 14-October 12 — Mexicans besiege American army at Puebla

September 16 — Santa Anna resigns as President

September 26 — Manuel de la Pena y Pena becomes acting President of Mexico

October 7 — Santa Anna relieved of command by Mexican Government

October 9 — Battle of Huamantla

November 11 — Pedro Maria Anaya elected ad interim President by Mexican Congress; Naval landing party from the *Congress, Cyane,* and *Independence* seize Mazatlan

November 25 — Zachary Taylor relieved as army commander and returns to U.S. to begin a campaign for the Presidency

1848

January 8 — Pena y Pena becomes acting President once again in place of Anaya

January 13 — General Scott relieved of command in Mexico

February 2 — Treaty of Guadalupe Hidalgo signed

March 10 — Treaty ratified by U.S. Congress

March 16 — Colonel Sterling Price attacks Mexican forces at Santa Cruz de Rosales south of Chihuahua

April 5 — Santa Anna leaves Mexico and goes into exile in Havana, Cuba

May 30 — Treaty ratified by Mexican Congress; Jose Joaquin de Herrera once again becomes President of Mexico

June 12 — U.S. troops evacuate Mexico City

July 15 — General Worth and last U.S. troops depart Vera Cruz

ROUGH AND READY

CARRICITOS RANCH AND FORT BROWN

"Hostilities may now be considered as commenced."
General Zachary Taylor to President Polk

Captain Seth B. Thornton, of the U.S. Second Dragoons, led his command into the Rancho de Carricitos on the Rio Grande during the morning of April 25, 1846 in search of Mexican cavalry. The scouting party included Thornton's own Company F and Captain William J. Hardee's Company C, also from the Second Dragoons, totalling four officers and fifty-six men. The Carricitos Ranch was named for the fields of *carriza* (reed grass) that were commonly found in the area and was located on the northern bank of the Rio Grande, some thirty miles west of the main camp of the American Army of Occupation at Fort Texas (later Fort Brown) under General Zachary Taylor.

The 2nd Dragoons were a proud unit with a devil-may-care attitude and had seen service in the Second Seminole War from 1836 to 1842. They rode with a characteristic swagger and wore their hair long with mustaches and full beards, totally against regulations. They caused more than their fair share of problems while in camp, as Lt. Colonel Hitchcock wrote in his diary, "...since the arrival of the 2d Dragoons there have been several disgraceful brawls and quarrels, to say nothing of drunken frolics. The dragoons have made themselves a public scandal. One captain has resigned to avoid trial, and two others have had a dirty brawl. Two others still are on trial for fighting over a low woman." Despite their well deserved reputation for hell-raising they considered themselves ready for anything, especially Mexican cavalry.

The Mexican cavalry that Thornton's reconnaissance mission was about to find belonged to General Anastasio Torrejon, who had crossed the river the day before with a mixed brigade of cavalry and infantry numbering some 1600 men. Actually, the dragoons had been discovered first, by a four man patrol of Torrejon's Presidial cavalry under Lieutenant Roman Galeon, early in the morning on the 25th. The Dragoons were on the same narrow road that the Mexican force was coming up. Torrejon had wasted no time once alerted, and had marched his men quickly to the ranch to prepare an ambush

for the Americans. His force included veteran regulars of the Second Light Infantry, the Battalion of Sappers (Zapadores) and the crack Seventh Cavalry Regiment, among others.

Thornton and his command were in Texas, according to the U.S. government, but Mexico disputed the boundary. Even though the two countries were not yet at war, the dragoons maintained silence on the march and tried to keep their sabres from jingling. Local inhabitants had already warned the patrol that the Mexicans had crossed the river in force and Thornton's Mexican guide had refused to go any further earlier that morning. Thornton didn't really believe that the Mexicans would cross the river though, or that they would fight even if they had ventured across. This attitude was typical of the dragoons, and is illustrated by a Sergeant of the 2nd Dragoons, later in the war, encouraging the men of his small patrol to charge when outnumbered five to one by Mexican guerrillas, "No firing, men! If twenty dragoons can't

---

RANCHO CARRICITOS, APRIL 25, 1846

Mexican Forces: Brig-Gen. Anastasio Torrejon (1606)
Infantry Detachment: Col. Jose Maria Carrasco
   Battalion de Zapadores (250)
   2nd Light Infantry (150)
   Rifle Company of the Villas del Norte (80)
First Cavalry Brigade: Col. Cayetano Montero
   Light Mounted Regiment of Mexico (201)
   7th Cavalry (198)
   8th Cavalry (255)
Second Cavalry Brigade: Gen. Antonio Canales
   Cavalry Regiment of the Villas del Norte (322)
   Squadron of Presidial Cavalry (150)
This entire Brigade was in the area but not all may have engaged in the skirmish.

American Forces
Reconnaissance Patrol of the Second Dragoons
Captain Seth B. Thornton (60) (63) (65) (80)*
   Company F: Captain Seth B. Thornton
   Company C: Captain William J. Hardee
   Other officers present: Lieutenants George T. Mason
   & Elias K. Kane

---

* In all the orders of battle, strengths are given like this when there are different estimates of troop strength. The author's opinion is that the first number is most likely.

whip a hundred greasers with the sabre, I'll join the Doughboys (the infantry) and carry a fence rail (a musket) all my life."

The Carricitos Ranch was enclosed by a high chaparral fence that ringed off a field of about three hundred acres with the Rio Grande as its southern side. It was surrounded by chaparral on the other three sides with the road running alongside the outside of the fence. The only way in was at a barred gate located in the southwestern corner. Inside there was swampy bottomland close to the river and a large field with three other fences dividing it. There were several ranch buildings by the riverbank close to the gate. The dragoons were approaching from the east, following the road around the ranch.

The advance guard of ten men under Lieutenant George T. Mason had skirted the fence and found no means of entry. Meanwhile Thornton himself, with the main body, remarked that about five hundred horsemen had recently used a path leading into the chaparral north of the fence. Eventually the advance guard came upon the draw bar gate and Thornton joined them, leaving the main body to come up behind on their own. Thornton rode into the field and when he saw Mexicans running to one of the ranch buildings he signalled for the advance guard to follow him in. Meanwhile, the main body had come up and they too entered the ranch upon seeing Thornton's signal. Orders had not been given to post sentries at the gate as Thornton had assumed that the main part of the command would remain outside the enclosure. Thornton did order the advance guard to capture a Mexican and bring him to him for questioning. The rest of the dragoons promptly spread out with some dismounting to tend to their horses or get water from the river while others explored buildings or simply rested on the ground.

While Thornton was in the midst of questioning his Mexican prisoner, Torrejon sprung the ambush. The Mexican infantry sealed off the draw bar gate and opened fire on the disorganized dragoons. Thornton ordered an immediate charge, while Hardee tried to form his men up. The fire from the Mexican riflemen panicked some of the horses and caused the disordered sabre charge to recoil back to the inside of the chaparral fence. Thornton ordered the fence breached, as it was too high for the horses to jump over, but no one complied. In desperation to save part of his command he finally ordered every man to "look to his own safety." His own horse had gone out of control and eventually fell, pinning him underneath.

Captain Hardee, who had kept a cooler head, was trying to rally remnants of the shattered dragoons. He was able to lead about twenty-five men towards the river, but realized that it was not possible to make their way down to the water from where they were and so an escape could not be made by crossing. Fearing that the Mexicans would show no quarter, Hardee formed the men into a line of battle and was preparing for a last desperate charge "to sell their lives as dearly as possible." When he urged his men to fight, some of them pointed out that further resistance was hopeless because they were surrounded and many had lost their weapons.

Carricitos Ranch

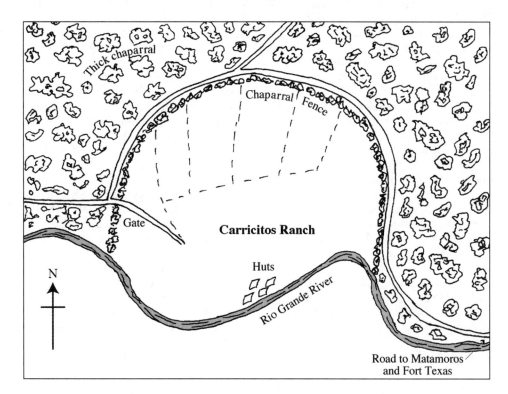

Hardee decided to come to terms and surrendered on the condition that his men were made prisoners of war. The fight at Rancho Carricitos was over.

Lieutenant Mason and nine other dragoons had been killed, with four others wounded. The Mexicans marched forty-six men into Matamoros as prisoners, including Captains Hardee and Thornton. Hardee had thought Thornton dead and the report he wrote to General Taylor the next day gave the General the same impression. Thornton's own report written the following day was shorter and more general, and attempted to shift the blame for the debacle to others including his Mexican guide and even General Taylor himself.

Hardee was well treated by General Arista while in Matamoros and he and Thornton, along with the rest of their command, were exchanged for prisoners held by the Americans within three weeks. Hardee insisted on a court of inquiry to look into his conduct during the action in a desire to clear his name of any wrongdoing, which it did, while Thornton was court-martialled in July and found not guilty of all charges. However, Thornton's career was already tarnished beyond repair and another court martial after Cerro Gordo, where he was arrested by none other than Hardee, earned him a reprimand in general orders. On August 18, 1847 Seth Thornton's career ended when he was the first American killed entering the Valley of Mexico on a scouting patrol with General Scott's army.

The Mexicans claimed the defeat and capture of Thornton's command as a great victory and it provided fuel for the fires of the faction that wanted a war with the United States. In Washington President James K. Polk had already accepted the fact that war with Mexico was probably inevitable but he wanted the Mexicans to commit the first aggressive act. Taylor realized that it was only a matter of time before the presence of his army would somehow provoke the Mexicans. Thornton seemed to recognize his role as a victim in this strategy when he stated at his trial that "Our little army was compelled under its instructions to keep up a peaceable attitude until the first blow should be given by them [the enemy]. It was my misfortune to receive that first blow upon my devoted head; but it had to be received, and why not by me"? On April 26, 1846 General Taylor was able to write in a communication to President Polk that "Hostilities may now be considered as commenced." The Mexican-American War had begun.

Brevet Brigadier General Zachary Taylor was ordered to move a "Corps of Observation" into Texas in the summer of 1845 as a precaution against any negative reaction that Mexico might display towards the annexation of Texas by the United States. When diplomatic efforts to settle the issues in dispute with Mexico failed, Taylor was ordered to the Rio Grande with his "Army of Occupation" to show the Mexicans that the United States would protect what was now American territory. Although still on a peaceful mission, Taylor and his superiors in Washington knew that unless the Mexicans backed down (which they were expected to do), it would not be long before some type of incident on the border would occur. The middle of January of 1846 had seen General Taylor, with approximately half of the total army of the United States, camped at Corpus Christi, Texas. Taylor began moving his "Corps of Observation" here from Ft. Jesup, Louisiana in July. By the middle of October the newly renamed "Army of Occupation" was organized into three brigades and totalled some 3,922 officers and men. This left the United States Army with only three regiments remaining to patrol some 1,500 miles of Indian territory and one additional regiment to patrol the 2,000 mile long border with Canada. The "Army of Occupation" was the largest assembly of American troops since the War of 1812. The men spent most of their time on the parade ground practicing drill and tactics. Many of the regiments had not had all of their companies assembled together for a period of years, and the opportunity was used by the officers to practice their skills of maneuvering and fighting with such a large unit in the field.

The total American army at the beginning of the war consisted of eight regiments of infantry, two regiments of cavalry (dragoons) and four regiments of artillery. Each regiment of artillery had only one company outfitted as a field battery with guns, the other nine companies serving as infantry. The army was composed of all regular soldiers that had freely enlisted and came with the experience gained during long hard marches and duty at isolated frontier posts in Indian country. They wore their fatigue uniforms of sky blue kersey jackets and trousers and dark blue caps. Even the officers had left their full dress uniforms behind and wore dark blue frock coats and light blue trousers.

The field officers had seen service dating back to the War of 1812 and none of them had attended the Military Academy at West Point. They had gotten much of their experience on the frontier and fighting in Florida against the Seminoles. The junior officers were mostly graduates of the Academy and were anxious to prove themselves in combat.

The infantry were mostly armed with the reliable flintlock muskets with only a few companies carrying the new percussion cap weapons which were looked at skeptically by many of the older officers. The cavalry was the weakest arm numerically speaking but they were well mounted and trained to fight as dragoons, mounted or on foot. The artillery was the most up to date of any army at the time. They were well led and had been well trained in the newest methods of maneuver and combat by Major Samuel Ringgold, whose ideas would make the "flying artillery" famous. Then Captain Sam Grant would later comment that "a better army, man for man, probably never faced an enemy."

The leader of this small army was Brevet Brigadier General Zachary Taylor. He was sixty-one years old and held the regular rank of Colonel of the Sixth Infantry. Born in Virginia and raised near Louisville, Kentucky, Taylor had very little formal education. He served as a volunteer as early as 1806 and ended the War of 1812 with the rank of Brevet Major. His promotion to Colonel came in 1832 after more than twenty years of service. He took part in the Black Hawk war and commanded Illinois militia volunteers that included a young Captain by the name of Abraham Lincoln. His next assignment was in Florida fighting the Seminole Indians where he was awarded the rank of Brevet Brigadier General. It was at some point during that conflict that he earned the title that would follow him to Mexico, "Old Rough and Ready" from a soldier's letter that had been published in the papers. Most of Taylor's experience in the military had been gained on the frontier fighting Indians. He was not one to emphasize drill and training but instead put his faith in hard marching and bayonet charges.

General Taylor was not fond of proper military etiquette. A volunteer from one of the Illinois regiments gave a description of the general that was common: "Taylor is short and very heavy, with pronounced face lines and gray hair, wears an old oil cloth cap, a dusty green coat, a frightful pair of trousers and on horseback looks like a toad." Usually he could be found in a long coat, coarse linen trousers, old shoes and a floppy palmetto hat sitting outside his tent or wandering around camp chatting informally. Taylor had been described as looking: "...more like an old yankey Farmer than the General in command of the American Army." Sam Chamberlain of the Second Dragoons tells of a Lieutenant of the First Virginia Volunteers who was a member of one of the first families of that state (F.F.V. according to Chamberlain), and how he came to meet "Old Zack" one day. Apparently the Lieutenant went up to Headquarters to catch a glimpse of the General when he saw a bronze-faced old man hard at work in his shirt sleeves cleaning a sword. In his dignified, high-toned voice he asked, "I say, old fell, can you tell me where I can see General Taylor?"

The old "fell" without rising replied, "Wull, stranger, thar is the old hoss's tent," pointing to the Headquarters.

"Lieutenant, if you please," said the F.F.V. "And so that is the humble abode of the great hero. Can I see him? And by the way, my old trump, whose sword is that you are cleaning?"

"Wull Colonel," replied the old man, "I don't see there is any harm in telling you, seeing's you are an officer. This sword belongs to the General himself."

"Ah! Then this is the victorious blade of the immortal hero! And I suppose then, my worthy man, that you work for the General?"

The worthy man replied, "I reckon, and doggone hard, and little thanks and small pay I get too."

At this point the Lieutenant took off his own sword and said, "My good man, I would like to have you clean my sword, and I shall come tomorrow to see the General and then I will give you a dollar."

When the Lieutenant came back the next day his old friend was standing and talking with some other officers. The F.F.V. beckoned for him to come over, which he did, bringing the young man's sword. The Lieutenant thanked the old man and poked him in the ribs and said, "Come, old fatty, show me General Taylor and the dollar is yours."

The "old fatty" drew himself up and said, "Lieutenant! I am General Taylor, and I will take that dollar!" The next day the embarrassed Lieutenant was properly introduced to the General.

Stories like these were common and Taylor came to be loved by the men, especially the volunteers who saw that he had more in common with them than most of the other regular officers did. His appearance on the battlefield provided inspiration to the troops when they needed it most. At the same time many of the other officers of the regular army doubted his judgement and military skills. The fact that he neglected to scout the surrounding countryside that the army would be likely to advance into led Lieutenant Colonel Hitchcock, commanding the Third Infantry, to write to his brother that if Taylor succeeded it would be by accident. General Worth, his second in command, wrote of Taylor "Whether an idea, strategic or of any other description, has had the rudeness to invade the mind or imagination of our chief is a matter of doubt," he went on, "We are literally a huge body without a head."

Brevet Brigadier General William Jenkins Worth was ten years younger than Taylor and had also seen service in the War of 1812. He was General Scott's aide-de-camp in 1814 at the Battle of Chippewa and at Lundy's Lane. The war ended with Worth a Brevet Major. He served as Commandant of Cadets at West Point from 1820 to 1828 and also saw service on the Canadian border. His vigorous campaigning as a Colonel of the Eighth infantry was instrumental in bringing the Second Seminole War to a conclusion in 1842 when he was awarded the rank of Brevet Brigadier General. He was named to be second in command to Taylor when the army was ordered to Texas. Worth was a dashing figure sometimes described as the 'Ney' of the army, a reference to Napoleon's marshal, Michel Ney, known as the "bravest of the brave." He worked the men hard and he had summed up his philosophy in an order during the Second Seminole War that said, in part "Scorn the exposed points in every direction, - keep the men in constant motion - tax their strength to the utmost." His men eventually came to admire and respect him when they realized that he was a skilled commander that was always reluctant to squander the lives of his soldiers in battle.

Worth had his share of problems with Taylor and the army, mostly due to his own pride. The worst of it had come to a head over Worth's Brevet rank of Brigadier General. Taylor had decided that Colonel David E. Twiggs was senior to Worth due to the fact that his regular rank preceded Worth's even though Worth's Brevet rank was higher. Worth and his supporters maintained that Brevet rank should predominate while in the field, a point that General Scott agreed with. The question was submitted to Washington and ultimately came down against Worth's argument. Taylor could not manage to smooth things over and Worth ended up leaving the army in early April. Once the actual fighting started he was back promptly, although he missed the first two field battles of the war.

Colonel David Emanuel Twiggs, the officer that Worth had his disagreement with over brevet rank, was fifty-six years old and had seen some service during the War of 1812, with the rank of major at

the end of the war. He saw action in the Black Hawk War and was promoted to be the first Colonel of the Second Dragoons in 1836. He was a large man with broad shoulders, white hair and a fierce looking reddish face framed by heavy white whiskers and mustachios. His rough troopers enjoyed having him in command and called him 'Old Davy' or the 'Bengal Tiger' and would brag that he 'cursed them right out of their boots.' He was an excellent disciplinarian that could get his men to accomplish more work than any other group in the army. He was usually anxious for a fight and was willing to rush at the enemy headlong without giving much consideration to the alternatives. Scott did not think him fit for an army command as a result of this tendency.

Most of the officers of the American Army of Occupation did not think that the Mexicans would actually go to war. There had been plenty of rumors of Mexican troops being massed at Matamoros, but none of them had proved to be true. When the men were not busy drilling and training they found other ways to keep themselves amused. There were the usual drunken brawls, and horse racing with Mexican mustangs was also popular. Some officers even put on stage performances at a newly built theater seating 800 people that had been organized by Captain John B. Magruder.

During the winter months conditions became miserable with the rains flooding out tents and the men barely being able to keep warm. Uncontaminated drinking water was scarce and the soldiers began to contend with an enemy that would take more lives than the Mexicans over the next two years, dysentery.

The order to march for the Rio Grande reached General Taylor on February 3, 1846. Taylor took his time, as he was not under any immediate pressure to move. The next couple of weeks were spent scouting out a route of march to Matamoros, which was 150 miles away and testing the ability of the roads to handle wagon traffic. When the army finally set out on March 8th morale was high, for they were finally leaving Corpus Christi! The dragoons and Ringgold's battery started out, followed on successive days by each of the three brigades. They were glad to be on the move and the country they were traversing was very beautiful in the spring. They advanced about ten miles per day but as they approached the border the going got tougher. The ground became sandier, the water holes farther apart. The sun and wind burned their cheeks and lips, and Mexican guerrillas had burned large patches of grass, causing the marching men to raise irritating clouds of ash and dust.

On March 19th the American army reached the Arroyo Colorado, a four foot deep salt lagoon about

---

UNITED STATES ARMY OF OBSERVATION IN NOVEMBER OF 1845
Brevet Brigadier General Zachary Taylor
General Staff (24)

1st Brigade: Bvt. Brigadier General William Jenkins Worth
   8th Infantry (447): Col. William G. Belknap
   1st Artillery (236)
   2nd Artillery (233)
   3rd Artillery (219)
   4th Artillery (235)
   (total of 12 companies of artillery): Bvt. Lt-Col. Thomas Childs
2nd Brigade: Lt-Col. James S. McIntosh
   5th Infantry (573): Lt-Col. James S. McIntosh
   7th Infantry (442): Major Jacob Brown
3rd Brigade: Col. William Whistler
   3rd Infantry (533): Lt. Col. Ethan Allen Hitchcock
   4th Infantry (511): Col. William Whistler
2nd Dragoons (596): Col. David E. Twiggs
2 Companies New Orleans Artillery
Texas Rangers

By March of 1846
Company A of the 2nd Artillery: Captain James Duncan
Company C of the 3rd Artillery: Major Samuel Ringgold
Company E of the 3rd Artillery: Captain Braxton Bragg

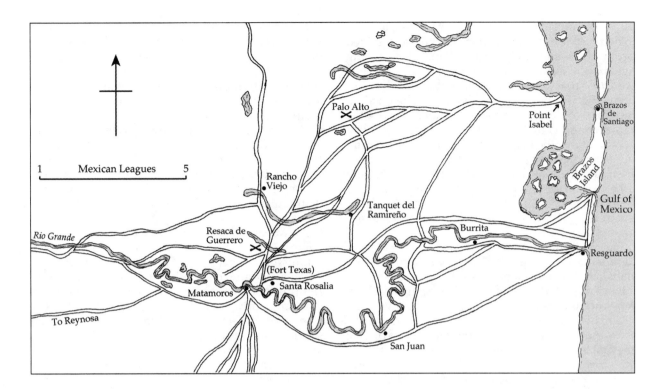

a hundred yards wide. The Mexicans were supposedly on the other side in force and apparently would contest any further advance by Taylor's army. The next morning as the Americans prepared to cross, Mexican Captain Jose Barragan issued a proclamation from his commander in Matamoros calling on the inhabitants of the frontier to oppose the "degenerate sons of Washington." The Mexican officer claimed that any crossing would be contested, to whit Taylor announced that he would begin the crossing immediately. Under the cover of Ringgold's and Duncan's batteries General Worth and his staff waded into the water followed by four light infantry companies led by Captain Charles F. Smith. The Mexican horsemen, of which there had been only a few, were seen beating a hasty retreat.

After waiting for the remainder of the army and the supply train to catch up Taylor proceeded towards Matamoros. A base was set up at Point Isabel on the coast, so that Taylor would have a supply link with the American Navy. The Mexicans had set fire to the buildings here just before they had hastily departed the area. The new garrison consisted of two artillery companies under Major John Munroe who began work on a fort to protect the incoming supplies. The army then continued on to a point opposite the town of Matamoros on the north bank of the Rio Grande, reaching there and making camp on the 28th of March. Taylor immediately sent word to the Mexican commander that his mission was a peaceful one. The Mexican General Mejía began work on the fortifications that he had previously

scorned. This led Taylor to begin construction of a permanent camp and a star shaped earthwork fort, designed by Captain Joseph K. F. Mansfield, that could hold 800 men. The six-sided fort had earthen walls nine feet tall and fifteen feet thick at the base with a deep dry moat surrounding it. This was to be called Fort Texas and its batteries would be able to engage those in Matamoros and bombard the city.

Now that the American army was on the border with Mexico, the ongoing problem of desertion among the ranks became worse than ever. Men swam the river in broad daylight towards the Mexican senoritas on the other side. Some obtained passes to attend church and neglected to mention that they were planning on crossing the river to do so. Taylor was frustrated and ordered that anyone attempting to desert would be shot as they were escaping, which was done on several occasions. Many of the American soldiers were foreign born immigrants and they felt very little loyalty to the service. The strict discipline and hard life made the prospect of escaping to a foreign land more enticing to some. The rate of desertion from the army during the Mexican War reached a high of 8.3% overall, compared to approximately a 4.1% desertion rate for the Vietnam War. The total number of men that left the army, both regulars and volunteers, was a little more than 9,200 throughout the course of the war. Desertion had always been a problem for the army. On the frontier, or in Indian territory it was often difficult to accomplish, but now the Mexicans made it as easy as possible. The Mexican government

19

offered grants of land to anyone who deserted and joined the Mexican Army. Many soldiers also gained promotions and higher rates of pay for serving against their own countrymen. In addition, they were told that they could serve together under their own officers. The Mexicans also used religion as an incentive to the many foreign Catholics among the ranks of the U.S. Army. At one point they were confident that the majority of the 7th Infantry would desert en masse because of its large contingent of Irish and German immigrants. They were hoping for a lot more deserters than they actually got. Many who deserted simply vanished from the scene entirely, not wishing to serve in either army anymore.

One of the myths of the Mexican War is that of the deserters known as the San Patricio, or Saint Patrick's Battalion. It was claimed at the time that these were a band of Irish deserters led by a man named John Riley. In truth the San Patricios began as an unofficial group of deserters that was gathered together from the various soldiers crossing over to Mexico during the first few months of the war. There were less than 40% Irish in the group at any time and they fought together as artillery crews long before they were organized as official militia companies later in the war. Also included in their ranks were any other foreigners who wished to fight for Mexico, creating a Mexican version of the French Foreign Legion. John Riley was a Lieutenant in the San Patricios and did organize a company of Irishmen in Matamoros to fight for Mexico after he deserted from the 5th U.S. Infantry. He is the American soldier that is most often associated as the leader of the San Patricios. In fact there were several Mexican officers that commanded the companies throughout the war. In June of 1847 the unit was made official by a Presidential decree that created two companies of the Foreign Legion organized in the same manner as the active militia. During the course of the war the San Patricio units distinguished themselves in several major battles.

The Mexican Army that Taylor was facing and that some of his men were so eager to join was an impressive one on paper. Their uniforms were very impressive and colorful, being made in a style reminiscent of the army of Napoleon. Dressed predominantly in dark blue with facings of every color in the spectrum and wearing tall shakos the Mexican army presented a fantastic spectacle when arrayed for battle. In reality there were many weaknesses that it had to overcome in order to be victorious against the Americans. The Mexican Army of the North, commanded by Brigadier General Francisco Mejia numbered a little more than 3,000 men and twenty pieces of artillery. Within a few days

---

MEXICAN ARMY AT MATAMOROS IN MARCH 1846
The Army of the North: Brig-Gen. Francisco Mejia (replaced by Maj-Gen. Mariano Arista on April 15, 1846)

4th Division
1st Brigade: Brevet-General Col. Antonio Maria Jauregui
  1st Line Infantry (273): Col. Nicholas Mendoza
  2nd Light Infantry (356): Lt-Col. M. Fernandez
  7th Cavalry (263): Lt-Col. J. Fernandez
  Company of Guias (9): Lieutenant Francisco Barragan
  Artillery (64 crew)
2nd Brigade: Brevet-General Col. Mariano Garcia
  10th Line Infantry (290): BattalionCommander Manuel Montero
  Zapadores (318): Colonel Jose M. Carrasco
  Artillery (55 crew)
A total of 20 artillery pieces available for the 4th Division

In Matamoros (Presidial Companies)
  1st Company of Tamaulipas (50): Captain Plaza
  5th Company of Tamaulipas (25): Capt. Jose Maria Garcia
  Tampico Cavalry Company (26): Capt. Francisco Munoz
  Regiment de las Villas del Norte (271): Gen. Antonio Canales
  (the northern settlements or villages)
  National Guard Battalion of Matamoros (500)

Colorado Basin observing U.S. forces in Corpus Christi (Presidial Companies)
  2nd Company of Tamaulipas (48): Capt. Antonio de la Garza

Permanent Company of La Bahia (12)
Auxiliary Company of La Bahia (31): Capt. Juan Antonio de los Santos
3rd Squadron, Regiment de las Villas del Norte (89): Squadron Commander Jose Maria Cardenas

Arriving at Matamoros March 31, 1846
6th Line Infantry
Marines of Tampico
Tampico Coast Guard Battalion
Veteran Coast Guard Company of Tampico

Arriving at Matamoros April 11, 1846
Operational Division Commander Maj-Gen. Pedro De Ampudia (scheduled to take command of the Army of the North but superseded by Arista only four days later)
  Light Mounted Regiment of Mexico (191): Col. Luis Noriega

Arriving at Matamoros April 14, 1846
Brevet General Colonel Anastasio Torrejon
  4th Line Infantry (670): Col. Andres Terres
  1st Active Militia Regiment of Mexico (506): Lt-Col. Francisco Berra
  Active Militia Regiment of Puebla (504): Lt-Col. Jose M. Correa
  Active Militia Battalion of Morelia (236): 1st Adjutant J. Salgado
  Active Militia Squadron of Chalchicomula (101): Commandante Juan Espino
  8th Cavalry (226)
  Artillery (80 crew) (6 guns)

of the American incursion they were reinforced by a division under General Pedro de Ampudia and other forces under the command of Brigadier General Anastasio Torrejon. This brought the total Mexican Army in Matamoros up to about 175 artillerymen, 3500 infantry and 1100 cavalry. In addition there were about 500 volunteers from Matamoros and another 400 or so irregular horse under General Antonio Canales. This gave the Mexican commander on the scene an army of some 5700 officers and men, a force far superior in numbers to the Americans.

Unlike the Americans, the Mexican forces on the Rio Grande represented only a small portion of the total Mexican Army, which was estimated to number as many as 35,000 soldiers. There were twelve regular line infantry and four regular light infantry regiments as well as nine regular cavalry regiments. There were also three brigades of foot artillery and a brigade of mounted artillery. In addition to the regular forces there were at least as many Presidial and Active Militia regiments, battalions and companies of infantry and cavalry under arms and available for service. The individual Mexican states could also call on National Guard units for home defense if and when the need arose. Mexicans and Europeans alike thought that the Americans would be defeated by a combination of the vast distances of Mexico, the numerical advantage and superiority in combat of the Mexican Army and the unwillingness of the army of a democracy to fight.

In actuality the Mexican Army suffered from some serious problems that observers on the spot frequently noticed and wrote about. The soldiers were courageous enough, generally, and many were veterans of skirmishes and battles of the frequent revolutions that took place. But they were, for the most part, poorly trained conscripts equipped with inferior weapons. The gunpowder used was of poor quality and the flintlock muskets the army used were mainly those discarded from the British army. Marksmanship was nonexistent, with no ammunition available for practice, and many men entered battle without having previously fired their weapons. The cavalry were excellent horsemen, but were not usually effective in shock combat (except for those armed with lances). The artillery was well served, but continual problems with powder and ammunition (as well as outdated guns) plagued this arm. The most glaring problem was the weak leadership exhibited at all levels. Political intriguing over the last twenty years had forced most of the sharper military minds out of the service. Despite its problems, the Mexican Army was a determined force that would still have to be reckoned with on the field of battle.

General Ampudia replaced General Mejia on April 12th and made a formal demand that the Americans withdraw back to the Nueces River. Taylor argued that his was a peaceful mission and that he could not withdraw without orders from his government. Ampudia was planning to start an offensive on the fifteenth of April but cancelled his plans when he found out that General Mariano Arista was en route to take over and would arrive on the 24th. When Arista arrived he immediately notified Taylor that he considered hostilities to have commenced. On the same day he dispatched General Torrejon with a force of about 1600 men to cross the river and strike the American supply line and support the main army.

Meanwhile, Taylor had already provisioned Fort Texas and now sent his supply train back to Point Isabel. Tensions had increased lately as the Americans had lost three men killed over the last two weeks when they were away from camp and were ambushed by Mexican bandits. When Taylor learned of the crossing late on the 24th he sent

---

FORCES AT THE SIEGE OF FORT TEXAS (LATER FORT BROWN) FROM MAY 3-MAY 9, 1846

Mexican: Maj-Gen. Pedro de Ampudia (1230)
    4th Line Infantry
    Active Militia of Puebla
    Zapadores (2 companies)
    Irregular Cavalry (200): Brig-Gen. Antonio Canales
In Matamoros: Brig-Gen. Francisco Mejia (1600)
    Active Militia of Mexico
    Active Militia of Morelia
    Artillery (18-20 guns of which 7- 12lb. guns are largest)

U.S. Forces: Major Jacob Brown (550)
    7th Infantry: Major Jacob Brown
    Company E, 3rd Artillery: Lieutenant Braxton Bragg
    (2- 6 lb. guns & 2- 12 lb. howitzers)
    Company I, 2nd Artillery: Captain Allen Lowd
    (4- 18 lb. siege guns)

Fort Texas

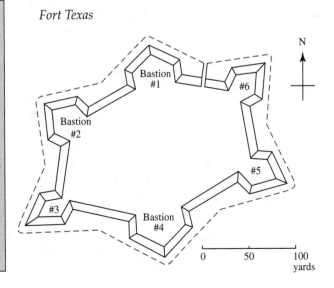

Thornton and his dragoons to investigate. On the morning of the 26th Taylor learned of Thornton's fate when his Mexican guide returned to camp. Then on the 29th he received news from Major Munroe that Torrejon was now threatening Point Isabel. What Taylor did not know was that Torrejon had decided to rejoin Arista and the main body of the army which had begun crossing the river on April 30th. General Mejia was left behind in Matamoros with about 1,400 men to man the city and its batteries of artillery. When Taylor learned of the crossing on May 1st he lost no time in gathering the army and marching to the relief of Point Isabel and the supply depot which

General Ampudia

he assumed would be Arista's main objective. Taylor had left behind about 500 men of the 7th Infantry along with Captain Allen Lowd's battery of four eighteen pounders and Lt. Braxton Bragg with his battery under the command of Major Jacob Brown to complete and hold Fort Texas.

When the Mexican Army had completed crossing the Rio Grande on May 2nd Arista sent General Ampudia with the 4th Infantry, the Active Militia of Puebla, two companies of sappers, and about 200 light cavalry (totalling some 1200 men) to attack Fort Texas. Early on the morning of May 3rd the attack began with a bombardment from the artillery batteries in Matamoros. The American response was accurate enough to score a hit on a twelve pounder which forced the Mexicans to relocate some other guns. The Mexican fire continued until midnight but the Americans had ceased firing a couple of hours earlier to conserve ammunition. The bombardment continued throughout the fourth, fifth and sixth with

the Mexican cavalry cutting the road to the coast and the infantry investing the fort to prevent escape. The Mexican guns were not powerful enough to breach the sides of the earthworks that made up the fort and allow it to be taken easily. Ampudia was reluctant to launch an assault on the fort directly, fearing the heavy losses that his brigade would suffer in the process. Major Brown received a mortal wound on the sixth and command passed to Captain Edgar S. Hawkins. Hawkins respectfully declined Arista's invitation to surrender the fort a short time later and for good reason. As long as he had adequate supplies the fort could hold out until Taylor returned. The bombardment lasted through the seventh and then Arista called on Ampudia to join him in confronting Taylor's army returning from Point Isabel on the eighth. The defenders of Fort Texas had sustained only one other man killed, besides Major Brown, and nine wounded. On the afternoon of the eighth they heard the booming of cannons to the east and they knew Taylor was on his way back from the coast.

PALO ALTO AND RESACA DE LA PALMA

"Take those guns, and by God, keep them!".
General Taylor at Resaca de la Palma

Taylor and his men had heard the bombardment of Fort Texas begin on the 3rd of May but they could not leave Point Isabel until sufficient reinforcements had arrived to hold the small fort there. The army finally set out on the afternoon of May 7th trying to cover the thirty or so winding miles to Fort Texas as quickly as possible. This was made more difficult because Taylor had chosen to attach the more than 200 wagons of the supply train to the column along with two 18-pound guns pulled by oxen. The column marched about seven miles that day and then made camp. When Arista got word of Taylor's movements

Key to Palo Alto Map	
L	Light Cavalry
P	Presidial Cavalry
T	Tampico Coast Guards
Z	Zapadores
B	Baggage camps
H	Hospital
Lt	Light Mounted Regiment of Mexico
W	Wagons
R	Ringgold's battery
C	Churchill's battery
D	Duncan's battery
M	May's Dragoons
K	Kerr's Dragoons
▮	Infantry first position
▯	Infantry later position
◪	Cavalry first position
◩	Cavalry later position
◫	Cavalry interim position

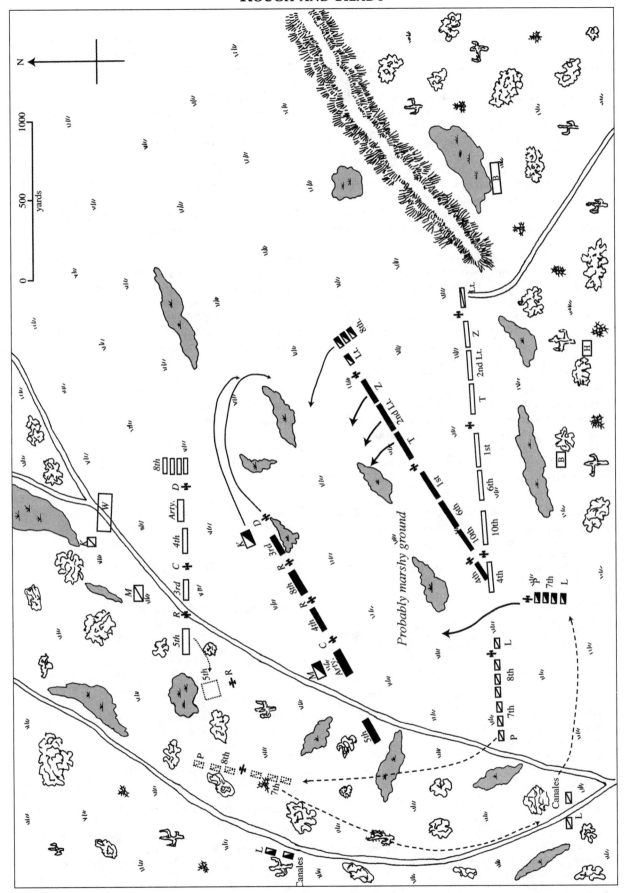

The Battlefield of Palo Alto, May 8, 1846

he made plans to intercept him and he quickly recalled Ampudia from the siege of Fort Texas to join him in facing the American army. The Americans continued their march the next morning and after going about eleven miles, at around noon on May 8th, the Mexican army came within view, already deployed, on a plain called Palo Alto.

The plain of Palo Alto was named for the stands of tall timber that began here and extended southwards towards the Rio Grande. The trees had chaparral and open patches of ground intermixed with them. The plain itself was about a mile and a half wide or larger, flat and covered with stiff, sharp pointed grass reaching to shoulder height that made movement difficult and limited visibility for soldiers on foot. There were several shallow, marshy depressions that contained runoff water scattered around the field. The road that Arista had come in on entered the field from the southeast and a ridge ran from here off to the northeast. The western edge of the field was fringed with more chaparral and small depressions. The road Taylor was travelling entered the field from the north and continued on to the southwest towards Matamoros. When the Americans arrived the Mexican army was arrayed along the southern edge of the plain.

When the supply train caught up to the halted troops Taylor ordered a move forward once again until the American line was only about three-quarters of a mile away from the Mexicans. The men were able to fill their canteens while the wagon train moved into a defensive position on the road, guarded by a squadron of dragoons. The rest of the men began to deploy in column of divisions, off the road. On the left of the line was the 1st Brigade under Lt. Colonel William G. Belknap with the 8th Infantry on the extreme left with their own left refused back, away from the Mexican line, to protect their exposed flank. They were supported by Captain James Duncan's Company 'A' of the 2nd Artillery. To the right of them was the regiment formed from the ten artillery companies serving as infantry led by Lt. Colonel Thomas Childs. To the right of these 'red-legged' infantry was the 4th Infantry which was the easternmost unit of General Twiggs' command. The 3rd Infantry was just to the right of the 4th and to the east of the road where the two 18-pounders under the command of Lt. William H. Churchill were set up. To the right of the road holding the American right flank was Major Samuel Ringgold's Company 'C' of the 3rd Artillery (this fully mounted artillery company was the one most well known as the "flying artillery") and the 5th Infantry. The two squadrons of the 2nd Dragoons under Captain Croghan Ker and Captain Charles A. May were kept in reserve. It would appear from the deployment that the American army was preparing to push its way past the Mexicans and continue down the road to Matamoros. Taylor's total army numbered somewhere around 2,200 men and he had instructed them that "their main dependence must be in the bayonet."

MEXICAN ARMY AT PALO ALTO ON MAY 8, 1846
Maj-Gen. Mariano Arista (3709) (6000)

Right Flank Forces
   Light Mounted Regiment of Mexico (201-150): Col. Luis Noriega
   1 - 4 lb. gun
   Zapadores (304)
   2nd Light Infantry (240)
   Tampico Coast Guard Battalion (130): Col. Juan Mateos
   Veteran Coast Guard Company of Tampico (71): Captain Arana
Right Flank Brigade: Brig-Gen. Romulo Diaz de la Vega
   5 - 4 lb. guns
   1st Line Infantry (270)
   6th Line Infantry (245)
Left Flank Brigade: Brig-Gen. Jose Maria Garcia
   10th Line Infantry (292)
   2 - 8 lb. guns
   4th Line Infantry (481): Colonel Jose Lopez Uraga
Cavalry Brigade: Brig-Gen. Anastasio Torrejon
   2 - 4 lb. guns
   1st Cavalry - 1 squadron (35)
   7th Cavalry - 3 squadrons (198)
   8th Cavalry - 2 squadrons (255)
   Presidial Cavalry - 1 squadron (150): Col. Sabariego
Reserve Cavalry: Col. Cayetano Montero
   Mounted Auxiliary of las Villas del Norte (322-200): Squadron Commander Rafael Quintero

Present but not participating in the battle
   Irregular Cavalry (425): Brig-Gen. Antonio Canales

U.S. ARMY AT PALO ALTO ON MAY 8, 1846
Brig-Gen. Zachary Taylor (2228) (2288)

Right Wing: Col. David E. Twiggs
   5th Infantry: Lt-Col. James S. McIntosh
   Company C, 3rd Artillery: Major Samuel Ringgold (4 - 6 lb. guns)
Garland's Brigade: Lt-Col. John Garland
   3rd Infantry: Captain Lewis N. Morris
   2 - 18 lb. guns: Lieutenant William H. Churchill
   4th Infantry: Major George W. Allen
Cavalry (250): Captains Croghan Ker and Charles A. May
   Companies B, C, D, E, F, H & K, 2nd Dragoons

Left Wing
1st Brigade: Lt-Col. William G. Belknap
   Artillery Regiment (as Infantry): Lt-Col. Thomas Childs
   (Companies B, D & E, 1st Artillery & Companies C & K, 2nd Artillery & Companies A & I, 3rd Artillery & Companies D, E & I, 4th Artillery)
   Company A, 2nd Artillery: Captain James Duncan (3-6 lb. guns & 1-12lb. howitzer)
   8th Infantry: Captain William A. Montgomery

While Taylor began deploying, Ampudia arrived on Arista's left to unite the Mexican forces. Arista did nothing to hamper Taylor's movements but simply waited in line of battle. His forces consisted of General Torrejon's 7th and 8th Cavalry along with a squadron of Presidial troops on the extreme left of the line deployed slightly forward of the main position. A couple of small guns were set up on their right with the 4th, 10th, 6th, and 1st Infantry extending the line to the right supported by seven guns and a company of sappers. To their own right were the Tampico Coast Guard Battalion along with their Veteran Company, the 2nd Light Infantry with the support of a 4-pound gun, and another detachment of sappers. On the extreme right of the Mexican line rode the Light Mounted Regiment of Mexico. Arista only had some local militia cavalry as a reserve and they played no part in the battle. Estimates of the size of these units vary but Arista had somewhere between 3,000 and 4,000 men on the field that day. Arista used his best units, the Sappers, 4th Infantry and the 2nd Light Infantry to anchor his flanks, while some of the more questionable units were kept together in the center. His plan seemed to be defensive in nature, placing himself astride the path that Taylor must take to return to Fort Texas and thereby forcing the Americans to attack. With his infantry holding the center of the line and cavalry on both flanks he could trap any force that might advance into his reach.

The Mexican artillery opened the battle while the Americans were moving up in columns. Taylor halted and deployed into line about a half mile from the Mexicans. The Mexican guns did not have a long enough range to be effective at this distance and the men were actually able to dodge many of the solid shot cannonballs as they bounced or rolled along the ground. About 3:00 p.m. the battle began in earnest with both Ringgold's and Duncan's batteries advancing to within 700 yards of the enemy positions and opening a deadly fire on the formed lines of Mexican infantry. Arista ordered Torrejon with his cavalry on the left to attack around the American right flank. This attack was slowed down a great deal by the chaparral and marshy ground and by the time the horsemen emerged from the rough terrain they were facing the 5th Infantry that had formed in square just behind their original position in anticipation of the attack. The cavalry lacked firepower and several volleys from the square at less than 50 yards range proved too much for them. When Torrejon tried to push past the square on towards the wagon train he saw the 3rd Infantry beginning to deploy with a section of Ringgold's guns under Lt. Randolph Ridgely in support. Torrejon pulled his men back without any success.

Arista had tried to launch a similar attack from his own right flank but the destruction caused by Duncan's battery had proved too disruptive to allow

it to move forward. The Mexican infantry stood up remarkably well to the punishment they were taking from the guns. Everytime a swath would be cut by artillery fire ripping through the ranks it would be closed up by the files of men moving in from behind or dressing ranks from each side. But Arista knew that his men could not take too much more of this. About 4:00 the battle was interrupted by the grass being set on fire in front of Duncan's battery. This was most likely an accidental fire from a burning wad coming out of one of the guns. The smoke was intense and began drifting across the battlefield towards the Mexican lines. For nearly an hour neither side could see well enough to continue the fight. The American artillery crews used the time to bring up more ammunition while the Generals on each side began to re-align their men.

Taylor moved his right wing forward about 1000 yards down the road and had his left face shift accordingly to maintain a straight line. In effect the Americans pivoted their army counterclockwise. Arista had done virtually the same maneuver with his troops attempting to bring his entire line closer to the road by advancing with the right and holding with the left. The end result was that the armies were in the same relative positions when the artillery battle began again about five o'clock. The American 4th Infantry was now taking a severe pounding at the hands of the Mexican batteries and fell back. It was replaced in the line by the Artillery Battalion which managed to hold its ground. The Mexican guns were concentrating on Ringgold's battery and they were doing a good job of it. Ringgold was mortally wounded, a cannonball passing through both thighs and the withers of his horse, and he would linger for three days before dying. His battery was forced to fall back. The Mexicans guns kept up their pounding for an hour and a half, and then ran out of ammunition. They had expended virtually all of the 650 rounds that they had brought to the battlefield. Torrejon had tried to press another attack but the Artillery Battalion managed to beat him back.

Meanwhile, on the Mexican right flank their own troops were continuing to take severe punishment from Duncan's guns. The men demanded to be ordered to attack or fall back outside of range. Arista ordered an immediate attack. Duncan managed to get a section of guns in front of the now advancing Mexicans and was able to fire on their flank at the same time as the 8th Infantry, forcing the Mexicans to fall back. At this time the American guns limbered up and moved to within 300 yards of the Mexican right flank and fired down the line of troops rolling them back to the west. The Mexican Light Cavalry on this flank rode through their own infantry in their flight and almost caused a general panic. Arista realized that no further attacks could succeed and before any more damage was done he ordered a withdrawal to the high ground behind his own right flank. It was about seven o'clock and the troops on both sides were exhausted. Taylor did not order any pursuit, but was content to hold the battlefield, on which the Americans camped for the night.

The battle of Palo Alto had ended. It had been an artillery duel that the Americans had won by a wide margin. The new doctrine of Ringgold's "flying artillery" had been demonstrated on the battlefield for the first time and was a complete success. Taylor was duly impressed with this arm which he hadn't given much credence to at first. His faith had always been placed totally in the bayonet and the infantry wielding it. Taylor had also had little experience facing cavalry forces in the numbers that the Mexicans fielded them. He may have been somewhat intimidated by these mobile troops into maintaining a defensive stance throughout the action. Since he was outnumbered already, this turned out to be a good move, for whatever reason it was adopted. His veteran regulars had not encountered this type of foe in the past either, but they were well trained in how to deal with the situation and they performed admirably.

The Mexicans had not taken advantage of their superiority in numbers, or their cavalry, while their artillery had been completely outclassed. In order to be successful, cavalry had to be supported in its attack and the Mexican infantry and artillery had failed to do this. The unexpected devastation wrought by the American artillery can account for much of this failure. Throughout the war Mexican cavalry would continue to attack without proper support and this fact, combined with a frequently demonstrated reluctance to close into combat, caused them to be held in contempt by the American infantry during the war. The Mexican infantry performed well under fire but they were not launched into the assault until it was too late. A better effort to coordinate an attack by Arista may have altered the outcome of the battle.

With battle being joined for the first time both sides had learned something about their enemy. The Americans had gained some respect for the steadiness of the Mexican soldier while the Mexicans had seen that the enemy artillery was something to be feared, although these basic lessons would often be repeated before the end of the campaign. Mexican casualties were approximately 102 killed, 129 wounded and 26 missing in action although American claims ran much higher. The Americans themselves claimed to have lost 9 killed, 44 wounded and 2 missing. This came out to about seven percent of the total Mexican force engaged but only two and one-half percent of the American force. Taylor had won the tactical battle and taken possession of the field, but he did not have an open road to Matamoros, and Arista's army was still a force that had to be dealt with. Arista had stopped Taylor from going any farther, but the American army had not been defeated. Palo Alto was an American victory, albeit not a decisive one.

The armies both spent that moonlit night camped on the battlefield. Arista decided not to renew the battle the next day at the same site. He issued orders for the remaining troops taking part in the siege of Fort Texas to march to join him at the Resaca de Guerrero about five miles towards Matamoros from Palo Alto. This was a shallow ravine that had once been a channel of the Rio Grande. Arista's army marched early on the ninth, and the Americans only caught sight of the end of the retreating Mexican column shortly after daybreak. Taylor decided to continue on to Fort Texas and pursue the Mexicans, instead of waiting for any reinforcements from the coast. He decided to leave the wagons behind this time, so that they would not slow the advance or hinder his deployment. The men buried the dead, collected the wounded, and built a breastwork for their two 18-pounders and two 12-pounder guns that were to be left with the wagons. In addition, the "red-legged" infantry and Captain Ker's squadron of dragoons would stay behind to guard the supply train. A patrol of dragoons and 220 light troops commanded by Captain George A. McCall of the 4th Infantry were sent to maintain contact with the retreating Mexicans. The American army marched from Palo Alto at about two o'clock, advancing in high spirits, as the victory of the day before had been a tremendous boost to morale. At about this same time McCall's skirmishers made contact with the Mexican artillery guarding the road going through the brush-covered riverbed at a place the Americans called Resaca de la Palma.

The position that Arista had chosen was a strong one. The banks of the ravine made a natural breastwork about three or four feet deep and the thick chaparral on either side was almost

Key to Resaca de la Palma Map	
T	Mounted militia Villas del Norte
P	Presidial Cavalry
LM	Light Mounted Regiment of Mexico
7	7th Regiment
8	8th Regiment
2	2nd Light Infantry
2A	2nd Light Infantry - 2nd position
4	4th Infantry - 1st position
4A	4th Infantry - 2nd position
●	Arista's tent
G	Tampico Coast Guards
1	1st Infantry
6	6th Infantry
10	10th Infantry
N	Zapadores
□	small boxes are independent companies of larger units

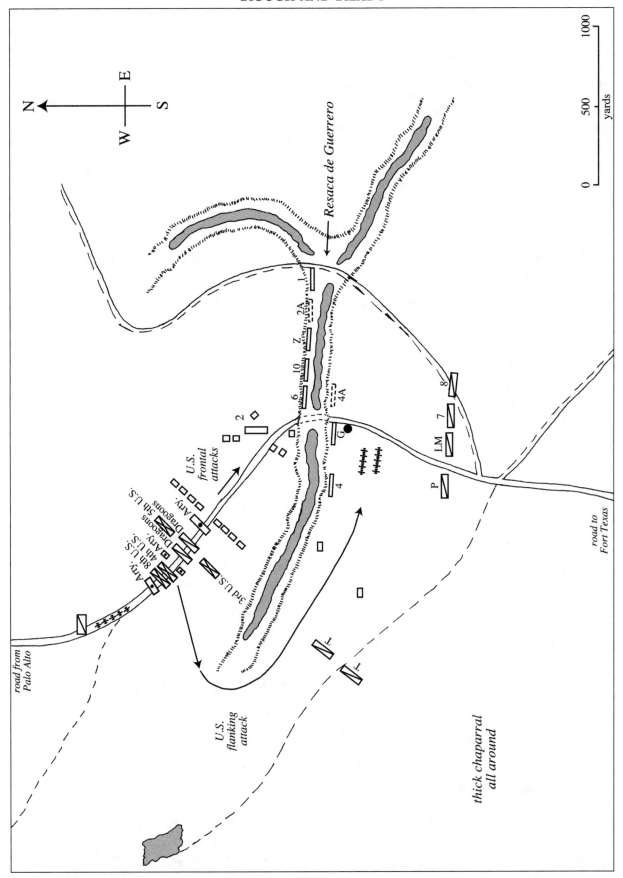

The Battlefield of Resaca de la Palma, May 9, 1846

impenetrable. The bottom was covered with brush and somewhat cluttered by stagnant pools of runoff water and twisted palm trees. At this point the road ran from north to south and the depression extended about 1000 yards to the west and about 1500 yards to the east of the crossing point. To Arista's left, or west of the road, was the 4th Infantry, the Tampico Coast Guard Battalion and their Veteran Company, a detachment of Sappers and four small 4-pound guns. These troops were actually on the Mexican side of the ravine and Arista's headquarters was here too, close to the road. On the right or east side of the road the 2nd Light Infantry was deployed on the opposite side of the ditch close by the road. In the Resaca itself were the 10th, 6th and 1st Infantry along with other Sappers. Brigadier General Rómulo Díaz de la Vega would later declare, "If I had with me… $100,000 in silver, I would have bet the whole of it that no 10,000 men on earth could drive us from our position". Torrejon was with the cavalry in reserve south of the ravine on the road. If anything, the position may have been too large for the troops available to occupy it. Another problem with the position was that the artillery had extremely limited fields of fire and range due to the close terrain. But this would also limit the deadly artillery of the Americans as well. The morale of the Mexican army was still shaky from their trials of the day before and the broken terrain served to isolate units from each other. What's more, it had been at least twenty-four hours since the Mexican soldiers had eaten.

At a range of somewhere between three and four hundred yards, the American light troops came into view of the Mexican battery covering the road. It opened fire briefly and forced the American troops to take cover. It wasn't until about four o'clock that Taylor appeared on the scene with the rest of the army coming up behind him on the road. He promptly ordered McCall to advance and engage the flanks. The general told him, "I will push the regiments in to support you as they come up." While McCall deployed on either side of the road, Lt. Ridgely, now in charge of Ringgold's battery, moved his guns up the road and into position. He was immediately charged by some of Torrejon's lancers, but the attack was driven off. The guns opened up with grapeshot on the Mexican 2nd Light Infantry deployed on the north side of the Resaca and drove them across the ravine.

When the American infantry began arriving they moved off piecemeal into the chaparral to engage the enemy. The 8th and the 5th Infantry were to the east of the road and the 3rd and 4th Infantry went to the west. The battle became one of many different small unit actions, isolated from each other by the rough terrain. Individual companies moved and fought on the initiative of their junior officers. The Americans, aggressive and well led, were suited for this type of engagement. The Mexican 4th Infantry and the 2nd Light Infantry both fought with a great deal of tenacity, but the Americans eventually gained the upper hand. In the confused terrain, some of the American 4th Infantry managed to find a way around the left flank of the Mexicans. Some captured Mexican guns, while others ended up at Arista's headquarters tent.

Meanwhile the fight along the road was reaching a climax. Ridgely had called for assistance against the Mexican battery in the road and Taylor had ordered May and his squadron of dragoons to

MEXICAN ARMY AT RESACA DE LA PALMA (RESACA DE GUERRERO) ON MAY 9, 1846
Maj-Gen. Mariano Arista (3758)

1st Line (East of road)-Right Flank (1274)
 1st Line Infantry
 2nd Light Infantry
 Zapadores
 10th Line Infantry
 6th Line Infantry
2nd Line (West of Road)-Left Flank (651)
 Tampico Coast Guard Battalion: Col. Juan Mateos
 Veteran Coast Guard Company of Tampico: Capt. Arana
 4th Line Infantry
 4 - 4 lb. guns: Capt. Delores Ramires
Flank Guard & Reserves (1103)
 4 - 4 lb. guns
 Mounted Auxiliary of las Villas del Norte
 Light Mounted Regiment of Mexico
 1st Cavalry
 7th Cavalry
 8th Cavalry
 Mounted Presidial Companies

UNITED STATES ARMY AT RESACA DE LA PALMA ON MAY 9, 1846
Brig-Gen. Zachary Taylor (1700) (2222)

1st Brigade: Lt-Col. William G. Belknap
 4th Infantry: Major George W. Allen
 8th Infantry: Captain William A. Montgomery
2nd Brigade
 3rd Infantry: Captain Lewis N. Morris
 5th Infantry: Lt-Col. James S. McIntosh
Attached
 2nd Dragoons (1 squadron): Captain Charles A. May
 Company C, 3rd Artillery: Lt. Randolph Ridgely (4 - 6 lb. guns)
In Reserve (from Palo Alto)
 Company A, 2nd Artillery: Capt. James Duncan (4 - 6 lb. guns)
 2nd Dragoons (1 squadron): Captain Croghan Ker
 Artillery Regiment (as Infantry): Lt-Col. Thomas Childs (Companies B, D & E, 1st Artillery & Companies C & K, 2nd Artillery & Companies A & I, 3rd Artillery & Companies D, E & I, 4th Artillery)

U.S. Grant saw action at Resaca de la Palma

charge. As May moved his men up to the American guns he called to Ridgely asking, "Where are they? I am going to charge". Ridgely replied: "Hold on, Charlie, till I draw their fire". At that the guns fired and the Mexican battery immediately replied. The dragoons were off at once, charging down the road in a column of fours and reaching the Mexican guns before they could be reloaded. The dragoons kept going though and couldn't halt and reform until they were several hundred yards past the Mexican lines. They returned through the guns and captured General Díaz de la Vega among others. The Mexican gunners returned to their guns as soon as the dragoons went by. Another charge was made, with the same results, again accomplishing little or nothing. Finally Taylor realized that only the infantry could take the position and hold it and he ordered Colonel Belknap to use the 5th and 8th Infantry and "Take those guns, and by God keep them"! Musketry combined with hand-to-hand fighting carried the Mexican positions on the road just as their left flank was collapsing with the capture of the army headquarters tent. Arista and Torrejon led a last ditch cavalry charge down the road to try to salvage the situation, but it was of no use. The Mexican infantry scattered and fled the field. Taylor ordered his only fresh troops, the Artillery Battalion and Captain Ker's Dragoons, to pursue. By the time they came

up, however, the Mexicans were well on their way to Matamoros, escaping as best they could. While some of the fleeing troops were able to find boats or scows to help them cross the river, many of the Mexicans drowned trying to swim the swift currents. Arista and the cavalry made their escape by fording the river downstream.

Captain Ulysses S. Grant, of the 4th Infantry, was in the fighting at this battle, which he later described in his *Memoirs*: "The balls commenced to whistle very thick overhead, cutting the limbs of the chaparral right and left. We could not see the enemy, so I ordered my men to lie down, an order that did not have to be enforced… There seemed to be a few men in front and I charged upon them with my company. There was no resistance, and we captured a Mexican colonel, who had been wounded, and a few men. Just as I was sending them to the rear with a guard of two or three men, a private came from the front… The ground had been charged over before". It turned out that Captain Grant had captured Mexicans who had already been captured before and it was this fact that convinced him to write: "that the battle of Resaca de la Palma would have been won, just as it was, if I had not been there".

The men in Fort Texas had heard the gunfire and now were treated to the spectacle of the Mexican army in headlong flight. They did not try to interfere. Arista later reported that he had lost 154 men killed, 205 wounded and 156 missing. This may have been as much as fifteen percent of his force. The American casualties had been lighter with 49 dead and 83 wounded, or about nine percent of those engaged. Captain May had claimed and gotten credit for the capture of General Díaz de la Vega, for which he became virtually a national hero. It turned out though (and it was common knowledge in the army in Mexico) that he was actually taken prisoner by one of the buglers with May at the time.

The American victory was complete this time. There were no longer any Mexican troops north of the Rio Grande. The battle had been fought as a series of independent actions led by the junior officers and infantrymen on the spot. There was not much chance to display any generalship on either side. Unfortunately, Taylor did not immediately follow up his victory, partly because he had no transport to carry his equipment across the river.

The day after the battle of Resaca de la Palma, a prisoner exchange was arranged that brought Thornton, Hardee, and the rest of the captive Americans back to the army. Taylor renamed the fort at Point Isabel Fort Polk on the twelfth and Fort Texas officially became Fort Brown on the seventeenth. By the eighteenth the Americans had managed to piece together a means of crossing over into Matamoros. The dragoons and some Texas Rangers were the first to make the passage, only to find that the Mexican army had already left. Arista had fled south with what remained of the army towards Monterrey, the capital city of the state of Nuevo Leon. Taylor accepted the surrender of the city from the civil authorities on the eighteenth.

MONTERREY

"Old Zack's at Monterrey,
Bring out your Santa Anner;
For every time we raise a gun,
Down goes a Mexicanner;"
Popular ditty in the streets

There had been a lighter moment in the campaign just after the battle of Resaca de la Palma, as a result of Taylor's reputation for not wearing regulation uniform. A meeting had been arranged with Commodore Conner at Point Isabel to discuss a joint operation to cross the Rio Grande. Taylor, realizing that the naval officer was always a stickler for form, dug out his full dress uniform and put it on (one of the few times he was seen in it) so as not to make Conner feel uncomfortable. Conner, meanwhile, in deference to Taylor's reluctance to wear uniforms, wore his civilian clothes to the meeting. The two

officers attempting to explain and apologize for the embarrassment this had caused was worth quite a laugh to their respective staffs.

The American victories, followed by the occupation of Matamoros, drew thousands of short term volunteers to Taylor's army. Some of the first had no sooner arrived on the scene when their three month enlistments expired. A few decided to stay, but the majority turned around and went back home. It was in this way that Taylor had acquired a great deal of manpower without the supplies necessary to support them. These volunteers brought little equipment and even less experience, along with a host of problems for Taylor to deal with. The lack of discipline exhibited by the volunteers was matched only by their total disregard for the basics of camp sanitation. The regulars were highly critical of the volunteers, many times for good reason. Second Lieutenant George B. McClellan wrote of the volunteers: "They plunder the poor inhabitants of everything they can lay their hands on, and shoot them when they remonstrate, and if one of their number happens to get into a drunken brawl and is killed, they run over the country, killing all the poor innocent people they find in their way, to avenge, as they say, the murder of their brother. This is a true picture, and the cause is the utter incapacity of their officers to control them or command respect". The

---

MEXICAN ARMY AT MONTERREY
FROM SEPTEMBER 21-23, 1846

Maj-Gen. Pedro Ampudia (5836) (5570) (7303)
  Gen-Col. J. Garcia Conde
  Commander of Engineers: Captain Luis Robles
  Commander of Artillery: Gen-Col. Tomas Raquena
  Surgeons (10)
  Zapadores (118) (229): Lt. Colonel Mariano Reyes
Artillery—29 guns total (211) (290)

1st Brigade of Infantry: Gen-Col. Simeon Ramirez
  3rd Light Infantry (512): Col. Nicolas Enciso
  4th Light Infantry (397): 1st Adjutant Prudencio Serrato
  Active Militia of Aguascalientes (383): 1st Adjutant Jose Ferro
2nd Brigade of Infantry: Gen-Col. Francisco Mejia
  2nd Light Infantry (220): Col. Jose Maria Carrasco
  6th Line Infantry (89): Battalion Commander Juan Espindola
  (2 Companies plus detachments from the 8th Line Infantry)
  10th Line Infantry (129): Battalion Commander Manuel Montero
  Active Militia of Queretaro (340): Lt. Colonel Jose Maria Herrera
3rd Brigade of Infantry: Col. Jose Lopez Uraga
  4th Line Infantry (187)
  1st Active Militia of Mexico (136): Lt-Col. Francisco Berra
  3rd Line Infantry (345): Lt-Col. Florencio Azpeitia

4th Brigade of Infantry: Colonel Nicolas Mendoza
  1st Line Infantry (186): Lt-Col. Gregorio Gelati
  Active Militia of Morelia (77): Lt-Col. Joaquin Orihuela
  Active Militia of San Luis Potosi (340): Battalion Commander Jose Salazar
Unattached
  Auxiliary Battalion of Monterrey (349)
  Defensores (militia) of Nuevo Leon (625)

Cavalry
1st Brigade of Cavalry: Gen-Col. Anastasio Torrejon
  Light Mounted Regiment of Mexico (80): Squadron Commander Mariano Valazquez
  1st Cavalry (93): Gen. Antonio Maria Jauregui
  7th Cavalry (attached to 1st Cavalry)
  8th Cavalry (99)
2nd Brigade of Cavalry: Gen-Col. Manuel Romero
  3rd Cavalry (140)
  Active Militia of Guanajuato (132): Col. Mariano Moret
  Jalisco Lancers (146): Lt-Col. Juan Najera
  Active Militia of San Luis Potosi (123)
Unattached
  1st Active Militia Company of Nuevo Leon (56)
  Auxiliary Squadron of Bejar (68)
  1st Permanent Company of Tamaulipas (41)
  2nd Permanent Company of Tamaulipas (9)
  Permanent Company of Lampazos (23)
  Permanent Company of Bejar (22)
  Permanent Company of La Bahia (1)
  these Permanent Companies may have been Presidial Companies

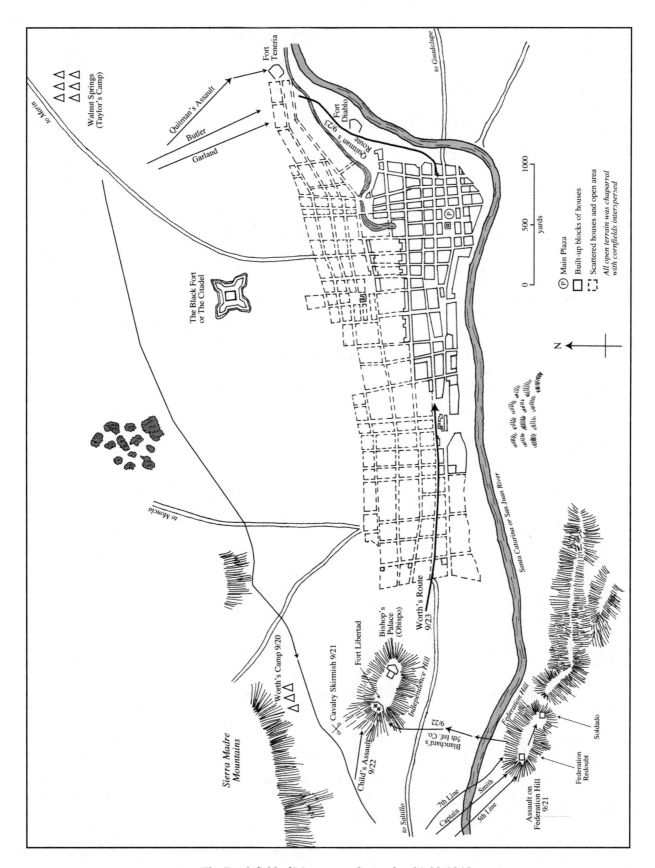

The Battlefield of Monterrey, September 21-23 1846

problems caused by the volunteers eventually reached a point where Taylor ordered some regiments to the rear in disgrace so as to get them away from the rest of the army. Disease also began to take a frightful toll due to the miserable living conditions suffered by most of the volunteers. McClellan wrote: "I have seen more suffering since I came out here than I could have imagined to exist. It is really awful. I allude to the sufferings of the Volunteers. They literally die like dogs". He elaborated in another letter from Camargo: "Already have they in almost every volunteer regiment reported one-third their number sick, and in many cases one-half the whole regiment, and I fear the mortality will be terrible among them, for their utter ignorance of the proper mode of taking care of themselves".

The volunteers were not only dangerous to the Mexican population of the area, but were also a danger to themselves. Later in the campaign when boredom had replaced the daily exertions required just to survive, the search for activities led the volunteers to begin fighting each other. An Ohio volunteer had claimed that he and his comrades had taken on a Tennessee battalion simply because they claimed that they had never been whipped and couldn't be, "by anything that lived". The 1st South Carolina, or "Palmetto", regiment refused to be brigaded or even bivouac in the same area as the New York Volunteers. When Irish and Scottish soldiers from two different companies of Georgia Volunteers began to fight among themselves some men of the Fourth Illinois Volunteers tried to break it up. The fight only got worse and ended up with one of the Georgia volunteers dead and several wounded on both sides including Colonel Edward D. Baker of the Fourth Illinois, who the Georgia troops blamed for making the situation worse by intervening.

The volunteers didn't always limit their energies to fighting among themselves. They generally disliked the regulars and the regular officers almost as much as the Mexicans. The innate American distrust of a standing army and the fact that many regular soldiers came from the lower strata of society made it easy for the volunteers to look down on the regular army. They may have admired many of the qualities that these experienced soldiers showed both on parade and in battle but they were careful not to show it. The regulars continued to complain that the volunteers did less than their share of the work and took more than their share of the credit for winning battles and the war. The volunteers often had no use at all for the regular officers or even some of their own, who they had elected themselves. There were some instances of officers being threatened by the men and it is possible that a few even perished at the hands of their own soldiers. This was a real problem, although not well documented, even among the regulars. Captain Braxton Bragg of the Third Artillery was particularly unpopular with the men under his command as he was a martinet who demanded strict adherence to the regulations at all times. There were at least two attempts made on his life during the course of the war. In one episode an eight-inch bomb shell was placed under his bed with a trail of gunpowder leading out of the tent, which was ignited after he retired for the night. There was a terrific explosion and even though his bed was penetrated by two chunks of metal he was not injured. Bragg believed that a disgruntled soldier from Ohio (who was a fugitive from the law there) may have made the assassination attempt, but he didn't have enough proof and charges were never filed.

Taylor had not left Matamoros for Camargo (about three hundred miles by river, but less than one hundred miles away by land) until August 4th. The delay had been due to the gathering of men and supplies and the necessity to scout the routes to be taken toward Monterrey, which Taylor had decided would be his next objective. He still did not have sufficient numbers of wagons or steamships to move the men and supplies on hand to Monterrey. It was at Camargo that the majority of the volunteers managed to catch up with Taylor, and eventually swell the size of the American camp to over 12,000 men. The camp at Camargo was also where the ranks of the volunteers were drastically thinned by disease, with an estimated 1,500 dead (about twelve percent) of the force gathered there. When Taylor finally moved out of Camargo he could only take about 3,000 volunteers with him out of a total of more than 7,700 on hand. To accomplish even this, he had to resort to mules to carry supplies instead of wagons. The remaining men were divided up as garrisons between Camargo, Matamoros, and other camps, with some 1,400 still in hospital. When pressed on the issue, Taylor blamed the Quartermaster Department for all of the delays in getting from Matamoros to Monterrey. The Army of Occupation marched by way of Cerralvo and Marin, about one hundred and twenty-five miles, finally reaching Monterrey on the morning of September 19th, four months after the fall of Matamoros.

The Mexicans had been given ample time to make preparations to defend the city. Some changes in leadership had taken place since May, with Arista being court-martialed for his failure to hold Matamoros and Ampudia taking over as commander of the Army of the North. The biggest change had been the return to Mexico of general Antonio López de Santa Anna himself in August. He had been given a safe passage through the blockade by the United States in the hopes that he could return from exile in Cuba, negotiate a peace and put an end to hostilities. Instead the self-styled "Napoleon of the West" was back in command of the Mexican Army and beginning to plan his next campaign to drive the Americans out. Santa Anna was aware of Taylor's plan to advance on Monterrey and he favored abandoning the city and pulling back to Saltillo to meet the Americans there if they continued to advance. Ampudia refused this advice, however, as he was confident that he could hold the northern province of Nuevo Leon and its capital city. To do so Ampudia had gathered as many as 7,000 men, most of them regulars, to man the city and the hills and forts that protected it.

The city of Monterrey had been turned into a fortress by the impressive Mexican defenses that had been built over the past several weeks. There were about 10,000 inhabitants in the city itself, which was built on the north, or left, bank of the Santa Catarina River, a tributary of the San Juan River. The city was bordered by the river on the southern and eastern edges with the road from Marin coming in from the northeast. The southern horizon was dominated by the wall of the Sierra Madre mountains which had their beginnings here. The road to Saltillo to the west and south was the only break in this rugged terrain. The stone buildings of the city stretched out for more than a mile from east to west and about half that distance north of the river. The northeastern part of the city was protected by Fort Teneria and Fort Diablo, both built to cover the approach from the Marin road. Directly to the north and about 1000 yards from the city itself was the Citadel, a quadrangular earthwork with walls thirty feet high commanding all of the approaches from the north and east. The fortress was manned by 400 men of the 4th Infantry and mounted only eight guns, although it was capable of holding thirty. It was soon dubbed the Black Fort by the Americans due to its dark and menacing appearance. The western approaches to the city were covered by Independence Hill which was a rugged 800 foot

---

UNITED STATES ARMY AT MONTERREY FROM
SEPTEMBER 21-23, 1846

Brigadier General Zachary Taylor (425/5795=6220)*
  Headquarters & Staff (22/23=45)
  Company A, 1st Artillery (3/24=27): Captain Lucian Bonaparte Webster
    (1 - 10" mortar & 2 - 24 lb. howitzers)
*(officers/men=total)

1st Division: General David E. Twiggs
  Hq & Staff (3/10=13)
  2nd Dragoons (10/228=238): Lt-Col. Charles A. May
    (Companies B, C, D & E)
  Company C, 3rd Artillery (3/75=78): Capt. Randolph Ridgeley
    (3 - 6 lb. guns & 1 - 12 lb. gun)
3rd Brigade: Lt-Col. John Garland
  Company E, 3rd Artillery (2/64=66): Capt. Braxton Bragg
  3rd Infantry (18/284=302): Maj. William W. Lear
    (Companies C, D, F, H, I & K)
  4th Infantry (16/287=303): Maj. George W. Allen
    (Companies A, B, C, D, E & I)
  Volunteer Company of Columbia (3/55=58): Capt. William R. Shivors
4th Brigade: Lt-Col. Henry Wilson
  1st Infantry (12/179=191): Maj. John J. Abercrombie
    (Companies C, E, G & K)
  Battalion of Maryland and District of Columbia Volunteers (20/314=334)(6 Companies): Lt-Col. Wlliam H. Watson

2nd Division: Brig-Gen. William J. Worth (93/1558=1651)
  HQ & Staff (5)
  Sick Call (7/45=52)
1st Brigade: Lt-Col. Thomas Staniford
  Company A, 2nd Artillery (68): Capt. James Duncan
    (1 - 12 lb. howitzer & 4 - 6 lb. guns)

Artillery Regiment (as Infantry)(532): Lt-Col. Thomas Childs (Companies C & E, 1st Artillery & Companies G & K, 2nd Artillery & Companies A & B, 3rd Artillery & Companies D, G, H& I, 4th Artillery)
  8th Infantry (331): Lt-Col. William G. Belknap
    (Companies A, B, D, E, H & I)
2nd Brigade: Col. Persifor F. Smith
  Company K, 1st Artillery (70): Lt. William W. Mackall
    (4 - 6 lb. guns)
  5th Infantry (280): Maj. Martin Scott
    (Companies E, F, G, H, I & K)
  7th Infantry (282): Captain Dixon S. Miles
    (Companies C, D, E, F, I & K)
  Volunteer Company of Louisiana (83): Capt. Albert C. Blanchard

Field Division (Volunteers): Maj-Gen. William O. Butler (148/1781=1929)
  Headquarters Staff (12)
  Sick Call (1/42=43)
1st Brigade: Brig-Gen. Thomas L. Hamer
  1st Kentucky Infantry (482): Col. Stephen Ormsby
    (10 Companies)
  1st Ohio Infantry (524): Col. Alexander M. Mitchel
    (10 Companies)
2nd Brigade: Brig-Gen. John A. Quitman
  1st Mississippi Rifles (452): Col. Jefferson Davis
    (8 Companies)
  1st Tennessee Infantry (459): Col. William B. Campbell
    (10 Companies)

Texas Division: Maj-Gen. Pinckney Henderson
  Headquarters & Staff (5)
  Surgeons (5)
  Sick Call (3/143=146)
  1st Texas Mounted Volunteers (32/376=408): Col. John C. Hays (10 Companies)
  2nd Texas Mounted Volunteers (35/527=562): Col. George T. Wood (10 Companies)

General Worth

height that overlooked the city and held Fort Libertad. This hill was referred to by the Mexicans as the Obispado, or Bishop's Palace which was located on the eastern end of the hill. Across the river was another hill about half as high that ran parallel to the Obispado called Federation Ridge, with Fort Soldado on its eastern end and a small redan to the west. Ampudia had plenty of ammunition on hand and no lack of troops to garrison the fortifications. Unfortunately, most of the strongpoints positioned around the city could not support each other very well. Ampudia had allocated all of his force to manning these bastions as well as barricades in the streets and outlying houses, to the point where he had no reserves to commit. There were about a thousand cavalry also present which were not going to be of much use for fighting in the city itself. Even so, the Mexican defenders outnumbered Taylor's attackers, who totalled just over 6,000 men.

Taylor's plan was to split his forces into two parts and attack the city from both the west and the east at the same time. He would send Worth's Division in a wide sweep north of the city toward the western side along the Saltillo road. This force consisted of the Artillery Regiment fighting as infantry and the 5th, 7th and 8th Infantry. There were two companies of field artillery along with Hay's unit of Texas Volunteers and some Texas Rangers. Worth's objective was to take Independence Hill along with the Bishop's Palace and so dominate the city from the western heights. The main body would make the direct assault on the forts that protected the eastern edge of the city in concert with Worth's

attack. This double envelopment would assure that the Mexicans would be cut off from their base and hard pressed to defend their entire perimeter. In practice, it was difficult, if not impossible, to coordinate attacks by two such widely separated forces.

Worth began his flanking march on the afternoon of September 20, but there was no way he could keep his movements from being seen by Ampudia. General Torrejon with a large force of cavalry was sent to try to keep communications open along the supply line and reinforcements were sent to Independence Hill immediately. The Americans were able to travel about six miles before dark when they camped close to the Pasqueria road. There were three more miles to go before reaching the Saltillo road and they would be under fire from the guns on Independence Hill. Meanwhile, Taylor had spent the day with the main body deployed on the plain to the northeast of the city, in full view of the Mexican defenders, in an attempt to create a diversion. Besides drawing a few wasted cannonshots from the city, nothing else was accomplished on this flank.

Worth's advance continued on the 21st with the Texans out front to screen. The advance guard of the Mexican cavalry was about 200 men of the Jalisco Lancers and the Guanajuato Active Militia. They charged into the fire of the Texans who had dismounted and found cover behind a fence. Worth's artillery also got into the brief action, which was over in about 20 minutes. The gallant Mexican charge had been repulsed with the loss of about thirty horsemen including the commander of the Jalisco Lancers, Lt. Colonel Juan Nájera. The march then continued, with the column reaching the Saltillo road before 9:00 a.m. Worth wrote to Taylor: "The town is ours."

With Monterrey now cut off from supply and Worth's men in position, the assault could begin. With little hesitation Worth decided to take Federation Hill and the works on top of it. His men found a crossing of the Santa Catarina a bit further to the west of his position and began fording the river under a hail of grapeshot from the batteries on the hill, but no one was injured. Captain C. F. Smith led a storming party of about 300 men, mostly Texas Rangers, to a position on the south side of the hill and began to scout the best approach. In the meantime, Worth had already decided to reinforce this small group. He sent Colonel Persifor F. Smith's brigade consisting mainly of the 5th and 7th Infantry regiments. Colonel Smith's men had followed a more direct route and had not been fired on, possibly because the Mexican gunners were distracted with Captain Smith's men already at the base of the hill. Together the two Smiths led their combined force in a charge up the hill with the regulars and Texans both vying for the lead. The shaken Mexican defenders fled, abandoning their 9 pounder cannon, and the 5th Infantry claimed the honor of being the first to the top. The captured gun was then turned to fire on Independence Hill after the Mexicans had been chased out of Fort Soldado at the other end of Federation Hill. It was late afternoon and Worth's victorious men were rejoicing in their accomplishments. Storm clouds were building up even as they received sporadic fire from the Mexican batteries on Independence Hill. There was no food, but some men tried to get some sleep to be able to renew the attack in the morning.

While Worth and his men had been storming the heights, Taylor had been having a hard time on the northeastern side of the city. Taylor had intended to launch only a diversion, but the orders he gave to Colonel John Garland (who was in command of Twigg's division while he was ill) specified that if he thought he could take any forts using the bayonet then he should do so. Garland moved up with the 1st and 3rd Infantry and the Maryland and District of Columbia Volunteers, known as the Baltimore Battalion, a force of about 800 men. As they advanced towards the city through a cornfield, the 3rd Infantry was on the right, the 1st Infantry was in the center, and the Baltimore Battalion was on the left. When they emerged from the partial cover of the field they were still 500 yards from their objectives of the forts on the outskirts of town. The Mexicans opened fire from Fort Teneria to their left front and the Citadel from the right flank. Maneuvering under fire proved to be too much for the Baltimore Battalion and they broke and ran. Their commander, Lt. Colonel William H. Watson, with about 70 men were all that remained to continue the advance. The regulars made it through the withering fire into the outskirts of town, where they quickly lost cohesion. The Mexicans were firing from the rooftops and houses as well as from behind barricades in the streets. Captain Bragg managed to bring some guns to bear on the town, but it was futile to remain under the intense fire from all around. Garland was forced to give the order to withdraw. The only bright spot was that three companies of the 1st Infantry had captured a tannery located behind Fort Teneria and managed to hold it in the face of a Mexican counterattack, but this was unknown to Garland at the time.

Taylor saw that Garland was having problems. He sent in the 4th Infantry along with the 1st Ohio Volunteers to aid in the assault. Further east he also ordered Brigadier General John A. Quitman's brigade to reinforce as well. This was made up of the 1st Mississippi Rifles and the 1st Tennessee who would refer to themselves after Monterrey as the "Bloody First." Unfortunately, they all arrived after Garland had withdrawn and consequently they were subjected to the same punishment as the first attack had suffered. The 4th Infantry on the right side of the advance was severely pounded by the guns from

General Wool

Fort Teneria and the Black Fort and they were forced to withdraw after taking heavy casualties, taking the 1st Ohio with them. Quitman's brigade had been farther east and had avoided the fire from the Citadel as they moved to attack Teneria directly. They were assisted in this by the companies of the 1st Infantry that had taken refuge in the tannery. Casualties were heavy, but the Fort fell with about 30 Mexicans being taken prisoner. This was Taylor's only success that day and it had cost 394 men killed or wounded. The 21st ended with the Americans in possession of Federation Ridge and Fort Teneria, which Garland's Brigade had taken over from Quitman.

Something occurred here that would be repeated on many battlefields in the not too distant future. At the height of the action Quitman's brigade of Mississippi and Tennessee Volunteers braved the galling fire of the Mexican artillery while attacking Fort Teneria. The charge by the leading elements of the regiments of Colonel Davis and Lieutenant Colonel McClung had gained entry to the ramparts of the fort causing the entire brigade to rush forward. As they did so, according to Samuel Reid, "a yell and shout of triumph rose above the din of battle …which sent forth the "harbinger of victory". The result was that "The Mexicans fled in dismay…" The wild sound that was heard here for the first time would also send a chill down the spine of many Northern soldiers in the Civil War. They even had a name for it, the "Rebel Yell".

The night of the 21st-22nd was cold and rainy. Worth's men lay exposed to the weather on the open hills above the town. About 3:00 a.m. Lt. Colonel Childs, with a picked force of Texas Rangers, red-legged Infantry, and men from the 4th and 8th Infantry set out for the slopes of Independence Hill to surprise the defenders there. A short hand-to-hand fight before dawn put the Americans in control of Fort Libertad on the west end of the hill. The Obispado, however, remained in Mexican hands. A 12-lb. howitzer was dragged up the slope and placed in Fort Libertad to bring this position under fire. When a Mexican counterattack from the Palace collapsed, the Americans pursued and took the Obispado without much of a fight. It was late afternoon and Worth's men now held control of the western approaches to the city.

Meanwhile, Taylor had spent the 22nd resting his exhausted troops and trying to hold on to what little they had gained. Fortunately, Ampudia did not launch any counterattacks or try to retake lost ground. That night he as much as admitted defeat by withdrawing his men from all of the outer defenses except the Citadel and concentrating them at the Plaza Mayor.

September 23rd saw a renewal of the attack by both Worth from the west and Quitman from the east. The fighting was street-to-street and house-to-house, but resistance was not as heavy as before, and the Americans from both flanks made progress into the city. By late afternoon, Taylor had decided to order his men out of the city again, however, so as not to expose them to any counterattacks at night in the confused labyrinth of the streets. Early in the morning of the 24th Ampudia sent word to Taylor that he was ready to discuss terms for surrender. The assault on Monterrey was over.

The surrender terms that Taylor agreed to were not popular with any of his men, or with the politicians back home. The Mexicans were given ample time to withdraw and an eight-week armistice was agreed to whereby Taylor would not advance much further south than he already was. Taylor was most likely thinking of the condition of his men and his supply situation, neither of which were in very good shape. Taylor may also have been influenced by the objective to "conquer a peace" which had been used as a catch phrase for what the American army was supposed to be doing in Mexico. The battle had cost the Americans 120 men killed, 368 wounded and 43 missing, which was a heavy price to pay. The Mexicans had lost 367 men killed and wounded and they abandoned some 25 pieces of artillery when they withdrew. In addition Ampudia had completely lost the will to fight, which may have been what determined the final outcome. By the end of September Ampudia and his men had withdrawn to Saltillo and were on their way further south towards San Luis Potosí, which would be their new base of operations.

The Division of the Center

"What is to be gained by going to Chihuahua? …all that we shall find to conquer is distance."
General Wool

Once war had actually been declared, the Polk administration lost no time in planning for the seizure of much of the northern territory of Mexico. It was hoped that this loss would convince the Mexicans to come to favorable terms quickly and put an end to the war. With this in mind, an expedition to the town of Chihuahua, capital of the state of the same name, was launched with Brigadier General John E. Wool in command. Wool was sixty-two years old in 1846 and he was the third ranking officer in the army. He had been commissioned captain in 1812 and ended the war with a rank of Brevet Lieutenant Colonel. He was promoted to Brigadier General in 1841. Wool was considered harsh by some, but his methods were effective in molding his command into a well trained force with more discipline than most. His objective was 350 miles northwest of Monterrey and 200 miles south of El Paso. It was the nearest sizeable Mexican outpost after Santa Fe, New Mexico. Wool's force would eventually total some 3,400 men, with only 500 of them being regulars, the rest volunteers. Wool

---

U.S. Division of the Center in September of 1846—Wool's Expedition to Chihuahua

Brig-Gen. John E. Wool (2961) (2829) (3400)
  Brig-Gen. James Shields
  Inspector General: Colonel Sylvester Churchill
  Assistant Quartermaster: Captain Osborn Cross
  Corps of Engineers: Capt. William D. Fraser & Capt. Robert E. Lee
  Aide de Camp: Lieutenant Irwin McDowell

U.S. Dragoons (300): Lt. Colonel William S. Harney
  1st Dragoons (Companies A & E): Capt. Enoch Steen & Capt. William Eustis
  2nd Dragoons: Lt-Col. William S. Harney (Companies A, G & I)
Company B, 4th Artillery (100): Capt. John M. Washington (8 guns)
6th Infantry (100) (3 Companies); Maj. Benjamin L. E. Bonneville
1st Illinois Infantry (574) (8 Companies): Colonel John J. Hardin
2nd Illinois Infantry: Colonel William H. Bissell
Arkansas Mounted Volunteers (750) (6 Companies): Col. Archibald Yell
Independent Company of Kentucky Mounted Volunteers (90): Capt. John S. Williams
attached to Illinois Regiments:
  Independent Texas Rifle Company: Capt. P. Edward Connor

---

first received his orders in mid-June, but due to the many difficulties in assembling troops and supplies (as well as a means to transport them), the first part of the army did not leave San Antonio until September 23, the day before the fall of Monterrey.

With the majority of his force consisting of volunteers, Wool had his work cut out for him. He was a strict disciplinarian and would not tolerate breaches of military behavior, especially when it came to the treatment of Mexican civilians. Upon preparing to cross the Rio Grande Wool had issued strict orders about the conduct of the men.

"Tomorrow you will cross the Rio Grande, and occupy the territory of our enemies. We have not come here to make war upon the people or peasantry of the country, but to compel the government of Mexico to render justice to the United States. The people, therefore, who do not take up arms against the United States, and remain quiet and peaceful at their homes, will not be molested or interfered with, either as regards their persons or property; and all those who furnish supplies will be treated kindly, and whatever is received from them will be liberally paid for.

It is expected of the troops that they will observe the most rigid discipline and subordination. All depredations on the persons or property of the people of the country are strictly forbidden; and every soldier or follower of the camp, who may so far forget his duty as to violate these injunctions, will be severely punished".

Though this did not make him any more popular with the volunteers, his march saw fewer problems arise from them than Taylor's advance had. In two weeks the advance guard reached the Rio Grande near present day Eagle Pass, Texas. On October 10, Captain Robert E. Lee of the Engineers helped to fashion a pontoon bridge across the river from specially built boats brought from San Antonio. A small Mexican force patrolling the area had dispersed the day before when Lt. Colonel William S. Harney and his dragoons had waded across to reconnoiter. Now that the army was underway and into Mexico, Wool discovered that there was no direct route that was suitable for wagons or artillery going to Chihuahua from the Rio Grande, where he was at. The lack of adequate water for a force of his size was also a consideration in taking a more roundabout route to the south. The first part of the journey took him to Monclava, which he reached by the end of October. The army had marched in several detachments and was finally brought together here. Among the newly arrived from Camargo was Brigadier General James Shields from Illinois, who brought word with him of the fall of Monterrey. He brought some balance to the force as second in command after Wool, for he gave the volunteers someone to look to besides the regular officers, who

Shields is remembered more for his defeat by Stonewall Jackson in the Shenandoah campaign.

they detested. Shields was a lawyer that had been born in Ireland and had served in the Illinois militia during the Black Hawk War in 1832. He was recognized as one of the best volunteer generals in the army and was well liked by the men. There had been many disputes and problems between the men and their officers and Wool was not at all popular with the volunteers by this time.

A good example of what Wool was up against with the volunteers comes from Sam Chamberlain of the 1st Dragoons at Monclava:

"One day when I was on General Wool's guard, he with his staff rode into town to dine. As we approached the guard line a "Sucker" on post was seated on the ground with a roguish looking Senorita, engaged in eating 'frijoles' and 'pan de maiz'. The sentinel coolly eyed the cavalcade, and with no thoughts of rising to salute, he remarked, "Good day General, hot riding out I reckon".

The General thundered out, "Call the officer of the guard"!

The man just raised himself on his elbow and drawled out, "Lieutenant Woodson, come here right quick, post nine, for the old General wants you"! He then turned to his companion with a self-satisfied air, as if he had discharged his duty in the most exemplary manner.

The officer of the guard made his appearance without belt or sword, coat unbuttoned and a straw hat on. The General gave him a severe reprimand for his own appearance as well as the unsoldierlike conduct of the guard, whereupon the officer broke out, "Jake Strout, yer ain't worth shucks. If you don't git right up and salute the General, I'll drive yer gal away, doggone if I don't".

The gallant sentinel riled up at this and replied "that if the General wanted saluting the Lieutenant might do it, he wasn't agoing to do anything of the kind".

From Monclava the only practical way to Chihuahua was by the road from Parras, a detour of 200 miles to the south to be able to go north again to the objective. Wool inquired of Taylor, "What is to be gained by going to Chihuahua?... all that we shall find to conquer is distance". He then requested that new orders be issued so that he could leave Monclava. After almost four weeks there the army was ordered to march south to Parras and the Chihuahua expedition was cancelled. By December 5, Wool's column had reached Parras after having marched a great distance fighting false alarms, the hostile environment, and amongst themselves all the way. On December 12 a note from General Worth

arrived summoning Wool and his army to Saltillo immediately with word of an imminent attack by Santa Anna. Wool and his army were on the road in two hours, a level of readiness that was the result of many long hours of training and discipline. The march took four days to bring them to Agua Nueva in the vicinity of Saltillo, by which time the rumors of attack had proved false. Wool had thus joined up with Taylor's army after a march of 900 miles through enemy territory.

The news of the armistice agreed to by Taylor was not very well accepted in Washington. Taylor was instructed to terminate it as soon as possible but it was mid-November before he considered it proper to make any movements. By this time the Polk administration had decided that their limited war strategy had failed to accomplish its objective of "conquering a peace." Mexico would not submit just because her northern territories were occupied and her armies there had been defeated. A new plan was needed that would re-activate the war and strike at the heart of the country to bring the Mexicans to the bargaining table. It was decided that the army would land on the gulf coast at Vera Cruz and march on Mexico City itself. The major effort of the war was to be taken away from Taylor, who had fallen out of favor with the administration. After much political maneuvering Winfield Scott, the commanding general of the U.S. Army, was chosen to command the expedition.

Major General Winfield Scott was sixty years old at the time of his appointment. He stood six foot, four inches tall and had a large build that made him quite an imposing figure of a soldier, especially when mounted. His insistence on the finer points of military etiquette and decorum had earned him the nickname of "Old Fuss and Feathers", but he was deeply respected by the men serving under him. He had obtained his first commission as a captain of light artillery from President Thomas Jefferson in 1808. He served in the War of 1812, most notably at the Battle of Lundy's Lane in 1814 where he was severely wounded. He ended the war with the rank of Brevet Major General and was recognized as somewhat of a national hero. He spent much time in writing and revising the army's military manuals and was very involved trying to improve the discipline and training of the troops. Scott was a meticulous planner and an excellent strategist. In 1841 he became the commanding general of the army with the rank of Major General. He had supported Taylor for command of the army in the field, but he soon saw that the northern strategy was not going to win the war. He was anxious to see action in Mexico and to lead the army to victory there.

Scott arranged to leave for Mexico as soon as possible, boarding a steamer before the end of

---

UNITED STATES FORCES AVAILABLE ON OCTOBER 27, 1846 (NOT WITH GENERAL TAYLOR)

At Camargo: Maj-Gen. Robert Patterson
2nd Brigade: Maj-Gen. Gideon J. Pillow
    2nd Tennessee Infantry (350): Col. William T. Haskell
    Alabama Volunteer Regiment (400): Col. John R. Coffey
Ohio & Kentucky Brigade: Brig-Gen. Thomas Marshall
    2nd Kentucky Infantry (400): Col. William R. McKee
    2nd Ohio Infantry (500): Col. George W. Morgan
Illinois Brigade: Maj-Gen. James Shields
    3rd Illinois Infantry (370): Col. Ferris Foreman
    4th Illinois Infantry (330): Col. Edward D. Baker
    2nd U. S. Infantry & Mounted Rifles (on foot) (500): Lt-Col. Bennet Riley
At Reynosa: Capt. Henry Swartwout
    Company H, 2nd Artillery
    1st Indiana Infantry (2 Companies)
At Matamoros: Col. Newman S. Clark (6th Infantry)
    3rd Ohio Infantry: Col. Samuel R. Curtis
    Company I, 2nd Artillery: Capt. Allen Loud
    Battery of Artillery: Capt. Norman
    Battery of Artillery: Capt. Vanness
At Camp Belknap:
    Indiana Brigade: Brig-Gen. Joseph Lane
    2nd Indiana Infantry (600): Col. William A. Bowles
    3rd Indiana Infantry (650): Col. James H. Lane
At the Mouth of the Rio Grande:
    1st Indiana Infantry (550): Col. James P. Drake
At Brazos Island:
    Battery of Artillery: Capt. Giles Porter (4th Artillery)
At Point Isabel:
    Company of Artillery: Maj. John L. Gardner (4th Artillery)

November and arriving at the Rio Grande shortly after Christmas. In corresponding with Taylor, Scott had not been specific as to what his mission was in coming to Mexico, only that he was not going to supersede Taylor in his present command. He also informed him that he would be taking away a large part of Taylor's force to be used on a different line of operations. Scott had written that he hoped to meet Taylor somewhere in Mexico to discuss these matters personally, but the meeting never took place. The schedule that Scott was on was a tight one, and he had been delayed several weeks by the time he reached Mexico. Besides that, Taylor's communications were not as reliable as they might have been and he only received word of the proposed meeting when it was already apparently too late to arrange it. Taylor was also very unhappy about the fact that part of his army was being taken away and he was expected to act only defensively. He had planned to renew his campaign to Saltillo and consolidate his gains with outposts all along the new frontier that he had conquered. Further friction was caused by the fact that Scott, in the interest of saving time, did not go through Taylor directly when he requisitioned the troops he wanted. Taylor was only sent a copy of the orders after the fact. By the end of January Worth's and Twigg's divisions along with many of the volunteers under Major General Robert Patterson had already marched for the coast at Tampico, which had fallen to the navy in mid-November. Taylor was left with a skeleton force until additional units would arrive to reinforce him.

Taylor was shocked when he discovered that he was to be left with a force of less than a thousand regulars and several regiments of the newly raised volunteers. He had already had reports of a Mexican army gathering to the south at San Luis Potosí under Santa Anna that could possibly threaten his position. Now he was to be left virtually defenseless, the way he saw it. Meanwhile, Scott had sent him orders to pull back all the way to Monterrey and not to undertake any other offensive actions in the near future. By the end of January reports were reaching Taylor in Monterrey that Santa Anna had returned to Mexico City and the Mexican army at San Luis Potosí was too short of supplies to initiate any action. With this threat now seemingly removed Taylor felt confident enough in his position that he chose to ignore his orders completely. He began to concentrate his forces just south of Saltillo to further consolidate his position in the event the opportunity arose to resume the offensive.

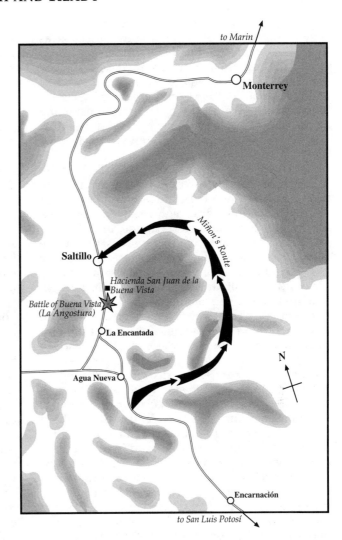

The approach to Buena Vista

General Taylor established his new camp at a site known as Agua Nueva, more than 16 miles south of Saltillo. His intent was to make Saltillo his base of supply, at the same time denying its use to the Mexicans. This would prevent any attack being made on Monterrey, about 50 miles to the north-east. This position would also allow Taylor to offer battle in the open to any forces that might march north from San Luis Potosí. It is clear Taylor did not expect Santa Anna to launch a strike towards him with virtually the entire Mexican Army.

While the Americans were shifting troops and planning new strategy, the Mexicans, now under the leadership of Santa Anna, had not been idle. Only two weeks after the fall of Monterrey Santa Anna reached San Luis Potosí, about 300 miles to the south, with the lead elements of the army that he would build there. Santa Anna had contemplated an attack north to Saltillo in December, which is what had triggered the alarm that brought Wool to that vicinity. The attack was called off when its chances of success were assessed as negligible due to the number of American troops now in the area. Then on January 13, 1847 Lieutenant John A. Richey was ambushed and killed while acting as a courier from General Scott to Taylor. He carried with him Scott's orders for transferring Taylor's troops out of the area by way of the coast. Santa Anna now knew that Taylor was left with only a small force to defend what he had won. The decision was therefore made to attack Taylor with as much of an army as could be mustered before Scott's new theater of operations could be opened up. A victory in the north might push the Americans all the way back to the Rio Grande and force the cancellation of any new offensives that were planned, or at least allow the Mexicans to meet any new threat on better terms. At the same time, a victory would put Mexico, and Santa Anna himself, in a much better bargaining position.

The problems that Santa Anna faced in raising an army were enormous, but this was what he did best of all. To begin with there was virtually no money to be had and very little popular support. At the same time the citizens in Mexico were clamoring for something to be done to stop the foreign invasion and hostile occupation of territory. Against popular opinion Santa Anna pulled back all of the northern garrisons, including the troops at Tampico, which allowed the Americans a free hand in the area. He began concentrating these forces at San Luis Potosí along with whatever other troops could be mustered. He put a great deal of pressure on the clergy for money, to be secured by Church property. He also tapped into every other available source of income and supply to be found to put together this supreme effort. He even contributed funds from his private estate to help finance the army and equip them with new uniforms. In the end, just over 21,000 men were raised and had begun training at San Luis Potosí before the end of January. It was an unbelievable achievement given the circumstances, and Santa Anna is to be given full credit for putting together the largest single army that Mexico would field during the war.

Santa Anna's plan called for the army to march over some of the most barren wastelands in Mexico during the most inhospitable season of the year in order to surprise Taylor's army at Saltillo. It was similar to what he had accomplished almost exactly eleven years before when he had surprised the Alamo defenders at the end of February, 1836. He issued a general order before the departure of the army to inspire the men and remind them of what they were fighting for.

"Companions in Arms! The independence, the honor, and the destinies of the nation depend, in this moment, on your decision! Soldiers! the entire world is observing us... Privations of all kind await you; but when has want or penury weakened your spirit or debilitated your enthusiasm?... the Mexican soldier is well known for his frugality and capability of sufferance... Today you commence your march, through thinly settled country, without supplies and without provisions; but you may be assured that very quickly you will be in possession of those of your enemy, and of his riches; and with them, all your wants will be superabundantly supplied...", he further exhorted them to "wipe away from our soil the vainglorious foreigner who has dared to pollute it with his presence".

The leading elements of the army began marching out of San Luis Potosí on January 27, heading north.

UNITED STATES FORCES AT BUENA VISTA ON FEBRUARY 22 & 23, 1847

Brig-Gen. Zachary Taylor (4792)
Brig-Gen. John E. Wool
Headquarters Staff (41)
Sick Call (364)
Regulars
1st Dragoons (133): Capt. Enoch Steen (Companies A & E)
2nd Dragoons (76): Col. Charles A. May (Companies D & E)
Company C, 3rd Artillery (75): Capt. Braxton Bragg (4 - 6 lb. guns)
Company E, 3rd Artillery (75): Capt. Thomas W. Sherman (4 - 6 lb. guns)
Company B, 4th Artillery (117): Capt. John M. Washington (1 - 4 lb. & 3 - 6 lb. guns & 1 -12 lb. howitzer)
Volunteers
1st Illinois Infantry (580): Col. John J. Hardin

2nd Illinois Infantry (573): Col. William H. Bissell
Texas Volunteer Company (61): Capt. P. Edward Conner
1st Mississippi Rifles (368): Col. Jefferson Davis
2nd Kentucky Infantry (571): Col. William R. McKee
Arkansas Cavalry Regiment (479): Col. Archibald Yell
Texas Rangers (27): Capt. Ben McCulloch
1st Kentucky (330): Col. Humphrey Marshal (2 squadrons mounted & 4 companies on foot)
Indiana Brigade (1253): Gen. Joseph Lane
2nd Indiana Infantry: Col. William A. Bowles (8 companies)
3rd Indiana Infantry: Col. James H. Lane (8 companies)
4 Rifle Companies: Col. Gorman (2 each from 2nd & 3rd Indiana)
In Saltillo
Company A, 1st Artillery: Capt. Lucian B. Webster (2 - 24 lb. howitzers)
Company B, 4th Artillery: Capt. John Paul Jones O'Brien (1 - 4 lb. & 1 - 6 lb. gun & 1 - 12 lb. howitzer)
1st Mississippi Rifles (2 companies)
Illinois Infantry (4 companies)

THE MEXICAN ARMY AT BUENA VISTA ON FEBRUARY 22 & 23, 1847

The Order of Battle for the Mexican Army at Buena Vista is one of the most difficult to obtain a clear picture of. Many isolated facts and bits of information are presented here that will hopefully enlighten rather than confuse.
Note: numbers in parenthesis indicate (chiefs/officers/troops), chiefs probably refers to officers of Colonel and above while officers could be any below this rank.

Generalissimo Antonio Lopez de Santa Anna
  Army General Staff (5/16/-): Gen. Manuel Micheltorena
  Engineers-General Staff: Gen. Ignacio de Mora y Villamil
  Military Medical Corps (11/15/35): Inspector Pedro Vanderlinden

unattached units
  Zapadores (2/11/311): Gen. Santiago Blanco
  San Patricio soldiers (deserters) (80) with 3 - 16 lb. guns were attached to the Zapadores
  Hussars of the Guard of the Supreme Powers (2/42/422): Lt-Col. Miguel Andrade
  Artillery (11/55/518): Gen. Antonio Corona
Light Infantry Brigade: Major-Gen. Pedro de Ampudia
  1st Light Infantry
  2nd Light Infantry
  3rd Light Infantry
  4th Light Infantry
  Reinforcements on night of 2/22
  4th Line Infantry
Vanguard Division (14/207/4618) (8 - 8 lb. guns): Maj-Gen. Francisco Pacheco
  1st Active Militia of Guanajuato
  2nd Active Militia of Guanajuato
  one brigade commander was Brigadier General Francisco Mejia
  mostly raw recruits, total of Guanajuato units at San Luis Potosi was 5,000
Center Division (22/249/4029) (5 - 12 lb. guns): Maj-Gen. Manuel Lombardini
  1st Line Infantry
  3rd Line Infantry
  5th Line Infantry
  10th Line Infantry
  11th Line Infantry
  mostly veteran troops
Rear Guard Division (18/209/2970): Maj-Gen. Luis Guzman then Major General Jose Maria Ortega
  Fijo de Mexico
  12th Line Infantry
  Tampico Coast Guard Battalion
  Veteran Coast Guard Company of Tampico
  Active Militia of Puebla
  ?? Brigade Commander General Anastasio Parrodi

1st Cavalry Brigade (15/101/1302): Gen. Vincente Minon
  4th Cavalry
  Active Militia Cavalry of Puebla
  Mounted Rifles (Cazadores)
  Jalisco Lancers
2nd Cavalry Brigade (13/107/974): Gen. Julian Juvera
  5th Cavalry

  9th Cavalry
  Active Militia Cavalry of Morelia
  Tulancingo Cuirassiers
3rd Cavalry Brigade (12/90/706): Gen. Anastasio Torrejon
  3rd Cavalry
  7th Cavalry
  8th Cavalry
  Active Militia Cavalry of Guanajuato
4th Cavalry Brigade (2/53/335): Gen. Manuel Andrade
  Presidial troops only

Observation Division
Infantry Brigade (11/117/1655): Brig-Gen. Ciriaco Vasquez
  Republicano Battalion (National Guard ?)
  Auxiliaries of Peejamo (National Guard ?)
  Active Militia Squadron of San Luis Potosi
Cavalry Brigade (8/95/2121): Brig-Gen. Jose Urrea
  Irregulars (2000)

Other units present but not yet accounted for
  Mixed of Santa Anna (remnants of the 6th, 7th & 8th Infantry)
  Active Militia Infantry of Aguascalientes, Celaya, Guadalajara, Jalisco, Lagos, Leon, 1st Mexico, 2nd Mexico, Michoacan, Morelia & Queretaro
  1st Cavalry
  Light Mounted Regiment of Mexico
  Active Militia Cavalry of Michoacan & Oaxaca
  It is assumed that these units were part of the larger formations listed above but specific information was not found that would place them in their proper place.

Note: It appears from the list above that most of the units of the Mexican Army took part in this battle. While this is true in one sense because it was a supreme effort it should be kept in mind that many of these units were only represented by detachments.

Miscellaneous facts
  Zapadores & Artillery combined total 900 (20 guns).
  1st & 3rd Light, 1st, 3rd, 4th, 5th, 10th & 11th Line total (6240)
  4th Light, Mixed of Santa Anna, Active Militia of Celaya, Lagos, Guadalajara, Queretaro, 1st Mexico & 2nd Mexico total 3200.
  12th Line, Active Militia of Puebla, Tampico Coast Guard Battalion, Veteran coast Guard Company of Tampico total 1000.
  Active Militia of Guadalajara commanded by Colonel Perdigon Garay
  Total guns available to the army from San Luis Potosi:
  3 - 16 lb. bronze guns (not mounted), 5 -12 lb. bronze guns (not mounted), 2 - 12 lb. iron guns, 7 - 8 lb. bronze guns, 4 - 8 lb. iron guns, 3 - 6 lb. bronze guns, 14 - 4 lb. bronze guns, 1 - 7" howitzer

Mexican Army Totals (162/1379/19,996) (39 guns) or, Infantry (13,432) in 28 battalions, Cavalry (4338) in 40 squadrons, Artillery (413) for a total of (18,183) or, Officers (1104), Men (14, 048) = total of (15,152) or, Aggregate (21,553); Leaving San Luis Potosi (18,000); At La Encarnacion (14,000) with (4,000) stragglers and deserters

The army soon began to pay a terrible price in manpower due to the extreme conditions they had to face. Indian recruits from some of the southern regions that were unaccustomed to the colder climate froze to death at night. Despite extra efforts to stop desertions, men still straggled and fell out of the column and never returned to their units. In addition the health of many of the conscripted soldiers was not good to begin with and many caught sick and died on the march. Estimates varied, but the army may have lost as many as 4,000 men somewhere between leaving San Luis Potosí and arriving at Encarnacion on February 18 and 19. This was a fortified hacienda held by the Mexicans which was located less than 40 miles south of Saltillo. Besides losing twenty-percent of his force on the march the rest of the men had been driven hard over terrible terrain and were badly in need of rest and provisions when they arrived. Despite all of the hardships they had been through, the men still showed a great deal of confidence and enthusiasm and they had arrived in the area undetected by the Americans based at Saltillo.

Santa Anna's strategy was fairly simple. General Urrea, operating with a force of about 1,500 cavalry and mounted guerrillas would cut off Taylor's communications between Monterrey and Matamoros by seizing Victoria and interfering with supply trains on the roads. General Minon with another cavalry force would stay in contact with Taylor and attack any targets that presented themselves, such as bases of supply. In addition this cavalry would screen the movements of the main body under Santa Anna himself. The "Napoleon of the West" as he styled himself, would then proceed to use his superior numbers to crush Taylor's army in open battle and chase the Americans out of Mexico.

Santa Anna's basic plan was sound, but implementing it would place a great deal of stress on his army, already under some very difficult conditions. If these could be surmounted, victory was possible.

In fact, as early as January 23, General Minon and his screening cavalry had met some success. An American cavalry patrol had been captured without a fight at the Hacienda of Encarnacion. This small group of five officers and sixty six men, from both the Arkansas and Kentucky Mounted Volunteers, had failed to post pickets the previous night when making camp. They had been sent on a scouting mission by General Wool to locate the Mexican Army that he suspected was already approaching. The first view they had of the Mexican troops was when they awoke to find themselves surrounded by five hundred of Minon's lancers.

Another patrol of Kentucky cavalry was likewise captured without a shot on the 27th. All these prisoners were marched south into the interior where they undoubtedly got a good view of Santa Anna's army headed north.

Despite the failure of the American patrols to locate the main body of the Mexican army, rumors of its imminent arrival persisted at Agua Nueva. General Wool, who had been put in charge of the camp by Taylor, had looked over much of the ground in the area since arriving in late December. The camp at Agua Nueva seemed ideal for the army as it was located on a wide plain with plenty of water. But it was soon evident that the position could be bypassed on either side by roads leading off through the hills. Wool had already chosen a much better place to deploy for battle, but Taylor would not sanction a retreat in the face of the enemy in order to occupy it. The terrain that Wool thought would make an ideal defensive position was about five miles south of Saltillo at a place known as La Angostura (the narrows).

This pass was located about a mile and a quarter south of the Hacienda San Juan de la Buena Vista. The position would effectively block any advance by the Mexicans as it could not be easily outflanked. The terrain was restricted enough to diminish any advantage the Mexicans might have with superior numbers, and also rugged enough to neutralize the effects of cavalry, of which the Americans had very little. It was not until the morning of February 21st, when Taylor received definite word that Santa Anna had reached Encarnacion, that he gave in to Wool's logic and authorized a retreat to the pass.

The reports that convinced Taylor came from two different sources. Brevet Colonel Charles A. May with two squadrons of the 1st Dragoons as well as several hundred volunteer cavalry led a scouting mission to the Rancho at Hedionda, about 15 miles south-east of Agua Nueva. On the morning of February 20th, here they encountered Minon's cavalry in force, moving to outflank the camp. Some of the troopers also observed vast clouds of dust in the distance, along the road to the south. This was evidence enough of a large army on the move. May and his men headed back to camp, arriving just before dawn on the 21st.

Further confirmation came shortly after dawn in the person of Captain Ben McCulloch, a Texas Ranger. McCulloch and one of his men, disguised as local rancheros, had ridden through the heart of Santa Anna's camp at Encarnacion. Their report that the Mexican army numbered some 20,000 men and was moving north spurred the American camp into action.

Leaving the Arkansas Mounted Regiment behind to load the wagons with the army's supplies and baggage, Taylor told Wool to dispose of the army as he saw fit in the position in the pass. Meanwhile Taylor coninued on to Saltillo with May's dragoons and the 1st Mississippi Regiment to ensure the security of his base from Minon's raiders. Wool and his troops began to prepare whatever defensive positions they could in the pass. This included two wagons loaded with rock that could be moved to block the road at the proper time.

While this was being done, some of May's dragoons were sent back towards Agua Nueva to discover why the army's supplies had not yet come up. When they arrived around midnight they found that the Arkansas "rackensackers" had found the duty of loading the wagons to be too demeaning, and they were lounging around the deserted camp or playing cards. Suddenly gunfire was heard from the road to the south, and in no time at all the Arkansas cavalry had fled. The dragoons were forced to set fire to the entire stock of supplies and wagons, and withdraw hastily north as Mexican lancers moved into the area.

When Santa Anna arrived at Agua Nueva on the morning of February 22nd he was convinced that the entire American army was in flight, and he hurried his troops forward. By midmorning Santa Anna and his staff had arrived at La Angostura pass with only an escort of cavalry to reconnoiter. He had not counted on finding the Americans occupying a position of such natural strength. Santa Anna disliked the idea of having to fight in this type of terrain and he would have preferred to maneuver around this "pass of Thermopylae" as he called it. The hasty American retreat may have convinced him that if he could press Taylor's army hard now, it would break. He also enjoyed a numerical superiority of at least three to one and had hopes his cavalry could exploit any gaps that might open in the American lines. A quick victory would be good for the morale of the army as well as doing wonders for his career. Santa Anna chose to fight.

The Mexicans would call the battle to be fought here La Angostura because that is where most of the fighting took place. To the Americans it would simply become known as Buena Vista.

BUENA VISTA

"A little more grape, Captain Bragg!"
General Taylor to Captain Bragg (popular version).
"Tell him to give 'em hell, God damn 'em."
General Taylor's actual message to Captain Bragg.

February 22nd, George Washington's birthday, was a beautiful sunlit morning with a gentle mountain breeze stirring the flags in the valley. The watchword among the American soldiers was "Honor of Washington" and the bands were playing Hail Columbia when a large dust cloud rose up on the road to the south. The Mexicans had finally arrived. Taylor's army consisted of about 4,750 men that had not marched off to the coast, including the sick. Out of these only about 700 had ever seen any action before, the rest were completely untried in battle. The only regulars present were two companies each from the 1st and 2nd Dragoons and three batteries of artillery. The volunteers consisted of the 1st Arkansas and the 1st Kentucky Cavalry regiments along with some Texas Rangers under Captain Ben McCulloch. The volunteer infantry was made up of the 1st and 2nd Illinois, the 2nd and 3rd Indiana, the 2nd Kentucky, and the 1st Mississippi Rifles. This last unit, commanded by Colonel Jefferson Davis, was the only volunteer regiment that had been in battle before, at the assault on Monterrey.

The ground that this untried army was defending had been well chosen by General Wool. The field of battle was in a valley a little over two miles wide, flanked on both sides by ranges of the Sierra Madre mountains. The main road from San Luis Potosí to Saltillo passed through this valley, which was only some forty feet wide at one point. To the west of the road, on the American right flank, the ground had been sculpted by a creek flowing from south to north into a network of gullies with nearly vertical banks rising twenty feet high, making this area virtually impassable. Further west of this was a line of high hills rising into a rugged ridge that was traversed only by a few narrow paths. It would have been possible, though extremely difficult, for small groups to have moved through this area and around the American right flank. Taylor did originally send a detachment from the 2nd Kentucky into the hills as a precaution, but the Mexicans never attempted any movements on the west side of the road. The east side of the road had several small and two large ravines running east and west that served to divide the area into three distinct areas. The northern most plateau had Buena Vista at its northwestern edge where the road entered the valley. There was a middle ground which contained the largest open areas extending to the base of the mountains. This plateau extended almost 800 yards north and south along the western side, where the road passed through. It was only half that wide along the eastern edge where the ground rose more and more steeply, eventually becoming the precipitous slopes of the Sierra Madres. The third area extended south along the base of the foothills and towards the road to Agua Nueva and then San Luis Potosí. The ravines in this area were almost impossible for artillery and cavalry to traverse and very difficult for infantry with some of them having steep sides forty or fifty feet high where they had eroded down to the floor of the valley close by the road. Large numbers of troops would find it difficult to deploy and bring their weight to bear. It was an ideal position for the greatly outnumbered American army to defend.

General Wool was responsible for deploying the

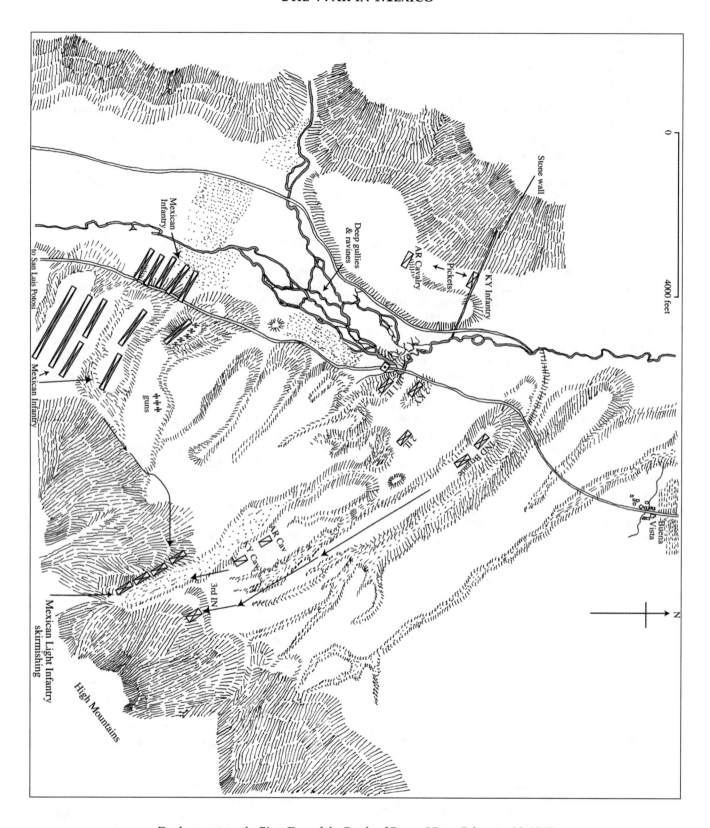

Deployment on the First Day of the Battle of Buena Vista, February 22 1847

*This representation of the second day of the battle exaggerates the terrain,
but it gives a good idea of the importance of the ravines.*

army in the pass. He placed a five gun battery under Captain Washington on the road itself at the narrowest point and facing south. Above them on the heights and to their left was the 1st Illinois behind some makeshift breastworks. A hill that was just behind the guns was held by the 2nd Kentucky. About a half mile behind them and to their left was the 2nd Illinois. The Indiana brigade was formed up on a ridge line directly behind the first line of defense. The Arkansas and Kentucky mounted volunteers were stationed to the left of this position between the road and the mountains to the east. Wool kept two squadrons of dragoons and a company of Texans as a reserve.

Shortly after 9:00 A.M. the first cavalry units of the Mexican army began to appear to the south. The troops had covered some forty-five miles in the last twenty-four hours and were tired and thirsty. It soon became clear that the Americans intended to stand and fight at La Angostura and the army would attack with a minimum amount of advance preparation. At about this time, according to Santa Anna's aide de camp Major Génaro Miranda, while the general was inspecting the American positions through his filed glasses, the first gun was fired and a cannonball struck and killed his horse. The subsequent fall

caused him a great deal of pain in the stump of his amputated leg. The main body of the Mexican army would take quite some time to arrive and deploy, and while this was going on Santa Anna issued the Americans an ultimatum directed to General Taylor, who had just arrived on the scene, along with his escort from Saltillo.

"You are surrounded by twenty thousand men, and cannot in any human probability avoid suffering a rout and being cut to pieces with your troops; but as you deserve consideration and particular esteem, I wish to save you from a catastrophe, and for that purpose give you this notice, in order that you may surrender at discretion, under the assurance that you will be treated with the consideration belonging to the Mexican character; to which end you will be granted an hour's time to make up your mind, to commence from the moment when my flag of truce arrives in your camp. With this view, I assure you of my particular consideration. God and Liberty"!

Taylor's first reaction may not have been as polite as his actual reply, which was sent back soon after:

"In reply to your note of this date, summoning me to surrender my forces at discretion, I beg leave to say that I decline acceding to your request".

The Mexican artillery was placed on the road

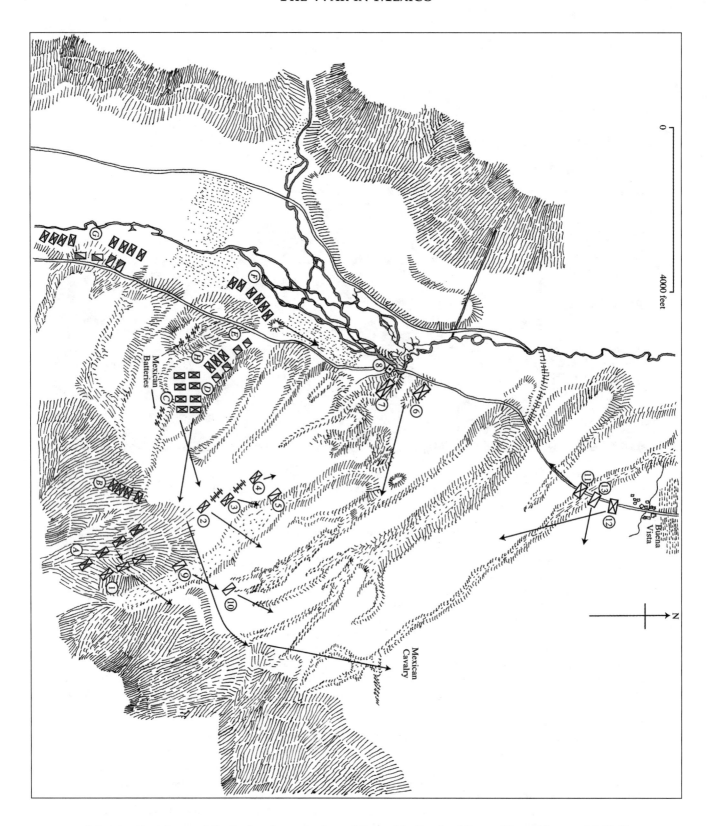

Morning Positions and Early Attacks on the Second Day of the Battle of Buena Vista, February 23 1847

opposite the American guns but beyond effective range. The Mexican infantry began coming up behind this position and would eventually form into two lines. The battle did not begin until after 3:00 P.M. with General Ampudia taking his brigade of light infantry to the slopes on the American left and working his men up into the hills in an attempt to outflank the position. Wool dispatched Colonel Humphrey Marshall with three companies of Kentucky cavalry and four dismounted rifle companies from the Arkansas cavalry, along with Major Willis A. Gorman with four companies from the 3rd Indiana, to counter the threat. The opposing forces were separated by a deep ravine extending up the mountain. All afternoon there was skirmishing in this area, but to no real effect. Ampudia and his light troops had managed to gain a foothold on the American left flank. Both sides would remain on the mountainside throughout the night. There were no other major efforts made on either side before nightfall. The Mexicans were still in the process of aligning their army and looking over the ground and Taylor was satisfied that his position was a strong one. The main attack would come in the morning.

The night of the 22nd was windy and cold, with alight rain falling. There were no fires lit in either army. The Mexican soldiers consumed the last of the rations they carried. The Americans ate hardtack and raw bacon.

Early in the morning of the 23rd Santa Anna ordered the Mexican buglers to sound reveille individually, one corps after another, to give the Americans an idea of just how vast his army was. the sight that met the Americans as the sun came up was one that impressed many of them. One of the observers was Sam Chmaberlain of the 1st Dragoons:

"I doubt if the "Sun of Austerlitz" shone on a more brilliant spectacle than the Mexican army displayed before us—twenty thousand men clad in new uniforms, belts as white as snow, brasses and arms burnished until they glittered like gold and silver. Their cavalry was magnificent—some six thousand cavaliers richly caparisoned in uniforms of blue faced with red, with white plumes and glittering weapons, advanced towards us as if they would ride down our little band and finish the battle at one blow. They formed in one long line with their massed bands in front, and then a procession of ecclesiastical dignitaries with all the gorgeous paraphanalia of the Catholic Church advanced along the lines, preceded by the bands playing a solemn anthem…" The Mexicans were celebrating mass which caused Chamberlain to remark that, "…there was not a chaplain in our army!"

The battle of February 23rd opened with attacks on the road and the plateau at the same time. In addition Ampudia had been reinforced during the night and his efforts to outflank the American position continued. On the main road General Santiago Blanco led an assault column including the 12th Infantry, the Tampico Coast Guards, the Fijo de Mexico, some Zapadores (engineers), and the Puebla Battalion into the fire of Washington's guns supported by the 1st Illinois. This attack was soon turned back with heavy losses, the Mexicans not even being able to deploy effectively due to the havoc wrought by the American artillery. The Mexican artillery in support had not managed to put enough pressure on the defenders to affect their fire. This attack had been but a diversion, however, with the main effort coming further east on the plateau to the American left.

The divisions of Francisco Pacheco and Manuel Lombardini had been advancing to their right in the hopes of smashing through the American positions between the road and the mountains. The Mexican infantry moved up through deep ravines where they were not seen by the Americans occupying the plateau that was their objective. This movement was also being supported by a battery of eight 8-pdr guns commanded by General Manuel Micheltorena deployed on the right of the Mexican attack.

To avoid being outflanked on his left, General Wool had made some adjustments to his positions of the previous day. He had sent two companies of Illinois troops along with some Texans to assist Colonel Marshall against the advancing light infantry of Ampudia in the hills. The 2nd Indiana, under Colonel William A. Bowles, along with three guns from Captain Washington's battery commanded by Captain John Paul Jones O'Brien, took up a position on the plateau to the far left of

Key to Buena Vista Map for the morning of the Second Day

A Mexican Light Infantry (Ampudia)
B Reinforcements sent during the night to Ampudia
C Lombardini's Division
D Pacheco's Division
E Mexican Cavalry
F Blanco's Column
G Reserves (Mejia)
H Ortega's Division

1 Dismounted Kentucky & Arkansas Cavalry
2 2nd Indiana & O'Brien's guns
3 2nd Illinois & Sherman's guns
4 2nd Kentucky
5 2 troops of Dragoons (Steen) & McCulloch's Texas Rangers
6 3rd Indiana
7 1st Illinois
8 Washington's battery
9 Kentucky Cavalry & 1 squ. of Dragoons
10 Arkansas Cavalry & 1 squ. of Dragoons
11 Taylor
12 1st Mississippi
13 May's Dragoons

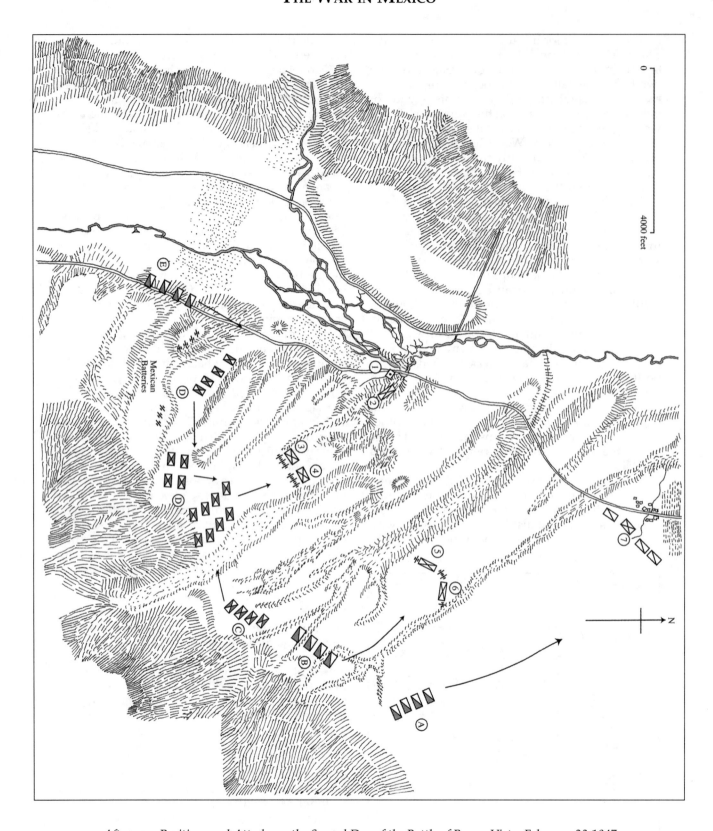

Afternoon Positions and Attacks on the Second Day of the Battle of Buena Vista, February 23 1847

the American position. Wool was hoping that from this location they could support Marshall on the slopes and close off any gap on the left flank. The 2nd Indiana was now the furthest forward unit of the American army. To their right and rear was the 2nd Illinois, under Colonel William H. Bissell, along with Captain Thomas W. Sherman's artillery battery. Further to the right and rear of the 2nd Illinois was Colonel William R. McKee's 2nd Kentucky. In addition two troops from the 1st Dragoons, under Captain Enoch Steen, along with some of Ben McCulloch's Texas rangers, tried to cover the gaps between the infantry formations.

The men of the 2nd Indiana were now under fire from Mexican batteries as well as the advancing troops. General Lane ordered them further forward once more to position themselves to be able to stop the Mexican advance. Pacheco's inexperienced brigade of Guanajuato militia was on the verge of retreat and appeared to be in a growing disorder.

O'Brien and his gunners began to move forward under the heavy fire. Bowles either did not hear or did not understand the order and when he saw O'Brien preparing to move his guns, he ordered his Indiana regiment to "Cease fire and retreat." Instead of an orderly withdrawal, the men of the 2nd Indiana broke, and along with some of the Arkansas volunteers in the vicinity fled for the rear. O'Brien was forced to withdraw as he was now without any support. In the process he lost a 4lb gun to the advancing Mexican infantry. Pacheco was able to turn the American left flank and begin the advance to roll up the line. The Americans on the slopes were completely cut off from the rest of the army and they

withdrew, both mounted and on foot, back towards Buena Vista. Lombardini's division was in close support of Pacheco, also advancing onto the plateau. The American line here was quickly turned to face the oncoming Mexicans in a fighting withdrawal. The 2nd Illinois and the 2nd Kentucky backed up towards the road with the batteries of Bragg, O'Brien and Sherman in close support. Although the main position on the road was still secure, the American left flank was gone and the route to the rear was wide open.

It was at this point, about 9 A.M., that Taylor arrived back from Saltillo with his escort of dragoons and the 1st Mississippi Rifles. When they arrived, Colonel Jefferson Davis's men proceeded to partially clear the northern portion of the plateau of Mexican troops heading for Buena Vista, forcing Ampudia and the supporting cavalry back temporarily. Seeing that the Mississippi regiment was not enough to hold the flank by itself, Wool now sent the 3rd Indiana, Colonel James H. Lane, to reinforce Davis on his own right flank. The battle had reached a critical point. Taylor had lost his left flank and the way to the rear was open. Santa Anna's men had gained the plateau in some strength. The Americans had suffered heavy losses including the routing of the 2nd Indiana. The cavalry brigade of General Juvera tried to make the most of the confusion on the plateau by heading straight for Buena Vista. There the remnants of the Arkansas and Kentucky horse, as well as some dragoons tried to hold the Mexican cavalry at bay. Most of the volunteer cavalry fled at the first charge. Some of those that didn't, including Colonel Yell from Arkansas, were cut down by lancers. Once the cavalry reached the walls of the hacienda and were charged in the flank by May's dragoons they decided to look elsewhere for action.

Meanwhile, Colonel Davis and his red-shirted Mississippi Rifles were fighting virtually alone on the northwestern plateau as the 3rd Indiana struggled through the ravines and rough ground to come to their aid. There may have been as many as 4,000 Mexican troops that had made their way onto the plateau and now were getting ready to advance on Davis and his men. The mass of Mexican troops on the plateau now became the target for the batteries of Sherman and Captain Braxton Bragg. They were deployed on the middle plateau where, along with the 2nd Illinois and 2nd Kentucky, they had managed to bring Lombardini's attack to a halt and force his troops to take cover. The artillery began to have a murderous effect on the Mexican formations. Combined with the accurate fire of the Mississippians, it was enough to cause the advance to break down. Many of the Mexican infantry began to seek shelter from the intense artillery fire in the ravines. This was the point at which Davis and his men, along with the 3rd Indiana, launched a charge, during which the Mississippi regiment received

Key to Buena Vista Map for the afternoon of the Second Day

A Mexican Cavalry attack Buena Vista
B Mexican Cavalry attack the V
C Mexican Infantry from Mountain Skirmish
D Combined Mexican Infantry for Final Assault
E Mexican Cavalry attack Washington's Battery and are repulsed

1 Washington's Battery
2 1st Illinois
3 2nd Kentucky with Sherman's Battery
4 2nd Illinois with Bragg's Battery
5 3rd Indiana
6 1st Mississippi
7 Arkansas & Kentucky Cavalry, Dragoons and remainder of 2nd Indiana

49

most of its casualties from the battle, including Colonel Davis, who was wounded in the heel but remained in action. Davis's advance succeeded in clearing the plateau and, at least temporarily, secured the American left flank.

Santa Anna had now realized that his initial attacks had not broken the American army. While his right flank had pushed far onto the northern plateau, it had been stopped short of a breakthrough, and had now lost much of its earlier gains. in the center, his infantry had been brought to a standstill. The San Patricio soldiers had manhandled their bulky 16lb. guns onto the middle plateau to support Lombardini's attack, but it was not enough to overcome the American artillery and musket fire. Santa Anna had his second horse shot from under him during this action.

However, the "Napoleon of the West' was not finished yet. Still enjoying superiority in numbers and with the Americans lacking any immediate reserves, Santa Anna launched what he thought would be the decisive blow. General Torrejon's cavalry brigade was ordered to force a passage through the American left flank on the northern plateau and break through to the Saltillo road. His forces would be able to link up with some of Ampudia's men coming from the hillsides to the plateau. In addition, he would have general Juvera's lancers returning from their foray to the Hacienda Buena Vista. Altogether about two thousand cavalry, supported by infantry, would make the assault. Meanwhile, in the center, General Jose Maria Ortega would lead the reserves along Pacheco's previous route onto the middle plateau to crush the remaining defenders there. Unfortunately for Santa Anna the rugged ground made it impossible to coordinate these attacks. The cavalry would strike first.

The military academy graduates, among which was Colonel Jefferson Davis, would have said the best defense for infantry being attacked by cavalry was to form a hollow square with bristling bayonets facing the enemy on every side. Davis, however, found himself with two regiments of volunteers not trained to the standards of regulars in field maneuvers. In addition, the Whitney rifles carried by his Mississippians did not even have bayonets. In the limited time available, Davis was able to deploy one of Sherman's artillery pieces along with the 3rd Indiana to his right. The unusual formation that resulted was directly in the path of Torrejon's horsemen.

This cavalry massed and approached their position. The Mississippi Rifles and 3rd Indiana were now angled in the shape of an inverted "V" facing the plateau. The cavalry began a cautious advance

Jefferson Davis

towards the open end of the "V" while the volunteers stood fast. At a distance of only eighty yards the volunteers fired a devastating volley that decimated the head of the cavalry column and threw its advance into confusion. The masses of cavalry from this attack as well as other troops returning from the attack on Buena Vista were turned into a mob of men and horses falling back towards the mountains. Some 2,000 of these men had become trapped in a ravine, unable to break out to rejoin their army. A young Mexican lieutenant with three other officers rode out with a white flag which caused the Americans to stop firing. The men were suspiciously conducted to Taylor under this impromptu flag of truce. There they demanded to know, in the name of Santa Anna, "what General Taylor wanted." Taylor was puzzled but it soon became clear when the Mexican heavy batteries continued to fire, that the entire thing was a clever ruse. The brief lull in the battle on that flank had allowed many of the trapped Mexican troops to escape back towards their own lines.

At this point Taylor figured that one last attack could finish the Mexicans. He ordered an advance that was taken up by both the 1st and 2nd Illinois as well as the 2nd Kentucky on the west end of the plateau. The Mexicans were far from finished at this point, however. It was almost 1:00 P.M. and the Mexican reserves under Ortega were making their appearance on the plateau after approaching out of sight through the ravines. Santa Anna had also ordered one last push with everything that was available, including some of wounded Lombardini's veterans, commanded now by General Francisco Perez, and the two assault forces ran into each other on the plateau. The Colonels of the 1st Illinois and the 2nd Kentucky were both lost in this fight, as well as O'Brien's guns that were in support. The situation had suddenly become desperate for the Americans. Bragg and Sherman raced to the plateau with their guns and began pouring fire and steel into the Mexican flanks, wreaking terrible destruction, but the units kept coming. The guns had gone into action without any infantry support and there were no reinforcements to be had. When Bragg arrived on the scene his guns unlimbered and went into action, but he also sent an aide-de-camp to Taylor to advise him of his situation and ask him what he should do. As Bragg remembers it, Taylor's reply to the aide was simply, "Tell him to give 'em hell, God damn 'em". This remark was to become famous later, mostly by being misquoted by many other writers who were not present. It came down in one variation or another as, "A little more grape, Captain Bragg" or with Taylor and Bragg conversing and Taylor suggesting that Bragg should, "...double-shot your guns and give 'em hell". In any case it is doubtful that there was much chance for such polite conversation. What's more, anyone who had been around Taylor and was familiar with the type of language that he was in the habit of using knew that the stories in the paper were pure fabrication. In any case Bragg's artillery did save the American position, and the battle, as it turned out. The Mexican attack finally was repulsed with horrendous losses due to the fire it had taken from the artillery on the plateau. The Mexican columns had recoiled back down into the ravines and away from the plateau to escape the carnage.

The day's fighting was over. While the battle had raged, General Minon and his cavalry had managed to reach Saltillo itself, but they were not able to successfully attack the fortifications there. Instead of returning by Buena Vista, where he might of been of some use to Santa Anna, Minon withdrew to the south-west.

As night fell, the American army still held the field but it was expected that the Mexicans would renew their attacks in the morning. Some of the soldiers searched the battlefield for missing friends who might be wounded or dead. A sergeant from the 1st Mississippi wrote about what he saw: "We there saw the mangled bodies of our fallen comrades... There was not a heart among us which did not for a moment cease to beat on beholding that horrible scene... Parties were engaged in burying the dead, but there were still hundreds of bodies lying still and cold with no covering save the scanty remnant of clothing which the robbers of the dead found too valueless to take from them. I saw the human body pierced in every place. I saw expressed in the faces of the dead almost every passion and feeling. Some seemed to die execrating their enemies, and cursing them with their last breath—others had the most placid and resigned expression; some appeared to have died defending their lives bravely to the last, while others evidently used their last words in supplicating for mercy. Here lay youth and mature age calmly reposing in untimely death."

After another cold night the Americans awoke to see the last of Santa Anna's army withdrawing to the south. The Americans had paid a high price but they had won the battle of Buena Vista.

The armies had both lost heavily at Buena Vista. The Americans held the field while losing some 272 killed, 387 wounded and 6 missing as well as several hundred scattered and disorganized. The Mexican losses had been more than twice as heavy with 591 killed, 1,048 wounded and some 1,894 missing. The Mexican army was completely spent. The Americans had reinforcements and fresh supplies arriving daily, while the Mexicans could only look forward to a retreat that would be a repeat of their long grueling march north. Santa Anna withdrew from the area and hurried south to face the new threat of invasion that he knew was coming. He claimed victory when he arrived in Mexico City and displayed captured guns and flags to prove it. The soldiers marched on past Mexico City and headed directly for the coast and further battles. The Buena Vista campaign had been a failure for Santa Anna. No decisive victory had been won and the army had suffered severely in the campaign. While the Mexicans had been close to victory several times during the 23rd, the Americans managed to hold on just long enough to stop them. The mostly untried volunteers, supported once again by the amazing American artillery had won the day for Taylor.

The credit for the victory at Buena Vista was all given to General Taylor even though it had been General Wool's choice of position and deployments that had made it possible. The opinion expressed by Colonel William Campbell of the 1st Tennessee Volunteers, upon hearing of Taylor's victory at Buena Vista, was one which most regular officers would have shared. He wrote, "Old Zack is the most lucky man alive. he is brave, kind, and good, and clever, but especially he is lucky."

Another man who achieved far reaching fame from the victory was Taylor's former son-in-law, Jefferson Davis. Brigadier General Joseph Lane, commander of the Indiana brigade at Buena Vista, wrote, "In a battle so fierce and protracted as this, where there were so many exhibitions of coolness and bravery, it is a difficult and delicate task to particularize. But Justice compels me to mention Colonel Davis and his regiment of Mississippians, who so nobly and so bravely came to the rescue at the proper time to save the fortunes of the day".

Davis acquired such fame from the success of his Mississippians that he became convinced that he had considerable military talent. There was a school of thought after the Civil War that attributed the downfall of the Confederacy to Davis's inflated view of his own abilities. The Richmond Examiner near the end of the conflict went so far as to say that posterity would recognize that "if ever the Confederacy perishes, it will have perished of a V", referring to the angle formed at Buena Vista.

Although the Americans were victorious, there was no further action in the north. The remainder of the war saw many volunteer and some regular units sent to this theater for training and garrison duty. Most of their time was spent in chasing down guerrillas and local bandits or in fighting among themselves. In addition they had to contend with the inadequate supply situation and the unforgiving elements that continued to cause hardships for the American soldiers. The end of the American offensive here was mostly as a result of General Scott's campaign in the south rather than being due to the efforts of Santa Anna.

THE WAR IN MEXICO

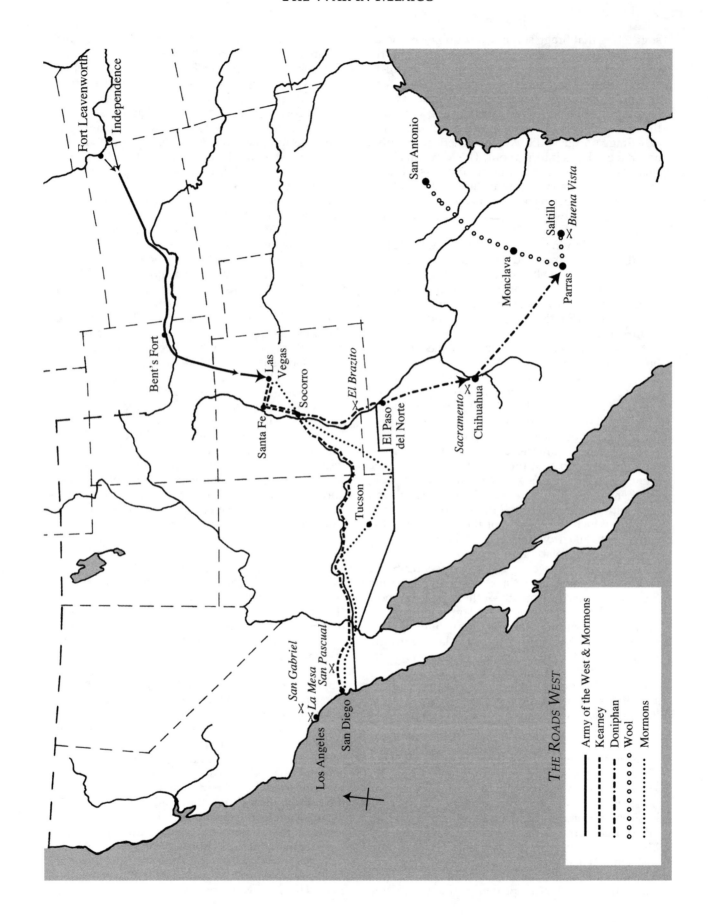

Fort Leavenworth

Independence

San Antonio

Saltillo
Buena Vista

Monclava

Parras

Bent's Fort

Las Vegas

Socorro

El Brazito

Sacramento Chihuahua

Santa Fe

El Paso del Norte

Tucson

San Gabriel
La Mesa
San Pascual

Los Angeles

San Diego

THE *ROADS WEST*

Army of the West & Mormons
Kearney
Doniphan
Wool
Mormons

THE ARMY OF THE WEST

THE TRAIL TO SANTA FE

"It is enough for you to know, Sir, that I have captured your town." Brigadier General Stephen W. Kearny in New Mexico

The day that the United States declared war on Mexico, May 13, 1846, President James K. Polk met with Secretary William L. Marcy and General Winfield Scott to chart the future course of the war as they saw it. One of their first acts was to order Colonel Stephen W. Kearny, then commanding the 1st Dragoons at Fort Leavenworth, to protect the trade caravans along the Santa Fe trail and simultaneously arrange for the seizure of the New Mexico territory in the name of the United States. It was well known in Washington that this area contained many disaffected citizens with closer economic ties to St. Louis than Mexico. The conquest of New Mexico and California may have taken place even without a war against Mexico being fought. These areas had been coveted by the United States long before the annexation of Texas. It was thought by many Americans that a part of their "Manifest Destiny" was to rule the continent from the Atlantic to the Pacific. Some even believed that Mexico itself should be taken over and governed by the United States. It was for these reasons that the Polk administration lost no time in ordering Kearny with the "Army of the West" on its mission. There was not expected to be much resistance to the conquest but Kearny was to raise 1,000 mounted volunteers from Missouri to augment his small force of regulars.

Colonel Kearny was fifty-one years old and was recognized as one of the ablest men in the army at the time. He saw his first active service during the War of 1812 in which he had achieved the rank of captain. He served for most of his career in the Great Plains region and at many posts on the western frontier. He was promoted to colonel of the 1st Dragoons in July of 1836. Somewhat of a perfectionist, he personally oversaw their rigorous recruitment and training in an effort to make them the elite of the army. An old anecdote regarding Kearny the disciplinarian made reference to the time when a subordinate had addressed a military unit as "gentlemen." Kearny had quickly admonished him by replying, "There are colonels, captains,

lieutenants and soldiers in this command, but no such persons as gentlemen". Kearny was known for vigorous action and well respected by the men. He was a good choice for the difficult task that lay ahead.

The force that was eventually mustered for the expedition numbered some 1,600 men, mostly from Missouri. In addition to the five companies of the 1st Dragoons there was a full regiment of mounted volunteers, two companies of artillery, a two company battalion of infantry as well as an independent mounted company from St. Louis and fifty Delaware and Shawnee Indians. The supply train for the army included 1,556 wagons, 459 horses, 3,658 draft mules and 14,904 cattle and oxen which had mostly been gathered together by Kearny's efforts and the Quartermaster office in St. Louis. General Scott also authorized Kearny to recruit men from the traders and settlers along the trail as needed. He also informed him that an additional regiment of another 1,000 Missourians would be joining him as soon as possible as well as whatever infantry could be raised from among the Mormons fleeing persecution in Illinois. Scott also directed Kearny that he was to see that New Mexico was safely garrisoned and then lead a force by the southern route to California and effect the capture of Monterey and San Francisco with the aid of local recruits.

Kearny was anxious to be off and so the first units left Fort Leavenworth, located on the Missouri River about 300 miles west of St. Louis, beginning June 5th. By the end of June all of the various detachments that had arrived here had set out for their first rendezvous at Bent's Fort, a march of about 650 miles from Fort Leavenworth. This protected trading post was located on the Arkansas River near the site of present day Las Animas, Colorado, about 250 miles northeast of the capital of New Mexico at Santa Fe, which was Kearny's objective. The march to get here had been a grueling one and many of the horses had died along the way. The men were exhausted, sick and hungry but they had made it this far without any serious losses. On August 2nd the united force set out for Santa Fe amid rumors that the Mexicans, under the command of Governor Manuel Armijo, intended to fight. Upon reaching the small village of San Miguel less than two days march from Santa Fe the alcalde informed Kearny that he would not submit to the jurisdiction of the United States until after the fall of the state capital. Upon hearing this Kearny sternly replied, "It is enough for you to know, Sir, that I have captured your town."

The rumors of resistance came from the willingness of many citizens to take up arms against the invader if they were organized and led. August 8th had seen about 3,000 Mexicans and Indians gathered at Apache Canyon, a defensive position commanding the approach to Santa Fe, in answer to a summons to fight, waiting for Armijo or Colonel Manuel Pino to take charge of the defense. Despite further rumors of 1,500 dragoons riding to their support from the south, which turned out be totally unfounded, the two men in charge wavered with uncertainty as to how they should proceed and the makeshift army dispersed. On the 17th of August Armijo was heading towards the pass leading another armed force of about 300 men and eight small guns when he decided that the Americans would be too strong to fight. He headed south for Chihuahua with all possible speed taking his mounted bodyguard with him.

Later that day Kearny and the Army of the West got the word from a local alcalde that they could rest easy and continue their advance into Santa Fe because, "Armijo and his troops have gone to hell and the Canyon is all clear." The army marched into Santa Fe on August 17th after travelling almost 900 miles in eight weeks without firing a shot. Kearny declared himself military governor of the province and had the people swear an oath of allegiance to the United States. Mexico had lost her territory without making any effort to put up a fight. Fortunately for this small force composed mostly of irregulars, very little organized resistance was encountered. The long march to Santa Fe is mainly

Kearny

remembered for the hardships encountered on the trail rather than the empty threat of a battle at the end of it. New Mexico was beyond effective control or defence from Mexico. The only forces available were a handful of frontier troops and the local inhabitants. The entire territory had developed closer economic ties with the United States through the caravans to St. Louis than they had enjoyed with Mexico in quite some time. It would have most likely been only a matter of time before New Mexico would have broken away from Mexico entirely and followed the example set by Texas. Perhaps the war with Mexico had only hastened the inevitable.

Kearny was now free to pursue the second part of his mission, which was to advance to California and effect another conquest there.

SANTA FE TO CHIHUAHUA

"Charge and be damned"
Colonel Alexander Doniphan at El Brazito

The 1st Missouri mounted volunteers in the Army of the West were commanded by Colonel Alexander Doniphan, a tall, red-haired frontier lawyer and born leader. Doniphan had not had any previous military experience but he was quickly able to adapt to being in command. After the departure of Kearny he had contacted and successfully concluded peace with the Navaho in New Mexico by the end of November. By mid-December his forces were once again concentrated on the Rio Grande at Valverde and ready to advance south to Chihuahua.

The advance took place in stages, with the advance guard departing on December 14th. All of the contingents set out across the Jornada del Muerto

---

The Army of the West in June of 1846

Brig-Gen. Stephen Watts Kearny (1658) (1458)
1st Dragoons (300): Maj. Edwin V. Sumner (Companies B, C, G, I & K)
1st Missouri Mounted Volunteers (856): Col. Alexander W. Doniphan (8 Companies)
St. Louis Volunteer Artillery (250): Maj. Meriwether Lewis Clark (2 Companies with 12 - 6 lb. guns & 4 - 12 lb. howitzers)
Missouri Infantry Battalion (145): Capt. William Z. Angney
Laclede Rangers (107): Capt. Hudson (mounted men from St. Louis)
Delaware & Shawnee Indians (50)
Following Later
2nd Missouri Mounted Volunteers (1200): Col. Sterling Price (14 Companies)
Mormon Battalion (500): Lt-Col. James Allen (5 Companies)

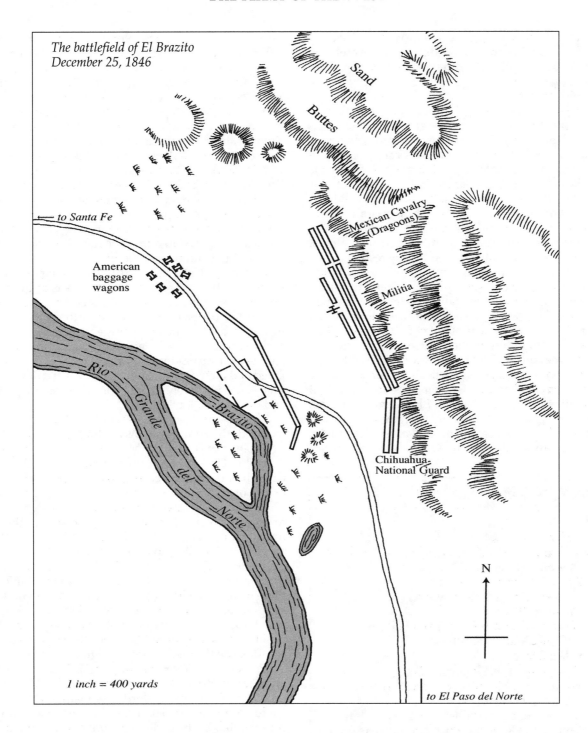

The battlefield of El Brazito
December 25, 1846

Sand Buttes

← to Santa Fe

American
baggage
wagons

Mexican Cavalry
(Dragoons)

Militia

Rio Grande del Norte

Brazito

Chihuahua
National Guard

N

1 inch = 400 yards

to El Paso del Norte

(Journey of Death) which was a dried out desert valley that had once been the bed for the Rio Grande itself. This shortcut saved time and distance over following the river to El Paso but it was a difficult march to make as there was little water or vegetation. On December 25th, with his forces almost completely together, Doniphan reached a point about thirty miles north of El Paso. Here the Brazito River flowed into the Rio Grande and the land around was fairly level. The troops were halted and preparing their supper when the call to rally was sounded. A cloud of dust had been spotted approaching from the south that turned out to be Major Antonio Ponce de León with a Mexican army prepared for battle. The accounts vary considerably as to how many men were in the major's force although it did contain some regulars as well as militia. Doniphan, with less than 900 men estimated that the enemy numbered more than 1200 strong including lancers and an artillery piece.

A Mexican lieutenant carried forward a black flag and called for the surrender of the American commander. Otherwise they would be forced to charge and take him, without giving any quarter. Doniphan, who was not intimidated by threats such as this, replied, "Charge and be damned." During this time the Americans were gathering their arms and organizing for battle while the Mexicans maneuvered into position. The Mexicans placed their howitzer in the center of their line supported by the El Paso militia. The infantry from Chihuahua was on the left and the cavalry on the right. The Mexicans did launch a charge and they began firing ineffectively at about 400 yards in the process. The Americans were in a crescent shaped line, almost all on foot, with both ends secured by resting on the banks of the river. Doniphan had his men hold their fire until they were well within range and then they opened up with a devastating volley that emptied quite a few saddles. The Americans launched a charge of their own with about twenty men who had been able to round up their horses. They were able to put the lancers to flight on the Mexican right flank. The entire skirmish was over in about thirty minutes, the Mexicans having lost their appetite for a fight and dispersing. The 'battle' of El Brazito was over. The Americans had seven men in need of medical care and the Mexicans reportedly lost eleven men killed and seventeen wounded, although Doniphan's men claimed over a hundred casualties inflicted. The road was now opened to El Paso which they entered on December 27th.

Colonel Sterling Price of the 2nd Missouri Mounted Volunteers was having his own problems back in Santa Fe while Doniphan was at El Paso. An Indian uprising on January 19, 1847 at Taos, about eighty miles north of Santa Fe, had resulted in the massacre of seven Americans, including Governor Charles Bent, who had always been a friend to them. Price quickly gathered together what troops he could, some 350 men and four small howitzers and headed north to stop the rebellion from spreading. There may have been as many as 1,500 New Mexicans opposed to him in the field, but they were all untrained and not well led.

After several indecisive skirmishes along the way his forces encountered the dug in rebels at Puebla de Taos on February 3rd. In a siege and assault lasting the better part of two days the Americans managed to dig out the insurgents and break the back of the resistance. There were at least fifty killed and the rest surrendered. The Americans lost seven killed and forty-five wounded. The insurrection had been squashed before it could spread by Price's quick and decisive action.

When Doniphan had reached El Paso he had learned that General Wool had not gone to Chihuahua and that the Mexicans were willing to defend it. His artillery, under Major Meriwether L. Clark had been delayed by Colonel Price until the extent of troubles originating in Taos was known. The guns and their commander were finally ready to go by February 5th and Doniphan set out three days later. His command included about 900 soldiers, six artillery pieces and some 300 civilian teamsters and traders organized into a makeshift battalion under 'Major' Samuel Owens. In addition there were over 300 wagons with merchants goods, supplies and ammunition. After a long and tiring march the small army came within a days march of Chihuahua on February 27th, when they learned that the Mexicans were prepared to fight.

The Mexican Governor Angel Trias had expected an attempt to take Chihuahua and had been preparing for it by mustering as many men as he could to oppose it. The army he had raised was commanded by Brigadier General José A. Heredia and totalled almost 4,000 men. There were about 1,200 cavalry, 1,500 infantry, 1,000 rancheros and some ten to twelve guns of different sizes. The troops were of varying degrees of reliability but it was an impressive array that outnumbered the Americans by at least three to one. The Mexicans had chosen to defend the point where the El Paso road crossed the Rio Sacramento about fifteen miles north of Chihuahau and they had constructed twenty-three separate defensive positions there. The weak point

---

Forces at El Brazito on December 25, 1846
(30 miles north of El Paso on the Rio Grande)

Mexican
Major Antonio Ponce de León (500) (1200) (1300)
  Mounted Dragoons (320) (514) *
  Active Militia Company of El Paso (70)
  Artillery (15) (1 - 2 lb. howitzer)
  Infantry (108)
  National Guard Infantry from El Paso & Chihuahua (700-800)
United States
Col. Alexander W. Doniphan (500) (856)
  1st Missouri Mounted Volunteers (rifle armed): Capt. John W. Reid
  LaClede Rangers (from St. Louis)
  Chihuahua Rangers (95): Capt. Thomas B. Hudson

Based on the descriptions given by Hughes of this unit as the 'Veracruz & Zacatecas Cavalry' this could be a part of the 2nd Line Cavalry Regiment. However the uniform description of blue pants and green coats trimmed in scarlet would point to the 9th Line Cavalry Regiment instead. No other information has been found to clarify this matter, but this unit apparently was line cavalry, not militia.

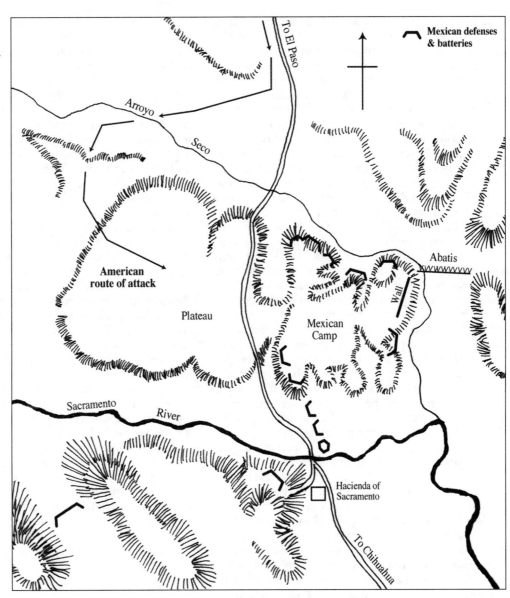

The battlefield on the Sacramento River, February 28, 1847

Mexican defenses & batteries

To El Paso

Arroyo

Seco

American route of attack

Plateau

Mexican Camp

Wall

Abatis

Sacramento River

Hacienda of Sacramento

To Chihuahua

Forces at the Sacramento River, February 28, 1847 (15 miles north of Chihuahua)

Mexican
Brig-Gen. José A. Heredia (3819) (4220)
Cavalry Commander: Gen. Pedro García Conde (1200)
   2nd Squadron of Durango (255)
   Conde's Cavalry (700)
   Presidial Troops
Infantry Commander: Gen. Mauricia Ugarte (1500)
   7th Line Infantry (70): Col. Pedro Horcacitas
   Chihuahua Battalion (250): Governor Angel Trias

Artillery Commander: Gen. Justiniani (119)
   10-12 guns ranging from 4 lb. to 9 lb.
Mounted Rancheros (1000)

American
Col. Alexander W. Doniphan (924) (1164)
   1st Missouri Mounted Volunteers (700) (800):
      Lt-Col. David D. Mitchell
   (only two companies still mounted) Capt.
      Monroe M. Parsons & Capt. John W. Reid
Artillery (100) (117): Maj. Meriwether L. Clark
   4 - 6 lb. guns & 2 - 12 lb. howitzers
Chihuahua Rangers (97): Capt. Thomas B. Hudson
Battalion of Teamsters & Traders (300) (150): Maj. Samuel C. Owens (2 companies)

that apparently was not taken into account was that the position could be turned and bypassed if the Americans chose not to continue their advance on the road and clash head on with the defenders. The Mexican leaders thought that this route to the west was impossible for the wagons to traverse and therefore would not be utilized. Everything was ready when the American column began to approach on the morning of February 28th, a Sunday.

Doniphan's scouts quickly realized that the Mexican position was very strong and they began to search for an alternate route to the west of the road. They soon discovered that the wagons could be manhandled through the area at a point to the west of the dug in Mexicans. That is the direction Doniphan took, veering to the right with the Mexican line off to his left guarding the road. When the force was almost all the way past the Mexican position Doniphan began to engage them with his artillery, one post at a time, working his way back north to clear out the redoubts. The artillery would close within about fifty yards and set up to fire point blank to open a way for the mounted men to attack and clear each position in hand to hand fighting. Heredia had ordered a charge by his cavalry to halt the movement of the wagons, advancing four abreast, but they were forced back without accomplishing their mission. By five P.M. the Mexicans were beaten. They withdrew from their remaining positions and fled south with some of Doniphan's men in pursuit.

The battle of the Sacramento had been the best chance yet for the Mexicans to inflict a defeat on the American Army of the West. Their completely static position combined with a very weak will for fighting helped to lose them the battle. Doniphan claimed 300 killed and another 300 wounded while capturing about forty others along with a great deal of equipment and artillery. The tactics employed by the Americans were very unconventional and unexpected by the Mexicans. The determination exhibited by Doniphan's men in pushing forward the wagons and fighting the battle had been unstoppable. The Missourians lost only one man killed and eight wounded. Doniphan and his men took possession of Chihuahua on March 1, 1847. There was no further resistance.

Doniphan did not want to stay in Chihuahua any longer than he had to and so he sent to General Wool, his immediate commander, for further orders. In the meantime scouts were sent out to determine if there were any further threats from the Mexican army. Although not in any danger at present Doniphan figured that his position would only get worse, and without any chance of reinforcement, he was anxious to be on his way. The people of Chihuahua were not interested in becoming part of the United States and would not consent to remain neutral. The collapse of the Mexican army in the northern provinces made it unlikely that organized forces would meet the Americans in battle after the Sacramento fight, but the Army was vulnerable to guerilla action that would have cut them off from their communications and supply. The Americans pulled out of Chihuahua on April 28th after receiving orders to march for Saltillo to join up with the forces of Wool and Taylor. They reached Parras on May 11th and reached Monterrey shortly before the end of their enlistment term, which was the last day of May, 1847. General Taylor sent them on to New Orleans to be discharged and paid for the first time in a year.

Doniphan's small army had marched more than 2,000 miles and fought two battles, a great achievement for a small force. The taking of Chihuahua was symbolic in that it showed that Mexico could not protect its northern provinces. This fact could be used at the bargaining table to assure that the Americans were awarded the concessions they desired, such as New Mexico. In that respect the expedition was a complete success, even though Chihuahua itself was abandoned not long after it was taken. Doniphan's achievement was a remarkable one that could have met with disaster had serious resistance been offered by the Mexican forces available.

The last action that Colonel Price was to see during the war came more than a year after the Puebla de Taos incident when he launched his own campaign into what he called the 'lower provinces of New Mexico.' Rumors had been circulating that a large Mexican force was being gathered in Chihuahua to strike north. Price left El Paso on March 1, 1848 heading south with three companies of the 1st Dragoons, four companies of the 3rd Missouri (they had taken over garrison duties from the 2nd

A Mexican Lancer

Missouri) and two howitzers. In reality Governor Angel Trias with about 800 men and eight artillery pieces was just north of Chihuahua and was aware of the peace treaty that had already been signed in Mexico City. His attempts to convince Price of the fact that hostilities were at an end were to no avail as the American suspected that it was a trap of some kind. Trias withdrew in the face of the American advance and Price was able to occupy Chihuahua. The Mexican forces were at the small town of Santa Cruz de Rosales on March 16th when Price struck them. The Americans took the town in house to house fighting with the loss of four killed and nineteen wounded. The Americans claimed that they had inflicted more than 300 casualties on the Mexicans, which was highly unlikely. It was not until the 15th of April that Price received confirmation of the peace and orders to withdraw. He was given a slap on the wrist for exceeding his orders and he was instructed to restore all captured property.

California

"Steady my Jacks, reserve your fire, front rank kneel to receive cavalry." Brigadier General Stephen W. Kearny at San Gabriel.

Once Santa Fe was taken the newly promoted Brigadier General Kearny wasted no time in preparing to continue his march to California. He set out on September 25th with 300 mostly mule-mounted dragoons, a small wagon train, and a group of topographical engineers to accomplish the military conquest of California. If New Mexico had been on the brink of being lost to Mexico then California was already over the edge. Once again the experience of Texas was being repeated, at least in Alta California. The Mexican government was simply too weak and out of touch to offer any effective government to its far flung territory. Kearny's expedition to California would thrust him into a situation that was already a lost cause as far as Mexico was concerned. The resistance movement was mainly to keep the Americans out of control so that the Californios could govern themselves. Unfortunately, there was no government that they could agree on. At this time Kearny was completely ignorant of the personalities involved or the events that had taken place there in the last several months.

On hand in California at the beginning of hostilities was Brevet Captain John C. Fremont of the Topographical Engineers. He was only thirty-two years old and he had already earned fame and respect as an explorer, becoming known as the "Pathfinder" for his exploits. He was brave and decisive as well as egotistical, headstrong and ambitious. He dealt in a highhanded manner with most of those he came into contact with and he

A very formal Kit Carson

believed that he was a law unto himself. His current expedition had arrived in California at the end of 1845 and he had assured the Mexican authorities there that his mission was a peaceful one. General José María Castro granted him permission to camp in the Sacramento Valley until the spring. The men with Fremont included some very famous scouts and mountain men such as Kit Carson and Tom Fitzpatrick (known as "Broken-Hand").

In March of 1846, Fremont had made an unsuccessful bid to take over Monterey, but upon learning that Castro was coming after him with artillery, he thought better of it and headed north for Oregon. Fremont's action had started a chain of events that could not be stopped. By the time he returned in early June the territory was in open rebellion. After scattering part of the Mexican forces around San Francisco bay, Fremont and his party declared California independent on July 4th under the Bear Flag of his California Battalion. The new Republic was to last fifteen days.

On July 7th the U.S. Navy entered the action with the seizure of Monterey by a naval landing party. Two days later they were in San Francisco. Fremont and his men came in and re-enlisted in the service of the United States now that hostilities had begun, ending the short-lived Bear Flag Republic. Just over a month later, on August 13th Fremont and his men, marched into Los Angeles which had been captured by a naval landing party after the Mexicans had fled the area. California had been taken, or so it appeared at the time.

The American hold on California was not as strong as it appeared. Over the next several weeks unrest continued to grow, made worse by some of the

THE WAR IN MEXICO

California

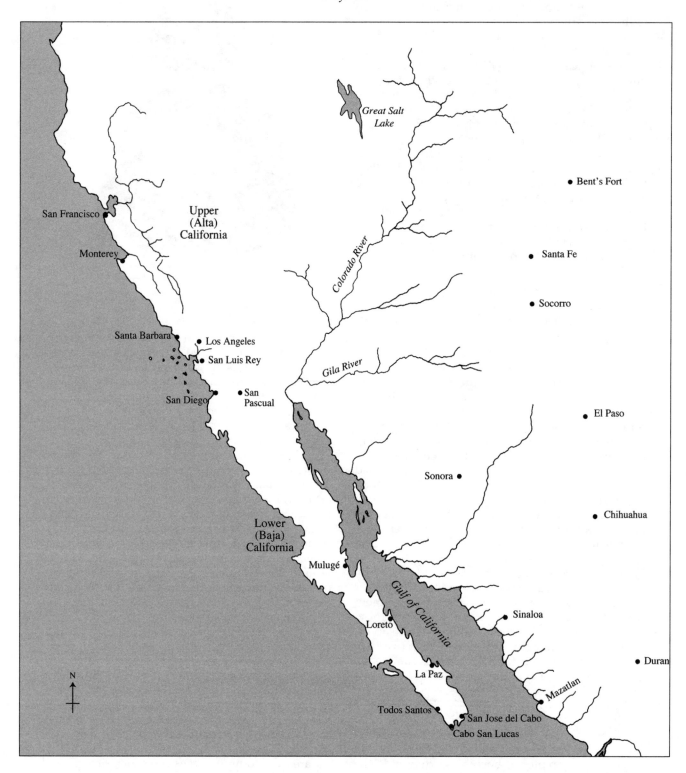

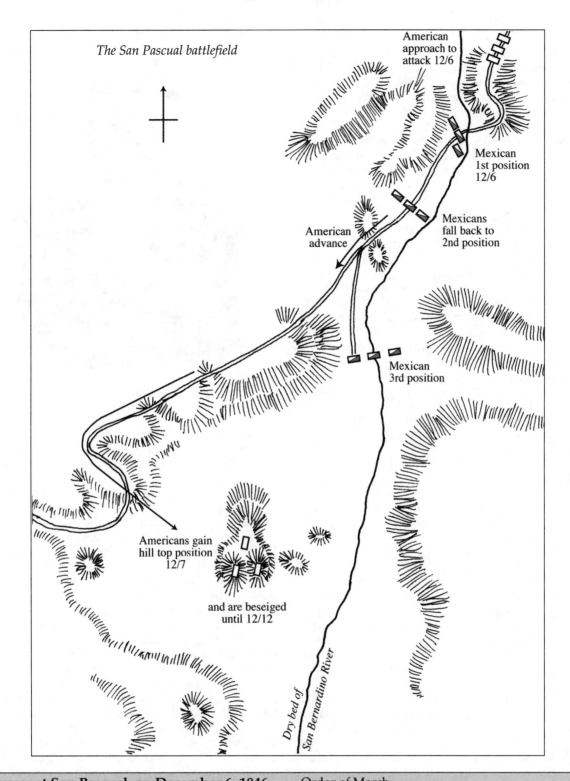

The San Pascual battlefield

American approach to attack 12/6

Mexican 1st position 12/6

Mexicans fall back to 2nd position

American advance

Mexican 3rd position

Americans gain hill top position 12/7

and are beseiged until 12/12

Dry bed of San Bernardino River

Forces at San Pascual, on December 6, 1846	Order of March
	Advance Guard (12): Capt. Abraham R. Johnston
Mexican	Dragoons (50): Capt. Benjamin D. Moore
Mounted Rancheros (75) (100): Andrés Pico	Volunteers (38): Capt. Archibald H. Gillespie
United States	USMC
Gen. Stephen W. Kearny (150)	Artillery (1 - 4 lb. gun & 2 Mtn. howitzers): Lt.
1st Dragoons, Company C (80)	John W. Davidson
	Rearguard (50): Maj. Thomas Swords

personalities involved who basically disliked the Californios and let it show in their dealings with them. One of these men was Captain Archibald H. Gillespie who was in charge of the forty-eight man garrison at Los Angeles. After many rumors the uprising broke out in earnest on September 23rd when shots were exchanged and Gillespie found himself besieged by about 150 Californios led by Captain José María Flores. By the 30th Los Angeles was back in Californio hands and Gillespie had withdrawn his men by ship. Within a few days American control of southern California was lost.

When the news of the fall of Los Angeles spread both Commodore Stockton and Captain Fremont began to mobilize men to retake it. Stockton made his base at San Diego after landing further troops to garrison Monterey. Fremont took more time and eventually headed south out of Monterey at the head of 300 men by November 17th. Flores had spent the intervening time trying to recruit and further organize the resistance, but his men had little enthusiasm for the cause. Supplies were low and there was very little money. His main chance lay in conducting guerrilla operations, forcing the Americans to stay close to their naval support on the coast and thus lose control of the inland areas until the Californios could consolidate. Besides Stockton and Fremont, Flores now had a third force to deal with as Kearny and his miniature Army of the West had finally entered California.

Kearny had gotten word of the successful American takeover of California on October 6th when he encountered a small group of horsemen heading east carrying the news to Washington. This prompted him to send two thirds of his force back to Santa Fe and continue on with just an escort of two companies, about one hundred men. He also prevailed upon one of the couriers, Kit Carson, to turn around and lead him and his men to California, while Tom Fitzpatrick took the dispatches on to announce the news of the conquest. The small force continued west, confident that their mission upon reaching California would be to simply assist in setting up an orderly government and keeping the peace.

On November 23rd, Kearny's men encountered a Mexican messenger whose information dashed any hopes the expedition had of a peaceful journey. His letters told of the overthrow of the Americans at Los Angeles and other places. Kearny was now faced with the fact that he would have to fight for California after all, and with a very small force. He continued on, nevertheless, and reached a place called Warner's Ranch or Agua Caliente on December 2nd, almost a thousand miles from Santa Fe. It was here that the information about the uprising was confirmed and Kearny was able to get a better picture of the current situation. He decided to continue on and on December 5th he was joined

Pico besieged Kearny at San Pascual

by Gillespie at the head of some thirty-five sailors and marines, bringing his total force to about 150 men. Gillespie also warned him that Andrés Pico was in command of about one hundred men that were out to intercept him before he reached San Diego. The prevailing opinion was that the Californios would not put up much of a fight.

During the early morning hours of December 6th Kearny entered the valley of San Pascual near the village of the same name. It was still dark when the two forces collided with the dragoons leading the charge. There was a brief fight and then some of Pico's men feigned flight, a tactic that the Plains Indians would later perfect, and the dragoons gave chase, becoming separated from the foot soldiers and artillery. This was when the Californios turned to stand and fight, wreaking havoc with their lances among the dragoons. The fight lasted only fifteen minutes before the lancers withdrew, taking with them one of Kearny's howitzers whose mule team had strayed into their lines. The Americans had lost eighteen men killed and thirteen wounded, including Kearny, who had taken a lance in the groin. The Californios had about a dozen men wounded in the brief fight. The Battle of San Pascual was over.

Pico and his men did not leave the scene, however. They knew that Kearny's force was crippled and they hovered nearby, just out of range, waiting for an opportunity to strike. Kearny was besieged with his wounded on a small hill until help arrived on the eleventh, forcing Pico to leave. The combined force marched back to San Diego on December 12th.

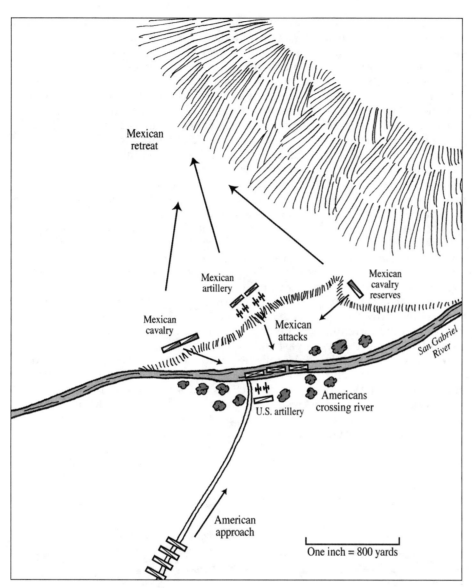

The San Gabriel battlefield

Mexican retreat

Mexican artillery

Mexican cavalry reserves

Mexican cavalry

Mexican attacks

San Gabriel River

Americans crossing river

U.S. artillery

American approach

One inch = 800 yards

Forces at San Gabriel on January 8, 1847

Mexican
Capt. José María Flores (600) (450)
Artillery (1 - 2 lb., 1 - 3 lb. & 1 - 6 lb. gun)

United States
Commodore Robert F. Stockton (607) (565)
Maj-Genl. Stephen W. Kearny
1st Division: Lt. Jacob Zeilin USMC
   Company C, USS Portsmouth (musketeers)
   Company E, USS Cyane (carbineers)
   Company G, USS Congress (carbineers)
2nd Division: Capt. Henry S. Turner
   1st Dragoons (Company C)
   Company D, USS Cyane (musketeers)

1st Dragoons (Company K)
Artillery Battalion: Lt. R. Lloyd Tilghman
(6 guns) Army & Navy gunners
3rd Division: Lt. William B. Renshaw USN
   Company A, USS Congress (musketeers)
   Company B, USS Savannah (musketeers)
4th Division: Capt. Archibald H. Gillespie USMC
   California Battalion of Mounted Rifles (54)
   Californios (ranchers) (30)

Totals
   Dragoons (57)
   Sailors & Marines as Infantry (407)
   Sailors manning Artillery (47)
   Miscellaneous men from other units (54)
   Corps of Topographical Engineers (3)

Kearny and Stockton now began to plan joint operations with Stockton in overall command, since most of the men available were sailors and marines, and Kearny as his executive officer who would exercise field command. The sailors and marines were trained to operate in a hollow square formation whenever they were in sight of the enemy. This was a simple system that would help keep the men together and better able to defend themselves, particularly against cavalry attack. The total force came to about 600 men. The makeshift army was ready by the end of December to launch the expedition to retake Los Angeles.

Captain Flores was not well prepared to defend Los Angeles from attack. He had somewhere between 450 and 600 men who were poorly armed and not well motivated, along with four artillery pieces. On January 8, 1847 the Californios placed themselves on a low ridge overlooking the banks of the San Gabriel river to await Stockton's army. The hollow square of the Americans moved toward the river and began fording the knee deep stream, successfully fighting off cavalry attacks launched by Flores. The American artillery took a heavy toll while the guns of the Californios were virtually useless and had inadequate powder available for a fight. Within ninety minutes the Californios had withdrawn towards Los Angeles, the Americans failing to pursue. Each side had lost two killed and nine wounded.

The next day the Americans continued the advance towards Los Angeles and once again encountered Flores with what remained of his army. There were about 300 Californios and four guns deployed in a line across a wide, dry plain known simply as La Mesa. The hollow square of the sailors and marines advanced as before and once again the Californios' weak artillery fire and halfhearted cavalry charges failed to make any impact on it. After a short time the army of the Californios dispersed and no further resistance was offered to the advance. On January 10th the Americans marched in to Los Angeles and took control once again, this time to stay. A peace treaty was signed on January 13th at the Rancho Cahuenga, orchestrated by Fremont, who actually had no authority to do so. Nevertheless, it was accepted by both sides and the fighting in California came to an end.

Most remarkable about the California campaign is that despite all of the victories and defeats suffered on both sides, the Americans gained control over a vast and rich territory with only a handful of men. A motley combination of marines, sailors, soldiers and volunteers accomplished their mission amid the complete chaos of California politics and the local resistance it fostered. Once again Mexico had lost a valuable possession due to its inability to mount any creditable force to protect it.

The battlefield of La Mesa

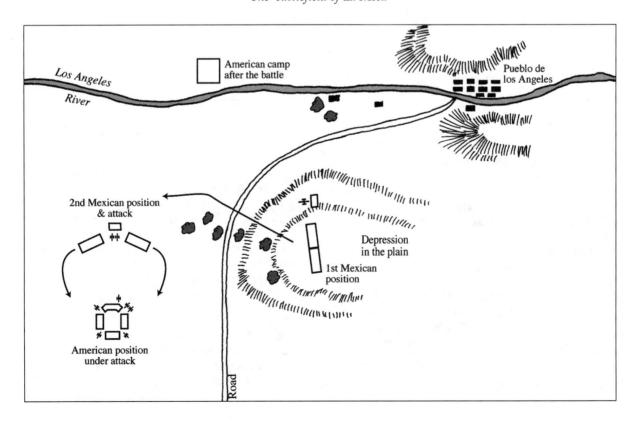

THE NAVAL WAR

WAR IN THE GULF

"If Santa Anna endeavors to enter the Mexican ports, you will allow him to pass freely."
Orders to Commodore Conner, May 1846

The naval war against Mexico was fought in two distinct theaters, the Gulf of Mexico by the American Home Squadron and off of the west coast of Mexico and California by the Pacific Squadron. In both theaters the Mexican Navy was virtually non-existent when it came to contesting the objectives of the U.S. Navy.

The naval war in the Gulf of Mexico was a very different kind of war from that being waged in the interior. The main duty of the United States Home Squadron stationed off of the east coast of Mexico was the monotonous one of manning a blockade of Mexican ports. The Mexican Navy was far too small to contest control of the sea lanes and only a few privateers made any attempts at harassing American ships. In addition to maintaining the blockade the United States Navy also served as the means of transportation for most of the American troops going to Mexico throughout the war. Naval landing parties made up of sailors and marines from the fleet raided and captured Mexican ports and goods as well. The navy played a vital part in prosecuting the war against Mexico.

Commodore David Conner had been ordered into Mexican waters as early as March of 1845 to help protect the annexation of Texas from any interference by sea. Once hostilities had commenced a blockade was declared against the major ports of Alvarado, Tabasco (actually San Juan Batista), Tampico, Tuxpan, Soto la Marina and Vera Cruz. In addition the port city of Matamoros was taken early on and the port of Carmen was neutralized by the revolution in Yucatan. Except for Vera Cruz, which really had no harbor to speak of, all of the other ports were located up shallow-mouthed rivers emptying into the Gulf.

These shallow waters allowed only light ships to pass and blockading ships could not find refuge from the "Northers" or storms that frequented the Gulf from October to April and struck without warning. Another danger of blockade duty off the coast of Mexico was the prevalence of the *vómito* or yellow fever during the wet season from April to October. The disease could be deadly to a single ship or the entire fleet as it could spread rapidly. The only solution was to steer clear of these waters as much as possible if outbreaks were reported.

General Taylor had requested a blockade of the Rio Grande in mid-April of 1846 to prevent supplies from reaching Matamoros when his army was camped opposite the port city. The blockade was effective and in early May 500 sailors and Marines were landed at Point Isabel to help man the fort while Taylor engaged the Mexican Army at Palo Alto and Resaca de la Palma. In the meantime, the blockade was being established along the coast as ships became available to man it. The two largest ships in the Mexican Navy, the *Guadaloupe* and the *Montezuma*, had set sail on May 18, 1846 from Alvarado. They were flying the British flag as they had been repossessed by their former owners, who sailed them to safety in Havana. The escape of these two ships was disappointing to Conner because they would have made welcome additions to his squadron if they had been captured. Most of the smaller vessels of the Mexican fleet had taken refuge at Alvarado or Tampico.

The Polk administration was hopeful from the outset that if Mexican General Santa Anna, in exile in Cuba, could be returned to power an early peace could be brought about that would be favorable to the United States. On May 13, 1846, while the blockade was being established Commodore Conner had been ordered: "If Santa Anna endeavors to enter the Mexican ports, you will allow him to pass freely." Santa Anna did arrive at Vera Cruz on August 16, 1846 on the British mail packet *Arab*. He was allowed free passage by the blockading squadron and upon landing proceeded with his plans to return to power, but without any intention of honoring his pledge of peace with the United States.

The main U.S. base for maintaining the blockade was the anchorage at Anton Lizardo, located about twelve miles south of Vera Cruz. Here the vessels from the fleet could find refuge from storms because a chain of islands, reefs and shoals about nine miles long broke the fury of the sea. Supplies could be transferred from ship to ship and even stored on the islands in relative safety. Fresh water, fruit and coal for the steamships were the most vital supplies that had to be shipped in or somehow procured from the area. Numerous skirmishes resulted when shore parties in search of these items encountered Mexican soldiers. Eventually, these expeditions were halted altogether.

On August 7th Commodore Conner bombarded the port of Alvarado and, even though Mexican response was limited, there was no attempt to capture any ships or land a raiding party due to the onset of adverse weather conditions. The fleet withdrew leaving the now alerted Mexicans to prepare for the next attack. On August 10th the Navy had been authorized by the Polk administration to increase its strength from 7,500 men to 10,000 men for the duration of the war. Problems recruiting seamen made it impossible to fulfill this quota, and the Navy never exceeded a strength of 8,000 men during the course of the war. A second attack on Alvarado was attempted October 15th against a well prepared garrison. The American squadron became split in two when the first half crossed the bar into the river and the first ship of the second column unexpectedly grounded. Conner was reluctant to engage with only half of his ships and he ordered the attack called off. The grounded ship was recovered without being damaged, but the fleet sailed back to Anton Lizardo.

Commodore Conner, in search of a successful operation to offset the failures at Alvarado decided to accept Commodore Matthew C. Perry's idea of attacking Tabasco. Perry was given command of the *Mississippi, McLane, Vixen, Bonita, Forward, Nonata* and the *Reefer* which became separated from the squadron in a storm and did not take part in the attack. In addition, a landing force of 253 men under Captain Forrest was carried along. Tabasco itself was located seventy two miles from the coast along the Tabasco River. The port of Frontera was at the entrance to the river, which had a very shallow bar lying across its approach. The garrison of Tabasco was not very strong, consisting of only one company each of infantry and cavalry with twenty-three artillerymen and a militia battalion. The total was less than 300 men with four 24-pounders at a small fortification called Fort Acachapan. In command was Lieutenant Colonel Juan Bautista Traconis, the provincial governor.

On October 23rd with his flag flying in the shallow drafted *Vixen* Perry crossed the bar into the river. He was followed by the *Bonita* and the *Forward* with the *Nonata* bringing up the rear. The *McLane* had run aground, a repeat occurrence of what had happened at Alvarado, and the *Mississippi* could not enter the shallow waters. The *Nonata* also had the boats with the landing party in tow. The *Vixen* made for the Frontera wharf and managed to capture the schooner *Laura Virginia* and the steamers *Petrita* and *Tabasquena.* The schooner *Amado* had already fled upriver. A small force was left to garrison Frontera

with the support of the still grounded *McLane* and the more distant *Mississippi.* The next day, with Forrest's men embarked on *Petrita* the force continued up the river with *Bonita* effecting the capture of the schooner *Amado*. On the morning of the 25th Fort Acachapan was sighted and could have created severe problems for the American squadron if the garrison had not fled upon spotting the enemy ships rounding the bend in the river. A landing party was quickly sent ashore and spiked the guns in the fort. The squadron was anchored off the town of Tabasco by 1:00 PM that day and demanded the surrender of the town. Traconis refused and led the defenders a short distance out of the town. The Americans fired several warning shots at the barracks, knocking down the flag. Forrest then led his men ashore and began skirmishing with the defenders in the town itself. The ships provided support wherever they could. Meanwhile, the Americans had captured the brigs *Rentville* and *Yunaute,* the schooners *Alvarado* and *Tobasco,* and the sloops *Campeche* and *Desada* that were lying in the river. Finally as darkness was falling Perry recalled the landing party so as not to expose them to night attack in an unfamiliar town. The fleet remained at battle stations during the night in case of attack.

The next morning found the Mexican defenders more entrenched than before inside the town and still unwilling to discuss surrender. It was doubtful if Perry had enough men to take the town and then hold it once he had. He decided to withdraw back to Frontera with his prizes. The fleet traded shrapnel with musket fire issuing out of the town until a request from foreign merchants convinced Perry to agree not to fire unless fired upon. The fleet began to retire down river when the *Desada* ran aground and began to draw fire. A boat from the *Vixen* helped her to get free and with a parting bombardment of Tabasco, continued on to Frontera. The total casualties had been one officer and three seamen killed and two men wounded for the Americans. The Mexicans had lost five soldiers and four civilians killed. The prize ships were of great value and made the mission a success. Two of the ships, *Petrita* and *Laura Virginia* were added to the American squadron, several of the others being lost in a storm at sea. The success of Perry's attack on Tabasco gave a much needed boost to the morale of the fleet.

The Americans next decided to attack Tampico, a base that would be more useful for further operations in the south than the Rio Grande. Upon hearing of American plans to attack, Santa Anna ordered the town evacuated. On November 14th the Americans sent ashore a landing party of some 300 men and occupied the town without any resistance. Eventually seven companies of the Second Artillery, about 450 men, were transferred from Matamoros to garrison the town. The capture of Tampico did

The expeditionary force landing at Tabasco, by Henry Walke.

not assist the army of Zachary Taylor in any way, as there was no easy supply route from this part of the coast into the interior as the Americans had originally thought. It did however, serve as an important staging point for the invasion of Vera Cruz the following spring.

A pro-Mexican revolution in Yucatan made it necessary to occupy the port of Carmen, to put a stop to the illicit trade into Mexico. On December 21st Perry was able to accept the surrender of the city without any opposition. Only a few days later word came that the pro-American party was back in power and the need to blockade the entire coast of Yucatan was over. Occupation forces were kept in place in Carmen just the same.

Preparations for the amphibious invasion of Mexico at Vera Cruz had already begun in Washington at this time. One of the most important items being requested by General Scott were the flatboats, or surfboats, required for actually carrying the assault troops to shore. There were three sizes, designed so that they could be stacked aboard ship, and they carried from 40 to 45 men each along with an eight man crew. The cost was $795 each and a total of 141 boats were ordered. These were the first specially built amphibious craft ever bought by the American armed forces.

Despite a shortage of transports the invasion of Vera Cruz took place on March 9, 1847, the thirty-third anniversary of Winfield Scott's being promoted to the rank of General. The landings were an unqualified success with the largest fleet yet assembled putting ashore more than 8,600 men in only five hours without any loss of life. There was no Mexican resistance to the landing and the Americans were able to invest the city of Vera Cruz and the Castle of San Juan de Ulloa offshore. Additional troops and supplies continued to land on the beaches to support Scott's army in its first battle ashore, the siege of Vera Cruz.

March 21st saw Commodore Perry relieve Commodore Conner of his command of the Home Squadron as the limit of his term had previously expired and the Secretary of the Navy would not continue to extend it indefinitely. Perry was taking command of the largest squadron ever assembled by the U.S. Navy up until that time. One of the first actions that Perry took was to arrange the landing of naval guns and crews to support the bombardment of the city. These had previously been offered to General Scott by Commodore Conner and the General had decided to accept, but informed the Navy that he would provide the artillerymen. Commodore Perry agreed to Scott's request for a battery of six guns but stated that the Navy would provide the crews to man them. When Scott said that all he needed were the guns Perry insisted saying, "Certainly, General, but I must fight them." Scott had no choice but to accept the terms. Perry knew that it would be good for morale and add to the prestige of the navy. The sailors on board the ships clamored to go ashore to man the guns and a rotating schedule was set up to allow as many different men as possible to take part in the bombardment.

Vera Cruz and San Juan de Ulúa were considered to be some of the strongest fortifications in North America. They capitulated to the American Army on March 29, 1847 after a bombardment lasting one week. The loss to the Americans had been only fourteen killed and fifty-nine wounded. The capture of the port was the first step in the advance to Mexico city that all hoped would end the war.

With the Americans in control of Vera Cruz, the Mexican garrison at Alvarado withdrew and on March 31st the city was captured by a lone steamer, the *Scourge.* After a brief action the fortifications at Tuxpan were taken and destroyed on April 19th. The town was not occupied by the Americans but it was now useless to the Mexicans. Meanwhile rumors of trade between Yucatan and Tabasco were once again circulating. When the American fleet showed up in mid-May the government of Yucatan assured them that they were now neutral and would take no further part in the war. This proved to be true.

Commodore Perry decided that the last major Mexican port must now be taken. He led an expedition on June 16th that included a landing party of more than 1,000 men against Tabasco. After some hard marching and a brief skirmish the landing force arrived at the town to find that the ships in the river had overcome the obstacles in their way to get

there first and receive the surrender. Mexican guerrilla bands continued to enter the town and harass the defenders. On July 22nd, the Americans withdrew from Tabasco because of these continuous attacks and also because yellow fever had broken out in the area and it was not thought wise to expose the men needlessly. The port of Frontera continued to be cut off and blockaded as did other smaller ports along the coast. Mexico was thus completely cut off from outside trade coming through the Gulf.

Commodore Perry's operations for the remainder of 1847 were drastically curtailed by several problems over which he had no control. One of them was a shortage of men and officers that the Navy had simply not been able to fill. In addition many of his ships were lost to the need for repairs. By far the worst problem to affect the fleet was an outbreak of yellow fever in July that incapacitated so many men that the fleet was crippled for the next few months. The Commodore himself was a victim and had not fully recovered six months later. Fortunately not many lives were lost to the disease, but many ships were forced to operate with reduced crews or sail to cooler climates away from the fever zone.

Meanwhile, in the interior of the country, the successful advance of the American army towards Mexico city proceeded even when cut off from its main base of supply at Vera Cruz. Guerrilla bands had taken control of the countryside and prevented passage from the coast inland to all except heavily armed expeditions. The fleet could not have any effect beyond the range of its guns and the need for further operations was limited. By the end of the summer when the fleet had begun to recover from the epidemic, the hopes for a peaceful settlement to the war made the squadron reluctant to plan any other major moves. The last mission of the fleet in the Gulf was during the summer of 1848 when the American army was transported home from Vera Cruz at the end of the war.

The blockade in the Gulf of Mexico had accomplished the vital mission of keeping Mexico cut off from the rest of the world so that supplies and war materials could not be imported. The American navy had faced difficulties with weather, disease and the number of ships and sailors available for duty. Despite these problems the U.S. navy gained control of the sea quickly and the blockade was very effective. The navy was also able to contribute to the campaigns on land by using sailors to seize ports and garrison posts along the coast. After the invasion at Vera Cruz, which the navy had made possible by transporting the troops, the major objective of the fleet was to keep open the lines of supply for the army. The fleet once again succeeded in its mission, the main difficulties being the transport of these men and materials from the coast to the army inland.

MEXICAN ARMY EVACUATES TAMPICO ON OCTOBER 27-28, 1846

General Anastasio Parrodi
(1000) (1200) + 200 on sick call

12th Line Infantry
Active Militia of Puebla: Gen. Joaquín Morlet
Tampico Coast Guard Battalion
Veteran Coast Guard Company of Tampico
6th Cavalry (1 Company)
National Guard of Tampico (Tamaulipas?) (200)
120 guns of all sizes (?)

The Naval War

War in the Pacific

"This port, with its valiant soldiers ...will defend itself ...until the last drop of blood has been shed."
Captain Manuel Pineda, Muleje, Baja California

The United States government had made offers to Mexico to acquire the area known as Alta (upper) California dating back to 1835. California was undergoing a transition similar to what was happening in Texas at the time but at a slower pace due to its distance from the populated portion of the United States. More and more Americans were moving into the area and settling down with their homes and businesses, becoming landholders. American ships were often seen off the coast plying their trade in hides and furs. The California coast had also become an important stop for the Pacific whalers as well by the early 1840s. The *United States*, an American frigate, had gone so far as to seize the port city of Monterey in 1842 when Commodore Thomas ap C. Jones got what he thought was reliable information that the United States and Mexico were at war. The mistake was promptly corrected and the American government disavowed the action completely. But the handwriting was on the wall for the Mexican government to see.

The end of 1842 saw the central government attempt to regain some control over the territory by sending General Manuel Micheltorena to act as governor. By the beginning of 1845 the Californians had ousted him and set up their own state government, which was chaotic at best, but which Mexico eventually recognized. The distance from California to Mexico City had proven too great to allow for an effective government to function that would satisfy the needs or solve the problems of the people living there. The Californians, for the most part, were not looking to become a part of the United States, they simply wanted some of the protection and peace that a stable form of government could offer.

The Polk administration was prepared to take action, in the event of the commencement of hostilities with Mexico, to assure that California would become part of the United States. In July of 1846, with word of a rebellion already underway on shore, Commodore John D. Sloat decided to seize the port of Monterey even though he had received no direct confirmation that war existed with Mexico. A general order was read to the crews of the ships involved on the morning of July 7:

"We are about to land on the Territory of Mexico, with whom the United States are at war. To strike her Flag, and to hoist our own in the place of it, is our duty.

It is not only our duty to take California but to preserve it afterwards as a part of the United States, at all hazards; to accomplish this, it is of the first importance to cultivate the good opinion of the inhabitants, whom we must reconcile.

I scarcely consider it necessary for me to caution American Seamen and Marines against the detestable crime of plundering and maltreating unoffending inhabitants.

That no one may misunderstand his duty the following regulations must be strictly adhered to, as no violation can hope to escape the severest punishment.

1st. On landing, no man is to leave the shore until the Commanding Officer gives the order to march.

2d. No gun is to be fired or other act of hostility committed without express orders from the Officer Commanding the party.

3d. The officers and boat keepers will keep their respective boats as close to the shore as they will safely float taking care they do not lay aground, and <u>remain</u> in them, prepared to defend themselves against attack and attentively watch for signals from the ships as well as from the party on shore.

4th. No man is to quit the ranks or to enter any house for any pretext whatever without express orders from an officer. Let every man avoid insult or offense to any unoffending inhabitant, and especially avoid that eternal disgrace which would be attached to our names and our country's name by indignity offered to a single female even let her standing be however low it may.

5th. Plunder of every kind is strictly forbidden. Not only does the plundering of the smallest article from a prize forfeit all claim to prize money, but the offender must expect to be severely punished.

6th. Finally let me entreat you one and all, not to tarnish our hope of bright success by any act that we shall be ashamed to acknowledge before God and our Country".

The landing party was made up of 85 Marines and more than 140 sailors from the *Cyane, Levant* and *Savannah*. They were unopposed, and the Stars and Stripes were run up the same flag pole that had been used some four years previously, only this time it would not be taken back down. The Mexican military commandant, Captain Mariano Silva, had not even had his own flag to be able to surrender to the Americans. The Marines paraded through town, led by a brass band to celebrate the town's change of ownership.

Commodore Sloat had also issued orders to Commander John B. Montgomery aboard the *Portsmouth*, for the capture of San Francisco, which he accomplished two days later with a naval landing party, also unopposed. On July 29, Commodore Sloat transferred the command of the Pacific Squadron due to reasons of ill health and immediately sailed for home. His second in command, Commodore

Robert F. Stockton took over and issued a proclamation that all Mexican officials should recognize his authority. This did not go over very well with many of the Mexicans that did not support the rebellion and was a complete turnabout from the relatively conciliatory tone that Sloat had initiated.

July 29th also saw the occupation of San Diego by a naval landing party from the *Cyane* with Captain John C. Fremont and some of his men taking possession shortly thereafter. August 4th saw the occupation of Santa Barbara and a garrison of sixteen men was left here to defend the post. On August 6th, the port of San Pedro was occupied by a small party of U.S. Marines under the command of Lieutenant Jacob Zeilin. Commodore Stockton then formed a large naval landing party of some 360 men, only ninety of which had muskets, for the march to Los Angeles. They took control of the town on August 13th, after the Mexican officials and their small army of less than a hundred men had fled. It was not until four days later that Commodore Stockton officially learned that war had broken out between the United States and Mexico.

Now that Alta California seemed to be safely in American hands, Stockton declared a blockade along the entire west coast of Mexico on August 19th. This was totally unenforceable due to a lack of ships available and was thus against the normal policy of the United States. This also violated the rules of war at the time. The blockade here would be difficult, if not impossible to maintain with the limited forces available, but the commerce was more limited here than in the Gulf. Stockton sent the *Cyane* and the *Warren* to begin the blockade by going to San Blas and Mazatlan. On September 3rd, Commander Samuel F. Du Pont, the captain of the *Cyane* captured the Mexican sloop *Solita* and the brigantine *Susana* off San Blas where he proclaimed the blockade to be in effect. At Mazatlan on September 7th, the *Warren* under Commander Joseph B. Hull, captured the Mexican brig *Malek Adhel* in the harbor. The next day the brig *Carmelita* bound for Mazatlan, was captured by Hull, who had officially declared the blockade in force here. The *Cyane* had sailed across the Gulf of California to the port of La Paz, Baja California to declare the blockade. On September 14th, Du Pont captured the Mexican brigantines *Correo*, *La Paz*, and *Manuela*, schooners *Adelaide*, *Eliza*, *Julia*, *Mazolea*, and *Victoria*, and the sloop *San Jose* in the harbor there.

Stockton had been making plans for an attack on Acapulco, which would deny that base to any privateers wanting to operate against American shipping. He also envisioned being able to launch an advance on Mexico City from there, hoping to recruit the necessary manpower from California, augmented by most of the complement of his available ships. All of these plans were put on hold, however, when it was learned that Los Angeles had been re-taken by an insurrection led by the Mexican Captain José María Flores and his band of about 150 Californians. The Americans had lost control for the time being, but the rebellion was not very organized.

During this time the *Cyane* had been keeping busy in Baja California. On October 1st she captured the

The U.S. Navy at work: a naval landing party heads for shore

Mexican schooners *Fortuna* and *Libertad* at Loreto, the next day it was the schooner *Rosita* at the same place. Two days after that she captured the sloops *Alerto* and *Chapita* at Muleje. And on October 7th she launched a boat expedition at the harbor of Guaymas and burned the Mexican brig *Condor* and the gunboats *Anahuac* and *Sonorese*. The 10th saw her take over the blockade at Mazatlan until November 1st when the ship was forced to withdraw to reprovision. This left no American ships in the Gulf of California to enforce the blockade. The problem was the severe lack of available ships, combined with insurrection of the Californians that had to be dealt with. The campaign entered a new phase when General Stephen W. Kearny with his portion of the American "Army of the West" finally entered California on December 2nd, guided by the scout "Kit" Carson.

Shortly after the resolution of the problems on land a new commander took over from Commodore Stockton. On January 22, 1847, Commodore W. Branford Shubrick in the *Independence* had anchored at Monterey to assume overall command of the Pacific Squadron. Naval operations did not get under way again until March 30th, however, when a landing party from the *Portsmouth* seized the port of San Jose del Cabo at the tip of the Baja peninsula. On April 13th the capital of Baja California and the only sizeable town on the entire peninsula, La Paz, was seized by a landing party from *Portsmouth*. The town was eventually occupied in July by two companies of the New York Volunteers that had reached California.

The only resistance to the Americans in Baja came at Muleje on October 1st when the Mexican commander Captain Manuel Pineda refused to remain neutral to Mexico as the Americans demanded. Instead he boasted that, "This port, with its valiant soldiers who have their instructions, will defend itself, and they will maintain their arms until the last drop of blood has been shed". A landing party returned to their ship before nightfall after some inconclusive skirmishing with the garrison ashore. The main purpose of trying to take Muleje had been to cut off the Baja peninsula completely from the west coast of Mexico, especially the port of Guaymas.

At Guaymas on October 20th, after an hour long bombardment from the *Congress* and the *Portsmouth*, the town surrendered. The garrison and most of the townspeople had already withdrawn or fled inland. The Americans destroyed the fortifications in the town and then re-embarked. No permanent garrison was left here as the manpower was simply not available. The town was also accessible from the interior and any garrison would be vulnerable to attack from larger Mexican forces. A ship was kept off shore to maintain trade under American

supervision and to keep the Mexicans from using the port. Attempts were made to re-occupy the area by the Mexican garrison with new landing parties engaging them along with the support of the naval guns from the *Dale*. Eventually, a lack of supplies and desertion by many of the Mexican soldiers served to end any major threat, but Guaymas was an embattled town until the end of the war.

Commodore Shubrick issued a proclamation on November 4, 1847 that the United States was about to begin active operations in Baja California and meant to retain control of the territory even after the war was over. Shubrick hoped that this would encourage the Bajacalifornios to assist the American cause in any way that they could, since they were eventually to become citizens. Some residents did take this to heart, but many of them had to leave for the United States to avoid retribution from their neighbors after the war when Mexico took over again.

On November 11, the Americans occupied Mazatlan with a naval landing party of some 730 men. It was decided to leave a permanent garrison here to prevent the Mexicans from retaking the port. Lieutenant Henry W. Halleck laid out the fortifications that were to be built to accommodate a 400 man garrison. Over the next two months there were a couple of skirmishes in the area with local Mexican forces, but once the fortifications were complete the Americans could not be dislodged without a major effort, which was impossible for the Mexicans to mount.

Meanwhile, Baja California was showing renewed signs of revolution. The fiery Captain Pineda had shown himself to be an able organizer with the will to fight, something that not many Mexicans along the coast had possessed. He had decided to launch his own offensive against La Paz and San Jose del Cabo, both under American control with small garrisons. The attack on La Paz began before daylight on November 11th with Pineda and about 120 men forcing their way into the town. They were repulsed by American artillery and had to withdraw. A second attempt six days later also failed. The Mexicans had suffered about ten casualties while the Americans had lost one man killed and two wounded during the skirmishing.

Another force of about 150 men under Lieutenant José Antonio Mijares of the Mexican Navy, among others, moved against San Jose del Cabo on November 19th. The garrison was made up of four officers and twenty Marines under the command of Lieutenant Charles Heywood along with twenty California volunteers. The Mexicans approached and offered terms of surrender, which were refused. That night and the following night the Mexicans assaulted the old mission where the garrison had holed up. They suffered several casualties in the action,

U.S.S. Dale landing marines on the Baja California coast

including the death of Lieutenant Mijares. The morning of the 21st saw two ships standing into the harbor which prompted the Mexicans to withdraw as they knew that they could not fight with any chance of success against a garrison that had support from naval gunfire and landing parties.

When the Mexicans withdrew from San Jose del Cabo they joined up with Pineda still outside La Paz. This gave the Captain a combined force of nearly 350 men, with which he decided to make another attempt to capture the town. The garrison numbered 112 men from the two New York volunteer companies under the command of Colonel Henry Burton. On November 27th the Mexicans made an all out assault on the town, which the Americans fended off while inflicting severe losses to Pineda's army. The arrival of the *Cyane* insured the final withdrawal of the Mexicans from the area. Pineda was not beaten yet. He marched his force back to San Jose del Cabo, whose garrison had been only slightly increased to about sixty-three men. The second siege here began on January 22, 1848 and the Americans were hard pressed to hold out in the absence of their naval power, which had sailed off a couple of weeks before. The siege was finally broken by Commander Du Pont in *Cyane* which arrived on

February 14th. A strong landing party helped to push the Mexicans out of the town and relieve the garrison.

Colonel Burton was preparing his own offensive at this time in an effort to end the resistance in Baja once and for all. He acquired horses and saddles to mount some of his men and also received another 115 men as reinforcements. On the 25th of March they fell on Pineda's main encampment and the gallant Captain was severely wounded in the fight. Command in Baja passed to the governor, Mauricio Castro. Castro's army was broken up several days later in a vicious, thirty minute fight near Todos Santos during which he was captured. Commodore Shubrick was able to report on April 8, 1848 that the Mexican forces in Baja California had been totally dispersed and resistance was at an end.

Shubrick received word on March 30th of the armistice that had gone into effect around Mexico City, pending the ratification of the treaty of Guadalupe Hidalgo. All further plans were put on hold while awaiting this development. The only other action was when the New York Volunteers at La Paz and San Jose del Cabo began to mutiny due to the enforced inactivity. The ringleaders were brought off by landing parties from the *Independence*

THE NAVAL WAR

and the *Cyane* respectively. The war against Mexico in the Pacific was over.

CONCLUSION

In retrospect, the United States Navy had done well in accomplishing its mission in the war against Mexico. The Mexican Navy had not challenged its command of the sea at all but other obstacles to victory had to be overcome. A chronic shortage of manpower led to the inability of the navy to man the number of vessels it needed for duty on both coasts. Many times the necessity to rotate ships for reprovisioning made it difficult just to maintain the blockade, much less launch other operations. The Navy also had difficulty supplying its squadrons distant from their home ports for long periods of time. There had been little appreciation of what was involved in maintaining numerous ships at sea while they enforcing a blockade. Despite these handicaps, the blockade was maintained effectively and privateering on behalf of Mexico was kept at a minimum. Mexico was virtually cut off from the outside world when it came to supplies of war materials and munitions.

The navy had performed well on land as well with commanders on both coasts making good use of traditional landing parties to secure important objectives. This was possible because of the small and scattered nature of the resistance offered by the Californios. Stockton in California had gone so far as to equip a small army and campaign inland in support of the forces ashore. The sailors and Marines of the fleet saw a great deal of action, even though they were rarely faced with serious opposition. The navy had accomplished a great deal by the time Kearny arrived to take over. Thus the navy was able to protect the army ashore and its supply line from enemy interference by sea, which was a prime objective. It was also able to achieve its other main objective, that of seizing important points on the coast to deny them to the enemy and further assist the invading forces. Naval support had made it possible to control the coast, and eventually all of the richest territory in Alta California.

The experience of the Mexican war led to expansion of the navy in recognition of the important role that it had played. It was also necessary to protect the expanding commerce from the Pacific coast to the Far East. In addition the experience gained by many of the junior officers present in Mexico would be put to use when they were in command during the Civil War, a mere thirteen years later.

Another Mexican War veteran that could not cope with the American Civil War, the frigate Cumberland. The Merrimack sank her in Hampton Roads

73

Ships of the American Navy 1846-1848

Home Squadron

Albany—First class sloop. 1042 tons. 4 - 8" shell guns & 18 -32 pdrs. 210 man crew. Lost at sea in the West Indies in 1854.

Bonita—Schooner. 74 tons. 1 - 32 pdr. carronade. 40 man crew. Sister ship to the Petrel and the Reefer. Sold 10/11/48.

Cumberland—First class frigate. 1708 tons. 8 - 8" shell guns & 42 - 32 pdrs. 480 man crew. Sister ship to the Potomac, Raritan and Savannah. Sunk by the CSS Virginia (Merrimack) on 3/8/62 in Hampton Roads, VA.

Decatur—Third class sloop. 566 tons. 16 - 32 pdrs. 150 man crew. Sister ship to Dale and Preble. Sold 8/17/65.

Electra—Ordnance storeship. 248.5 tons. 2 - 18 pdr gunnades. 21 man crew. Sold 11/17/49. Ex- Rolla.

Etna—Bomb brig. 182 tons. 1 - 10" columbiad. 47 man crew. Sold 10/11/48. Ex- Walcott.

Ewing—Revenue cutter. 170 tons. 6 - 12 pdrs. Transferred to the Coast Survey, 1848.

Falcon—Schooner. 74 tons. 1 - 24 pdr. 40 man crew. Captured by U.S. at Tampico 11/14/46. Probably a sister ship to the Bonita, the Petrel and the Reefer. Sold 10/18/48. Ex - Isabel.

Falmouth—Second class sloop. 703 tons. 22 - 24 pdrs. 190 man crew. Sold 11/7/63.

Flirt—Schooner. 150 tons. 2 - 18 pdr carronades. 33 man crew. Transferred to the Coast Survey in 1851.

Forward—Revenue cutter. 150 tons. 6 - 12 pdrs. Sold 10/65.

Fredonia—Storeship. 800 tons. 4 - 24 pdr. carronades. 37 man crew. Wrecked at Arica, Peru on 8/13/68.

Germantown—First class sloop. 942 tons. 4 - 8" shell guns & 18 - 32 pdrs. 210 man crew. Burned to avoid capture at Norfolk Navy Yard on 4/20/61

Hecla—Bomb brig. 195 tons. 1 - 10" columbiad. 47 man crew. Sold 10/18/48. Ex- I. L. Richardson.

Hunter—Steamer. 96 tons. Iron hull. Wrecked on Isla Verde, near Veracruz on 3/21/47.

Iris—Third class steamer. 388 tons. 1 - 32 pdr carronade. 48 man crew. Side wheeler. Sold 3/8/49.

John Adams—Second class sloop. 700 tons. 22 -24 pdrs. 190 man crew. Sold 10/5/67.

Lawrence—Brig. 364 tons. 2 - 32 pdrs & 8 - 32 pdr carronades. 80 man crew. Sold in 1846.

Legare—Revenue steamer. 364 tons. 1 - 18 pdr., 1 - 12 pdr., 1 - 9 pdr. & 2 - 4 pdrs. Transferred to the Coast Survey 11/12/47.

McLane—Revenue steamer. 369 tons. 6 - 12 pdrs. side wheeler. Converted to lightship at New Orleans on 12/17/47.

Mahonese—Schooner. 100 tons. Captured by U. S. at Tampico on 11/14/46. Sold 10/15/48.

Mississippi—First class steamer. 1732 tons. 2 - 10" shell guns & 8 - 8" shell guns. 257 man crew. side wheeler. Sunk by Confederate batteries at Port Hudson, LA on 3/14/63.

Morris—Schooner. Captured by U.S. at Frontera on 10/23/46. Ex- Laura Virginia.

Nonata—Schooner. 122 tons. 4 - 42 pdr. carronades. Captured by the Porpoise in the Gulf of Mexico on 8/

21/46. Ex- Belle, ex- Nonata (Mexican Navy).

Ohio—Ship of the Line. 2757 tons. 12 - 8" shell guns, 28 - 42 pdrs. & 44 - 32 pdrs. 820 man crew. Also served in Pacific Squadron. Sold 9/27/83.

On-ka-hy-e—Schooner. 200 tons. 2 guns. Wrecked on Caicos Reef in the West Indies, 6/21/48.

Perry—Brig. 280 tons. 2 -32 pdrs. & 6 - 32 pdr. carronades. 80 man crew. Sold 8/10/65.

Petrel—Schooner. 74 tons. 1 - 32 pdr. carronade. 40 man crew. Sold 10/18/48.

Petrita—Steamer. 200 tons. 1 - 24 pdr. carronade. Side wheeler. Captured by U.S. at Frontera on 10/23/46. Foundered in the Alvarado River on 4/15/48. Ex-Champion, ex- Secretary, ex- Petrita (Mexican Navy).

Porpoise—Brig. 224 tons. 2 - 9 pdrs. & 9 - 24 pdr. carronades. Lost at sea in the East Indies in 1854.

Potomac—First class frigate. 1708 tons. 8 - 8" shell guns & 42 - 32 pdrs. 480 crew. Sister ship to the Cumberland, Raritan and Savannah. Sold 5/24/77.

Princeton—First class steamer. 672 tons. 1 - 8" shell gun & 12 - 42 pdr. carronades. 166 man crew. Broken up in 1849.

Raritan—First class frigate. 1708 tons. 8 - 8" shell guns & 42 - 32 pdrs. 480 man crew. Sister ship to the Cumberland, Potomac and Savannah. Scuttled at Norfolk Navy Yard on 4/20/61.

Reefer—Schooner. 74 tons. 1 - 32 pdr. carronade. 40 man crew. Sister ship to the Boniat and the Petrel. Transferred to the Coast Survey in 1850.

Relief—Storeship. 467 tons. 4 - 18 pdr. gunnades & 2 - 12 pdr. gunnades. 44 man crew. Sold 9/27/83.

St. Mary's—First class sloop. 958 tons. 4 - 8" shell guns & 18 - 32 pdrs. 210 man crew. Sold in 1908.

Santa Anna—Revenue cutter. Acquired from the Republic of Texas.

Saratoga—First class sloop. 882 tons. 4 - 8" shell guns & 18 - 32 pdrs. 275 man crew. Sold 8/14/1907.

Scorpion—Third class steamer. 339 tons. 2 - 8" shell guns & 2 - 18 pdr. carronades. 61 man crew. Sidewheeler. Sold 10/18/48. Ex- Aurora.

Scourge—Third class steamer. 230 tons. 1 - 32 pdr. & 2 - 24 pdr. carronades. 61 man crew. Iron hull. Sold 10/7/48. Ex-Bangor.

Somers—Brig. 259 tons. 10 - 32 pdr. carronades. 80 man crew. Capsized off Isla Verde, nr Veracruz on 12/8/46.

Spencer—Revenue steamer. 398 tons. 1 - 18 pdr. carronade. Converted to a lightship in 1848.

Spitfire—Third class steamer. 241 tons. 1 - 8" shell gun & 2 - 32 pdr. carronades. 50 man crew. Sidewheeler. Sister ship to the Vixen. Sold 10/11/48.

Stromboli—Bomb brig. 182 tons. 1 - 10" columbiad. 47 man crew. Sold 10/18/48. Ex- Howard.

Supply—Storeship. 547 tons. 4 - 24 pdr. carronades. 37 man crew. Sold 5/3/84.

Tampico—Schooner. 75 tons. 1 - 24 pdr. 40 man crew. Captured by U.S. at Tampico on 11/14/46. Sold 10/11/48. Ex- Pueblano.

Truxton—Brig. 331 tons. 10 - 32 pdr. carronades. 80 man crew. Wrecked near Tuxpan on 8/14/46.

Union—Schooner. 74 tons. 1 - 24 pdr. Captured by U.S. at Tampico on 11/14/46. May have been a sister ship to the Bonita, Petrel and Reefer. Wrecked off Veracruz on 12/16/46.

Van Buren—Revenue cutter. 112 tons. 4 - 12 pdrs. Sold 6/1/47.

Vesuvius—Bomb brig. 240 tons. 1 - 10" columbiad. 47 man crew. Sold 10/11/48. Ex- St. Mary's.

Vixen—Third class steamer. 241 tons. 3 - 32 pdr. carronades. 50 man crew. Sister ship to the Spitfire. Transferred to the Coast Survey on 7/21/48.

Washington—Coast Surevey brig. 1 - 42 pdr. Seized at New Orleans by the State of Louisiana on 1/31/61.

Water Witch—Third class steamer. 255 tons. 1 - 8" shell gun & 2 - 32 pdrs. 54 man crew. Sidewheeler. Expended as a target in 1851.

Woodbury—Revenue cutter. 112 tons. 4 - 12 pdrs. & 1 - 6 pdr. Sold 6/1/47.

Pacific Squadron

Columbus—Ship of the Line. 2480 tons. 8 - 8" shell guns, 56 - 32 pdrs. & 22 - 32 pdr. carronades. 780 man crew. Burned to avoid capture at Norfolk Navy Yard on 4/20/61.

Congress—First class frigate. 1867 tons. 8 - 8" shell guns & 46 - 32 pdrs. 480 man crew. Sunk by the CSS Virginia (Merrimack) in Hampton Roads on 3/8/62.

Cyane—Second class sloop. 792 tons. 20 - 32 pdrs. 200 man crew. Sister ship to the Levant. Sold 7/30/87

Dale—Third class sloop. 566 tons. 16 - 32 pdrs. 150 man crew. Sister ship to the Decatur and the Preble. Sold 11/30/1904.

Erie—Storeship. 611 tons. 4 - 9 pdrs. 43 man crew. Sold 11/26/50.

Independence—Razee. 1891 tons. 8 - 8" shell guns, 48 - 32 pdrs. 750 man crew. Sold 11/23/1914.

Julia—Schooner. Captured by the Cyane at La Paz, Baja California on 9/14/46. Probably sold in 1847.

Levant—Second class sloop. 792 tons. 4 - 8" shell guns & 18 - 32 pdrs. Sister ship to the Cyane. Lost at sea off Hawaii in 1860.

Lexington—Storeship. 691 tons. 4 - 9 pdrs. & 2 - 32 pdr. carronades. 43 man crew. Sister ship to the Warren. Sold in 1860.

Libertad—Schooner. 1 - 9 pdr. Chartered in 10/47 at La Paz, Baja California. Returned to owner.

Malek Adhel—Brig. 114 tons. 2 - 9 pdrs. & 10 - 6 pdrs. Captured by the Warren at Mazatlan on 9/7/46. Sold 9/47.

Portsmouth—First class sloop. 1022 tons. 4 - 8" shell guns & 18 - 32 pdrs. 210 man crew. Sold 7/12/1915.

Preble—Third class sloop. 566 tons. 16 - 32 pdrs. 150 man crew. Sister ship to the Dale and Decatur. Burned at Pensacola, FL on 4/27/63.

Savannah—First class frigate. 1708 tons. 4 - 8" shell guns, 28 - 32 pdrs & 22 - 42 pdr. carronades. 480 man crew. Sister ship to the Cumberland, Potomac and Raritan. Sold 0n 9/27/83.

Shark—Schooner. 198 tons. 2 - 9 pdrs. & 10 - 24 pdr. carronades. 100 man crew. Wrecked at the mouth of the Columbia River on 9/10/46.

Southampton—Storeship. 567 tons. 2 - 42 pdr. carronades, 4 - 18 pdr. carronades & 2 - 12 pdr. gunnades. 43 man crew. Sold about 1855.

Warren—Second class sloop. 691 tons. 24 - 32 pdrs. 190 man crew. Sister ship to the Lexington. Sold 1/1/63.

Whiton—Bark. Chartered or impressed into service in 1847 in the Gulf of California. Probably returned to owner in 1848.

THE MEXICAN NAVY 1846-1848

Aguila—Schooner. 130 tons. 6 - 18 pdr. carronades. 40 man crew. Scuttled in the Alvarado River in April of 1847.

Anahuac—Schooner. 105 tons. 1 - 12 pdr. Burned at Guaymas October 7, 1846.

Guadaloupe—Steamer. 775 tons. 2 - 68 pdrs. & 4 - 12 pdrs. Sidewheeler with an iron hull. The first metal hull construction ship to be used in the Western Hemisphere. Repossessed by the British in May of 1846 for defaulting on the purchase contract.

Guerrero—Schooner. 48.5 tons. 1 - 24 pdr. 25 man crew. Sister ship to the Victoria. Scuttled in the Alvarado River in April of 1847.

Isabel—Schooner. 74 tons. 1 - 24 pdr. 25 man crew. Sister ship to the Pueblano and the Union. Captured by U.S. squadron at Tampico on November 14, 1846. Name changed to USS Falcon.

Libertad—Schooner. 89 tons. 1 - 12 pdr. Captured from Yucatan. ex-Campecheno. Scuttled in the Alvarado River in April of 1847.

Mexicano—Brig. 208 tons. 14 - 18 pdr. carronades & 2 - 8 pdr. howitzers. Captured from Yucatan in October of 1842. ex-Yucateco. Scuttled in the Alvarado River in April of 1847.

Montezuma—Steamer. 1111 tons. 1 - 68 pdr., 2 - 32 pdrs, 4 - 32 pdr. carronades & 1 - 9 pdr. Sidewheeler.

Repossessed by British in May of 1846 for default on the purchase contract.

Morelos—Schooner. 59 tons. 1 - 12 pdr. Scuttled in the Alvarado River in April of 1847.

Pueblano—Schooner. 74 tons. 1 - 24 pdr. Sister ship to the Isabel and the Union. Captured by the U. S. squadron at Tampico on November 14, 1846. Name changed to USS Tampico.

Queretana—Schooner. 1 - 24 pdr. Scuttled in the Alvarado River in April of 1847.

Sonorense—Schooner. 27 tons. 1 - 12 pdr. Burned at Guaymas on October 7, 1846.

Union—Schooner. 74 tons. 1 - 24 pdr. Sister ship to the Isabel and the Pueblano. Captured by the U. S. squadron at Tampico on November 14, 1846. Name changed to USS Union.

Veracruzano Libre—Brig. 174 tons. 1 - 32 pdr., 6 - 18 pdr. carronades & 2 - 12 pdr. howitzers. 70 man crew. Scuttled in the Alvarado River in April of 1847. ex-Santa Anna.

Victoria—Schooner. 48.5 tons. 1 - 24 pdr. Sister ship to the Guerrero. Scuttled in the Alvarado River in April of 1847.

Zempoalteca—Brig. 6 - 12 pdr. carronades. Captured from Yucatan. Scuttled in the Alvarado River in April of 1847.

FUSS AND FEATHERS

VERA CRUZ

"Providence may defeat me, but I do not believe the Mexicans can." General Scott to General Taylor

On October 11, 1846 word reached Washington of the armistice agreed to by General Taylor with General Ampudia at Monterrey that would effectively suspend operations for eight weeks. President Polk was extremely upset about this and ordered the truce suspended immediately. He had been working for peace with Mexico since the beginning of hostilities and had seen every overture that he had made rebuffed. The success of Taylor's campaign in the northern provinces had not accomplished anything towards "conquering a peace". With the strategy of campaigning in northern Mexico failing to bring the Mexicans to terms it was realized that the only way to end the war was to strike at the heart of the country. This meant an expedition to take Mexico City itself, which would force the Mexicans to accept a peace that would be favorable to the United States. The problems of supply over the distances involved, plus the resistance that would be encountered along the way, made it impractical for Taylor's army to advance on Mexico City from Monterrey. An alternative approach was needed to end the war. Fortunately there was already a plan in the works, as well as a man who was to implement it.

The man chosen for the task of leading the army into the heart of Mexico was Major General Winfield Scott. Scott was sixty years old and had been in the military for almost forty years. He saw service during the War of 1812 and was a national hero with the rank of Brevet Major General by the end of that conflict. He had spent quite a bit of time writing and revising the army training manuals and trying to improve discipline in the service. He was too late reaching the area to participate in the Blackhawk War of 1832, and he only saw short service in Florida during the Second Seminole War in 1836. Scott became the commanding general of the army with the rank of Major General on July 5, 1841. He was known as a meticulous planner and organizer and his insistence on exact military etiquette and decorum earned him the title of "Old Fuss and Feathers." He was deeply respected by his men, whose welfare he looked out for as much as possible. While Scott was an excellent military strategist, he was not experienced at politics and his frank comments and criticisms, as well as petty feuds resulting from clashing personalities, often got him into trouble with the administration. Ironically, when Santa Anna had been passing through Fredericktown, Maryland on his way to Washington in 1836, he chanced upon a court of inquiry that was then investigating the conduct of General Scott. In Mexico Scott would show that he was one of the best generals ever to command the U.S. Army.

Before October Major General Scott had been working out the details of an operation that would have the United States Army and Navy combine to launch the biggest amphibious invasion attempted in history, to that time. The concept was to approach Mexico City from the east by landing at, and seizing, the port city of Vera Cruz and then marching by the most direct route to the capital. This would be basically the same route that Cortes and his conquistadors had followed more than three hundred years before when they had conquered Montezuma and the capital city of the Aztec empire. Scott estimated that he would need at least ten thousand men for the operation. The landing would be carried out as soon as possible to get the troops on the march and out of the coastal region before the onset of the wet season in April when the dreaded *vómito* (yellow fever) began to make its appearance. The troops would come from Taylor's army as well as newly raised units of regulars and state volunteers.

The city of Vera Cruz was guarded by the old Spanish fortress of San Juan de Ulúa located on an island about a thousand yards offshore. Commander David G. Farragut had observed the French bombard the fort in 1838 during the "Pastry War" with Mexico, when they took control of Vera Cruz. Due to the presumed difficulty of taking the fortress, the plan would be to land the army on the beaches some distance away from the city and then besiege the defenses into submission. It was expected that the island castle would have to be dealt with separately after the city had surrendered. Vera Cruz would then become a base of operations from which the army could start its march into the interior of the country. The navy would supply the shipping necessary to move the troops to the new theater of operations and then cooperate in maintaining a steady stream of supplies for the troops inland. Special flatboats were designed and built to be able to land the landing force on the beach. The invasion force would use the port of Tampico, which had not yet been secured, and the Brazos Santiago as its main staging point.

On November 23, 1846, Scott departed from Washington headed for Mexico. He also began to correspond with Taylor to arrange a possible meeting with him to discuss future plans. He was trying to prepare Taylor for the loss of most of his army to augment the invasion force being gathered. Scott reached Camargo on January 3, 1847 but Taylor was absent at Victoria at the time. Scott wrote to him informing him that he had already instructed General Butler to move troops that would cause Taylor to give up about 9,000 men from his army, including most of his regulars. In this letter Scott showed some of his lack of tact in political matters. Having just taken away most of Taylor's troops, and informing him only after the fact, he went on to declare optimistically that; "Providence may defeat me, but I do not believe the Mexicans can." The instructions that Scott sent to inform Taylor of what had already been ordered were intercepted on January 13th by the Mexicans and passed on to Santa Anna at San Luis Potosí. This was the information that would prompt Santa Anna to launch his campaign that would culminate in the battle of Buena Vista less than six weeks later.

After many delays transporting ships and troops to the proper positions, the invasion fleet finally set sail on March 2nd from Lobos Island (about sixty miles south of Tampico) where it had gathered. Scott had assembled almost 13,000 men for the expedition. General Worth commanded the First Division consisting of the 4th, 5th, 6th and 8th Infantry, the 2nd and 3rd Artillery fighting as infantry, a detachment of U.S. Marines, the Howitzer and Rocket Company of the ordnance department, and the Company of Sappers, Miners and Pontoniers.

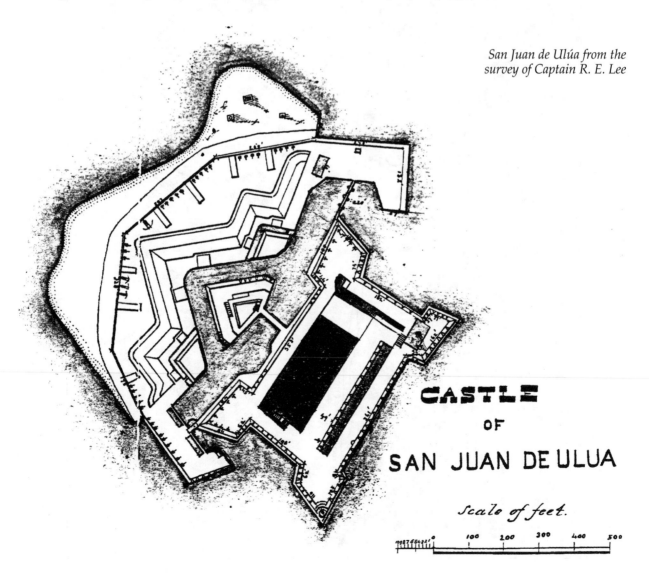

San Juan de Ulúa from the survey of Captain R. E. Lee

CASTLE
OF
SAN JUAN DE ULUA

Scale of feet.

0   100   200   300   400   500

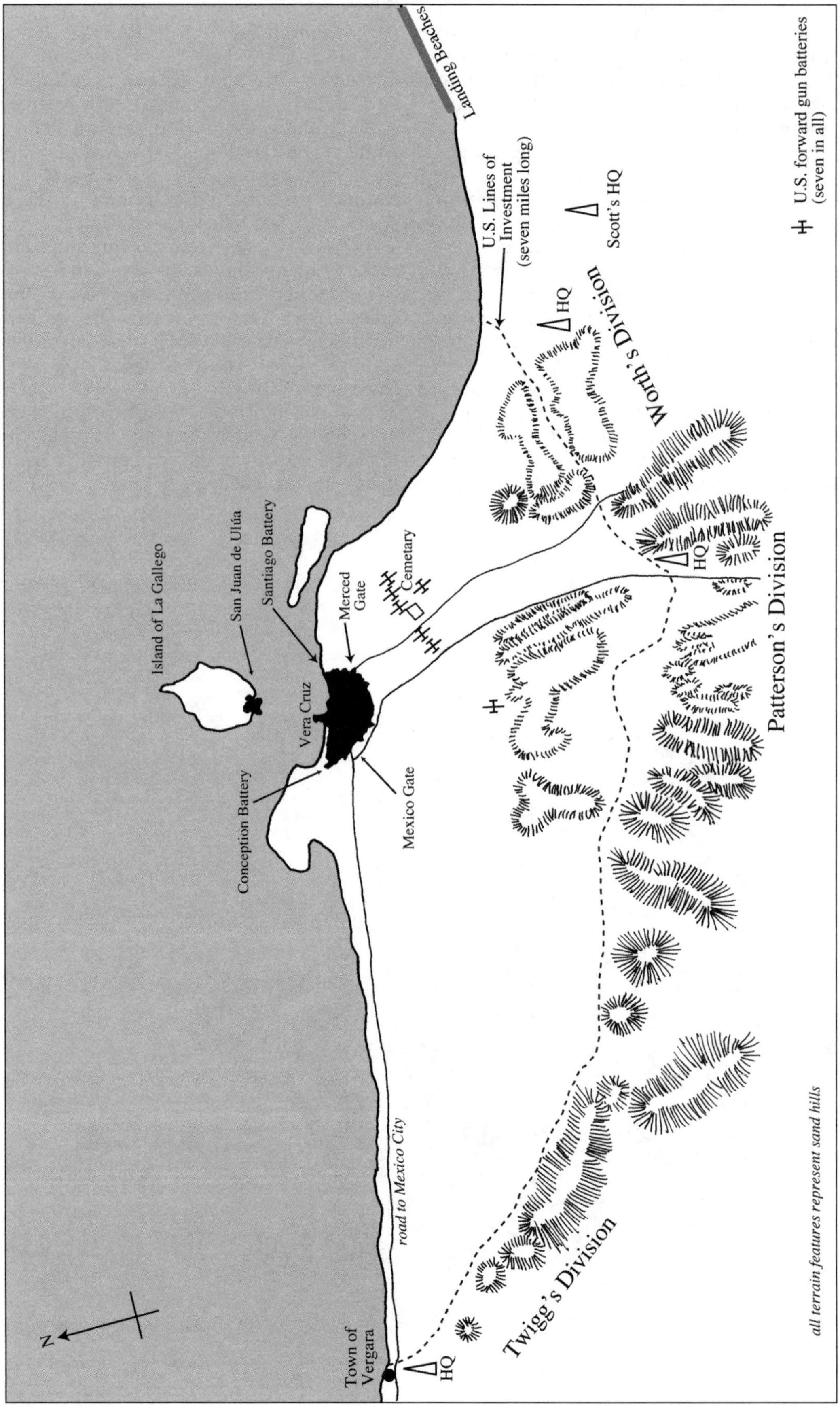

The Siege of Vera Cruz

all terrain features represent sand hills

Island of La Gallego

San Juan de Ulúa

Santiago Battery

Vera Cruz

Merced Gate

Cemetary

Conception Battery

Mexico Gate

road to Mexico City

Town of Vergara

HQ

Twigg's Division

Patterson's Division

HQ

Worth's Division

HQ

Scott's HQ

U.S. Lines of Investment (seven miles long)

Landing Beaches

U.S. forward gun batteries (seven in all)

N

The Second Division was led by General Twiggs and was made up of the 1st, 2nd, 3rd, and 7th Infantry, the 1st and 4th Artillery fighting as infantry, and the battery of Company K of the 1st Artillery led by Captain Francis Taylor. The Regiment of Mounted Riflemen, mostly on foot due to the loss of many of its horses during transport, was also attached to Twiggs' Division. The 3rd Division was the volunteer division of three brigades and it was commanded by Major General Robert Patterson. Patterson was an Irish-born, Pennsylvanian who was fifty-four years old and had seen service during the War of 1812. He returned to civilian life after that conflict and continued to serve in the state militia. He would acquit himself well as a subordinate although he did not have much experience in command. He could sometimes be overly cautious and he often lacked initiative. Patterson's brigade commanders were Brigadier General Gideon J. Pillow, Major General John A. Quitman and Major General James Shields. Pillow had the 1st and 2nd Pennsylvania and the 1st and 2nd Tennessee. Quitman led the 1st Alabama, 1st Georgia and 1st South Carolina, known as the Palmetto Regiment. Shields commanded the 3rd and 4th Illinois as well as the 2nd New York. In addition Colonel William S. Harney led a cavalry brigade consisting of companies from the 1st and 2nd Dragoons and the Tennessee Mounted Volunteers. This was the force embarked on the fleet that arrived in the vicinity of Vera Cruz on March 5th.

On the morning of March 6th, in order to scout out the best landing beaches to use, Commodore Conner had taken General Scott, along with some of his staff, onto the small steamer *Petrita* to go close

in to shore for a better look. In addition to Conner, Scott, Worth, Patterson and Twiggs, Captains Joseph E. Johnston and Robert E. Lee, and Lieutenants Pierre G. T. Beauregard and George G. Meade were all aboard. Unknown to the Mexican gunners, the future course of the war, as well as the future history of the United States, could have been drastically changed by the destruction of the lowly *Petrita* that day. The small ship did draw fire from the guns at the fortress of San Juan de Ulúa, but fortunately for the invasion and all on board the ship, no hits were scored.

The landing was set for the afternoon of March 9th at Collado Beach about two and a half miles south of the city and fortress. General Worth and his staff were the first ashore, followed by the rest of the first wave of some 2,595 men. The specially built surfboats ferried men ashore from the fleet and then returned to repeat the process. The invasion was completely unopposed and the next four hours saw the landing of the remainder of Scott's assault force of more than 8,600 men. The operation had gone flawlessly and the objectives of the first day were achieved without the loss of a single man.

The commander of the garrison at Vera Cruz, Brigadier General Juan Morales had decided not to oppose the beach landing and would save his strength instead for the siege that would follow. This was probably not the best course of action to take as it allowed Scott to land and organize his army without any interference. Morales may have overestimated the power of the Americans to support the invasion at the waters edge, when it was the most vulnerable to attack. In the city itself he commanded a garrison of some 3,360 men of which

---

MEXICAN FORCES AT VERA CRUZ, MARCH 9-28, 1847
Brig-Gen. Juan Morales (4390)

Veracruz garrison in City (3360)
    2nd Line Infantry (400): Col. Bartolo Arzamendi
      (includes various small detachments)
    8th Line Infantry (140): Col. José Felix López
    11th Line Infantry (41): Capt. Miguel Camargo
    3rd Light Infantry (150): Capt. Juan J. Sanchez
    Active Militia Battalion of Oaxaca (400): Col.
      Juan Aguayo
    Active Militia Battalion of Tehuantepec (60):
      Commander Manuel Prieto
    Puebla National Guard (350): Col. Pedro M.
      Herrera
    Orizava National Guard (500): Col. José
      Gutierrez Villanueva
    Veracruz National Guard (800): Col. José
      Luelmo
    Coatepec & other National Guard (109)
    Regular Artillery (150): Col. Antonio Ortiz
      Izquierdo

    National Guard Artillery (80): Lt. Antonio Sosa
    Marines (80)
    Zapadores (100): Commander José María Parra

    Cannons: 14 - 24 lb., 20 - 16 lb., 11 - 12 lb., 13 - 8 lb.,
    4 - 4 lb. guns & 4 - 4 lb. mountain guns
    Mortars: 3 - 42 lb., 6 - 13", 5 -12", 2 - 9" & 7 - 8"
    howitzers
    Total: 89 artillery pieces

Garrison of San Juan de Ulúa (1030)
    Active Militia Battalion of Puebla (180):
      Commander Fernando Urriza
    Active Militia Battalion of Jamiltepec (150): Col.
      N. García
    Active Militia of Tuxpan, Tampico & Alvarado
      (250) (2 companies): Capt. Miguel Argumedo
      & Capt. Eligio Pérez
    Artillery (250): Col. Mariano Aguado

    Cannons: 87 - 24 lb., 6 - 16 lb. & 4 - 8 lb. guns
    Mortars: 10 - 84 lb., 10 - 68 lb., 16 - 42 lb. & 2 - 14"
    Total: 135 artillery pieces

AMERICAN ARMY AT VERA CRUZ
FROM MARCH 9 - 28, 1847
Major General Winfield Scott (13,000)

General Staff ("little cabinet")
Chief of Engineers: Col. Joseph G. Totten
Inspector General: Lt-Col. Ethan Allen Hitchcock
Assistant Adjutant General: Capt. Henry Lee Scott
Engineer: Capt. Robert E. Lee

1st Division (3065): Gen. William J. Worth
4th Infantry: Lt-Col. John Garland (Companies A, B, C, D, E & I)
5th Infantry: Lt-Col. James S. McIntosh (Companies E, F, G, H, I & K)
6th Infantry: Col. Newman S. Clarke (Companies A, C, D, E, F & H)
8th Infantry: Maj. Carlos A. Waite (Companies A, B, D, E, H, I & K)
2nd Artillery: Col. James Bankhead (Companies B, C, D, F, G, H, I & K, as infantry)
3rd Artillery: Lt-Col. Francis S. Belton (Companies A, B, D, G & K, as infantry)
U.S. Marines (180): Capt. Alvin Edson, USMC
Company A, 2nd Artillery: Lt-Col. James Duncan (4 - 6 lb. guns)
Howitzer & Rocket Company: Maj. George Henry Talcott (Hale's Rockets & 12 lb. mountain howitzers)
1 Company of Louisiana Volunteers: Capt. Albert C. Blanchard (attached to 5th Infantry)
1 Company of Kentucky Volunteers: Capt. John S. Williams (attached to 6th Infantry)
Company of Sappers, Miners and Pontoniers (100): Capt. Alexander J. Swift

2nd Divison (2917): Brig-Gen. David E. Twiggs
1st Infantry: Col. William Davenport (Companies C, E, F, G, H & K)
2nd Infantry: Lt-Col. Bennet Riley (Companies A, B, D, E, F, G, H, I & K)
3rd Infantry: Capt. Edmund B. Alexander (Companies C, D, F, G, H, I & K)
7th Infantry: Lt-Col. Joseph Plymton (Companies C, D, E, F, I & K)
1st Artillery: Col. Thomas Childs (Companies B, F, G, H & I, as infantry)
4th Artillery: Maj. John L. Gardner (Companies A, D, E, F, G & H, as infantry)
Company K, 1st Artillery: Capt. Francis Taylor (4 - 6 lb. guns)
Regiment of Mounted Riflemen (on foot): Col. Persifor F. Smith (Companies A, B, C, D, E, F, G, H & K)

3rd Division: Maj-Gen. Robert Patterson
Field Battery, 3rd Artillery: Capt. Edward Jenner

Steptoe (4 - 12 lb. guns)
Pillow's Brigade (2500): Brig-Gen. Gideon J. Pillow
1st Tennessee Volunteers: Col. William Campbell
2nd Tennessee Volunteers: Col. William Haskell
1st Pennsylvania Volunteers: Col. Francis M. Wyncoop
2nd Pennsylvania Volunteers: Col. William B. Roberts
Quitman's Brigade (1000): Maj-Gen. John A. Quitman
1st Alabama Volunteers: Col. John R. Coffey
1st Georgia Volunteers: Col. Henry R. Jackson
1st South Carolina Volunteers: Col. Pierce M. Butler (known as the 'Palmetto' Regiment)
Shields' Brigade (1500): Maj-Gen. James Shields
2nd New York Volunteers: Col. Ward B. Burnet
3rd Illinois Volunteers: Col. Ferris Foreman
4th Illinois Volunteers: Col. Edward D. Baker

Harney's Cavalry Brigade (900): Col. William S. Harney
1st Dragoons (Company F)
2nd Dragoons (Companies A, B, C, F, I & K)
Tennessee Mounted Volunteers: Col. Jonas E. Thomas

Siege Batteries: Col. James Bankhead, 2nd Artillery
Battery #1: Capt. Horace Brooks, 2nd Artillery (4 - 10" mortars)
Battery #2: Lt. Muscoe L. Shackleford, 2nd Artillery (3 - 10" mortars)
Battery #3: Capt. John R. Vinton, 3rd Artillery (3 - 10" mortars)
Battery #4 (4 - 24 lb. guns & 2 - 8" howitzers)
Battery #5 (Naval Battery): Capt. John H. Aulick (3 - 32 lb. guns & 3 - 8"/68 lb. Paixhan guns)
*Capt. Vinton was killed on March 22nd and Battery #3 was then commanded by Lt. Stewart Van Vleit, 3rd Artillery.

American Navy at Veracruz in March of 1847
Home Squadron: Commodore David Conner
Albany (22 gun sloop): Capt. Samuel L. Breese
Bonita (1 gun schooner): Lt. Timothy G. Benham
Falcon (1 gun schooner): Lt. John J. Glasson
Petrel (1 gun schooner): Lt. T. Darrah Shaw
Petrita (1 gun steamer): Lt. Samuel Lockwood
Porpoise (11 gun brig): Lt. William E. Hunt
Potomac (50 gun frigate): Capt. John H. Aulick
Princeton (13 gun steam frigate): Comm. Frederick Engle
Raritan (50 gun frigate): Capt. French Forrest
Reefer (1 gun schooner): Lt. Isaac Sterrett
St. Mary's (22 gun sloop): Comm. John L. Saunders
Spitfire (3 gun steamer): Comm. Josiah Tattnall
Tampico (1 gun schooner): Lt. William P. Griffin
Vixen (3 gun steamer): Comm. Joshua Sands

only about a fourth were regulars. The majority of the troops available were National Guard units with some Active Militia for support. The city also had 89 different artillery pieces of varying size and quality. The castle/fortress of San Juan de Ulúa had its own garrison on the island of another 1,030 Active Militia with some 135 cannon and mortars. Supplies of ammunition, powder and provisions were short in both the city and on the island and many of the guns were unserviceable. Morales was not optimistic about trying to hold a city with deteriorating defenses and no hope of reinforcements arriving anytime soon. His decision was to remain on the defensive and reply to the inevitable bombardment with whatever artillery he could bring into action. The only action taken outside the walls of the city would be skirmishes by cavalry patrols encountering American scouting parties.

The Americans quickly set out to surround the city and began to emplace the artillery batteries necessary to reduce the defenses. There were frequent encounters during this time with small detachments of Mexicans trying to find weak points in the American lines to break into or out of the city. The guns from Vera Cruz fired on the working parties that were constructing the siege artillery batteries and bunkers. Once the siege had been going on for several days, some of the Engineers ventured out to view the results of their work. A young 2nd Lieutenant, Ulysses S. Grant of the 4th Infantry, had also gone forward to observe these professionals at close range. Lieutenant Beauregard was peering through his field glasses from the vantage point of a sand hill to get a better view of the Mexican artillery that was showering the American lines with shot and shell. He remarked to the other officers present that he was going forward to an old adobe house that would afford him a closer look. The other engineers present, Captain Robert E. Lee, 2nd Lieutenant George B. McClellan and Lieutenant Gustavus W. Smith stayed where they were, but Grant decided to go with him. While the two men were inside the abandoned house looking through the cracked walls, a shell came through the roof, buried itself in the dirt floor, and exploded. Fortunately, both men managed to scramble out of the wreckage completely unhurt.

Eventually there were five separate batteries established, including one of naval guns with crew from the ships to make up for Scott's overall shortage of siege guns. Among the sailors helping to man the guns was Lieutenant Raphael Semmes, USN, later to make his fame in the Confederate Navy as the Captain of the *CSS Alabama*.

The construction of the naval battery was overseen by Captain Robert E. Lee. This would be the first time that he would see action during his career in the army. One night while the siege was underway,

Captain Lee and Lieutenant Beauregard of the Engineers were returning to camp from a late reconnaissance in front of the advanced pickets. The sentries had been drawn in for the night but upon entering a small open spot in the chaparral the officers were hastily challenged by an unseen observer. Beauregard quickly shouted "Officers!" while Lee exclaimed "Friends!" but it was too late. An explosion lit the night as the man discharged his musket at point blank range, the ball passing within inches of Lee's chest and singeing his uniform. Before anything else could happen, the two men disarmed their assailant who claimed to be a sentry in search of his company after having gotten lost in the chaparral. The officers escorted him back to the unit where he belonged. Beauregard suspected all along that he was a deserter en route to the Mexican lines when they had happened by.

On March 15th the Americans received unofficial word of Taylor's victory over Santa Anna at Buena Vista in northern Mexico. This was good news, but many of the regulars were disappointed that they had missed the fight and that all of the glory had gone to the volunteers. There had also been a revolt in Mexico City, by the local garrison, that had been put down by loyal troops from the regular army and National Guard after three weeks of skirmishing. This event occurred while Santa Anna was away from the capital.

Scott issued a call for the surrender of Vera Cruz on March 22nd, which General Morales rejected. The American bombardment began in earnest later that same day, with Scott planning to assault the city if the bombardment did not cause the Mexicans to capitulate. But the shelling proved to be too much, and on March 26th negotiations for the surrender were initiated by Brigadier General José Juan Landero who had taken over from Morales when that officer resigned. The city was formally surrendered to the Americans on March 29th. The Americans had lost only thirteen killed and fifty-five wounded. Mexican losses are impossible to determine but most likely numbered several hundred of which many were civilians. Somewhat to the surprise and relief of General Scott was the fact that the fortress of San Juan de Ulúa was surrendered along with the city and so it did not have to be taken separately. This allowed the American army to begin using the port of Vera Cruz immediately to establish a base of supply for the march inland to Mexico City.

Scott's main priority now that Vera Cruz had fallen was to get the army on the march to Mexico City as soon as possible. The season for the dreaded *vómito* was drawing nearer and he wanted to have his army out of the unhealthy lowlands along the coast before they were exposed to the disease. The route he chose was that of the National Highway, the same route that Cortes and his conquistadores had used in 1519. The road went through Jalapa, Perote, Puebla, and on to Mexico City. There were many good defensive positions along this route that the Mexicans might try to hold, but Scott had few alternatives. The army set out on April 2nd, with Harney leading a mixed force scouting the road ahead. Twiggs' division marched on the 8th, followed by Patterson's volunteers. The morning of April 12th found Twiggs' men at the pass of Cerro Gordo, which was well defended by a reported 4,000 Mexicans. Twiggs was prone to use the simplest method he knew for clearing the pass and ordered an immediate attack for the next morning. He was persuaded to postpone this attack by General Pillow and General Shields, whose men were just coming up and were exhausted. Before the attack could be launched General Patterson wisely intervened from his sickbed and called off any attacks until further reconnaissance was done and the rest of the army had come up. It was fortunate for the Americans that he had, for Santa Anna had managed to fortify the pass and bring up almost 12,000 men to hold it.

REVOLT IN MEXICO CITY

Santa Anna had been extremely active since his return to San Luis Potosí on March 9th, the same day that the Americans had invaded at Vera Cruz. Leading his exhausted and depleted army back from Buena Vista he got word of an uprising in the capital on February 27th by some troops of the National Guard. The revolt was an attempt, supported by General Peña y Barragán, to oust the Acting President, Gomez Farías, while Santa Anna was away with the army. The primary support for the rebellion came from the wealthy and privileged upper classes of Mexico.

The city of Mexico had originally raised the Active Commerce Regiment of Mexico in 1835. The unit was to maintain order in the city. There were requirements that the officers had to be wealthy businessmen, successful professionals, or their sons. The non-commissioned officers had to be educated and have a record of proven good conduct, as well as being tradesmen or property owners. The units was nicknamed the Polka Dancers, or *Polkos*, by the populace in reference to the dance popular among the upper classes. The regiment had flashy uniforms, sometimes with more adornment than the regulations allowed. It had been disbanded in 1839 for rebellion, but was reformed the same year.

In September of 1846 the upper classes began to feel the sting of how very expensive the war would be for Mexico. They knew they would be asked to pay a large part of the bill, and if they did not pay willingly, it was possible that their assets would be subject to forcible seizure. To help protect their own interests they decided to raise a corps of militia for the National Guard. Four units were formed with the purpose of acting as a garrison for Mexico City and protecting property, especially that of the wealthy. The Victoria battalion was made up of wealthy professional men and merchants, while the Hidalgo battalion was mostly raised from clerks. The Bravos and Independencia battalions were recruited from artisans and tradesmen. These new battalions were also given the name of *Polkos*.

These units were prepared to act in the interests of the Puro party of 'pure' federalists or democrats. In opposition to them was the more conservative *moderado*, or moderate, party of the Government. These factions had been on the brink of civil war in October of 1846, but a crisis had been averted. Now in February of 1847 it looked like armed rebellion, in response to government policies, would be unavoidable.

In an effort to disarm the *puros* the government of Farías planned to send the National Guard units away from the city. The Independencia battalion, which was considered untrustworthy, was ordered to march against the impending invasion at Vera Cruz. The battalion refused to leave the city and it was quickly joined by the other three "elite" militia units in denouncing the government of Gomez Farías. The historian, Justin Smith, described the situation,

"...the city echoed with the cries, "Death to Gómez Farías!" "Death to the Puros!" Cannon were soon at the street corners, and the usual scenes of a Mexican insurrection, fatal chiefly to peaceful residents, were presently on exhibition..."

The situation was all too familiar to the inhabitants of any major city in Mexico at the time. There were

---

FORCES INVOLVED IN THE REVOLT IN MEXICO CITY ON FEBRUARY 27, 1847

Puros (revolutionaries)
Bravos Battalion* (300)
Hidalgo Battalion* (500)
Independencia Battalion* (800)
Mina Battalion (500)
Victoria Battalion* (600)
Zapadores (400)
Line Cavalry (150)
* These units were also called *Polkos*
Moderados (government)
Libertad Battalion (1000)
Line Grenadiers (1000)
Line Cavalry (300)
Artillery of the National Guard of Galeana, Guerrero, Matamoros & Verduzco (1000)
22 Artillery pieces

nine days of inconclusive skirmishing. A description by Francis Calderón of the rebellion of 1841 in Mexico City was very appropriate, "both parties seem to be 'fighting the city' instead of each other, and this manner of firing from behind parapets, and from the tops of houses and steeples, is decidedly safer for the soldiers than for the inhabitants."

The initial enthusiasm for the rebellion soon wore off when the *puros* and *polkas* realized that there was little popular support for their cause, not even in the other parts of the country they had hoped would aid them. The *moderados* under Farías managed to hold onto power. The army was itself divided with different units siding with each of the two factions, while other units remained neutral.

Santa Anna's return from his 'victory' at Buena Vista prompted both factions to send their own emissaries to him to plead their cause. The political system in Mexico was too vulnerable to the man commanding the biggest army. There was no guarantee that Santa Anna, an opportunist if ever there was one, would back his own vice-president in this dispute. Santa Anna vacillated for a time, but in the end, after 23 days of insurrection, he was able to force a compromise on both parties, and declared himself the saviour of Mexico once again.

The wealthy and the Church would end up paying huge sums of money towards the military effort, and Farías was out, to be replaced by Pedro Maria Anaya as the new president. There was little time to accomplish anything more as word had arrived that the Americans under General Scott had launched their attack on Vera Cruz. Both factions once more rallied to the "Napoleon of the West" to rid their country of the invaders.

Santa Anna left Mexico City on the day after Harney set out from Vera Cruz on his scouting mission. He had already diverted three brigades of infantry and one of cavalry, some of the survivors of the march back from Buena Vista, down the National Highway towards the coast to prepare a defensive position

CERRO GORDO

"Charge 'em to hell!"
General Twiggs at Cerro Gordo

The position chosen by Santa Anna was a strong one. The National Highway was dominated on both sides by hills with one of the largest being El Telegrafo near the village of Cerro Gordo. The large hill was at least 600 feet high with a flat top. It was on the north side of the road and became the Mexican left flank. At this point the road was built generally east to west with a few twists and turns as it wound its way through the passes. The Rio Del Plan, a substantial stream running to the south of the main position, presented an obstacle that would protect the Mexican right flank. In front of the main position was a hill with three distinct points from which steep cliffs descended to the level of the highway. These positions made ideal gun emplacements to protect against any advances along the road. North of the road, on the Mexican left flank, there seemed to be impassable terrain broken up by gullies and hills and with a solid covering of chaparral that would force any army to confine its advance to the road. A second, smaller, flat-topped hill called La Atalaya stood about a half-mile to the northeast of El Telegrafo, further from the highway.

The Mexican fortifications were well planned and built partly by labor from Santa Anna's own Encero estate close by. The front position of three points on a single hill held three batteries with at least nineteen

Scott's March to Mexico City

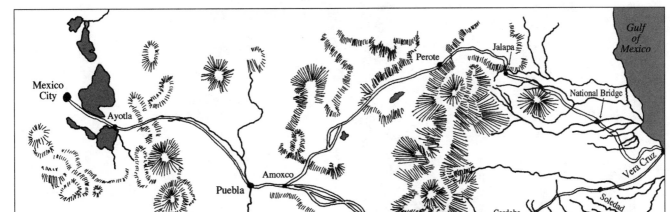

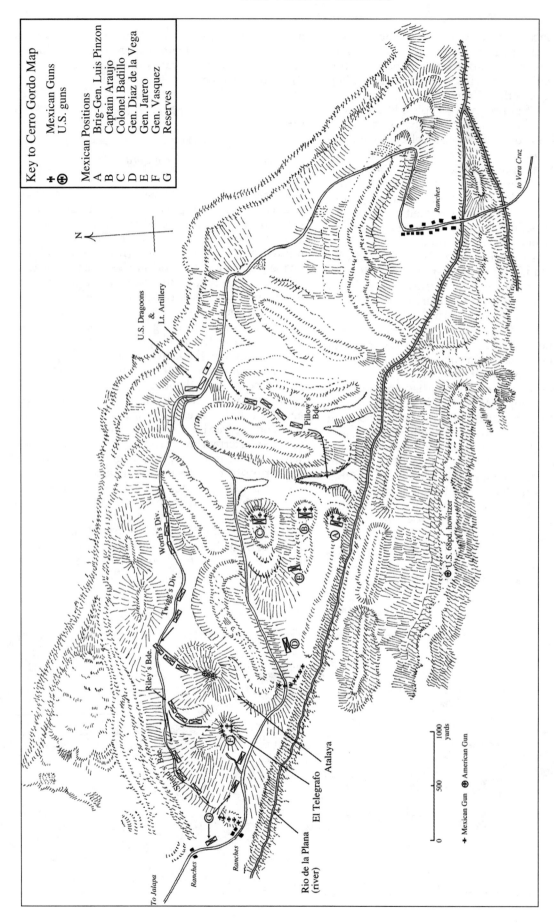

The battlefield of Cerro Gordo

Key to Cerro Gordo Map

Mexican Guns
U.S. guns

Mexican Positions
A   Brig-Gen. Luis Pinzon
B   Captain Araujo
C   Colonel Badillo
D   Gen. Diaz de la Vega
E   Gen. Jarero
F   Gen. Vasquez
G   Reserves

The battle is raging on El Telegrapho in the center, in this picture of Cerro Gordo by Nebel. The Atalaya is on the left.

guns and more than 1,800 men from the brigades led by Brigadier General Luis Pinzón, Colonel Badillo, Captain Buenaventura Araujo of the Navy and with Brigadier General José María Jarero in close reserve. Further back and astride the road a battery of guns with supporting troops was commanded by General Rómulo Díaz de la Vega, who had been captured at Resaca de la Palma and had recently been exchanged. On El Telegrafo itself was a small contingent of about a hundred infantry and four small guns commanded by General Ciriaco Vásquez. Finally, there were a great number of troops being held in reserve by Santa Anna in the main Mexican camp close to the village of Cerro Gordo. Santa Anna himself reported that he commanded a total of 12,000 troops in this well defended position.

Fortunately for the American army Twiggs' hasty attack had been postponed. General Scott came up on the afternoon of the fourteenth and ordered further reconnaissance by the engineers to discover what his options might be. Lieutenant Beauregard had already recommended that the smaller hill of Atalaya was the key to being able to attack the position. Now Captain Robert E. Lee discovered a path to approach it without exposing the army to

any undue fire from the Mexicans above. Lee had almost been captured while out on his scouting mission. He was forced to hide under a log within a few feet of Mexican patrols and actually overheard Mexican officers discussing the upcoming battle. On the morning of the seventeenth Twiggs' division moved out along the newly improved path made by the engineers towards Atalaya. Colonel Harney led the charge up the slope that swept away the handful of defenders there. Someone had asked Twiggs how far to charge and he had replied, "Charge 'em to hell!" This is what may have caused some of the men to continue on towards El Telegrafo, where they were pinned down by musketry and artillery fire. They were forced to withdraw as Twiggs' sole objective had been to gain a favorable position for the next days attack, not to bring on a general engagement.

The Mexicans thought that the Americans had been repulsed from their objective of El Telegrafo with the loss of only the smaller Atalaya. They reinforced El Telegrafo with extra guns and troops from the camp for the renewal of the fight in the morning, perhaps not appreciating the importance that Atalaya would play now that it was in enemy hands. Twiggs also got reinforcements in the form of Shields's brigade as it arrived on the field. The Americans were able to move guns, including three 24 pounder cannons to the top of Atalaya to support the attack on El Telegrafo the next day.

Scott's plan was to attack El Telegrafo as the Mexicans expected, but to launch another attack at the same time to go behind the hill and cut the road from Jalapa near the Mexican camp. The main defenses would thus be encircled and forced to withdraw or surrender. Twiggs had Harney, leading General Smith's brigade, charge the slopes of El Telegrafo at seven o'clock in the morning on the eighteenth. Meanwhile Shields and Riley led their men on the flanking maneuver towards the camp. After a very difficult ascent the breastworks were taken by the 7th Infantry and Captain John B. Magruder took over the captured Mexican guns and turned them on the defenders now fleeing down the hill. Meanwhile Shields had gained the Mexican camp but was severely wounded while taking the position on the road. His movement served to cut off the entire Mexican army where it stood. Riley was also involved in reaching the road from almost directly behind El Telegrafo. The American objective

had been achieved in only three hours of hard marching and fighting.

General Scott had also planned to launch a diversionary attack on the Mexican right flank so that Santa Anna would be deceived as to the real location of the main effort to turn his position. Brigadier General Gideon J. Pillow's brigade of volunteers from Pennsylvania and Tennessee was given this task. Pillow was forty years old and his only qualifications for the command that he held was that he had been President Polk's law partner and political advisor. He was not very popular with the men, who knew that his incompetence could cost them their lives. An earlier incident at Camargo had subjected Pillow to much ridicule in the army, especially among the West Point cadets. Pillow had ordered fortifications to be constructed for the defense of the town and its supplies. The men building the entrenchments had placed the earth on the outside of the fortifications and had dug the ditch on the inside. This was opposite of the way it was supposed to be constructed. Normally the ditch was on the outside, so that the enemy was kept out and the entrenchments could be well defended. The young cadets, recently graduated from engineering

---

AMERICAN FORCES AT CERRO GORDO ON APRIL 18, 1847
Maj-Gen. Winfield Scott (8500 engaged)

1st Division (2416): Gen. William J. Worth
1st Brigade: Col. John Garland
   2nd Artillery (Companies B, C, D, F, G, H, I & K, as infantry)
   3rd Artillery (Companies A, B, G, H & K, as infantry)
   4th Infantry (Companies A, B, C, D, E & I)
   Company A, 2nd Artillery: Lt-Col. James Duncan (4 - 6 lb. guns)
2nd Brigade: Col. Newman S. Clarke
   5th Infantry (Companies E, F, G, H, I & K)
   6th Infantry (Companies A, C, D, E, F & H)
   8th Infantry (Companies A, B, C, D, E, H & I)
Worth's Division was not engaged at this battle

2nd Division: Brig-Gen. David E. Twiggs
attached
   2nd Dragoons (Companies A, B, C, F, I & K)
   Artillery (6 - 24 lb. guns, 2 - 8" howitzers & 4 - 10" mortars)
   Howitzer & Rocket Company: Maj. George H. Talcott (Hale's Rockets & 12 lb. mountain howitzers)
1st Brigade: Gen. Persifor F. Smith
   1st Artillery (Companies B, F, G, H & I)(as infantry)
   3rd Infantry (Companies A, C, F, H, I & K)
   Regiment of Mounted Rifles (on foot)

(Companies A, B, C, D, E, F, G, H & K)
   Company K, 1st Artillery: Capt. Francis Taylor (4 - 6 lb. guns)
2nd Brigade: Col. Bennet Riley
   4th Artillery (Companies A, D, F, G, & H, as infantry)
   2nd Infantry (Companies A, B, D, E, F, G, H, I & K)
   7th Infantry (Companies C, D, E, F, I & K)

Volunteer Division (3367): Maj-Gen. Robert Patterson
1st Brigade: Maj-Gen. James Shields (attached to 2nd Division)
   2nd New York Volunteers
   3rd Illinois Volunteers
   4th Illinois Volunteers
   Field Battery, 3rd Artillery: Capt. Edward J. Steptoe (4 - 12 lb. guns)
2nd Brigade: Maj-Gen. Gideon J. Pillow
   1st Pennsylvania Volunteers: Col. Francis M. Wyncoop
   2nd Pennsylvania Volunteers: Col. William B. Roberts
   1st Tennessee Volunteers: Col. William Campbell
   2nd Tennessee Volunteers: Col. William Haskell
   U.S. Marine detachment

unattached
   Engineer Company (51): Maj. John Lind Smith
   Tennessee Mounted Volunteers: Col. Jonas E. Thomas

classes that taught the proper way to build such things, were greatly amused. Lieutenant James Stuart, of South Carolina, mounted a mustang and proceeded to leap both the parapet and the ditch at a fast gallop, showing the folly of their construction. Pillow may not have been directly responsible for this blunder, but it was done under his command and he was given full credit for it by the men.

Pillow's troops had about four miles to cover to reach their positions and even though they had set out by 6 o'clock in the morning they were not in position until almost 9 o'clock. This was largely due to Pillow issuing confusing orders for maneuvers that caused the rear of the column to miss the proper route completely at first. Once on the scene Pillow proceeded to split his forces between the faces of two ridges so that they could not support each other. What's more, the strung out column of march did not allow the second regiment in each attack the ability to arrive in time to accompany the first regiment in its assault. The men advanced carefully and undetected to the appointed spot where the voices of the Mexican officers at their positions could be clearly heard above them. At this point the men were trying to recover from some of the disorder caused by the march when a frustrated Pillow

Charge 'em to hell! Twiggs

MEXICAN ARMY AT CERRO GORDO ON APRIL 18, 1847
Generalissimo Antonio López de Santa Anna (9490) (12,000)

Extreme Right Flank (500): Brig-Gen. Luis Pinzón
  5th Line Infantry
  Atlixco National Guard Battalion
  1 - 12 lb. & 6 other guns
Center Right Flank: Capt. Buenaventura Araujo (Mexican Navy)
  Libertad Battalion (400)
  Zacapoastla National Guard Battalion (300)
  8 guns
Right Flank (250): Col. Badillo
  National Guard Company of Jalapa
  National Guard Company of Coatepec: Capt. Mata
  National Guard Company of Teusitlan
  9 guns
Matamoros Camp (close reserve) (450): Brig-Gen. José María Jarero
  National Guard Battalion of Matamoros
  National Guard Battalion of Tepeaca
  1 - 8 lb. & 4 other guns
Road Battery: Gen. Romulo Díaz de la Vega
  6th Line Infantry (900)
  Grenadier Guards of the Supreme Powers (460)
  4 - 16 lb. & 3 other guns
Left Flank on El Telegrafo: Gen. Ciriaco Vásquez
  3rd Line Infantry (100): Col. Azpeitia

  4 - 4 lb. guns (150): Col. Palacios
unattached
  Galeana National Guard Artillery
Reserve
Vásquez's Light Infantry Brigade (1700)
  1st Light Infantry
  2nd Light Infantry
  3rd Light Infantry: Gen. Baneneli
  4th Light Infantry
Ampudia's Brigade (780)
  4th Line Infantry
  11th Line Infantry
Cavalry Reserve: Gen. Valentín Canalizo
(the first four units listed totalled 1500)
  5th Cavalry
  9th Cavalry
  Active Militia Cavalry of Morelia
  Tulancingo Cuirassiers
  Active Militia Cavalry of Chalchicomula (1 squadron)
  Active Militia Cavalry of Jalapa (1 squadron)
  Active Militia Cavalry of Orizaba (1 squadron)
  Hussars of the Guard of the Supreme Powers (1 squadron)
arriving on April 18
Arteaga's Brigade (2000): Gen. Arteaga
  Active Militia of Puebla
  National Guard of Puebla

The San Patricio companies were also present but I have not discovered their location.

shouted at the top of his voice, "Why the Hell don't Colonel Wyncoop (the commander of the 1st Pennsylvania) file to the right"? Immediately a bugle sounded ahead of them and within minutes the column came under heavy fire from the artillery and musketry of the emplaced Mexicans.

The 2nd Tennessee under Colonel Haskell charged uphill unsuccessfully and suffered heavy losses in the process. They came streaming back down the hill disorganized and badly scattered. Some men bolted while others sought whatever cover was available. The 1st Tennessee under Colonel Campbell was halted to the rear and unable to support the attack. Colonel Campbell was now in command after Pillow had received a slight wound to the arm and left the field without giving any further instructions. Campbell was now in a rage amid the confusion and attempted to get the two Pennsylvania regiments that were standing ready next to each other into the action. As Sergeant Thomas Barclay of the 2nd

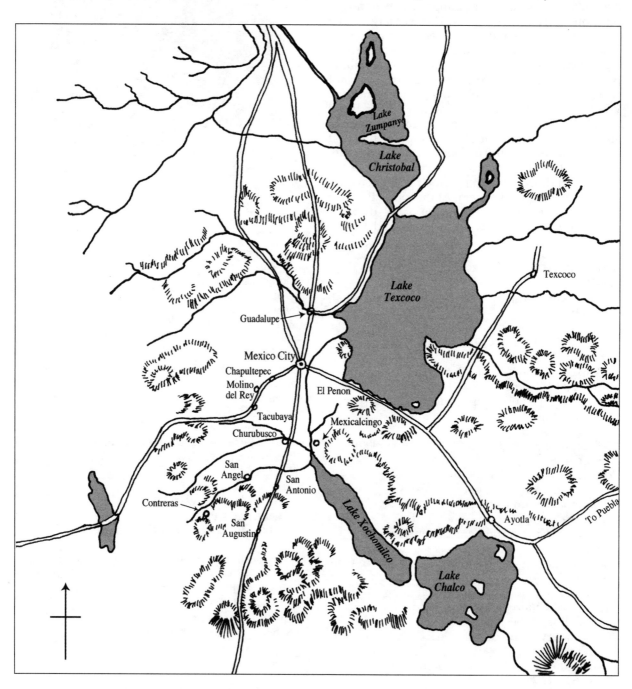

The Valley of Mexico

Pennsylvania told it: "Campbell orders the Pennsylvania regiment to charge. As he does not designate either the 1st or 2nd neither obey him. So he damns the Pennsylvanians for a set of cowards. He next inquired who commanded our Regiment. Being informed that it is Colonel Roberts, he now orders Colonel Roberts to advance with his Regiment. Roberts, who is on the right, does not hear him and there is no movement. Campbell jumps about, damns the Pennsylvanians, damns Colonel Roberts for a coward that he will expose him, etc. While Campbell is leaping about someone informs him that Roberts' Regiment is the supporting and not the charging Regiment and that Colonel Wyncoop commands the 1st Pennsylvania". Fortunately, even though the Mexicans continued to issue a heavy fire the troops were not fully exposed to it due to the cover offered by the growth of chaparral and the fact that the Mexican cannon could not be depressed enough to fire down the ridge. Before this new dilemma could be sorted out by the frustrated Colonel Campbell, new orders arrived that called for the suspension of the offensive because the Mexicans were withdrawing from their positions after being outflanked by the forces under General Twiggs.

By ten o'clock the Mexican army was defeated and had taken flight. Only about half of the troops were able to keep any sort of unit integrity afterwards and there are no reliable figures for actual Mexican losses in the battle. The Americans reported the capture of 199 officers (including the luckless Díaz de la Vega) and 2,837 men, most of whom were quickly paroled. American casualties were sixty-three killed and 368 wounded, which were relatively light considering the strength of the position that they had just taken.

During the battle a squad of men from the 4th Illinois led by Sergeant John N. Gill had gotten into the rear of the Mexican position. They eventually came upon a disabled coach that had been hastily abandoned by a Mexican officer who had unhitched one of its horses and ridden off. Inside the carriage the soldiers found a roasted chicken, a bag of gold worth thousands of dollars, and a wooden leg which turned out to belong to Santa Anna. This souvenir was taken back to Illinois and is still in the possession of the National Guard there.

General Scott was much relieved at having achieved such a great victory at so little cost and he was genuinely proud of his men. George Ballentine, an English soldier in the army, recalled what Scott told the troops gathered around:

"Brother soldiers, I am proud to call you brothers and your country will be proud to hear of your conduct this day. Our victory has cost us the lives of a number of brave men, but they died fighting for the honour of their country. Soldiers, you have a claim on my gratitude for your conduct this day which I will never forget."

If Pillow got his command because he was President Polk's law partner, the price was paid by the Confederacy at Fort Donelson many years later.

When he concluded his remarks the troops cheered him and he rode off bowing and waving his hat. Less than six weeks after landing at Vera Cruz Scott and his men had opened up the road to Mexico City and were on their way to the "Halls of the Montezumas".

PUEBLA

"Scott is lost! He cannot capture the city and he cannot fall back upon his base!"
Duke of Wellington when Scott's army was cut off from the coast

The day after the battle of Cerro Gordo, the American army occupied the pretty little town of Jalapa. Worth's division, which had not been engaged, continued on and entered Perote on April 22nd. The advance on Mexico City might have continued virtually unopposed if it weren't for some serious problems with his own army that General Scott had to deal with. First of all he was losing the majority of seven regiments of volunteers, due to the fact that their enlistments would expire in May. They had been raised under the provisions of the War Bill of May 1846 and could now determine for themselves whether or not they would serve for the duration or for only twelve months. Ninety percent of the men, more than 4,000 soldiers, chose not to re-enlist and went home instead. Scott decided to let them go as soon as possible, so that they could depart from Vera Cruz before the onset of the Yellow Fever season in the summer. The bulk of the American volunteers marched out of Jalapa on May 6th, leaving only a handful of detachments behind. One of these small groups was a company formed after great exertions by Lieutenant C. Roberdeau Wheat of Tennessee. He was elected their captain and they served until the end of the war. The same man raised the Louisiana Tigers in the Civil War. Despite a few men staying on, Scott's army had been reduced to just over 7,000 men, of whom many were sick.

The other major problem facing the American army was that of supply. Moving supplies from Vera Cruz to the army as it got farther and farther from the coast would prove increasingly difficult and take ever lengthening periods of time. While the Mexican army itself had been defeated and virtually destroyed, there were numerous guerilla bands forming throughout the country. They were bent on harassing the American supply trains, usually without any thoughts of patriotism, but simply for their own enrichment. The only way to safeguard these convoys was to make sure that they were going to be accompanied by troops along the way. Soldiers would also have to garrison cities and towns along the route to discourage any local enemy activity. There was simply no way that Scott could spare the troops necessary for these tasks. This is what made him consider alternatives to maintaining his lines of communication with the coast in the traditional manner. First of all, though, Scott wanted to secure a base of operations to concentrate his army closer to his objective of Mexico City.

The same day that the volunteers marched from Jalapa towards the coast, Worth set his division in motion for Puebla. He arrived there on May 15th and with the support of the Catholic priests, secured the city without a shot being fired. Scott arrived in Puebla himself on May 28, 1847 after leaving a small garrison behind in Jalapa. It was now that he decided that his best chance of keeping his small army intact was to cut his supply lines with the coast and concentrate his forces at Puebla. Washington had promised Scott that he would have 20,000 additional men by the end of June, but they were nowhere in sight at this time. His army would have to try to live off the land as best it could and hope that the reinforcements that were on the way would still be able to make it through on their own. On June 3rd he ordered the Jalapa garrison to march to Puebla to concentrate the army. Scott's army numbered somewhat less than 6,000 men with about a fourth of those being on the sick and disabled list at any

given time. When word of Scott's decision was publicized he was widely criticized for putting his army in such a precarious position. The Duke of Wellington, upon hearing the news, reportedly declared, "Scott is lost! He cannot capture the city and he cannot fall back upon his base!" The Duke was absolutely right in his assessment, for even with Scott setting himself adrift of his line of communications, his army was too small to accomplish anything if the Mexican army chose to put up any kind of determined resistance to his advance.

Fortunately for Scott his reinforcements were finally on the way. After quite a bit of confusion and delay the first troops raised by the Ten Regiment Bill of February were en route to Mexico, along with additional volunteers. Colonel James S. McIntosh led some 700 men out of Vera Cruz on June 4th. He was forced to call for Brigadier General George Cadwalader and additional troops to help fight his way past the National Bridge and through the Cerro Gordo area. Upon reaching Perote they halted to await the group following them that was being led by General Pillow, leaving Vera Cruz on the 8th of June. Together these troops marched on to Puebla without further incident, arriving there on July 8th. The next reinforcement group did not leave Vera Cruz until July 14th. This was commanded by Brigadier General Franklin Pierce and included both new recruits as well as new regiments. When this force arrived at Puebla on August 6th, Scott's army totalled about 14,000 men counting those on sick call. He had 10,738 effective officers and men for the final push. This was the army with which he intended to march on Mexico City and win the war.

The troops that had been at Puebla since late May and early June had spent much of their waiting time in training and re-equipping themselves. Local Mexican suppliers had been manufacturing uniforms to U.S. Army specifications, even if the materials on hand were not up to the quality of the originals. The troops were also getting acclimated to the country and they had gained a great deal of respect for and confidence in General Scott based on his achievements and the way that they had been treated by him. Supplies were stockpiled with great exertion and made ready for the campaign. The troops were becoming eager to advance even though they knew that there would be some tough times ahead. Finally, on August 5th, the day before General Pierce arrived, Scott gave the order to begin the march on Mexico City.

Scott organized his army into four divisions for the advance. General Worth commanded the 1st Division which included Colonel Garland's First Brigade of the 2nd and 3rd Artillery (fighting as infantry), and the 4th Infantry along with Lt. Colonel

Duncan's battery of the 2nd Artillery. The Second Brigade of Worth's Division was led by Colonel Clarke and was made up of the 5th, 6th, and 8th Infantry. General Twiggs had the 2nd Division also composed of two brigades. The First Brigade was led by Brigadier General Smith and included the Regiment of Mounted Rifles, fighting on foot; the 1st Artillery, also being used as infantry; the 3rd Infantry, and Captain Taylor's battery of the 1st Artillery. The Second Brigade under Twiggs was commanded by Colonel Riley and included the 4th Artillery, fighting as infantry, and the 2nd and 7th Infantry. The 3rd Division was under General Pillow with two brigades. General Pierce commanded the First Brigade with the 9th, 12th, and 15th Infantry supported by the newly formed battery of the 1st Artillery being led by Captain John B. Magruder. Pillow's Second Brigade was under the command of General Cadwalader with the 11th and 14th Infantry, the Regiment of Voltigeurs and Foot Riflemen along with the Rocket and Howitzer Company under Colonel Andrews for support.

Finally, the 4th Division was being led by General Quitman. His First Brigade was that of General Shields with the 2nd New York Volunteers (usually known simply as the New York Regiment, as the 1st New York had gone to California) and the 1st South Carolina (known as the 'Palmetto' Regiment). A field battery of the 3rd Artillery under Captain Steptoe filled out the brigade. Quitman's Second Brigade was led by Lt. Colonel Samuel E. Watson, USMC and included the 2nd Pennsylvania along with a newly organized unit of 300 Marines.

Brigadier General John A. Quitman was forty-eight years old. He had commanded a brigade of volunteers at Monterrey under Taylor and at Vera Cruz under Scott since March. He had recruited a company of volunteers for the Texas Revolution in 1836 but had not taken part in any action at that time. He was a New York native and a well respected militia officer in Mississippi, where he had been living for quite some time. Taylor had characterized him as 'unreliable' and of only 'mediocre ability' but he still managed to distinguish himself in Scott's

---

AMERICAN ARMY AT PUEBLA, AUGUST 6, 1847
Maj-Gen. Winfield Scott (10,738) (14,000)
  sick call (2500)
  convalescing (600)
General Staff
  Assistant Inspector General: Lt-Col. Ethan
    Allen Hitchcock
  Engineer Corps: Maj. John Lind Smith
  Ordinance Department: Capt. Benjamin Huger
  Topographical Engineers: Maj. William
    Turnbull
  Quartermaster Corps: Capt. James R. Irwin
  Subsistence Department:Capt. John B. Grayson
  Paymaster Department: Maj. Edmund Kirby
  Medical Department: Surgeon General Thomas
    Lawson

Cavalry Brigade: Col. William S. Harney
  1st Dragoons: Capt. Philip Kearny
  2nd Dragoons: Maj. Edwin V. Sumner
  3rd Dragoons: Capt. Andrew T. McReynolds

1st Division: Maj-Gen. William J. Worth
1st Brigade: Col. John Garland
  2nd Artillery (as infantry)
  3rd Artillery (as infantry)
  4th Infantry
  Company A, 2nd Artillery: Lt-Col. James Duncan
2nd Brigade: Col. Newman S. Clarke
  5th Infantry
  6th Infantry
  8th Infantry

2nd Division: Brig-Gen. David E. Twiggs
1st Brigade: Brig-Gen. Persifor F. Smith
  Regiment of Mounted Rifles (on foot)
  1st Artillery (as infantry)
  3rd Infantry
  Company K, 1st Artillery: Capt. Francis Taylor
2nd Brigade: Col. Bennet Riley
  4th Artillery (as infantry)
  2nd Infantry
  7th Infantry

3rd Division (3500): Maj-Gen. Gideon J. Pillow
1st Brigade: Brig-Gen. Franklin Pierce
  9th Infantry: Col. Trueman B. Ransom
  12th Infantry: Col. Henry Wilson
  15th Infantry: Col. George W. Morgan
  Company I, 1st Artillery: Capt. John B.
    Magruder (2 - 12 lb. guns & 1 small howitzer)
2nd Brigade: Brig-Gen. George Cadwalader
  11th Infantry: Col. Albert C. Ramsey
  14th Infantry: Col. William Trousdale
  Regiment of Voltigeurs & Foot Riflemen: Col.
    Timothy P. Andrews
  Rocket & Howitzer Company: Lt. Franklin
    Callender

4th Division: Brig-Gen. John Anthony Quitman
1st Brigade: Brig-Gen. James Shields
  2nd New York Volunteers
  1st South Carolina Volunteers (known as the
    'Palmetto' Regiment)
  Field Battery, 3rd Artillery: Capt. Edward J.
    Steptoe
2nd Brigade: Lt-Col. Samuel E. Watson USMC
  2nd Pennsylvania Volunteers: Col. William B.
    Roberts
  U.S. Marines (300)

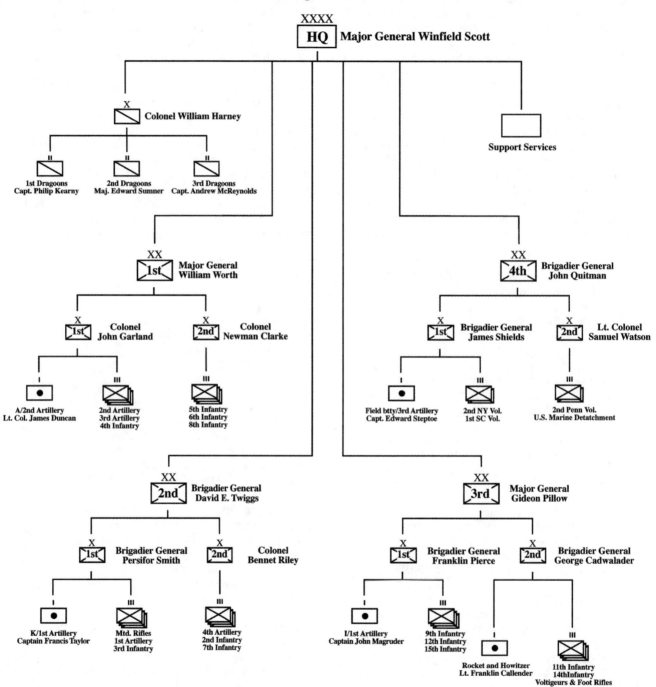

Organization of the
American Army at Puebla,
6 August, 1847

XXXX
HQ Major General Winfield Scott

X
Colonel William Harney

Support Services

II
1st Dragoons
Capt. Philip Kearny

II
2nd Dragoons
Maj. Edward Sumner

II
3rd Dragoons
Capt. Andrew McReynolds

XX
1st Major General William Worth

XX
4th Brigadier General John Quitman

X
1st Colonel John Garland

X
2nd Colonel Newman Clarke

X
1st Brigadier General James Shields

X
2nd Lt. Colonel Samuel Watson

I
A/2nd Artillery
Lt. Col. James Duncan

III
2nd Artillery
3rd Artillery
4th Infantry

III
5th Infantry
6th Infantry
8th Infantry

I
Field btty/3rd Artillery
Capt. Edward Steptoe

III
2nd NY Vol.
1st SC Vol.

III
2nd Penn Vol.
U.S. Marine Detatchment

XX
2nd Brigadier General David E. Twiggs

XX
3rd Major General Gideon Pillow

X
1st Brigadier General Persifor Smith

X
2nd Colonel Bennet Riley

X
1st Brigadier General Franklin Pierce

X
2nd Brigadier General George Cadwalader

I
K/1st Artillery
Captain Francis Taylor

III
Mtd. Rifles
1st Artillery
3rd Infantry

III
4th Artillery
2nd Infantry
7th Infantry

I
I/1st Artillery
Captain John Magruder

III
9th Infantry
12th Infantry
15th Infantry

I
Rocket and Howitzer
Lt. Franklin Callender

III
11th Infantry
14thInfantry
Voltigeurs & Foot Rifles

campaign and had just been Brevetted Major General for the capture of Puebla in May. He would serve the army well, if impetuously, in the days ahead.

Independent of the infantry divisions and attached directly to the army was Colonel Harney with his brigade of cavalry that included companies of the 1st, 2nd, and 3rd Dragoons. Colonel William S. Harney had been born in Tennessee in 1800 and had been with the 2nd Dragoons ever since they had been formed in 1836. He had been second in command under Twiggs and had seen much service in Florida against the Seminoles. He had taken over as Colonel of the 2nd Dragoons in June of 1846. His red hair and fierce-looking face were clues to his fiery temper, but he was an imaginative as well as an aggressive officer. He was resourceful enough to recognize the value of Samuel Colt's revolving carbine and obtained them for his dragoons as early as 1838, even though they had not been officially approved. Unfortunately Harney and Scott had clashed early on and they had long been antagonists without much trust between them. Regardless, Harney continued to perform his mission well, even though the campaign saw only limited opportunity for the employment of cavalry.

The army that set out from Puebla was the army that Scott would have to win the war with. There were other reinforcements still en route, but none that would arrive in time to participate in the battles around Mexico City. The latest group to leave Vera Cruz had departed on August 6th under the command of Major Lally of the 9th Infantry. The column included about 1000 men and sixty-four wagons carrying quite a bit of money for Scott's troops. The Mexican guerrillas in the area had discovered this fact and opposed the passage of the supply train and its escort. In a series of sharp engagements beginning before the National Bridge and extending all the way to Jalapa the Americans were forced to fight their way through. This was ample evidence that Scott's line of communications had been effectively cut by the guerrilla bands operating throughout the countryside. While Scott had been building up his forces and concentrating his army for the advance, the Mexicans had also been gathering their strength.

Santa Anna had used the time that Scott had granted him after the debacle at Cerro Gordo to do what he did best: raise another army. The confidence of the Mexican people in Santa Anna and his government had been severely shaken. At one point Santa Anna resigned the Presidency, thereby demonstrating his willingness to sacrifice everything for the nation. When it was discovered that there was virtually no one else willing or able to take over the reins of power, Santa Anna "sacrificed" himself and assumed the Presidency once again. The paper *Monitor Republicano* ridiculed his eloquence with their own sarcasm, as related by Justin Smith in "The War with Mexico":

"Mexicans, I shall be with you always—to the consummation of your ruin," was its paraphrasing, and then they went on: "What a life of sacrifice is the General's; a sacrifice to take the power, to resign, to resume; ultimate sacrifice; ultimate final; ultimate

---

ACTIONS ON THE ROAD FROM VERA CRUZ TO JALAPA
Ovejas Pass (Paso de Ovejas) 8/10/47; National Bridge (Puente Nacional) 8/12/47; Plan del Rio and Cerro Gordo 8/15/47; Las Animas & Jalapa 8/19/47. All fought by an American reinforcement column against Mexican guerrillas.

Mexican Forces
Gen. Don Juan Soto, Governor of the State of Vera Cruz
Padre Caledonio Domeco Jarauta (guerrilla leader)
Juan Aburto (guerrilla leader)
   1000-2000 guerrilla fighters including troops earlier paroled by the Americans after the fall of Vera Cruz.

American Forces
Maj. Folliot T. Lally, 9th Infantry (1000+)
Capt. Benjamin Alvord, 4th Infantry as Asst. Adjutant-General
   2nd Artillery: 2nd Lt. Henry B. Sears (Section A: 2 - 6 lb. guns)

4th Infantry: Lt. Henderson Ridgely & Sergeant H.L. Carter (Companies H & K)
5th Infantry: 2nd Lt. Clinton W. Lear (Companies C & D)
11th Infantry: Capt. Arthur C. Cummings (Company K)
12th Infantry: Capt. William J. Clark, Capt. Charles C. Hornsby & Lt. Charles R. Jones (Companies G, I & K)
15th Infantry: Capt. Frazey M. Winans (Company G)
Voltigeurs & Foot Riflemen: Capt. James N. Caldwell & Lt. John W. Leigh (Companies D & K)
Georgia Mounted Volunteers: Capt. John Loyall (1 Company)
Louisiana Mounted Volunteers: Capt. Lorenzo A. Besancon (1 Company)
64 wagons
Note: Mr. George D. Twiggs (nephew of General David E. Twiggs) en route to join his uncle and receive a commission on his staff was killed at the National Bridge action

more final; ultimate most final; ultimate the very finalist. But let him cheer up. He is not alone in making sacrifices. For twenty-five years the Mexican people have been sacrificing themselves, all of them in the hope that certain persons would do good to the country". He was counting on Mexican pride, along with the National Guard, to rally to the defense of the capital when it was at the mercy of the invading North Americans. Fortunately there were already some troops available in the city and once the urgency of the situation was realized, politics were made a secondary issue to military preparedness.

To begin organizing a viable defense force Santa Anna drew on some 4,000 veterans that had survived the Buena Vista campaign and were in the area of San Luis Potosí under General Valencia. Many of these units were no more than small detachments or the remains of full regiments that had suffered heavy losses during the previous campaign. Added to this hard core would be about 10,000 men from the National Guard along with several thousand regulars from other garrisons and the survivors of Cerro Gordo. Mexico City itself also provided quite a few troops from the local defense forces. Altogether Santa Anna had between 25,000 and 30,000 men available for the defense of Mexico City by the beginning of August. Despite these numbers, Santa Anna decided to remain on the defensive rather than attack the Americans when they approached. This was a sensible strategy considering the fact that most of his troops were poorly trained and equipped and were not very reliable. The other factor that was in favor of the Mexican Army was the nature of the terrain around the city. There were only a few restricted approaches to the capital along

---

MEXICAN ARMY DEFENDING THE VALLEY OF MEXICO AS OF AUGUST 14, 1847

Generalissimo Antonio López de Santa Anna
  Hussars of the Guard of the Supreme Powers
  Light Mounted Regiment of Veracruz

Army of the East: Maj-Gen. Manuel María Lombardini
Brigade: Brig-Gen. Andrés Terrés
  1st Active Militia of Mexico City
  2nd Light Infantry
Brigade: Brig-Gen. Martinez
  Active Militia of Morelia
  Corps of Invalids
Brigade (2000): Brig-Gen. Joaquín Rangel
  Grenadiers of the Guard of the Supreme Powers
  Mixed of Santa Anna (1500)
  San Blas Battalion
  National Guard of Morelia
  San Patricio Company
Brigade (3500-2500): Brig-Gen. Francisco Pérez
  1st Light Infantry
  3rd Light Infantry
  4th Light Infantry (1500)
  11th Line Infantry
Brigade: Brigadier Gen. Antonio León
  Active Militia of Oaxaca
  10th Line Infantry (detachment only)
  Active Militia of Queretaro
  Queretaro National Guard (500)
  Mina of the District National Guard (miners from the city)
5th Brigade of Mexico City National Guard: Gen. Pedro María Anaya
  Bravo Battalion
  Hidalgo Battalion
  Independencia Battalion
  Victoria Battalion

Brigade: Colonel Zerecero
  Battalion of Tlapa (detachment)
  Battalion of Libertad (detachment)
  Battalion of Acapulco
  Pickets from Aldama, Galeana & Matamoros
  General Andrade also had detachments in San Angel and Coyoacán

Army of the North: Maj-Gen. Gabriel Valencia
1st Division: Gen. Francisco Mejía
Infantry Brigade
  1st Line Infantry
  Fijo de Mexico
  Active Militia of San Luis Potosí
Cavalry Brigade: Gen. Romero
  7th Line Cavalry
  Active Militia Cavalry of San Luis Potosí
  Artillery (3 -12 lb. guns and 4 howitzers)
2nd Division: Gen. Parrodi
1st Brigade
  10th Line Infantry
  12th Line Infantry
  Tampico Coast Guard Battalion
  Veteran Coast Guard Company of Tampico
2nd Brigade: Lt-Col. Cabrera
  Auxiliaries of Celaya
  Active Militia of Celaya
  Active Militia of Guanajuato
  Artillery (6 - 8 lb. guns & 2 howitzers)
3rd Division (reserve): Gen. Salas
Infantry Brigade
  Active Militia of Aguas Calientes
  Zapadores
Cavalry Brigade
  2nd Line Cavalry
  3rd Line Cavalry
  8th Line Cavalry
  Active Militia Cavalry of Guanajuato
  Artillery (7 light guns)

narrow causeways that did not lend themselves to the maneuvers necessary to fight a pitched battle. If the Mexicans fortified these positions they would command the routes of entry and the Americans would be forced into costly assaults against prepared defenses. The self-proclaimed "Napoleon of the West" was counting on the fact that the size of Scott's army would preclude these types of tactics from being used and the Americans would be forced to admit defeat and withdraw.

The approach routes to Mexico City from Puebla were restricted by the location of three large lakes. Lake Texcoco to the north and east of the city was too large to detour around to the north and made it necessary to use one of the three causeways between it or the other two lakes. Lake Chalco was the furthest body of water east and south of the city with Lake Xochimilco being smaller and directly west of it. The western shore of Xochimilco was directly to the south of the city. The most direct route was the one that went between Lake Texcoco and Lake Chalco directly by the 450 foot high hill of El Peñón, seven miles from the city. El Peñón was where the main attack was expected to come and the Mexicans were prepared for it. This was where Santa Anna himself was stationed along with some thirty artillery pieces and almost 7,000 of his best troops. The second closest route was a bit further south of El Peñón and travelled along the northern shore of Lake Xochimilco and through the fortified village of Mexicalzingo, which was south and slightly east of the city itself. The guns on El Peñón could bear on this route to support the defenders here and help make it a costly one to follow for any attacking army. The third major route went to the south of Lake Xochimilco and into the village of San Augustín, about nine miles directly south of the capital. This area was also defended, but mainly by some of the more inexperienced troops as it was not expected to come under attack.

The American army marched out of Puebla on August 7th with Twiggs' Division leading the way and the men anxious for action in what they knew would be the deciding battles of the war. When the army reached Ayotla, 25 miles from Mexico City, a decision had to be made as to which route to follow. The engineers were sent out to scout the possibilities before the army advanced. Captain Robert E. Lee, along with Captain Mason and Lt. Stevens checked out El Peñón and informed Scott that it could be taken but that it would be very costly. Lieutenants Beauregard and McClellan reported that the Mexicalzingo route was also practicable, if heavily defended. Lee and Beauregard made another reconnaissance on the 13th with two companies of Dragoons led by Captain Phil Kearny to scout the road through Churubusco to San Antonio. The route that Scott liked the best was the indirect one, south of Lake Chalco coming out at San Augustín. Once

the roads here were found to be passable by the army his mind was made up. On the 15th Scott gave the order to move south of the lake to avoid the strongest Mexican positions on the eastern side of the city. The only hindrance to this maneuver was when the main body of the Mexican cavalry under General Alvarez briefly harassed the flank of Twiggs' advance. After seeing the American army he became discouraged at the difficulties of pursuing or attacking them and returned to Mexico City without further incident.

When Santa Anna realized that Scott had turned his main positions by going south and west he quickly ordered troops to cover this area. Among them was Major General Gabriel Valencia and his Army of the North that still included some veteran troops from the Buena Vista campaign. Santa Anna did not trust Valencia, but he had no other choice than to rely on him. Troops were deployed at San Antonio, directly north of San Augustín, and Valencia went to the south of San Angel, which was to the north and west of San Augustín along a minor road. Between these two positions the terrain was broken up by the 'Pedregal' (a large field of broken lava). The huge chunks and shards of dark rock outcroppings were almost impassable for men on foot, much less for horses and wagons. The Mexicans believed that this area was secure enough to leave unguarded except for a few pickets posted on its western edges. These were near the farm at Padierna in front of Valencia's main camp, which was located on the high ground astride the road leading to Contreras to the south.

On the 18th the engineers moved out to scout the approaches to San Antonio and the Pedregal. They quickly concluded that the only way to overcome the strong defenses on the road was to turn them by finding a route through the Pedregal. A force emerging here would ultimately come out behind San Antonio and render its defenses useless. General Valencia himself had taken up a position on the western edge of the lava fields on some high ground near Padierna farm. He had some 5,000 men and twenty-two guns at his command. Santa Anna had ordered him to move further north to San Angel so that he could not be cut off by any surprise move through the Pedregal. However, Valencia disdained to take this advice from his superior, whom he loathed. Between his position and the Pedregal the road ran from Contreras just to the south all the way to the crossing of the Churubusco River at the village of the same name. This was directly north of the position at San Antonio and would cut those troops off from the city if it was lost. The Americans decided that they would construct a passage through the Pedregal to outflank the Mexican defenses. The morning of the 19th of August saw Captain Lee and some 500 men hard at work carving a passage through the lava field that would allow artillery batteries to pass through. It was around noon that

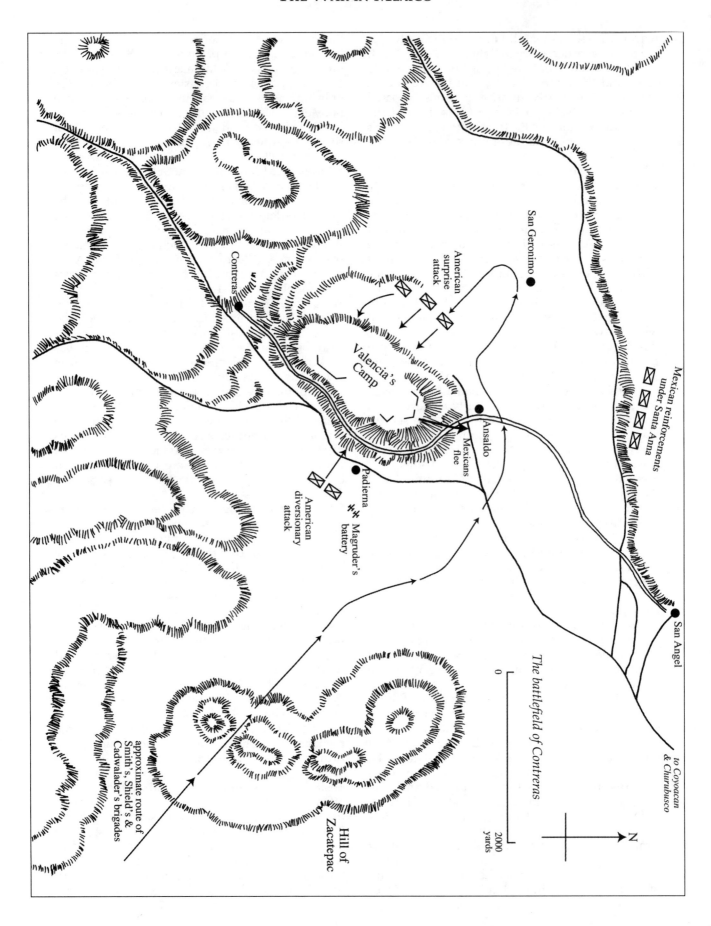

San Geronimo

American surprise attack

Contreras

Valencia's Camp

Mexican reinforcements under Santa Anna

Ansaldo

Mexicans flee

Padierna

Magruder's battery

American diversionary attack

The battlefield of Contreras

0

2000 yards

N

to Coyoacan & Churubusco

San Angel

approximate route of Smith's, Shield's & Cadwalader's brigades

Hill of Zacatepac

Plate 1

Americans at Palo Alto

Plate 2

Mexicans at Resaca de la Palma

Plate 3

Americans at Monterrey

Plate 4

Mexicans at Buena Vista

Plate 5

American Volunteers at Buena Vista

Plate 6

Mexican Cavalry at Buena Vista

Plate 7

Americans at Cerro Gordo

Plate 8

Mexicans at Churubusco

Plate 9

Americans at Chapultepec

Plate 10

Mexicans at Chapultepec

Plate 11

Americans at Puebla

Plate 12

Mexican Generals and Guard Troops

Plate 13

American Army of the West and in California

Plate 14

Miscellaneous Mexicans

Plate 15

American Flags

VIVA LA REPUBLICA MEXICANA.

BATALION FIJO

DE
CALIFORNIAS

ESCUADRON ACTIVO DE VERA CRUZ

Bat.n Act.o de Lagos.

GUARDIA NACIONAL

ARTILLERIA DE MINA

Plate 16

Mexican Flags

they met resistance in the form of Mexican outposts and pickets. The battle known as Contreras by the Americans and Padierna by the Mexicans had just begun.

CONTRERAS AND CHURUBUSCO

"It has taken just seventeen minutes."
Brigadier General Persifor F. Smith after the assault on Contreras

General Pillow was placed in command by Scott, and his Assistant Adjutant General was Captain Joseph Hooker. Captain Robert E. Lee of the engineers was in charge of the 500 man work party that was constructing a road through the Pedregal when the Mexican pickets began to press the men. Pillow's Division was being supported by Twiggs' Division, but despite being the junior of the two, Pillow was to assume command if any action took place, which General Scott thought unlikely. When the lead units of Twiggs' command came under fire in the early afternoon, he quickly ordered up two batteries of artillery. These were assisted in setting up for action by Captain Lee and 2nd Lieutenant McClellan. Captain Magruder, along with Lieutenant Thomas J. Jackson serving in the battery, gave a good account of himself but he was heavily outgunned by the Mexicans and was eventually

forced to withdraw. This gun duel was enough to keep Valencia occupied, and when the Americans had withdrawn he was certain that he had won a victory. While the Mexicans were preoccupied with this action to the east of their position at the edge of the Pedregal, other American forces were moving into position either unnoticed or unopposed.

Colonel Ransom with the 9th Infantry and Lt. Colonel Bonham with a battalion of the 12th Infantry moved across the road to the south of Valencia's position virtually undetected. Even Pillow was not aware of their position and they were left unsupported. Meanwhile, to the north of Valencia's position, Pillow had sent Colonel Riley with most of his brigade across the road and into the Mexican rear to cut their line of communications. Pillow realized that once they reached that point they might be too vulnerable, and so he sent Cadwalader's brigade by the same route to lend support. Eventually Shields' brigade was also sent by the same route when it was feared that Santa Anna would attack from the north with the reinforcements under his command. Instead, Santa Anna chose to do nothing, and the Americans who could have been completely cut off and surrounded, were no longer in any danger. Smith's brigade, supported by the only remaining reserve, the 15th Infantry, was to demonstrate in the front of the Mexican position and attack if the opportunity arose. General Pierce had been injured in a fall from his horse and his brigade

---

MEXICAN FORCES AT CONTRERAS (PADIERNA) ON AUGUST 19 - 20, 1847
Maj-Gen. Gabriel Valencia (486/5078) (officers/men)
Cavalry commanded by Gen. Anastasio Torrejon

1st Division: Gen. Francisco Mejía
   Artillery (3 -12 lb. guns & 4 howitzers)
1st Infantry Brigade (700)
   1st Line Infantry: Col. Nicholas Mendoza
   Fijo de Mexico
   Active Militia of San Luis Potosí
   National Guard Company of Acolhua
2nd Cavalry Brigade (400): Gen. Romero
   7th Line Cavalry
   Active Militia Cavalry of San Luis Potosí

2nd Division (1500): Gen. Parrodi
   Artillery (6 - 8 lb. guns & 2 howitzers)
2nd Infantry Brigade
   10th Line Infantry
   12th Line Infantry
   Tampico Coast Guard Battalion
   Veteran Infantry Coast Guard Company of
     Tampico
3rd Infantry Brigade: Lt-Col. Cabrera
   Auxiliaries of Celaya

   Active Militia of Celaya
   Auxiliaries of Guanajuato
   Active Militia of Queretaro

3rd Division (reserve): Gen. Salas
   Artillery (7 light guns)
4th Infantry Brigade (800)
   Active Militia of Aguas Calientes
   Mixto de Santa Anna
   Zapadores
3rd Cavalry Brigade (400)
   2nd Line Cavalry
   3rd Line Cavalry
   8th Line Cavalry
   Active Militia Cavalry of Guanajuato
   Auxiliary Squadron of Guanajuato
   Volunteer Company of Texcoco (on foot)

forces available but not engaged
Perez' Brigade (3500): Brig-Gen. Francisco Pérez
   1st Light Infantry
   3rd Light Infantry
   4th Light Infantry
   11th Line Infantry
Santa Anna with
   Hussars of the Guard of the Supreme Powers
   Light Mounted Regiment of Veracruz

---

was being commanded by Colonel Ransom at this time. Smith quickly saw that the position was too strong to attack frontally and so he too shifted forces to his right. He also crossed the road with most of his brigade and ended up in the rear of Valencia. By the end of the day the Americans had almost four brigades in Valencia's rear, virtually undetected. They had encountered parts of Santa Anna's forces briefly, but no attack had been pressed against them. Valencia was already celebrating his victory as the only enemy troops he had seen and fought had withdrawn back to the Pedregal.

During the night the American engineers were once again being kept busy. Captain Lee made his third crossing of the dangerous Pedregal in the dark. He had led some of Shields' men into position earlier and then carried messages to General Scott. The new plan was for a diversion to be launched on Valencia's front as soon as it was light while the rear of the camp was being assaulted simultaneously. Lee also led Twiggs and some of his men back during the night so that they could be a part of the diversion. Scott later characterized Lee's efforts that night as: "the greatest feat of physical and moral courage performed by any individual." The night had been cold and wet but the Americans continued to probe the area for a path to attack Valencia. They discovered a ravine that led directly into the rear of the Mexican camp. It was Smith who took over and decided on the plan of attack. At daybreak while a demonstration from the Pedregal got under way,

almost 4,000 Americans would attack from the Mexican rear and envelope the position. Smith did not know that Santa Anna had been in a position to crush the American brigades in the Mexican rear. Fortunately for these units, Santa Anna had ordered a retreat and was now out of range of the battle that was to take place in the morning.

At first light on the 20th Valencia's men realized that Santa Anna had pulled out, along with the reserves. They were disheartened by this but before they had any time to consider what this might mean they were under attack from the rear. Smith gave the word to attack shortly after daybreak. The Americans fired a volley and charged with fixed bayonets. Valencia's force disintegrated. Smith checked his watch when the assault was over and remarked, "It has taken just seventeen minutes." The battle of Contreras or Padierna was over that fast. The Mexican losses were 700 men killed and 813 taken prisoner, including four generals. The Americans lost only sixty men killed and wounded. They also recaptured two 6-lb. artillery pieces that the Mexicans had taken at Buena Vista when O'Brien's battery was overrun. Captain Simon Drum of the 4th Artillery was happy to have them back in American service. Meanwhile the remainder of Valencia's several thousand defenders scattered in all directions to escape pursuit. The road to Churubusco was now open and it led to the rear of the San Antonio defenses. Santa Anna knew that this river crossing must be held to allow the troops to

---

AMERICAN FORCES AT CONTRERAS (PADIERNA) ON AUGUST 19 - 20, 1847
Maj-Gen. Gideon J. Pillow

3rd Division: Maj-Gen. Gideon J. Pillow
1st Brigade: Brig-Gen. Franklin Pierce
  9th Infantry: Col. Trueman B. Ransom
    (Companies A, C, D, E, F, G, H, I & K)
  12th Infantry: Lt-Col. Milledge L. Bonham
    (Companies B, C & H)
  15th Infantry: Col. George W. Morgan
    (Companies A, B, C, E, F, H, I & K)
  Company I, 1st Artillery: Capt. John B.
    Magruder (2 - 12 lb. guns & 1 howitzer)
2nd Brigade: Brig-Gen. George Cadwalader
  11th Infantry: Col. William M. Graham
    (Companies D, E, F, H & I)
  14th Infantry: Col. William Trousdale
    (Companies B, E, F, G, I & K)
  Regiment of Voltigeurs & Foot Riflemen: Col.
    Timothy P. Andrews (Companies A, B, C, E, F,
    G, H, I & K)
  Rocket & Howitzer Company: Lt. Franklin
    Callender

2nd Division: Brig-Gen. David E. Twiggs
1st Brigade: Brig-Gen. Persifor F. Smith
  Regiment of Mounted Rifles (on foot): Maj.
    William W. Loring (Companies A, B, D, E, F,
    G, H, I & K)
  1st Artillery (as infantry): Maj. Justin Dimick
    (Companies B, D, F, G, & H)
  3rd Infantry: Capt. Edmund B. Alexander
    (Companies A, B, C, D, E, F, H, I & K)
  Company K, 1st Artillery: Capt. Francis Taylor
2nd Brigade: Col. Bennet Riley (1300)
  4th Artillery (as infantry)
    (Companies C, D, E, F & H)
  2nd Infantry
    (Companies A, B, C, D, E, F, G, H, I & K)
  7th Infantry
    (Companies A, B, C, D, E, F, G, H, I & K)

attached
Shields' Brigade (600): Brig-Gen. James Shields
  2nd New York Volunteers
  1st South Carolina Volunteers (the 'Palmetto'
    Regiment)
  Field Battery, 3rd Artillery: Capt. Edward J.
    Steptoe

withdraw from their southern defensive positions back towards the city. General Scott also realized the importance of taking the Churubusco position and so he lost no time in ordering a headlong pursuit to secure it. The result of the hasty movements of these two armies would be the second battle of the day, at the bridgehead and convent of Churubusco.

The Mexican position at Churubusco that would secure the bridge over the river consisted of two main defenses: the heavily defended San Mateo Convent, sometimes called by the Americans San Pablo, and the "tete de pont" that protected the main bridge itself. Santa Anna had crossed to the north as soon as he could and the troops with him formed a reserve that could possibly be used against any enemy force that had successfully crossed the river. In the meantime the fortified convent was being held by between 1500 and 1800 men of the Bravos and

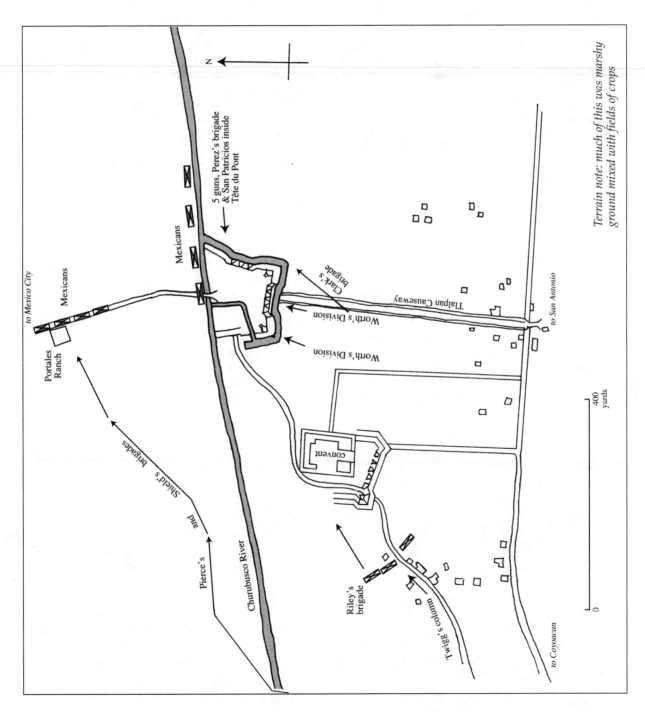

The battlefield of Churubusco

Independencia National Guard Battalions as well as the San Patricio Battalion, which was Mexico's Foreign Legion. They had seven artillery pieces among them, but the entire force was low on ammunition and supplies. The "tete de pont", which was about three hundred yards from the convent, was held by a regiment from Pérez' Brigade while two more regiments took up positions along the river bank.

Scott had ordered an immediate pursuit once he realized that Valencia's force had disintegrated. He also sent instructions to Worth, in front of San Antonio, to begin his attack at once. Worth got his division in motion and began a flanking move around the west side of the defenses at San Antonio, skirting through the edge of the Pedregal on a route that Lee had scouted for him. The Mexican defenders were already in full retreat on the road to the north. Worth was able to disrupt this force and capture some guns but at least half of the fleeing troops made it back to the bridgehead. The mass of Mexican troops streaming across the bridge looked like a rabble that would rout as soon as it was struck. Scott ordered Twiggs to attack the Convent and open the way for just such a strike. The furious action which followed was due to the failure of the Americans to scout the enemy position, as well as the tenacity of the Mexican defenders.

The assault on the convent went in as soon as the troops arrived on the field. They plodded through high cornfields and emerged disorganized within musket range of the walls of the convent. They immediately came under a fusillade of fire from the Mexican infantry. The Mexican artillery also wreaked havoc and forced the men back time after time, even causing Taylor's battery to withdraw after a fierce artillery duel. While this was happening Worth's men had joined the battle by hurriedly launching a frontal assault against the troops at the "tete de pont". This position was also well defended and heavy fire caused a distressing number of casualties among the American regiments. These attacks came to nothing and left the troops badly shaken. A third attack column was launched by the brigades of Pierce and Shields which managed to cross the river to the west of the convent and attempted to outflank the bridgehead. Santa Anna responded by shifting some of the troops along the riverbank to meet this threat. He also sent cavalry to operate on the American left flank and to threaten an attack there. The quick Mexican reaction and heavy musketry fire, combined with the broken terrain, caused this attack to grind to a halt as well.

The flanking maneuver had accomplished something, however. On Worth's flank, the defenders who had been shifted to the west sufficiently weakened the "tete de pont" position so that his attacks began to make headway. Soon the bridgehead was taken in deadly hand-to-hand fighting by the U.S. 8th Infantry, with support from elements of the 5th. With the bridgehead in American hands the convent could now be attacked from the east. The defenders were forced to shift guns and men and the southern wall was thereby weakened. There were simply not enough defenders to continue to completely man all of the positions. The U.S. 3rd Infantry managed to scale the southern wall and force the Mexicans back inside the convent building itself. The San Patricio soldiers pulled down three separate surrender flags put up by the other Mexican defenders, as they knew what their fate would be if captured. Finally the Americans put out their own white flag and the Mexican soldiers quit fighting. The convent had fallen. Across the river, Shields and

---

MEXICAN FORCES AT CHURUBUSCO ON AUGUST 20, 1847

Vicinity of bridge & road
Generalissimo Antonio López de Santa Anna
　　Hussars of the Guard of the Supreme Powers
　　Light Mounted Regiment of Veracruz
　　Tulancingo Cuirassiers

Cavalry of the Army of the North
Gen. Anastasio Torrejón & Gen. Jáuregui
　　2nd Line Cavalry
　　3rd Line Cavalry
　　7th Line Cavalry
　　8th Line Cavalry
　　Active Militia Cavalry of Guanajuato
　　Active Militia Cavalry of San Luis Potosí

Light Brigade: Brig-Gen. Francisco Pérez
　　1st Light Infantry
　　3rd Light Infantry
　　4th Light Infantry
　　11th Line Infantry

　　National Guard of Acapulco (pickets only)
　　National Guard of Lagos (pickets only)

From Garita at San Antonio: Gen. Nicholas Bravo
　　Hidalgo National Guard Battalion
　　Victoria National Guard Battalion

San Mateo Convent: Gen. Pedro María Anaya
　　Bravos National Guard Battalion (750-900)
　　Independencia National Guard Battalion (750-900)
　　National Guard Battalion of Tlapa (1 company)
　　San Patricio Active Militia Company (260): Lt-Col. Francisco Rosenda Moreno
　　Artillery (2 - 4 lb., 1 - 6 lb. & 4 - 8 lb. guns)

American infantry storm the Tete-de-pont

AMERICAN FORCES AT CHURUBUSCO

1st Division: Maj-Gen. William J. Worth
1st Brigade: Col. John Garland
  2nd Artillery (as infantry)
    (Companies C, D, F, G, H, I & K)
  3rd Artillery (as infantry)
    (Companies B, G, H, I & K)
  4th Infantry (Companies A, B, C, D, E, F & I)
  Company A, 2nd Artillery: Lt-Col. James
    Duncan
2nd Brigade: Col. Newman S. Clarke
  5th Infantry (Companies A, B, E, F, G, H, I & K)
  6th Infantry (Companies A, B, C, D, E, F, H & K)
  8th Infantry (Companies A, B, C, D, E, F, H, I & K)
A Light battalion was formed by Lt. Colonel Charles F.
Smith from 2 companies of the 2nd Artillery and 1
company each from the 5th and 8th Infantry.

2nd Division: Brig-Gen. David E. Twiggs
1st Brigade: Brig-Gen. Persifor F. Smith
  Regiment of Mounted Rifles (on foot)
    (Companies A, B, D, E, F, G, H, I & K)
  1st Artillery (as infantry)
    (Companies B, D, F, G, H, I & K)
  3rd Infantry (Companies A, B, C, D, E, F, H, I & K)
  Company K, 1st Artillery: Capt. Francis Taylor
2nd Brigade: Col. Bennet Riley
  2nd Infantry (Companies A, B, C, D, E, F, G, H, I &
    K)
  7th Infantry (Companies A, B, C, D, E, F, G, H, I & K)

attached to 2nd Division
Shields' Brigade: Brig-Gen. James Shields
  2nd New York Volunteers
  1st South Carolina Volunteers (the 'Palmetto'
    Regiment)
  Field Battery, 3rd Artillery: Capt. Edward J.
    Steptoe

3rd Division: Maj-Gen. Gideon J. Pillow
1st Brigade: Brig-Gen. Franklin Pierce
  9th Infantry: Col. Trueman B. Ransom
    (Companies A, C, D, E, F, G, H, I & K)
  12th Infantry: Lt-Col. Milledge L. Bonham
    (Companies B, C & H)
  15th Infantry: Col. George W. Morgan
    (Companies A, B, C, E, F, H, I & K)
  Company I, 1st Artillery: Capt. John B.
    Magruder
2nd Brigade: Brig-Gen. George Cadwalader
(not engaged)
  11th Infantry: Col. Albert C. Ramsey
    (Companies D, E, F, H & I)
  14th Infantry: Col. William Trousdale
    (Companies B, E, F, G, I & K)
  Regiment of Voltigeurs and Foot Riflemen: Col.
    Timothy P. Andrews (Companies A, B, C, E, F,
    G, H, I & K)

not attached
  1st Dragoons (Company F)
  Company of Engineers

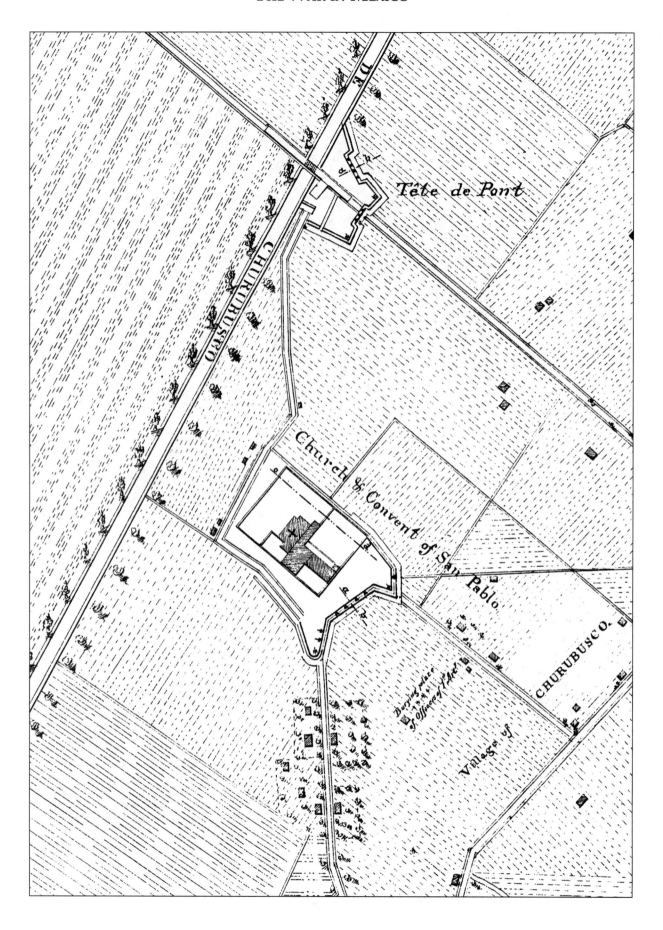

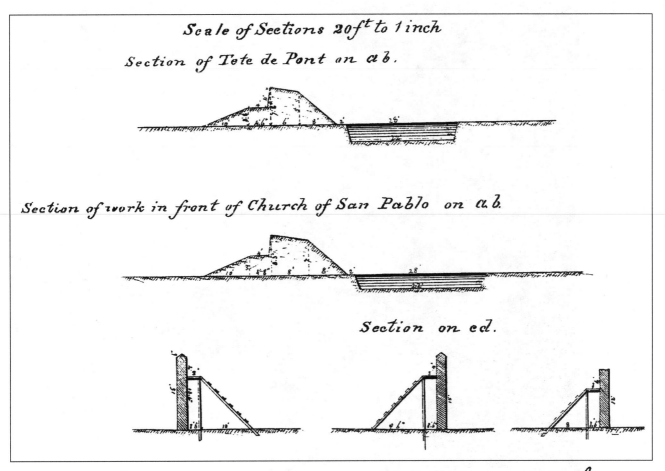

Scale of Sections 20ft to 1 inch

Section of Tete de Pont on a b.

Section of work in front of Church of San Pablo on a b.

Section on c d.

Details from the survey of the Churubusco battlefield made by Captain Mason and Lieutenants Beauregard, McClellan and Foster of the Corps of Engineers. approved Captain R.E.Lee, his signature to the right. Opposite is the area around the San Mateo Convent (here called San Pablo) and the Tête de Pont at a scale of 440 feet to the inch, and above profiles of the works.

Pierce were finally able to make some headway, at great cost in lives, now that the Mexican position was collapsing. Both the South Carolina and New York Regiments lost their commanding officers in the tough fighting before being able to link up with Worth's men on the road. The battle of Churubusco had lasted about three hours.

The Mexicans were once again in headlong flight, but the Americans were in no shape to press the pursuit any further. A few of the 1st Dragoons charged off in hot pursuit, against orders, all the way up to the gates of Mexico City itself. Among them was Captain Philip Kearny and about a dozen men, including Lieutenant Richard S. Ewell, who decided to charge a Mexican battery. The confusion was great and the Dragoons took the guns only to find out that they were but a handful of cavalry all alone amidst the Mexican army. They quickly remounted to withdraw but before they were out of range a piece of grapeshot mangled Kearny's left arm, which had to be amputated later. He was brevetted to Major

while Ewell won a brevet to Captain for his part in this action.

Santa Anna had suffered grievous losses in the last two days with the dual actions at Padierna and Churubusco. The Mexican army had lost at least 10,000 soldiers, about half of them captured, or about a third of the forces available for defense. Included among them were eight generals, two of whom were former presidents of Mexico. The army was in great disorder and would need time to regroup.

The Americans had also lost heavily. Total losses were 137 killed, including 14 officers, 865 wounded, of which 62 were officers, and 38 missing in action, almost twelve percent of the army engaged. It had been the toughest fight yet for Scott and his men. But the city of Mexico was now open for Scott to take on the run if he chose. As long as Santa Anna was not given time to organize new defenses the Americans could enter and end the war. But Scott's men were tired and hungry and he thought that discipline might break down upon entering the city.

In this picture by James Walker, U.S. troops parade past the captured convent at Churubusco.

He had also decided to give a negotiated settlement one more chance. Scott halted his victorious army at the gates to the city to give diplomacy a try once again.

General Scott was of the opinion that the Mexicans would now be ready to make peace. By halting the army outside the city he could spare them the humiliation of being completely conquered and so make it easier for their leaders to come to terms. He was also truly concerned about the discipline of his own army breaking down once the city was overrun, and that might lead to widespread pillaging and destruction. It was in this frame of mind that he agreed to a temporary truce signed on August 24th that would prohibit any military activity while terms were being discussed. What Scott had hoped would be the first steps towards peace ended up being only a delaying tactic by Santa Anna to reorganize his army. On September 6th Scott announced that the truce was ended, as no serious efforts had been made to negotiate and the Mexicans continued to violate the terms of the armistice. Now Scott began to study the situation and make plans for the attacks that would lead to the capture of the city.

MOLINO DEL REY

"I believe if we were to plant our batteries in Hell the damned Yankees would take them from us." Santa Anna.

The resumption of hostilities once again put the burden of attack on the Americans. The engineers, led by Captain Lee, began to study the possible approaches that could be used to gain entry into the city. There were several major causeways, or raised roads, that led into the city from the south and southwest, which was where the army was deployed. The ground lying between these causeways was either marshland or had been deliberately flooded by the Mexicans. At any rate, it was virtually impassable, especially for artillery. The causeways themselves were narrow and could be easily defended at their terminus points where they entered the city. These were the "garitas" or gates that Santa Anna had fortified for defense. On the west side of the city were the Garita de San Cosme and the Garita de Belén, approached by separate causeways that both originated at Chapultepec castle less than two miles to the southwest. The fact that Chapultepec would have to be taken first seemed to preclude this avenue of advance. The Garita de Belén was also the end point for the Piedad causeway from the south. On the south side of the city was the Garita de Niño Perdido on the west and the Garita de San Antonio which was at the northern end of the causeway from Churubusco. These were the two

areas that looked the most promising from which to launch an attack.

There were two reports on the evening of September 7th that encouraged Scott to change his plans for the attack. First of all, reconnaissance revealed that Santa Anna had been shifting troops to the two southern garitas to strengthen them. At the same time there was a large concentration of cavalry to the southwest of the city in the area called El Molino del Rey (the King's Mill), just west of Chapultepec (the Hill of the Grasshopper). Scott was informed that the Mexicans were using the mill as a foundry and melting down church bells there to cast them into cannon. The large stone buildings that made up the complex of the Molino del Rey were about 1,000 yards from Chapultepec and made up the westernmost end of the walled park of the castle grounds. Scott originally wanted to use a raid at night to destroy the works, but Worth convinced him to wait until daylight when a conventional attack could be launched.

The buildings of the Molino del Rey itself were about 300 yards long from north to south. This was manned by the Oaxaco Brigade of Brigadier General Antonio León and he was supported by another brigade under General Rangel. These were all troops of the National Guard. Another massive stone building known as the Casa Mata was 500 yards to the west of this position and had been fortified with earthworks by Mexican engineers. Here Brigadier General Francisco Pérez manned the defenses with 1500 regulars. A dry drainage ditch ran between the

---

MEXICAN FORCES AT MOLINO DEL REY ON SEPTEMBER 8, 1847

Left Flank (Molino del Rey itself)
  Oaxaco Brigade: Brig-Gen. Antonio León
  Libertad National Guard Battalion
  Mina National Guard Battalion: Colonel Lucas Balderas
  Querctaro National Guard Battalion
  Union National Guard Battalion
Center (behind dry irrigation ditch): Brig-Gen. Simeon Ramírez
  2nd Light Infantry (160) (2 companies)
  Fijo de Mexico
  1st Line Infantry
  12th Line Infantry
  Artillery (7 guns)
Right Flank (at Casa Mata): Brig-Gen. Francisco Pérez
  4th Light Infantry (600)
  11th Line Infantry (900)
Reserves
  3rd Light Infantry (700): Lt-Col. Miguel María Echegaray
  Cavalry Reserves (4000): Gen. Juan Alvarez

105

THE WAR IN MEXICO

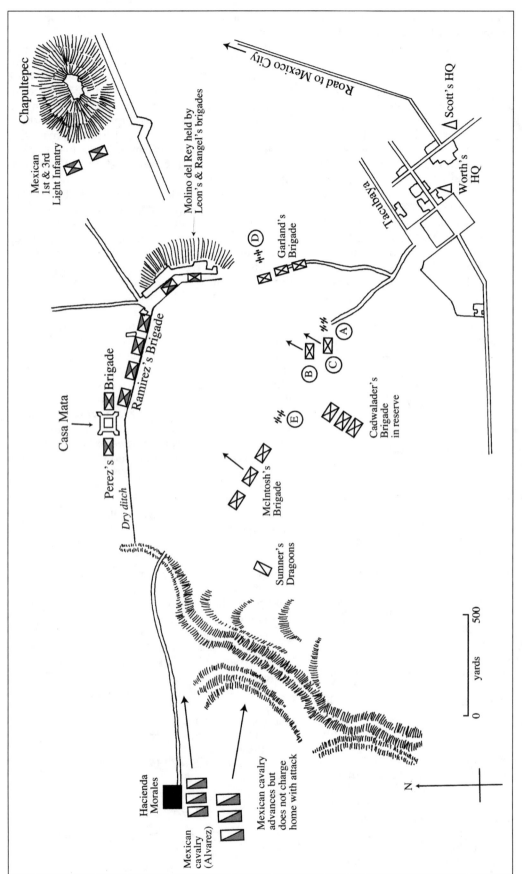

The battlefield of Molino del Rey

Key to Molino del Rey Map

A   Huger's battery of 2 - 24lb. guns
B   Storming party under Wright
C   Light Battalion under Smith
D   Drum's battery of 2 - 6lb. guns
E   Duncan's battery

two positions and this was manned by Brigadier General Simeon Ramírez and his brigade with seven artillery pieces. A mile further to the west of the Casa Mata was General Juan Alvarez and his cavalry brigade of almost 4000 men who were in position to outflank any attackers. The attack would have to come along almost 600 yards of gentle downward slope directly into interlocking fields of fire, with a minimum of cover available.

General Worth had been ordered to make the attack with his entire division on the morning of September 8th. Twiggs and Pillow would provide a feint by demonstrating towards the southern gates with some of their brigades. Worth's men began moving into position at about three o'clock in the morning with Garland's brigade on the right and Clarke's brigade on the left, temporarily commanded by Brevet Colonel James S. McIntosh. McIntosh was assigned to take the Casa Mata and Garland would assault the Molino del Rey itself. Major George Wright led a 'forlorn hope' of 500 picked men against the front of the buildings. Cadwalader's brigade from Pillow's division was in reserve and the left flank of the advance was screened by the cavalry under Major Sumner.

A bombardment was begun just before six o'clock but stopped short when it was reported that the Mexicans had abandoned the position. They had not. The first assault ran into a devastating fire that decimated Wright's assault column, putting eleven of his fourteen officers out of action. The Mexican 3rd Light Infantry seized the opportunity to launch an unplanned attack that shattered the remainder of Wright's ad hoc force. The Americans were thrown back. At Casa Mata, McIntosh was also running into heavy resistance, including local counterattacks that caused heavy losses. McIntosh himself was down and his second in command killed. Major Carlos A. Waite took over and was himself wounded. The attackers pulled back out of musket range and Duncan's battery began shelling the building, which was not supported by artillery. Duncan also threw a few rounds at Alvarez's cavalry which was hovering for an attack. This was enough to cause them to retire without pressing the attack that Santa Anna had ordered. The defenders of Casa Mata withdrew under Duncan's shelling and the recognition of the fact that the Molino itself was in danger of capitulating.

The attack continued to be pressed on the Molino del Rey by small units after Wright's storming party had failed. These persistent attacks included men of the 11th Infantry and the Voltigeurs, commanded by Lt. Colonel Joseph E. Johnston, from the reserve. Finally, the gates at the southern and northern ends of the compound were forced open and hand-to-hand fighting for the buildings began to rage. General León was killed in an attempt to regain his position where his artillery had been. The Mexicans were able to execute a fighting withdrawal from the buildings with the aid of counterattacks from the troops on Chapultepec. The battle came to an end

AMERICAN FORCES AT MOLINO DEL REY ON SEPTEMBER 8, 1847
Maj-Gen. William J. Worth (3154-3250)

1st Division (2000)
1st Brigade: Col. John Garland
  2nd Artillery: Maj. Patrick H. Galt
    (Companies C, D, F, G, H, I & K)
  3rd Artillery: Lt-Col. Francis S. Belton
    (Companies B, G, I & K)
  4th Infantry: Maj. Francis Lee
    (Companies A, B, C, D, E, F & I)
  Company A, 2nd Artillery: Lt-Col. James Duncan
2nd Brigade: Col. James S. McIntosh
  5th Infantry: Maj. John J. Abercrombie
    (Companies A, B, E, F, G, H & I)
  6th Infantry: Maj. Benjamin L. E. Bonneville
    (Companies A, B, C, D, E, F, H & K)
  8th Infantry: Maj. William R. Montgomery
    (Companies A, B, C, D, E, F, H, I & K)

An assault column of 500 men was formed from the 6 regiments listed above and commanded by Maj. George Wright, 8th Infantry.
A Light Battalion (185) of 2 companies of the 2nd

Artillery and 1 company each from the 5th and 8th Infantry was commanded by Capt. Ephraim Kirby Smith taking over for Lt-Col. Charles F. Smith who was ill.

Artillery (100)
  Ordnance Company: Capt. Benjamin Huger
    (2 - 24 lb. guns)
  Company G, 4th Artillery: Capt. Simon H. Drum (3 - 6 lb. guns)
Reserves
Cadwalader's Brigade: Brig-Gen. George Cadwalader (784)
  11th Infantry: Col. Albert C. Ramsey
    (Companies D, E, F, H & I)
  14th Infantry: Col. William Trousdale
    (Companies A, B, E, F, G, H, I & K)
  Regiment of Voltigeurs & Foot Riflemen: Col. Timothy P. Andrews (Companies A, B, C, D, E, F, G, H, I & K)
unattached
  Company of Engineers
U.S. Dragoons: Col. Edwin V. Sumner (270)
  1st Dragoons (Company F)
  2nd Dragoons (Companies A, B, C, F, I & K)
  3rd Dragoons (Companies E & K)
  Regiment of Mounted Rifles (Company I)

after two hours of the hardest fighting in the campaign so far.

Worth had accomplished his objective, but at a heavy price. He lost 116 men killed, including 9 officers, 665 wounded of which 49 were officers and 18 men missing in action. Clarke's brigade was the hardest hit, losing half of its officers and almost a third of its men. The Americans had captured 53 officers and 632 men along with three artillery pieces. There had been about 2,000 Mexican killed or wounded. The buildings of the Molino del Rey were found to be empty after all and Scott simply ordered them abandoned and destroyed. The Casa Mata blew up shortly before noon, causing a few more American casualties. By one o'clock that day the American troops had returned to their original positions without having much to show for their victory.

The loss of their defenses and the casualties incurred were both damaging blows to Mexican morale. The feeling among the troops must have echoed Santa Anna's earlier remark after witnessing the American troops assault a position when he said, "I believe if we were to plant our batteries in Hell the damned Yankees would take them from us".

General Scott now had to decide which direction the attack would take that was to break into Mexico City itself. Chapultepec castle had always been considered too difficult to attack and now the engineers were reporting that the southern approach routes had been greatly strengthened, with each one

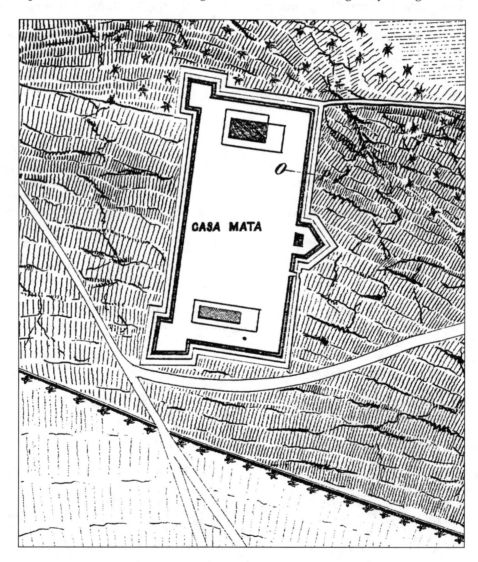

The Casa Mata and a profile of its ditch, as surveyed by Captain R.E. Lee and Lieutenants Beauregard and Tower of the Corp of Engineers.

having ten or more artillery pieces in direct support. The longer the Americans waited the worse things would get. Santa Anna was doing everything possible to make any assault very costly. Possibly to justify the attack on the Molino del Rey, Scott was actually now in favor of taking Chapultepec itself since the army was already deployed in that area. The only one of the engineers to agree with him was Beauregard, who was convinced that Santa Anna could be fooled into thinking that the attack would come elsewhere and the resulting surprise would lead to victory. Scott made up his mind to assault Chapultepec, and Beauregard would complain years later that he was never given the proper credit for his idea to attack the castle in the first place.

Scott had placed four siege batteries within range of the castle, which he hoped might be induced to surrender by bombardment alone. The bombardment began early in the morning of September 12th and was continuous. The castle roof was soon partially destroyed and the walls had been pierced in several places. The Mexicans, however, had not yet given up hope and they were not about to surrender. The assault was scheduled for the morning of the 13th.

Quitman

CHAPULTEPEC

"Brave Rifles! Veterans! You have been baptized in fire and blood and have come out steel!"
General Scott addressing the Regiment of Mounted Rifles

The castle of Chapultepec housed the Mexican Military College atop a two hundred foot tall hill that overlooked the causeways leading to the Garita de San Cosme as well as the Garita de Belén. The castle was part of an entire park whose grounds were walled off and formed a rectangle that was roughly three-quarters of a mile long by a quarter of a mile wide. The hilltop fort looked impregnable from below, but it could be cut off from water and supplies by occupying the grove of trees that ran to the west and ended at the Molino del Rey. What's more, the position had no other supporting defense works that could bear on an attacker to protect the castle. The

THE U.S. ARMY ON SEPTEMBER 18, 1847

Major General Winfield Scott's strength report following the battle at Molino del Rey, given in a communication of September 18, 1847, shows how some of the regiments have shrunk.

Total Army (7180)
1st Division
1st Brigade
  2nd Artillery (218)
  3rd Artillery (207)
  4th Infantry (376)
  Company A, 2nd Artillery (78)
2nd Brigade
  5th Infantry (355)
  6th Infantry (357)
  8th Infantry (480)
  Light Battalion (185)

2nd Division
1st Brigade
  1st Artillery (284)
  3rd Infantry (372)
  Regiment of Mounted Rifles (125)
3rd Division
1st Brigade
  9th Infantry (404)
  15th Infantry (384)
  Company I, 1st Artillery (100)
2nd Brigade
  11th Infantry (170)
  14th Infantry (303)
  Voltigeurs & Foot Riflemen (341)
  Rocket & Howitzer Company (100)
Volunteers
  2nd New York Volunteers (404)
  2nd Pennsylvania Volunteers (540)
  1st South Carolina Volunteers (423)
U.S. Marines (200)

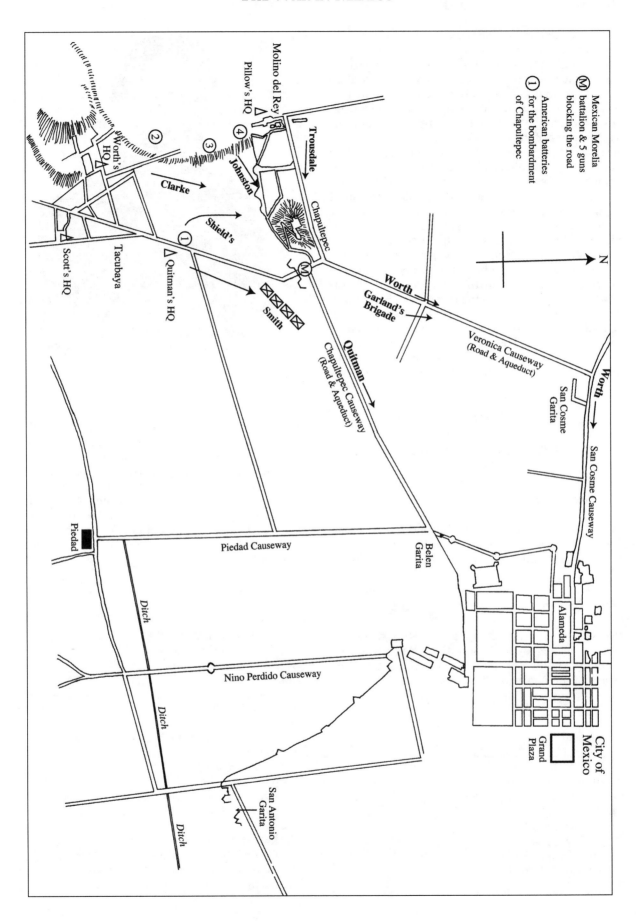

entire park area including the castle of Chapultepec could have held a garrison of 2000 men easily, yet General Nicolás Bravo had only 832 combatants and about 60 cadets to man the defenses. The western wall of the castle was protected by a ditch and a minefield. There were infantry breastworks and redans for artillery batteries placed along the approach roads and some were half way up the slopes of the hill. The brigades of Rangel and Ramírez were deployed to the east of the hill but found it difficult to lend any direct support.

The main assault would be made by Pillow's and Quitman's divisions with Worth and Twiggs in support and ready to follow up any breakthroughs that might occur. Twiggs' division provided Quitman with a "forlorn hope" of 265 men under Captain Silas Casey as well as Smith's brigade being on immediate call. Worth's division lent Pillow a similar size storming party under Captain Samuel Mackenzie to lead the attack. All of the assaulting troops were to be regulars. Pillow's men would assemble at the Molino del Rey and launch the attack from there with Pierce's brigade in the lead. Quitman's men would be to his right and move down the causeway from Tacubaya to the southeast corner of the position. Quitman would be responsible for scaling the walls and gaining entry via the winding path to the top of the hill fort. After the fall of Chapultepec the causeway leading to the Garita de Belén would be open.

The American artillery batteries began their bombardment on the 13th at dawn and continued shelling the castle for the next two and a half hours. Pierce's brigade jumped off from the Molino del Rey and made quick progress up to the western side of the hill, but the men with the scaling ladders were not with them. The attack slowed and came under fire from above. Colonel Ransom of the 9th Infantry was shot in the head and killed. Pillow was wounded in the ankle and quickly sent for help from Worth. On Pierce's right Lt. Colonel Johnston with the Regiment of Voltigeurs successfully attacked a sandbag redoubt and continued on up the hill to the approach road. They were then able to bring the defenders under musket fire.

Towards the northern side of the hill a section of artillery from Magruder's battery had gotten its guns stuck in a ditch and was under heavy fire from Mexican guns on the road and on the heights. A lone officer was walking back and forth amid dead or dying men and horses trying to encourage the rest of his crew to leave their shelter in the rocks and bushes and bring the guns back into action. "There's no danger! See, I'm not hit!" It was Lieutenant Thomas J. Jackson of the 1st Artillery. General Worth himself saw the situation and ordered Jackson to leave his position. Seemingly having no sense of danger he sent word back that it would be more dangerous for him to withdraw than to maintain his location. Instead he requested fifty soldiers so that he could take the barricade on the road just ahead. Jackson finally managed to enlist the aid of a sergeant and together they got their gun firing again. Shortly thereafter "Prince John" Magruder arrived with another gun for support and the Mexican fire began to slacken.

Quitman was the first to come to Pillow's aid with Casey's storming party and a detachment of Marines moving up the causeway from Tacubaya. The advance on the causeway itself faltered and was stopped by the Morelia Battalion and a five gun battery. Quitman then sent Smith's brigade off to the meadows to the right of the road to turn the Mexican position and open up the causeway. He sent Shields

---

MEXICAN FORCES AT CHAPULTEPEC CASTLE ON SEPTEMBER 13, 1847

Chapultepec Castle: Gen.Nicolás Bravo (892)
  10th Line Infantry (250): Lt-Col. Miguel Camargo
  Queretaro National Guard Battalion (115)
  Toluca National Guard Battalion (27)
  Mina National Guard Artillery Battalion (277)
  Union National Guard Battalion (121): Col. N. Aguayo
  Patria National Guard Battalion (42): Col. Fernando Martínez
  Cadets of the Military College (60)

Reserves east of Chapultepec
1st Brigade: Gen. Joaquín Rangel (1400)
  Matamoros de Morelia Battalion (200): Battalion Commander José Barreiro

San Blas Battalion (400): Lt-Col. Felipe Santiago Xicoténcatl
Grenadiers of the Guard of the Supreme Powers (400): Lt. Col. Miguel María Echegaray
Mixto de Santa Anna (200): Lt-Col. Agustín Zires
Matamoros National Guard Battalion (200): Lt-Col. Juan B. Traconis
2nd Brigade: Gen. Simeon Ramirez (1050)
2nd Light Infantry (300): Col. José M. Carrasco
  1st Line Infantry (300): Battalion Commander Pedro Quiroz
  12th Line Infantry (200): Battalion Commander José M. Cota
  Fijo de Mexico (250): Battalion Commander Manuel Vázquez
Artillery
  3 - 4 lb., 1 - 8 lb. & 2 - 24 lb. guns and 1 - 68 lb. howitzer
San Antonio Garita
  6 large and 4 small guns

with the New York and Pennsylvania troops to the left followed by the South Carolina regiment, to assist in the direct assault against Chapultepec.

Worth's veterans of Clarke's brigade arrived at the walls about the same time that Shields' men did. The fresh troops and scaling ladders provided momentum for the stalled attack. Lt. Lewis A. Armistead, 6th Infantry, was the first to leap into the ditch and was wounded in the hail of artillery and musket fire raining down from the Mexicans above. Meanwhile, when Lt. James Longstreet, 8th Infantry, was seriously wounded while scaling the slope Lt. George E. Pickett, of the same regiment, seized the colors from him and carried them over the works to the top of the castle. The tattered Voltigeur flag was raised first, followed by the Stars and Stripes after General Bravo surrendered to Lt. Brower of the New York regiment at nine-thirty.

The brave young military cadets, of whom there may have been as many as sixty present, had fought very well alongside General Bravo and the other soldiers. They had been ordered to abandon the academy because of their ages, which ranged from the youngest at thirteen to nineteen for the oldest, who would almost be ready for military service. During the course of the assault six of the cadets died fighting, heroically defending their posts and refusing to surrender. One of the youngest of the students was bayoneted while trying to ready his rifle to fire on the advancing Americans. Others were killed inside the palace walls. Juan Escutia, one of the older cadets at twenty, grabbed the flag of the garrison to prevent it from falling into enemy hands. He was shot and fell over the parapet onto the rocks far below, still clutching the flag in his hand. The full story of the defense and the part played by the cadets is almost impossible to document fully. Most of the existing information has been passed down by word-of-mouth and much of it is the stuff of legends. However, these six boys would go down in Mexican history as "Los Niños Heroes" (the heroic children) and become immortalized as national

AMERICAN FORCES AT CHAPULTEPEC CASTLE ON SEPTEMBER 13, 1847
Maj-Gen. Winfield Scott

3rd Division: Maj-Gen. Gideon J. Pillow
1st Brigade: Brig-Gen. Franklin Pierce
  9th Infantry: Col. Trueman B. Ransom (Companies A, B, C, D, E, F, G, H, I & K)
  15th Infantry: Col. George W. Morgan (Companies A, B, C, D, E, F, H, I & K)
  Company I, 1st Artillery: Capt. John B. Magruder
2nd Brigade: Brig-Gen. George Cadwalader
  11th Infantry: Col. Albert C. Ramsey (Companies D, E, F, H & I)
  14th Infantry: Col. William Trousdale (Companies A, B, E, F, G, H, I & K)
  Regiment of Voltigeurs & Foot Riflemen: Col. Timothy P. Andrews (Companies A, B, C, D, E, F, G, H, I & K)
  Rocket & Howitzer Company: Lt. Jesse L. Reno

4th Division: Brig-Gen. John A. Quitman
1st Brigade: Brig-Gen. James Shields
  2nd New York Volunteers: Col. Ward B. Burnet
  1st South Carolina Volunteers: Lt-Col. Adley H. Gladden
2nd Brigade: Col. William B. Roberts
  2nd Pennsylvania Volunteers: Lt-Col. John W. Geary
  U.S. Marines: Maj. Levi Twiggs, USMC

2nd Division: Brig-Gen. David E. Twiggs
1st Brigade: Brig-Gen. Persifor F. Smith
  Regiment of Mounted Rifles (on foot): Maj. William W. Loring (Companies A, B, D, E, F, G, H, I & K)
  1st Artillery (as infantry): Maj. Justin Dimick (Companies B, D, F, G & H)
  3rd Infantry: Capt. Edmund B. Alexander (Companies A, B, C, D, E, F, H, I & K)
  Company K, 1st Artillery: Capt. Francis Taylor

Assault Column (265): Captain Silas Casey

Reserves
1st Division: Maj-Gen. William J. Worth
1st Brigade: Col. John Garland
  2nd Artillery (as infantry): Maj. Patrick H. Galt (Companies C, D, F, G, H, I & K)
  3rd Artillery (as infantry): Col. Francis S. Belton (Companies B, G, H, I & K)
  4th Infantry: Maj. Francis Lee (Companies A, B, C, D, E, F & I)
2nd Brigade: Col. Newman S. Clarke
  5th Infantry: Maj. John J. Abercrombie (Companies A, B, E, F, G, H, I & K)
  6th Infantry: Maj. Benjamin L. E. Bonneville (Companies A, B, C, D, E, F, H & K)
  8th Infantry: Maj. William R. Montgomery (Companies A, B, C, D, E, F, H, I & K)
Light Battalion: Lt-Col. Charles F. Smith

Artillery
Battery #1: Capt. Simon H. Drum (2 - captured 16 lb. guns & 1 - 8" howitzer)
Battery #2: Lt. Peter V. Hagner (1 - 24 lb. gun & 1 - 8" howitzer)
Battery #3: Capt. Horace Brooks (1 - captured 16 lb. gun & 1 - 8" howitzer)
Battery #4: Lt. Charles P. Stone (1 - 10" mortar)

heroes.

The flag being raised to announce the fall of Chapultepec was also the signal for the execution of thirty men of the San Patricio Battalion that had been captured at the Churubusco Convent. The deserters had been tried and sentenced to be hung. Several days earlier sixteen San Patricios had been hung at San Angel. Scott had shown leniency where he could and thirty-nine others had gone free after being

whipped and in some cases branded. Now Colonel Harney waited for the Stars and Stripes to flutter in the morning breeze above Chapultepec castle. When the flag went up Harney lowered his sword and, with a cheer, all thirty men went to their deaths at the end of a rope at the same time. The cause they had deserted to fight for was lost.

The Americans in the castle now brought the gateway below under fire from the castle itself.

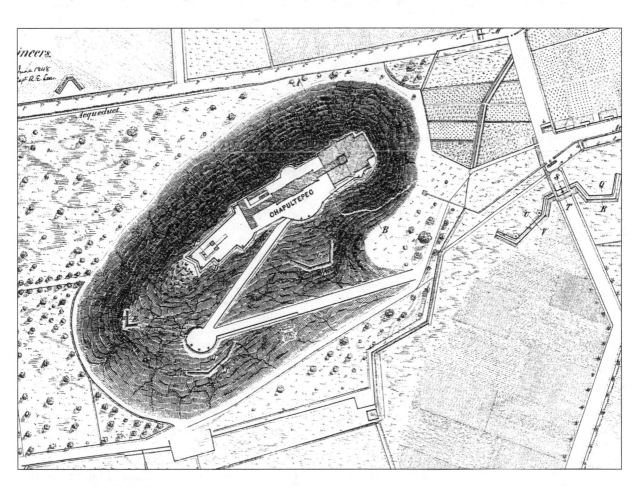

The Castle of Chapultepec and its profile, as surveyed by Captain R.E. Lee and Lieutenants Beauregard and Tower of the Corp of Engineers. His signature from the survey is to the right.

Scale of this section one inch to 100 feet.

Smith's brigade swept up the causeway amid the fleeing enemy and the Chapultepec position was secured. The entire assault had lasted just over two hours. But Quitman wasted no time in gathering most of the available troops and pressing the advance along the causeway to the Garita de Belén so as not to lose the advantages gained in the battle just won. The Mounted Rifles (on foot) led the way, taking a two gun battery and redan on the way and meeting tougher resistance the closer they came to the garita itself.

Brigadier General Andrés Terrés took command of the position with the Morelia Battalion and reinforcements provided by Santa Anna. There were also men who had withdrawn from the fight at Chapultepec and had managed to rally here. The garita was guarded by a ditch, parapet and redoubt with a three gun battery and substantial reserves were now available. With these troops a withering fire was poured into Quitman's advance, bringing it to a halt. The Americans brought up their own artillery for close support and with a rush the Mounted Rifles were over the parapet and by twenty minutes past one o'clock had raised their yellow banner over the garita. They would later be congratulated by General Scott for their efforts and they would make part of his exclamation their regimental motto: "Brave Rifles! Veterans! You have been baptized in fire and blood and have come out steel!"

The storming of the battery defending the garita at the Belén Gate had been a lively affair in which several men suffered minor wounds. Lieutenant Earl Van Dorn, General Quitman's aide, was wounded in the foot. Lieutenant Cadmus Wilcox, 7th Infantry, was hit with a musket ball that struck the side of his Colt revolver on his waist belt. The impact knocked him down, causing a severe bruise and the bullet was recovered from the ground by his side. The ball had been flattened and bore the imprint of the maker of his pistol and the place where it was made. Quitman was encouraged to abandon the assault by some, but he had decided to press on and was successful in the end.

Once past the garita Quitman's men ran into continued heavy resistance from the area know as the Ciudadela (Citadel). Santa Anna had reinforced this area that stood at the southwestern corner of the city itself with adequate men and guns to put up a respectable defense, which they proceeded to do. American artillery ammunition was now running low and the troops were not able to make any more headway. Quitman decided to wait for darkness to bring up more guns and ammunition, as well as to reconnoiter the position more fully.

On the night of September 13th, Captain Beauregard of the Engineers accompanied General Quitman in a reconnaissance of the terrain along the Piedad Causeway facing the Ciudadela. While searching for some high ground in the darkness they both tumbled in to the canal alongside, ending up standing in water that was waist deep. It was here that General Quitman lost his shoe and he was still without it upon entering the city on the following day.

Meanwhile, General Worth had launched his assault from Chapultepec towards the Garita de San Cosme at the northwest corner of the city. This was the advance that Scott wanted to make into his main thrust, with Quitman providing the feint. Colonel Trousdale with the 14th Infantry, supported by Lt. Jackson's guns from Magruder's battery, was meeting resistance on the causeway. Worth along with Garland's brigade, the light battalion under Lt. Colonel C. F. Smith, Duncan's artillery, the remainder of Magruder's battery, and Sumner's dragoons were all ordered to proceed along the Veronica causeway towards San Cosme. The brigades of Cadwalader and Clarke, as well as the siege guns with Huger, were also sent to Worth for his attack. By four o'clock Worth was within a half mile of the Garita de San Cosme, prepared to take it.

A hasty redoubt had been erected here with at least three cannon and additional troops to hold it. The rooftops of the surrounding houses were also occupied and used for firing platforms. Reinforcements had been sent as quickly as possible and once again a sizeable reserve force was at hand. The Americans were again subjected to devastating fire when they advanced in the open towards the garita. They were forced to try to flank the position by cutting their way through surrounding buildings and creeping around the arches of the aqueduct in small numbers to avoid drawing fire. One such small party was being led around the garita by Lt. Grant of the 4th Infantry.

Grant and his small group managed to drag a mountain howitzer to the belfry of a nearby church on the right flank and began to shell the Mexicans from above. Before long Lt. Raphael Semmes of the navy, who had been with Grant a bit earlier, had accomplished a similar feat on the left. This fire, combined with the renewed fire from the guns of Lt. Henry J. Hunt, 2nd Artillery and a fresh assault by Worth's troops, caused the defense to collapse. Worth entered the edge of the City of Mexico by six o'clock that night. His troops had halted at the garita for the night to prepare for what they believed would be the final bloody assault the next day.

On the morning of September 14th the Ciudadela opposite the Belén Garita raised the white flag of surrender. Captain Beauregard was sent to investigate and treat with the officer in charge. The Mexican officer offered to surrender everything provided he was furnished with receipts. Beauregard simply looked at him in utter amazement and told him that the Americans "gave our receipts with the points of our swords! That if he did not give up the

General Quitman leads the Marines through the Belen Gate of Mexico City. Quitman is shown missing one shoe because he and Beauregard had blundered into a ditch during a reconnaissance the night before. (Artist Tom Lovell, picture courtesy of the Marine Corps Gazette)

property under his charge willingly, we would take it." The officer then surrendered peacefully.

During the night Santa Anna, with perhaps 5,000 troops, had pulled out of the city toward Guadalupe Hidalgo to regroup. The main part of the city was without fortifications and was indefensible except by house to house fighting, which would surely destroy much of it. To avoid having the city bombarded and smashed into ruins Santa Anna had evacuated and would hope to join up with some 7,000 other troops close by to be able to eventually fight again. By dawn the city had been surrendered to Scott. His triumphal entry took place a few hours later to the cheers of his men. Quitman was appointed governor of the city and the United States Marines that had accompanied him in began patrolling the "Halls of the Montezumas." Scott's losses for September 12-14 were 130 killed, including 10 officers, 703 wounded, of which 68 were officers, and 29 missing in action. Santa Anna had probably lost about 1,800 men total in addition to losing the capital. The American army had been victorious, but the war was not quite over yet.

Santa Anna left the area of Mexico City with the remnants of an army that had been wracked by defeat and desertion. He had about 2,000 cavalry and only four light guns with him. General Alvarez still had about 600 infantry and cavalry and General Rea had about the same number of irregulars. Santa Anna knew that Puebla contained only a small garrison of American troops, most of them in hospital. He thought that if he took that city, Scott would have no hope of ever re-opening his supply lines to the coast. It was a last ditch effort, but Santa Anna decided to try to snatch a victory from the jaws of defeat. In the vicinity of Puebla itself he could also call on approximately 2,500 National Guard troops with two more field pieces.

The actual siege had begun on the same day that the Americans had taken Mexico City. Santa Anna and his army did not arrive until September 21st. Several attempts were made to breach the defenses over the next several days but none of them were successful. Colonel Childs had less than 400 men that were not on the sick list. Many of the slightly wounded helped to man the defenses during the siege. He was able to anticipate the Mexican maneuvers and reacted to the assaults in a timely fashion that threw the attackers back time after time. All the Americans could do was to hold out until a relief force drove off Santa Anna and his army.

Scott's forces at Mexico City were not able to move to Puebla due to the fact that heavy rains had made the roads virtually impassable, especially for wagons. The relief force would have to come from the reinforcements on the march from Vera Cruz. The latest group to set out was commanded by Brigadier General Joseph Lane of Indiana. He had commanded

the Indiana brigade in Taylor's army at Buena Vista. Lane was a shrewd backwoods lawyer with great energy, and was much admired by his men for his courage. He was a careless disciplinarian who often did not look to the comfort of his men in camp, or conserve their strength in battle. However, Lane had a real talent for waging partisan warfare that earned him the respect of his men as well as the title of the "Marion" of the war. This was a reference to the American General Francis Marion, "the Swamp Fox", from Revolutionary War days who fought a successful guerrilla war against the British from the swamps of South Carolina. Lane would earn his title beginning with the march from Vera Cruz.

Lane was aware of the situation at Puebla when he departed Vera Cruz on September 19, 1847. After fighting several skirmishes along the National Road and linking up with other detachments en route Lane was able to leave Perote on October 5th. Lane's total force numbered somewhere around 3,300 men and seven guns along with a large baggage train. During the difficult march to Puebla the column had to contend with the extremes of the Mexican climate, from deluges of rain that forced them to wade down submerged roads to travel across sun-baked plains where men could die of thirst and fatigue.

MEXICANS AT SIEGE OF PUEBLA FROM SEPTEMBER 14 - OCTOBER 12, 1847

Gen. Antonio López de Santa Anna (6000 total)
  Cavalry (2000)
  4 guns
  Maj-Gen. Juan Alvarez (600)
  Brig-Gen. Joaquín Rea (600)
  Puebla National Guards (2500)
  2 guns

AMERICANS AT SIEGE OF PUEBLA FROM SEPTEMBER 14 - OCTOBER 12, 1847
Colonel Thomas Childs (2193 total)
Hospital: Capt. Theodore F. Rowe, 9th Infantry, with (1800) men on sick call, leaving only about (393) effectives in the garrison.

1st Pennsylvania (250): Lt. Col. Samuel W. Black (6 companies)
Detachments from 2nd Infantry and Voltigeurs as well
Artillery (100)
  2nd Artillery: Capt. Henry L. Kendrick (Coy. B)
  4th Artillery: Capt. John H. Miller (Coy. A)
  Total of 5 - howitzers, 2 - 12 lb. guns & 1 - 10" mortar
3rd Dragoons (50): Capt. Lemuel Ford (Coy. D)
Mexican Spy Company
Detachments from 2nd Dragoons & Mounted Rifles as well

116

One of the men marching down the road from Vera Cruz cut quite an outlandish figure. Wearing a bright red flannel "fighting" shirt, coarse army issue trousers tucked into red-topped boots, a broad-brimmed sombrero, and a pair of large Mexican spurs at his heels, he was overly well armed with an artillery sabre, two large horse pistols in leather holsters, a couple of revolvers jammed into his belt, and a large butcher knife for good measure. The soldier was none other than 2nd Lieutenant Ambrose P. Hill of the 1st Artillery, newly graduated from West Point and like most of the other cadets, anxious to get into the war before it ended.

Meanwhile, Santa Anna was having trouble keeping his army intact at Puebla due to an ever increasing desertion rate. When he learned that Lane's column was already on the march, he decided that it must be destroyed before it could reach Puebla. To accomplish this, he gathered the most reliable of his cavalry along with six guns and headed east on the road to prepare to ambush Lane.

They met at a town called Huamantla. The advance guard for General Lane's column was made up of cavalry led by Captain Samuel H. Walker, the Texas Ranger who helped design the Walker-Colt revolver now becoming popular with the army. Walker had been with Taylor on the Rio Grande and his courage and daring had seen him through many tight spots during the war.

On the morning of October 9th, Walker and his men surprised the cavalry outposts of Santa Anna in Huamantla and charged headlong into action. When they reached the main plaza, they ran into the main body of Mexican lancers and were attacked from all sides. Walker was shot and killed but had time to issue a final order to his men; "Don't surrender boys; the infantry will soon be here". Lane did arrive shortly thereafter with the promised infantry support that turned the tide of the battle. This was the last battle fought by Santa Anna against the Americans. His luck had run out once again and soon after this fight he received word that he had been relieved of his command by President Peña. Lane continued on towards Puebla, reaching the outskirts of the city on October 12th and ending the siege.

All organized resistance in Mexico had now come to an end. The Mexican army had virtually ceased to exist. There were other skirmishes fought and minor expeditions launched to combat guerrilla bands and keep supply lines open. Additional reinforcements also continued to arrive to strengthen the occupying army while peace terms were being negotiated. Scott did not have a large enough army to occupy many of the outlying areas so the Americans remained fairly concentrated at the major cities they had captured. Towards the end of November, Zachary Taylor was relieved of his command and returned to the United States to

launch a successful Presidential campaign. In mid-January Winfield Scott was recalled amid much turmoil and bickering with his political and military foes. On February 2, 1848 the Peace Treaty of Guadalupe Hidalgo was signed bringing the war to an end. It took several months for both sides to ratify the treaty, but once this was accomplished the American army began a hasty withdrawal. By the middle of July the last troops had departed Vera Cruz and the War in Mexico was over.

EPILOGUE

"His campaign was unsurpassed in military annals. He is the greatest living soldier."
The Duke of Wellington

The war against Mexico started out as a very popular war in the United States. The rush of volunteers to enlist is good evidence of that. But it

---

HUAMANTLA, OCTOBER 9, 1847

Mexican forces under General Antonio López de Santa Anna (1000)
All cavalry and 6 guns

American forces at Huamantla
Brig-Gen. Joseph Lane (1800 total)
  4th Indiana: Col. Willis A. Gorman (10 companies)
  1st Pennsylvania: Col. Francis M. Wyncoop (4 companies)
  Company A, 3rd Artillery: Capt. George Taylor (5 - guns)
  9th Infantry: Maj. Folliot T. Lally (Companies D, E, F, H & I)
  Regulars*: Capt. Samuel P. Heintzelman, 2nd Infantry (6 companies)
Cavalry (200): Capt. Samuel H. Walker
  Regiment of Mounted Rifles (Company C)
  Louisiana Mounted Volunteers: Capt. Lorenzo Lewis (2 company)
  Georgia Mounted Volunteers: Capt. John Loyall (1 company)
Guarding the baggage train
  4th Ohio: Col. Charles H. Brough (10 companies)
  Regulars*: Capt. Seneca G. Simmons, 7th Infantry (3 companies)
  2nd Artillery: Lt. Henry C. Pratt (2 - 6 lb. guns)

* = companies of Regulars were H & K, 4th Infantry; A & K, 11th Infantry; G, I & K, 12th Infantry; G, 15th Infantry and K, Voltigeurs. In addition there were also detachments of recruits for the 2nd and 15th Infantry present

quickly lost most of its lustre when the campaign in northern Mexico, despite some astonishing victories, did not bring about a quick Mexican surrender. The United States under the Polk administration had tried to avoid a war with Mexico, even while accepting the fact that one would probably occur. The army was as ready as it could be under the circumstances, but no advanced preparations for war had been made. The debate for increasing the authorized strength of each company to one-hundred privates had been going on for six months before hostilities began. This is what the administration eventually passed, but if done in a more timely manner the American army of Zachary Taylor could have been twice as large as it was for the opening battles, and the need for expensive recruits to raise new regiments and units of troublesome volunteers would have been much less.

The regulars of the "old army" managed to fight and win with what they had until the newly enlisted regulars and volunteers could join them. The new regiments of regulars were not as well trained as the original establishment, but they acquitted themselves well in Mexico. The volunteers, with their comings and goings due to short term enlistments, almost complete lack of discipline and training and a tendency for contracting diseases, proved less valuable than they could have been. Many more volunteers were called to the colors than ever saw active service, with some of the early regiments having their enlistments expire before they had reached the scene of action.

The victory in Mexico did carry a heavy price, however. The regulars lost a total of 1,010 men killed in action or dying from wounds; 4,899 men dead from disease and other causes; 2,745 wounded in action; 2,554 discharged for disabilities and 5,331 as deserters. The volunteers lost a total of 711 men killed in action or dying from wounds; 6,256 men dead from disease and other causes; 1,357 wounded in action; 7,200 discharged for disabilities and 3,876 as deserters. These figures show that death in battle was the least likely cause of loss to the army in Mexico. Less than 1.5 percent of the men would fall to enemy action while five times this many would desert and almost seven times this many would succumb to some type of disease, which was the biggest killer.

Overall the American army performed much better than expected in the campaigns in Mexico. The administration and logistics still left a lot to be desired at the end of the war but the troops had earned the admiration and respect of their countrymen and the world. General Scott, in his official report summed up the results of the campaign in the Valley of Mexico well when he said: "…this small force (the American army) has beaten, in view of their capital, the whole Mexican army of 30,000 men, posted always in chosen positions, behind intrenchments or more formidable defenses of nature and art; killed or wounded of that number more than 7,000 officers and men; taken 3,730 prisoners, one-seventh officers, including thirteen

The victory parade through Mexico City

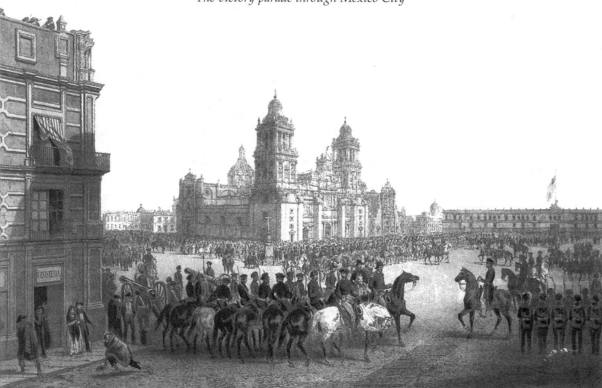

generals, of whom three had been Presidents of this republic; captured more than twenty colors and standards, seventy-five pieces of ordnance, …20,000 small arms, and an immense quantity of shot, shell, powder, etc". Much of the remainder of the Mexican army had been dispersed, disbanded, or had simply deserted and returned to their homes. The American achievement was quite impressive when the numbers are compared. The American victories in four major actions and several minor ones at the garitas had cost them a total of 2,703 casualties, killed and wounded, including 383 officers, or just over twenty-five percent of their force. It was an unprecedented accomplishment and assured Scott his place among history's greatest generals. The Duke of Wellington gave Scott high praise when, upon hearing of the results of the war, he had said: "His campaign was unsurpassed in military annals. He is the greatest living soldier."

The American officers and their men were very aware of the great victory that they had achieved, despite all of the odds against them. An officers club was formed in Mexico City called the "Aztec Club" that was open to any officers who had served in the war from Vera Cruz on. Membership in the club carried much prestige with it and its descendant still exists today. Eventually it came to number 160 members, many of whom would become more famous and achieve much higher rank in the war that would follow fifteen years later.

The war had cost the United States some $58 million in military expenditures along with the $15 million to be paid to Mexico under the terms of the peace treaty. In exchange for this the Americans gained over 600,000 square miles of territory, not including Texas. This area would eventually become the states of Arizona, California, Nevada, New Mexico and Utah and also included parts of Colorado and Wyoming.

The actual cost of the war to Mexico, beyond the loss of territory, has never been accurately calculated. Mexico was very poor at the beginning of the war

and afterwards it was virtually destitute. The lands that were taken by the United States had never been developed to anywhere near their full potential by Mexico and colonization by its citizens had been sparse. The discovery of gold in California shortly after the war was the first indication that the loss to Mexico was much greater than originally thought. In military terms the Mexicans had ultimately lost virtually every major battle that they fought against the Americans. Mexican leadership was to blame for this and the military hierarchy was discredited by its performance. Unfortunately for the nation, the military would continue to be a powerful institution whose aid and influence was necessary to gain and maintain governmental power.

The Mexican soldiers themselves had fought well but it had cost them dearly. The number of Mexican soldiers killed in battle was estimated as being at least 5000 or more. The amount of men wounded or missing in action has never been totalled. In addition the Mexicans were also subject to disease and other causes of casualties for which no numbers are available. The total extent of the suffering and loss from the war among both Mexican soldiers and civilians is beyond measure. Mexico had paid an extremely high price, in terms of both money and human misery, for its defeat at the hands of the United States.

The Mexicans began to develop an increasing distrust of the United States and its motives as a result of the war. Admiration for the Americans and their ideals was replaced by dislike and a wariness when it came to dealing with anyone north of the border. There were also many Mexicans who blamed their own political system and leadership and its failure to establish a stable government able to protect the homeland from invaders. This growing concern for the country and the way it was run would lead to a nationalist movement that would culminate with Benito Juarez and his democratic ideals coming to power within the next ten years. Mexico was not destined to be spared further suffering however, as it was forced to endure anarchy and civil war as well as another foreign intervention, this time by the French, during the time that the United States was engaged in its own civil war.

Perfect hindsight tells us that the war in Mexico was a war that did not have to be fought. Peaceful negotiations to settle boundary and monetary disputes between the two nations should have been preferable to a declaration of war. Both countries would have benefited from a settlement by the savings in money and human lives that would have been spared. The fact that the war seemed necessary and inevitable to both sides at that time is what set the participants apart from the thinking of our modern society as we would like it to be today.

THE MEXICAN ARMY AT THE END OF HOSTILITIES

Total of 109 officers, 817 non-commissioned officers and 6480 men

Combined Infantry and Cavalry (6688)
Artillery (514)
Zapadores (204)

A decree of December 1, 1847 reorganizing the army called for 10 Generals of Division and 20 Generals of Brigade to command 112 officers, 911 non-commissioned officers and 22,409 men

THE ORIGINAL MEMBERS OF THE AZTEC CLUB

Lt-Col. John J. Abercrombie
Capt. Thomas L. Alexander
Capt. Robert Allen
Lt. Samuel S. Anderson
Major Henry Bainbridge
Capt. John G. Barnard
Capt. Moses J. Barnard
Lt. Jenks Beaman
Lt. P.G.T. Beauregard
Lt. Barnard E. Bee
Lt-Col. Francis S. Belton
Capt. Charles J. Biddle
Lt. William B. Blair
Capt. George A.H. Blake
Capt. James D. Blanding
Capt. William Blanding
Col. Milledge L. Bonham
Lt. Andrew W. Bowman
Lt. John M. Brannan
Capt. Horace Brooks
Lt. William T.H. Brooks
Lt. Hachaliah Brown
Major Robert C. Buchanan
Brig-Gen. George Cadwalader
Capt. Albemarle Cady
Major G.A. Caldwell
Lt. Robert C. Caldwell
Lt. George W. Carr
Capt. Daniel T. Chandler
Lt. Henry Coppee
Capt. Lewis S. Craig
Surgeon Presley H. Craig
Lt. Alexander H. Cross
Capt. Joseph Daniels
Capt. George Deas
Asst Surgeon David C. DeLeon
Bvt. Lt-Col. James Duncan
Lt. Richard S. Ewell
Lt. Colonel Thomas T. Fauntleroy
Capt. Edward H. Fitzgerald
Lt. Robert Forsyth
Lt. William H. French
Lt. Daniel M. Frost
Major John P. Gaines
Lt. John W.T. Gardiner
Capt. Richard C. Gatlin
Major Patrick H. Gault
Lt. Alfred Gibbs
Lt-Col. Adley H. Gladden

Lt. John H. Gore
Lt. Henry D. Grafton
Lt. Ulysses S. Grant
Capt. John B. Grayson
Major Maxcy Gregg
Lt. Peter V. Hagner
Capt. O.P. Hamilton
Lt. Schuyler Hamilton
Lt. Richard P. Hammond
Lt. Edmund L. Hardcastle
Capt. William J. Hardee
Surgeon Benjamin F. Harney
Col. William S. Harney
Lt. John P. Hatch
Capt. John S. Hathaway
Lt-Col. Paul O. Hebert
Capt. William Hoffman
Lt. E.B. Holloway
Capt. Joseph Hooker
Capt. John E. Howard
Capt. Benjamin Huger
Capt. James R. Irwin
Lt-Col. Joseph E. Johnston
Lt. Llewellyn Jones
Capt. Philip Kearny
Major Edmund Kirby
Lt. George W. Lay
Capt. Robert E. Lee
Lt. Mansfield Lovell
Capt. Roland A. Luther
Capt. William W. Mackall
Capt. John B. Magruder
Lt. James R. May
Lt. Julian May
Lt. George B. McClellan
Lt. Philip W. McDonald
Capt. Samuel McGowan
Capt. Justus McKinstrey
Lt. George McLane
Lt. Robert M. Morris
Capt. Thompson Morris
Lt. Ferdinand S. Mumford
Bvt. Lt-Col. John Munroe
Capt. Abraham C. Myers
Lt. Anderson D. Nelson
Bvt. Capt. William A. Nichols
Capt. Theodore O'Hara
Capt. Franklin N. Page
Lt. Innis N. Palmer
Maj-Gen. Robert Patterson

Bvt. Capt. John C. Pemberton
Brig-Gen. Franklin Pierce
Major William H. Polk
Capt. Andrew Porter
Lt. Fitz-John Porter
Colonel William Preston
Maj-Gen. John A. Quitman
Lt. George W. Rains
Surgeon Burton Randall
Lt. Jesse L. Reno
Lt. Thomas G. Rhett
Lt. Roswell S. Ripley
Surgeon Robert R. Ritchie
Lt. Francis S.K. Russell
Capt. Henry L. Scott
Lt. Oliver L. Shepherd
Lt. Hamilton L. Shields
Capt. Henry H. Sibley
Assistant Surgeon James Simons
Bvt. Lt-Col. Charles F. Smith
Lt. Gustavus W. Smith
Lt. Martin L. Smith
Bvt. Brig-Gen. Persifor F. Smith
Lt. William Steele
Capt. Edward J. Steptoe
Lt. Charles P. Stone
Lt. James Stuart
Lt. George Sykes
Lt. Francis J. Thomas
Capt. Philip R. Thompson
Lt. Herman Thorn
Lt. James Tilton
Capt. John B.S. Todd
Lt. Zealous B. Tower
Surgeon Charles Tripler
Major William Turnbull
Brig-Gen. David E. Twiggs
Major Abraham Van Buren
Lt. Earl Van Dorn
Major Richard D.A. Wade
Lt. Cadmus M. Wilcox
Lt. John D. Wilkins
Col. John S. Williams
Lt. Thomas Williams
Colonel Jonas M. Withers
Capt. George W.F. Wood
Lt. Lafayette B. Wood
Lt. Frank Woodbridge
Major Samuel Woods
Bvt. Maj-Gen. William J. Worth

SEEING THE ELEPHANT: THE ART OF WAR IN MEXICO

"I came to Mexico to see the 'Elephant.' I have seen him..."
American soldier after the Battle of Buena Vista

The phrase "Seeing the Elephant" was a popular expression in use in America during the war with Mexico. It referred to a soldiers' actual experience of being in a battle and finding out what it was really like. The patriotic, flag waving, jingoist recruiting posters spoke only of duty, honor and the glory to be gained by anyone who went off to the war. The disappointment felt by the soldier and the dashing of any raised expectations of what war really was all about was the meaning of the phrase that one had "seen the elephant". The term came to refer to more than just the frightening knowledge of what conditions were like on the field of battle. The volunteers who joined up to go to Mexico expecting it be a lark or an enjoyable experience quickly discovered that war involved a great deal of boredom, sickness, fatigue, privations, and suffering. They too were said to have "seen the elephant", due to the demoralizing and sometimes deadly circumstances they often endured. Once most of them had experienced it, it was usually enough to dampen their enthusiasm about ever seeing it again. It is impossible to know what it was really like to have participated in a battle during that war, but the many firsthand accounts have left us enough information to get at least some inkling of what these soldiers went through.

The manner in which war was conducted in the 1840's was quite different from the contemporary conflicts that the modern reader is used to seeing on television, very often as they are occuring. The American and the Mexican armies were both organized, trained and led into battle with the same drill manuals that Napoleon had used for the French army more than thirty years before. The battlefield and the surrounding area served as a chessboard on which the generals attempted to outmaneuver their enemy. Scouts and spies roamed the countryside gathering information about the enemy and served as the eyes and ears of the commanders. Each army included infantry, artillery and cavalry, always in different proportions and often of varying quality from battle to battle. The weapons employed were similar, if not identical, as those that had been used

by the French Emperor and his enemies. The armies themselves were ponderous to move, either on or off the battlefield, as they were often encumbered by enormous supply trains. The columns of wagons and draft animals had to carry food and ammunition for the army and even more food for the draft animals themselves. A campaign that lacked for the proper logistical planning could drag on for weeks or even months and eventually might grind to a halt. A successful campaign would be one that would allow the army to engage the enemy in a decisive battle, hopefully on favorable terms, in order to inflict a resounding defeat on him and encourage him to sue for peace. Napoleon and his military machine were able to accomplish this feat time and time again. In Mexico, winning a decisive victory that would end the war would prove to be a very difficult task for either side to achieve. The best generalship, American or Mexican, found it almost impossible to overcome the myriad of obstacles on the path to ultimate victory. The similarities to their Napoleonic counterparts did not extend too far beyond the weapons and drill books in either army. The American and Mexican armies, despite being based on the French model, each had their own characteristics that made them very different from the armies of Europe.

The American army was an all volunteer force with a large percentage of immigrants, some of whom had previously served in the armies of Europe. Many of the regulars had been in service on the western frontier and were already used to the hardships and routine of life in the field. They formed the hard core of the army and set an excellent example for the volunteers to follow when it came to steadiness under fire and experience at being on campaign. The enthusiasm of the volunteers did not last very long when exposed to the rigors of campaigning in the field for months at a time. They found it difficult to adjust to camp life and paid a heavy toll in lives lost to carelessness and neglect that resulted in unsanitary conditions, among other things. One thing that the regulars and volunteers had in common was that few had ever taken part in any battles on the scale that would occur south of the border. Campaigns against the Seminoles in Florida, and other Indians on the plains could not compare with the size and scope of a war with

Mexico. The mustering of the U.S. Army for the campaign in Mexico was the first time that many of the men in the regular regiments of the army, not to mention the volunteers, had served together as complete units. It was also the largest gathering of United States military might since the War of 1812.

Only a few of the American officers had any actual experience at conducting the Napoleonic style of warfare that they had been schooled in. The lessons learned at the military academy at West Point would be put to the test by the junior officers, eager to see action. Many of the older field officers, such as Zachary Taylor among others, tried to use experience gained from leading isolated companies at far flung outposts and years of frontier soldiering to command brigades, divisions and even armies in the field. Meanwhile, at the top of the chain of command, General Winfield Scott, who had literally written the book on tactics for the American army, would have a chance to prove himself and his army on the field of battle.

The Mexican army had many veterans in its ranks at the opening of hostilities with the United States. Frequent political unrest continually tested the loyalty of the troops as well as their ability to campaign against their fellow countrymen. The common soldier was from the uneducated lower class and served in the ranks mainly because he had no other choice. Most were drafted legally or, when necessary, impressed into service. Very few were volunteers. There was very little time spent on training and only the basics were taught. The rigors of campaigning were learned while on the march or on the battlefield itself. The types of actions fought against other Mexicans were nothing like what they would face fighting the Americans. Battles were fought mostly at long ranges until one side or the other gained the upper hand. Normally very little blood was shed in the actions.

The Mexican officer corps represented mostly the politically ambitious rather than the militarily proficient. The majority were concerned with advancing their own careers and hardly cared about the welfare of their men. In theory, they had been schooled in Napoleon's art of war to the same degree as their American counterparts and with the same basic drill manuals. In practice, the rampant corruption in the army allowed the deal makers and hangers on to advance while forcing out many of the men with true military abilities. Mexican officers, including those at the highest level, were totally unprepared to wage the type of war that would be necessary to defeat the American invaders.

The Mexican-American war was fought with armies and tactics modelled on Napoleon's French army of thirty to forty years before. Any comparisons with Napoleonic warfare must account for the fact that there were very few similarities that could be drawn between fighting a campaign in Mexico as opposed to those fought by the French Emperor in Europe. Napoleon had routinely made the destruction of the opposing army the primary objective of his campaigns. Once this was accomplished the victorious French army would usually be able to march on the enemy capital before a new army could be raised to protect it. His opponents were usually forced to sue for peace rather than cause the continued existence of their government to be threatened.

The American objective at the beginning of the war was to capture territory in the form of the northernmost Mexican states to demonstrate to the leadership in Mexico city how vulnerable their country was to invasion. It was hoped that this strategy, to be carried out by General Taylor, would force a peaceful settlement on terms that were favorable to the United States. The failure of this plan to bring the war to a speedy conclusion led the Americans to change their goals and redirect their efforts. General Scott decided that the only way to end the war was to occupy the capital city and prove to the people of Mexico that suing for peace was their only option. Mexico fought mainly a defensive war with the objective of inflicting enough damage on the American army in battle to make it too costly for them to continue the war.

Mexico is a country of vast distances and varied terrain that presented many unique problems for the armies of the time. The extreme terrain that was sometimes fought over rendered much of the armies' drillbook training and military theory useless. There were not many battlefields in Mexico where the armies could be deployed along the Napoleonic model seen in Europe. Much of the country was only sparsely populated with limited access along poor roads. Once American objectives had been decided upon there were usually not many choices for the routes of march that must be taken. There were virtually no maps available for most of Mexico. The maps that the Americans could come by were not detailed enough to be useful in planning most military operations. The best maps of Mexico and the battlefields that were fought over were made by the American engineers either during or after the fighting. The American army was forced to travel by the most well known roads and landmarks so that valuable time would not be lost during needless detours. The limited options available, combined with their own scouting reports along the way, left no doubts among the Mexicans as to the current location and ultimate destination of the American army. Most of the time the only decision that had to be made by the Mexican leaders was where to give battle along the way. Despite this disadvantage the Americans, through extensive use of their engineers, still managed to outmanuever their opponents on several occasions. General Scott made every attempt to avoid a frontal assault on enemy positions if there were other alternatives available. The battles of Cerro Gordo and Contreras had both been preceeded by extensive American reconnaissance. In both cases the Americans advanced over terrain that the Mexicans had assumed was impassable to launch an attack onto the flank or rear of their positions. This "turning movement" was exactly the type of maneuver that Napoleon had used many times, with great results. The Mexicans were forced to fight these battles at a great disadvantage because they found themselves being attacked from an unexpected direction that also threatened their lines of communication and therefore escape. In these instances and others the American officers proved that they were much better at applying their studies of Napoleonic warfare than were their Mexican counterparts.

Once the battlefield had been determined and the armies had drawn together the resulting clash of arms resulted in a spectacle that would never be forgotten by those who had seen it. The soldiers of both sides began their preparations very early on the day when a battle was to be fought. Those who were able to have slept at all would be roused well before dawn to get ready. Fatigue would be a common factor among all of the men present. Quite often the days preceeding the battle would have been ones of hard marching with the men carrying their weapons and full packs. The grueling march to Buena Vista from San Luis Potosi may have cost Santa Anna the loss of almost a quarter of his manpower to straggling, exhaustion, exposure, disease and death before the

battlefield was reached. Troops in defensive positions were not exempt from fatigue either. The earthworks required for protection had to be dug by the men, often operating in continuous shifts to finish the work as rapidly as possible. The men usually slept out in the open when on the march and the damp and cold could deprive soldiers of sleep or contribute to their ill health. Veterans and volunteers, both Mexican and American, would most likely all be going into battle tired.

Uniforms were spruced up to provide an appearance that was as impressive as possible. New articles of clothing that had been saved for this occasion were brought out and put to use. A unit that presented a striking appearance could benefit by the confidence that this instilled in the men, who often translated image into a measure of ability. The Mexican army that fought at Buena Vista had been issued new uniforms shortly before the battle. The Mexican uniforms were formal in style and the regiments presented a very colorful spectacle when they were drawn up in full battle regalia. The positive benefit to the morale of the troops was also supposed to be augmented by the demoralizing effect that it might have on the enemy when faced by such an impressive array. The American fatigue uniform was designed to be much more practical in the field and was nowhere near as elaborate as a full dress uniform. General Taylor's troops generally presented a very professional, if workmanlike, appearance when in the field, and even the volunteers drew uniforms and equipment off of government supplies. The uniforms of the Americans under General Scott suffered much more during the course of the campaign because they

Nebel, who was an eyewitness, in his picture of the Battle of Churubusco depicted the U.S. Army to be better equipped and more uniform in appearance than some sources suggest.

123

were completely cut off from their base of supply.

Weapons also had to be repaired, cleaned, checked, and double checked to make sure that they would work properly when the time came. The smoothbore flintlock musket was the primary armament carried by the infantry of both sides and it was a fairly reliable weapon when properly cared for. Although maximum range was longer, the musket was most effective at ranges under 100 yards. This made it imperative that the infantry get as close as possible to the enemy to successfully engage them. Some special troops were armed with rifles, which had greater range and accuracy, but most firing was still done at close ranges. The ultimate close range infantry weapon which would decide the outcome of many actions was the bayonet. American officers put a great deal of faith in the bayonet charge to drive the enemy out of strongly held positions. The troops were ordered not to fire at all during the charge as the momentum of the advance would be halted while soldiers discharged their weapons. It was also very difficult to reload the musket with the bayonet attached and avoid injury. The American soldier did not hesitate to close into hand-to-hand combat to decide the issue with cold steel. They did so with efficiency and confidence. The Mexican soldier was not nearly as accustomed to delivering or receiving bayonet charges and rarely stood up to them in battle. Most of the combat experienced by Mexican soldiers before the war did not require them to expose themselves to such mortal danger at such close range.

The cavalry also used close range weapons for combat. Swords and sabres were used by both sides and were kept sharpened for action. The Mexican cavalry also counted the dreaded lance in its arsenal and they were trained to use it to deadly effect. Some American cavalry may have had the newest colt revolvers instead of the flintlock pistols that were common. The main advantage that the cavalry had was its mobility on the battlefield and the shock value that a cavalry charge had against an enemy. The Mexican horses were generally smaller than those used by the Americans, but they were hardy and well suited to the terrain that was being fought over. The U.S. Dragoons and other cavalry were never numerous enough to be used much in the traditional cavalry role and they played only a small part in most of the battles fought.

The artillery was potentially the deadliest branch of each army. The American guns and doctrine were virtually brand new, and unproven in the eyes of many, including General Taylor. Until this time artillery had been static on the battlefield, operating from where it was initially placed and rarely being moved during the actual battle. Major Ringgold and his "flying artillery" changed all of that. The light American guns were designed to be moved quickly into position and then relocated as the need arose.

The gunners themselves were highly trained in these new methods and were proficient at executing every order from their commander, who had instilled an excellent espirit de corps among the men. Artillery was a long range weapon at this time, but restrictions caused by the terrain and the positions of friendly troops often negated this asset. Most artillery in Mexico rarely engaged beyond 1000 yards range. The Americans were adept at bringing their guns even closer for a much more deadly effect.

The Mexicans artillerists were also very well trained and had some of the highest morale in their army. They were severely handicapped in their duties by being forced to use antiquated weapons firing with inferior ammunition and powder. Many of the guns dated back to the days when the Spaniards had ruled, while many fortress and siege guns were totally useless as there was no ammunition available for them. When it came to the question of mobility, the answer was simple-there was none. The Mexican army employed civilian drivers who provided their own means of transporting the guns and equipment. The heavy field pieces were dragged into place by mules, oxen, and manpower and rarely if ever moved until after the battle. The drivers would often retire with their teams to the rear areas to await the outcome of the fighting. The civilians did not want to get anywhere near where the action was hottest and so the Mexican guns could not normally be moved once a battle was underway.

On the day of the battle, the soldiers would eat a quick breakfast, if one was available, and then would assemble in ranks to form their companies and battalions. If defensive positions were being occupied the men holding them would have the advantage of not having to march anywhere before the battle began. They may have also had more of a chance to sleep and eat if they were not actively working on their own defenses. Sometimes the attacking troops moved to their starting positions while it was still dark. At other times getting the army organized could take most of the morning. The officers would know what positions their troops were to occupy and what the objectives would be for the battle to be fought that day. Moving the units to their starting points could often be difficult and very time consuming. The men would march in columns on the road or over open terrain, sometimes stretching out for miles towards the rear of the battlefield. Inadequate scouting reports, inaccurate maps and inhospitable terrain could all cause confusion and delay. A coordinated plan involving several different columns of troops converging on a common objective or set to attack in unison from different quarters required a lot of planning and a good deal of luck to be successful.

The artillery would normally open the battle with

an intense bombardment of the enemy positions. The guns would be trying to destroy fortifications or defensive positions containing enemy guns or soldiers. In an open field engagement they would bombard formations of troops in an attempt to disrupt them before they could engage. The range was usually less than a thousand yards and the artillery on both sides was almost always well served to deadly effect.

Infantry inside defensive works might not be affected much by artillery fire as long as they could take cover. The greatest damage would be done to the positions themselves or to exposed guns and crews that would be trying to return fire. The Mexican bombardment of Fort Texas (later Fort Brown), which was admittedly of a desultory nature, lasted for almost an entire week. During this time there were at least twenty guns firing at the fort, although none were heavy enough to destroy the works. The total American casualties were nine men wounded and two killed, one of which was the commanding officer, Major Jacob Brown.

Infantry formations in the open were usually expected to stand and take whatever punishment the guns could inflict until they were ordered to do otherwise. The Mexican infantry at Palo Alto stood in perfect ranks while the American "flying artillery" rained death and destruction on them. Their leaders finally demanded that they be sent into action before they were completely broken. It was at this battle that the Mexican regulars earned the well deserved respect of the American infantry veterans.

The Mexican artillery was rarely moved, once emplaced. Its position would remain fixed throughout most battles. This fact forced the Mexicans to use their artillery mainly as a defensive weapon, preferably set up in defensive works. The defenses of Matamoros, Monterrey, Vera Cruz, and Mexico City were all reliant on Mexican artillery in emplacements commanding the approaches. The Mexican position at Cerro Gordo was also set up to take advantage of dug in guns on the heights. The highly mobile American artillery was able to move to support an attack by the infantry, as they did during the battle for Mexico City, or re-deploy to add to the defense of a threatened sector, as at Buena Vista. Ammunition shortage was also a problem that plagued mostly the Mexicans if the engagement lasted for any length of time, or was particularly intense, as at Palo Alto. The Americans usually had adequate ammunition on hand as well as a way to move it up to the guns. The Mexicans were deficient on both counts.

The artillery bombardment "phase" of a battle could last anywhere from a few minutes to several days. Once the action got underway and the infantry closed into combat the artillery would have to cease fire for fear of hitting their own men. The opening fusillade from the guns on both sides would alert the troops that it was only a matter of time until the armies would clash. The smoke emitted from the guns would creep across the field and begin to obscure parts of it from view, while the intense noise would make it hard to hear shouted commands. The confusion that was a large part of every battle would start this way. Whether the troops were standing up as best they could under long range enemy fire or marching to get into position, the sound of the guns was the signal that the battle was beginning in earnest.

The Napoleonic style armies that fought in Mexico would place most of their hopes for victory on an effective combination of different types of troops. Ideally artillery, cavalry, and infantry would be able to work together in both attack and defense to defeat the enemy. This "combined arms" army and the theory behind its proper use were at the heart of Napoleonic warfare. All three branches had their own strengths and weaknesses when operating independently, but when correctly employed in combination, a general could greatly increase his chance of success on the battlefield.

It is the infantry that must take and hold a position against the onslaught of the enemy to deny him its use. Likewise it was the infantry that would be able to take and then occupy the ground necessary to win the battle. In theory, on the perfect battlefield (which never existed in Mexico), the infantry would be drawn up for battle facing the enemy at a distance of about a thousand yards. The regiments would march into position in columns, sometimes only four men abreast, which were easier to manage on the march and much better suited to more rapid movements. The column could also be used to attack with, especially if a position was to be taken with the bayonet and no fire was to be issued by the troops. With its small frontage the column was not suited to engage enemy battalions in line in a firefight as not many muskets could be brought into action, the ranks behind the first two being unable to fire. The column was also more vulnerable to enemy fire, especially artillery, as it presented a denser target with a high concentration of men in a small area. When threatened with enemy action or as they were about to engage, the columns would change formation and re-deploy as quickly as possible. The distance to the enemy could be three hundred yards or less at this point. This was where the endless drill on the parade ground was supposed to pay off.

Once they were in the proper position the columns would deploy into line formations of two ranks deep, both to be able to cover more ground and bring more muskets to bear on the enemy. Due to the inaccuracy of the small arms weaponry being used, it was only massed firepower at close range that could inflict the kind of damage necessary to shatter an opposing force. Hopefully the enemy battalions had suffered at the hands of friendly artillery fire and would already be weakened. In any case, infantry firefights were usually not prolonged affairs. At ranges that were often fifty yards or less, the men fired in unison and reloaded as quickly as possible to be able to fire again before the enemy could do likewise. Men would fall with every shot and others would step up to take their place or move over to fill in any gaps that might be formed by their loss. The Americans generally inflicted far greater destruction than the Mexicans in these deadly exchanges. Inferior gunpowder and outdated weapons, along with a tendency to aim high, if at all, doomed the Mexican soldier to defeat in a standup fight with an equal number of Americans. Poorly trained Mexican conscripts were also not able to fire as fast, but even when the volume of fire was very high the percentage of American casualties that it caused should have been much greater. These volleys of musket fire on both sides would generate great clouds of smoke and a tremendous amount of noise that would serve to isolate the soldier from the rest of the battlefield. Events taking place only a short distance away might be totally obscured to the combatants that were so fiercely engaged. This was where the mettle of the troops on both sides was severely tested. This was also when the state of mind of the troops engaged was most important.

The sight of friends being killed in close proximity or the loss of officers along with their leadership abilities might be enough to cause the men in the ranks to have doubts about the outcome of any further fighting they were about to engage in. Observing the enemy and whether or not he appeared to be affected by the results of the fighting could also be an important factor to consider. How tired, hungry or thirsty the men were could all enter into the equation that would determine how long they would stand up to the extreme punishment they were being subjected to. These and other imponderable factors comprised the morale of the men on both sides of the conflict. Soldiers who had experienced battle at close range before would be somewhat prepared for what they were about to go into, although that did not always make it easier. Veterans were less prone to overreact or panic in a given situation, realizing a minor problem or bit of bad luck for what it was and not being overly shaken up by adverse events. Troops that were untried in battle might not prove strong enough as a unit to withstand the pressure being put on them. This is why the U.S. Volunteers or the Mexican National Guard units could be so brittle in a fight and break with the least provocation. Conversely, there were also times when inexperienced troops acquitted themselves surprisingly well under terrible circumstances that would have been expected to destroy their morale. This was a phenomenon that would be seen once again in the American Civil War. It sometimes happened that "green" troops tolerated a bad situation and made the best of it simply because they hadn't the experience to know how bad things really were. They continued to function under the belief that whatever was happening to them must be what was to be expected in combat.

The culmination of the infantry firefight was supposed to be an attack with the bayonet to finish off an enemy who should already be weakened and wavering. Events rarely happened this way on the battlefield. Usually the soldiers on one side or the other would decide to call it quits and retreat at full speed away from the firefight. Often this might be triggered by additional forces coming up to join in the battle for the other side. It was also possible that enough officers became casualties and the men lacked the leadership by example that was necessary to keep them at the point of danger. Withdrawal in the face of the enemy was a very risky undertaking and it was usually successful only when friendly troops were close at hand to lend support. If the enemy was ready and willing to follow up their advantage at this vulnerable moment the retreat could become a rout. Later studies would prove that more casualties were suffered by retreating and routing forces than at any other time during a battle. In any case, it was rare for bayonets to be used in combat, especially in open field battles. The most common occurence of soldiers fighting with the bayonet are during an assault on an enemy held defensive position. The defenders may feel secure enough to hold on until their position has been breached at which time it is too late to retreat out of range of hand-to-hand combat with bayonets, knives and even fists. Usually it was an American bayonet charge being used to assault defensive works or fortifications. Time and again in Mexico the Americans showed a willingness to close into this type of deadly melee that the Mexicans were reluctant to emulate. The Mexican soldier came to fear the Americans because of their seeming disdain for death as they continued advancing through hostile fire to be able to cross bayonets with their adversaries. The bayonet attack was a major threat in any advance into close range, and because of that it became a great psychological weapon that preyed upon the morale and steadiness of the troops being faced by the prospect. In this way the bayonet was an effective offensive weapon even if it was not the cause of many casualties in most battles. Bayonets were also used defensively by the infantry of both sides when confronting cavalry.

The cavalry had many duties but was primarily the mobile striking force of a Napoleonic style army. European armies at this time had many different types of cavalry. The "heavy" cavalry were the cuirassier, carabinier, and dragoons which supposedly rode heavier horses and carried heavier equipment, including some armor. The "light" cavalry were the light dragoons, hussars, and lancers which were more lightly equipped for tasks requiring rapid movement. There were really no such designations existant in either the American or Mexican armies at the time. The American cavalry was universally labelled dragoons more for the fact that they were trained to fight mounted or dismounted which was a defining factor of the early dragoon regiments from the days of the Revolution. They were mounted on heavier horses than their Mexican counterparts but they would not have compared well to Napoleon's heavy dragoons which were trained as heavy "battle" cavalry for shock action. The Mexican cavalry included a regiment of cuirassiers which were troopers wearing protective helmets and breast plates. However, they were mounted on the same small horses that the rest of the Mexican cavalry used and they also would not have measured up to the French standards for "battle" cavalry. There were also Mexican hussars but this was more of an honorary title than a job description for them. The Mexicans also equipped a great deal of their cavalry with lances, which again, was more of a preferred weapon than a troop type designation as far as the units were concerned. The end result was that the cavalry on both sides was not as specialized as it was under Napoleon and any unit could be called upon to perform any task.

The cavalry was supposed to perform several different missions during the campaign, before a battle was to be fought. Patrols were responsible for scouting out the enemy positions and keeping track of his movements. The mounted arm also provided couriers to carry important communications back and forth between commands. The cavalry was also charged with the task of patrolling around the army to prevent ambushes, raids and surprise attacks, especially on the baggage train. There would often be encounters with groups of enemy cavalry trying to perform the same missions and countless small skirmishes resulted. In short, the cavalry acted as the eyes and ears of the army which was a essential to the success of the camapign.

On the battlefield the cavalry took on new responsibilities. The security of the army was even more important now, with the enemy in close proximity. Cavalry was usually assigned to protect the flanks and rear of the infantry and artillery formations as well as the baggage train, which was most vulnerable to raiding by enemy cavalry. The Americans rarely had enough cavalry available to ever be able to do much more than this. The proper mission for cavalry was, ideally, to eliminate or neutralize the opposing cavalry and then launch attacks on the enemy's infantry and artillery using mobility to take them in their flanks and rear, thus threatening their lines of communication and retreat. The Mexican cavalry, which was often numerous enough on the field, rarely if ever achieved much success in these areas.

The weapons of the cavalry were swords and pistols or sabres and lances with some short range carbines or small muskets for good measure. This meant that they had to actually come into contact with the enemy to be effective. Cavalry versus other cavalry, except on a very small scale, was a rare occurence in Mexico. The American cavalry often fought dismounted when attacked by cavalry. The Mexicans were also trained to fight on foot if necessary but this was rarely done. Cavalry engagements usually only occured when one side was ambushed or not prepared for a charge, as at Buena Vista when the Arkansas and Kentucky cavalry were attacked. These affairs tended to be short and not really very bloody. The horses would not crash at full speed into the enemy horsemen, as might be imagined from romantic paintings or movies depicting charging cavalry. In most cases the two units would open ranks enough to allow for a free passage through one another with the horsemen making their best thrusts and parries with sabre and lance as they passed to inflict damage on their foes. Once the regiments had broken through or away from the enemy the main task of the officers was to regroup to be able to bring the unit back into action. On more than one occasion Mexican cavalry charged and then left the scene in pursuit of fleeing foes or in search of loot or safer havens than the current battlefield.

Cavalry could successfully attack artillery positions if they were careful to time their approach so as to take the least amount of fire on the way in. The artillerists had no choice but to abandon their guns and seek cover or stand and die defending them. Most chose to run away and wait for an opportunity to return to the guns because even though a cavalry charge might overrun the position, it could not be held by the mounted troops alone. The Americans learned this at Resaca de la Palma when Mays' Dragoons repeatedly took the Mexican artillery battery, only to lose it again when they were forced to withdraw under pressure. Only when Taylor order the infantry forward the position taken and held. The key to success was always to support the mounted arm with infantry or artillery to follow up the advance.

When cavalry charged infantry the results could be much deadlier if the foot soldiers were not well prepared. The standard tactic was for the infantry to form a square to resist the mounted attack. In this way there would no longer be a vulnerable flank or rear to be attacked and a solid wall of bayonets facing outwards would be presented. This would stop the cavalry from charging home, for a horse, no matter how well trained, will refuse to impale itself on a sharp object if it can avoid doing so. The cavalry charge would be met by a volley of musketry from the side of the square facing the attack and then be forced to veer off to the side of the square. The American infantry at Palo Alto used this formation effectively to neutralize the Mexican cavalry attacks.

The ability of cavalry to force enemy infantry into square was the main role of the cavalry in the combined arms attack that a Napoleonic battle was supposed to utilize. Once the infantry was in this more vulnerable formation friendly infantry and especially artillery could bring the square under fire and wreak havoc with the densely packed soldiers. When the square was sufficiently weakened the infantry or cavalry, or both, could attack with a much greater chance of success and hopefully destroy the enemy units' fighting ability. This combined arms attack was the ideal situation to be employed given the troop types available for the battlefield commander. The war in Mexico does not have a single example of this occuring in any of the battles fought.

The typical battle in Mexico, if there ever really was one, did not usually last very long. The preparation period before a battle could last days or even weeks with supplies being moved, earthworks being dug and scouting missions to be undertaken. Most of the time the troops were just waiting for something to happen. When a battle was joined the action could last from a few minutes to several days. During this time the soldiers would be under tremendous pressure to perform well and follow the example set by their officers. The imminent danger of being killed or wounded in battle loomed over them all and heightened their senses and feelings about what they were being put through. This rush of emotion and adrenaline was something that most soldiers would never forget. It contrasted so greatly with the way most of their time was spent, in routine duties, that it left an indelible impression that they tried to describe to the folks at home. The bloody battlefield and the loss of friends that was the common aftermath of a battle also added to these feelings that they had been through something momentous. In time many of the painful memories would fade and it would be the exhiliration and spectacle of battle that would remain to be told and retold to anyone who would listen. This same generation of American soldiers would mostly be officers when they were put to the test once again in fifteen short years. Without giving much thought to the experience in Mexico the nation divided into North and South and once more went in search of the "elephant".

The Filson Club in Louisville, Kentucky has a reproduction of the Regimental Flag of the 4th U.S. Infantry, Grant's regiment. (The Filson Club Historical Society)

128

THE MEXICAN ARMY

In 1845 Minister of War Pedro Garcia Conde replaced the twenty two existing commandancies-general that had military jurisdiction throughout the country. His sweeping reorganization was the first in almost twenty years. There would ultimately be five territorial divisions and four commandancies-general to cover all of Mexico's states and territories. The commandancies-general were formed in areas where the population were virtually at war with the central government. In fact Mexican troops were trying to reassert government control in an all but independent Yucatan.

The Mexican army of 1846 was highly regarded by most contemporary observers, even though it had never been tested in battle against a foreign army. Many Mexicans and Europeans thought that Mexico would win a war against the United States. Closer scrutiny revealed many weaknesses in the system that were not readily apparent to outsiders. Decades of insurrections and revolutions had given the army combat experience fighting peasants, guerillas, Indians and among itself. The Mexican soldier had often fought his fellow conscripts in some uprising against the current government. Often, skirmishes in the capital had left the streets strewn with the corpses of the common soldiers while battalions from the outlying provinces arrived to support or oppose the loyal garrison. American minister Waddy

---

THE MILITARY REORGANIZATION OF 1845
The Territorial Divisions:
  1st Division: Mexico, Michoacan & Queretaro
  2nd Division: Oaxaca, Puebla, Tabasco & Vera Cruz
  3rd Division: Aguascalientes, Guanajuato, Jalisco, San Luis Potosi & Zacatecas
  4th Division: Coahuila y Texas, Nuevo Leon & Tamaulipas
  5th Division: Chihuahua, Durango & New Mexico (still a territory)
The Commandancies-general:
  Sinaloa & Sonora
  Alta & Baja California
  Yucatan
  Chiapas
* This small state was combined with Zacatecas later in 1845. (Note: Colima and Tlascala had not had their territorial status approved).

Thompson was very critical of the Mexican army and said that they "…may do well to fight each other, but in any conflict with our own or European troops, it would not be a battle but a massacre." Other observers had noted that the most impressive parts of most Mexican regiments were their military bands, which were quite good. The Mexican army had been reorganized in March of 1839 to consist of six divisions of two to four brigades with each one having two to four regiments, usually of mixed foot and mounted units. There were twelve regular line infantry regiments, three (later four) regular light infantry regiments, three foot artillery brigades, five foot artillery companies and one mounted artillery brigade along with a sapper battalion and eight regular cavalry and dragoon regiments as well as one additional squadron. There were also numerous formations of active militia, national guard and special units of varying size. The Chief of Staff of the Army had direct control of the Regular Army and the Active Militia, both infantry and cavalry. There was a separate Director of the Corps of Artillery and a Director of the Engineers. The National Guard units were under the control of their respective Mexican States. The Medical Corps and local General Staff detachments known as the Commandancies of Fortified Places (responsible for administrative duties in major forts, seaports and garrison towns) were also under the control of the Chief of Staff of the Army. The infantry was impressive in appearance while the artillery was numerous with well trained crews and the riding skills of the cavalry were unsurpassed. However, this colorful and varied force was to reveal its many weaknesses when finally put to the test.

A major problem for the Mexican Army since independence from Spain in 1821 was the weak leadership exhibited by its highest ranking officers. The primary leaders and organizers of the army were former Spanish and foreign born officers, many of whom had risen from the ranks dating back from before independence had been won. The majority of the officer corps was of pure caucasian blood from the Mexican ruling class and aristocracy called *gachupines* for those born in Spain and *criollos* for those born in Mexico. There were many generals and senior officers that were political and social appointees. The army suffered from a surplus of officers with as many as one hundred and sixty generals for an army of thirty thousand men, or about one general for every two hundred men or less. The Mexican War Office itself had criticized the number of awards of rank and decorations going to "...a multitude that does not know how to lead...." While every one of these "Excellencies," as they wished to be called, could issue glowing proclamations of intent to change allegiance during the latest political uprising, it was doubtful if any could actually handle a division or brigade in action. The number of colonels competent enough to lead a regiment were few and far between, with some not even qualified to lead a patrol. A typical battle was comparable to a mob fight ending with a cavalry charge. Observers on the spot claimed that maneuvers in the face of the enemy were never attempted. A self-respecting general would think it almost disgraceful to obey orders, especially while political trickery and scheming could be far more rewarding. Many men of real talent and honor had been driven from the service by the advancement of corrupt officers that had supported the winning side in the latest revolution. A strong and able junior officer was less valued than one who knew how best to serve the political ambitions of his superiors. On the eve of the war in April of 1846, a British diplomat described the Mexican officer corps as:

"...the worst perhaps to be found in any part of the world ... ignorant, incapable and insubordinate ... and their personal courage, I fear, is of a very negative character."

INFANTRY

The performance of the Mexican Army in battle depended a great deal upon the quality of its privates and non-commissioned officers. The Mexican manpower pool was not of itself bad material for an army. The population of roughly seven million may have had as many as four million Indians with another two million inhabitants of mixed white and Indian blood known as *mestizos*. These two groups formed the lower classes that made up the bulk of the army through conscription. Volunteers were virtually non-existent due to the hardships of soldiering that had to be endured. The draft law of January 26, 1839 stipulated that each department must contribute its quota to the army. Lots were drawn on the last Sunday of each October and the names posted in public for eight days. Citizens who were drafted in this manner could hire substitutes, but if the substitute deserted then the original draftee had to report for service or be judged as a deserter. The term of service began on the following December 15th and lasted for six years. Men from 18 to 40 years old who were single, childless widowers, married men not living with their wives or childless married men were all subject to the draft. There were many legitimate exemptions including

previous veterans, priests, college students, teachers, doctors, attorneys, elected officials and men engaged to be married. Anyone with money could avoid the draft, and very few men with education or from the upper classes served in the ranks. This system was not sufficient to meet the needs of the army, however, and more drastic measures were commonly used to fill the ranks. Press gangs were used to seize recruits by force from among the vagrants, petty criminals, poor Indians and laborers of the lower classes. After being rounded up they were marched in as prisoners in chains or roped in pairs, scantily clothed and barely fed.

Overall the conscripts could and did make good soldiers despite some serious shortcomings. The physical health of such draftees was not always very good, with diseases such as rickets and the "spotted itch" being reported. The height of the average soldier was below medium stature. Service papers from the time list men of five feet two and one-quarter inches, or five feet and one-half inch being common, with sixty Mexican inches being the minimum acceptable height. The pay scale established in 1839 was also small in stature for the average conscript. Monthly pay rates varied from 14 pesos for a drummer, 15 pesos for a private, on up to 26 pesos for a first sergeant in a grenadier company. Meanwhile a General of Division was being paid at the rate of 500 pesos per month in the field or more than 300 pesos while in garrison with extra rations and bonus pay for active command assignments. Wages were issued through the regimental officers and were frequently subject to embezzlement, as was the commissary. Soldiers were known to sell their weapons and accoutrements or work on the side to be able to afford adequate rations. It was said that, "If the Mexican soldier has something to eat, he eats it; if not, he goes without. That is all." Under such conditions desertion was often rampant with units on the march losing up to half of their combat strength before going into battle. Military discipline had to be severe. Soldiers could be put on rations of bread and water for lesser offenses or they could be shot outright for severe transgressions. Often their terms of enlistment were extended to an additional six or even ten years in the service. In the case of repeat offenders or sometimes with serious offenses the punishment was to be sent to serve in the hot coastal regions of the country where the extremely high incidence of disease was often equivalent to a death sentence.

Despite all of the problems that resulted from the miserable conditions of army life, the Mexican soldier managed to endure. The regular units of the army included many veteran troops that usually acquitted themselves well in battle. The conscripted Indians that composed most of the rank and file were uneducated and generally not well trained, but they managed to survive throughout unbelievable hardships and still fight bravely. Time and again Mexican armies were called on to make incredibly long and fast marches into battle, often without adequate food and water. With their strength already squandered through fatigue and hunger they still had the courage to face danger without fear and die on the field of battle. A phenomenon that would become more familiar during the American Civil War and even to some extent during more modern conflicts may also have influenced the Mexican conscripts. Raw recruits going into battle for the first time, not knowing what to expect, may sometimes tolerate terrible conditions in action better than veteran troops simply because they are unaware of what is really supposed to be happening. Mexican recruits, often ignorant of their plight on the battlefield, accepted their lot stoically and fought with a stubborn bravery. The Mexican soldier had little respect for his officers or loyalty to his government, neither of which had much stability. The soldiers' family or local village was where his allegiance was rooted and this is where he deserted to when defeated or despondent after losing confidence in a system that was foreign to him. When well led (which was rare) the Mexican soldier could be magnificent, especially in well prepared defensive positions. Morale was generally good but it was brittle and could crack easily and leave the soldiers prone to panic due to an unexpected turn of events or the loss of a key officer or position. Yet, even while depression and desertion took its toll, many veteran soldiers managed to keep their spirits up and hold out hopes for victory.

ORGANIZATION

The infantry regiment was the basic unit of the Mexican Army. In theory each regiment was led by a Colonel and included two battalions, one commanded by the Lieutenant Colonel of the regiment and the other by the Commandant. There is mention, during the hostilities in Texas in 1842, of both the first and second battalions of the same regiment being engaged. However, no evidence of two separate battalions of the same regiment is found in orders of battle during the war of 1846-1848. The fact that it had become common practice to break regiments into sections as small as companies for garrison duty in the cities and provinces may have obscured this organization. It is also possible that the second battalions were used as replacement cadres for their regiments and did not serve as independent units. Information on this subject is still very scarce.

The headquarters staff for an infantry regiment included a Colonel, Lieutenant Colonel, Commandant (equivalent to an Adjutant or Major), two Second Adjutants, two Lieutenants, two Ensign-Sub-Lieutenants, two Surgeons, two Chaplains, a Drum Major and a Bugle Corporal, two Pioneer Corporals with sixteen Pioneers (Sappers) and two

armorers. Each regiment also had a Second Sergeant as tailor and a Corporal blacksmith, mason and baker.

A battalion consisted of six fusilier companies, one rifle company and one grenadier company, although the distinctions between companies may not have been very pronounced in actual practice. Each company had eighty privates, a Captain, Lieutenant, two Sub-Lieutenants, one First Sergeant, four Second Sergeants, nine Corporals, a drummer, bugler and fifer in the fusilier companies, and four buglers in the rifle company. These figures represent the officially authorized strengths that were rarely achieved by units in the field. The practice of breaking units apart to serve in different areas along with the normal attrition from sickness and desertion meant that most battalions went into action at only a fraction of their paper strength.

On July 8, 1839 a law was enacted to reorganize existing infantry units into twelve regular regiments numbered consecutively by seniority and location. These regular formations were originally the product of an army reorganization of 1835 that had changed numbered units into battalions named after leaders from the War of Independence.

The First Line Infantry Regiment was formed with a first battalion from the Regular Morelos and a second battalion of the Active Militia of Guadalajara with its replacement cadre at Guanajuato.

The Second Line Infantry Regiment was formed from the Regular Hidalgo and a second battalion from Tres Villas with a replacement cadre at Vera Cruz.

The Third Line Infantry Regiment was formed from the Regular Allende and the Active Militia of Queretaro with a replacement cadre at Jalisco.

The Fourth Line Infantry Regiment was formed from the Regular Guerrero and the Active Militia of San Luis Potosi (a regiment that had been present at the siege of the Alamo in 1836) with a cadre at San Luis.

The Fifth Line Infantry Regiment was formed from the Regular Aldama (also present at the Alamo siege) and the Active Militia of Mexico with a cadre at Mexico. This regiment had been disbanded while in revolt and was reformed on the eve of war with the United States from the two battalions of the Active Militia of Celaya.

The Sixth Line Infantry Regiment was formed from the Regular Jimenez (also at the Alamo) and the Public Security Force Mexico with a cadre at Mexico.

The Seventh Line Infantry Regiment was formed from the Regular Matamoros (also at the Alamo) and the Active Militia of Puebla with a cadre at Puebla.

The Eighth Line Infantry Regiment was formed from the Regular Landero and the Yucatan Auxiliary with a cadre at Vera Cruz.

The Ninth Line Infantry Regiment was formed from the Regular Abasolo and the Active Militia of Chiapas with a cadre at Oaxaca-Chiapas.

The Tenth Line Infantry Regiment was formed from the Regular Galeana and the Active Militia of Yucatan with a cadre at Yucatan.

The Eleventh Line Infantry Regiment was formed from the Active Militia of Toluca (also present at the Alamo) and the Active Militia of Mextitlan with a cadre at Mexico-Queretaro.

The Twelfth Line Infantry Regiment was formed from the Active Militia of Tlaxcala and the Active Militia of Mexico with a cadre at Puebla-Tlaxcala.

The regular army also included four numbered regiments of Light Infantry organized along the same lines as the Line Infantry Regiments. The Fourth Light Infantry Regiment was formed on March 30, 1846 from the Third Line Infantry Regiment. The Third Line Infantry was subsequently reformed from the Active Militia Coast Guard Battalion of San Blas and was sometimes referred to as such during the war.

The largest unit organization in the army belonged to the Grenadier Guards of the Supreme Powers, an Active Militia battalion formed on December 7, 1841 in Mexico. The Guards had a paper strength of 1200 men with a minimum height requirement of five and one-half feet. Each company had a Captain, four Lieutenants, five Sergeants, twelve Corporals, two drummers, one bugler and the rest privates for a total of one hundred and fifty men per company. These men had been contributed by the departments of eight different states with half of the officers drawn from the regular army. The headquarters staff for the regiment had a Colonel, Lieutenant Colonel, three Adjutants, an armorer, surgeon, chaplain, drum major and bugle corporal.

There were also a variety of regional and reserve units that were used for garrisons and other miscellaneous duties. These included the Fijo de Mexico, (literally the Fixed Battalion of Mexico or Standing Battalion of Mexico also known as the Mexico Garrison Battalion) and the Fijo de California, (Fixed or Standing Battalion of the Californias). There was also a Battalion of Invalids of Mexico and a Battalion of Invalids of Puebla as well as Marine Infantry. There was an Active Commerce Regiment of Mexico with its officer corps being restricted to privileged men who were wealthy merchants or professionals. Preference was given to Sergeants who had proven good conduct and an education with men of property or a decent trade chosen first. The Regiment served without pay and its duties were limited to maintaining order and security for property or people in the area of the capital city.

The capital city of Mexico also had four militia battalions of its own raised in September of 1846 to protect the wealth and interests of citizens. They were Victoria, composed of merchants and professional men; Hidalgo, made up of clerks; Bravo and Independencia, both made up mainly of artisans. These four units, along with the Active Commerce Regiment were known by the people as the *polkos* or polka dancers, because of their colorful uniforms. Other cities and departments chose to raise their own National Guard regiments with organizations similar to the regular cadres that were located close to their areas.

The Active Militia had regiments named the First Mexico, Second Mexico, First Guanajuato, Second Guanajuato and Puebla that all presumably had the standard two battalions of eight companies each, although these may have been somewhat smaller than the regular regiments. The Active Militia also had individual named battalions from Aguascalientes, Chihuahua, Guadalajara, Lagos, Michoacan, Oaxaca, Queretaro, San Luis Potosi, Sinaloa, Sonora, Sur and Zacatecas. The Coast Guard Battalions were also part of the Active Militia and may have also been referred to as Garrison, Fixed or Standing Battalions. By 1835 there were a total of eight of these: one was located in Acapulco, Carmen Island, San Blas, Tampico, and two each in Tabasco and Bacalar. The elite companies of these battalions (the grenadiers and rifles) were called the Veteran Infantry Coast Guard Companies and were often detached from their parent unit. Sources list as many as fourteen battalions and eight companies of Coast Guard troops at the beginning of hostilities, but by 1847 there were only two Standing Companies remaining. The overall quality of these formations is questionable, although there are examples of them performing well in action. Generally these units were used for garrison duty and local defense. The Active Militia, even though serving and being paid by the central government, was probably not the equal of the regulars due to lack of experience in campaigning.

A presidential decree in June of 1847 created a Foreign Legion as part of the Mexican Army. There were to be two companies of infantry with the same organization as that of the regular army and uniforms that were the same as the Active Militia. They were know as the First and Second Militia Infantry Companies of San Patricio. Many deserters from the American army that had already been fighting as artillerists for Mexico were incorporated into this unit along with other various foreign residents in the country.

During the course of the conflict the Mexican army would also combine remnants of destroyed units into temporary battalions to be able to utilize all available manpower. The Mixed Santa Anna battalion is a good example of this practice. It was a combination of detachments from the Sixth, Seventh and Eighth Line Infantry regiments that fought as a unit as early as the battle of Buena Vista and afterwards. These recombinant units of infantry or cavalry were usually short lived.

WEAPONS

The Mexican soldiers went into battle poorly armed. Mexico had produced excellent quality muskets and pistols before becoming independent from Spain but the machinery was no longer in use as early as 1834. The majority of infantry weapons were out of date Spanish and British muzzle loading flintlock muskets. The British sold many of their old Tower factory muskets (collectively referred to as the "Brown Bess") that had been condemned as unserviceable to Mexico. These could have included several types such as the Pattern 1802 and the India Pattern musket used by the Honorable East India Company (John Company to the British) as well as some types of 'fusils' or light muskets. These various weapons had similar characteristics with walnut stocks and brass fittings, weighing between nine and a half and twelve pounds with barrels from thirty-nine to forty-two inches in length. The smoothbore barrels were of 0.753" caliber (No. 11 bore) while the ball they fired was only 0.71" in diameter (No. 14 bore) weighing about one and three-sixteenths of an ounce (commonly known simply as the ounce bullet). The large bullet had great 'stopping power' that would almost always incapacitate or kill any man that it hit. The space between the ball and barrel, known as 'windage', helped to make loading easier and faster but reduced the range and accuracy drastically. The guns had no rear sights and were aimed simply by looking down the top of the barrel. British tests in 1841 had established the range of these weapons at between 100 and 700 yards with a variation of up to 300 yards at any given elevation of the barrel. In actual practice the maximum effective range under optimum conditions was between 100 and 200 yards with the deadliest effect only at 50 yards or less. Colonel Hanger, an expert marksman, had written of these weapons in 1814 that "A soldier's musket, if not exceedingly ill bored (as many are), will strike a figure of a man at 80 yards - it may even be at 100, but a soldier must be very unfortunate indeed who shall be wounded by a common musket at 150 yards provided his antagonist aims at him: and as to firing at a man at 200 yards with a common musket you may as well fire at the moon and have the same hope of hitting your object. I do maintain and will prove whenever called upon that no man was ever killed at 200 yards by a common musket by the person who aimed at him." It was possible for a good marksman to hit a man at 100 yards and a massed volley by a line of men would have some chance of hits on a mass of troops at 200 yards, but by 300 yards the fire was totally ineffective and the bullet was no longer lethal. The tactics in use at the time did not encourage aimed fire by individuals but rather the output of a great volume of fire at a mass target. The rate of fire for experienced troops could be as high as five rounds per minute with misfire up to fifteen percent of the time, but this rate was difficult to maintain due to fatigue and the fouling of the gun barrel. A more realistic rate of fire might be more like one round per minute, taking into account the tendency of the piece to foul and require cleaning.

The bayonets on these weapons, when in British Service, would commonly be about fifteen inches in length, consisting of a triangular-sectioned blade attached to a cylindrical socket which would fit on the end of the musket barrel. The fixed bayonet might reduce the rate of fire due to the individual soldier taking more care in loading so as not to impale himself while ramming home the cartridge. These socket-bayonets were held in place by a right-angled slot passing over the foresight of the musket which was very insecure without some sort of locking ring which these British made weapons lacked. Regulation pattern socket-bayonets were not equipped with handguards.

Rifle companies were armed with the Baker flintlock rifle which the British had replaced by 1838. The Baker rifle was forty-six inches long with a thirty inch barrel weighing in at nine and one-half pounds without the bayonet. The caliber could vary from 0.615" to 0.70" with seven groove rifling having one turn in 120 inches. It fired a spherical soft lead 350 grain bullet with a muzzle velocity of 1200 feet per second and it had adjustable sight. The ramrod was heavy requiring the soldier to place the butt of the rifle between his feet to ram the bullet down by using both hands. The normal ball used was slightly smaller than the bore and required a greased leather patch to achieve a snug fit. The accuracy of these rifles was much better than the muskets in use with them being described as "deadly in the hands of troops up to 200 yards." This gave the rifle about twice the effective range of the musket but the overall range was actually not very much greater. The rate of fire and reliability of these weapons was less than the musket due to a lower tolerance for fouling in the barrel. The Baker rifle had a twenty-three inch long broad blade sword bayonet with a brass handle attached to the side of the barrel by spring-clips.

TACTICS

Considerable studies in tactical theory had been carried out up to 1835. These tactics were already outdated, being based on Spanish and French military manuals from the Napoleonic era. In open terrain an infantryman with knapsack occupied two paces (about four feet) of frontage. Intervals in line of battle were 20 yards between battalions, columns or regiments. Brigades had 30 yards between them and divisions 50 to 60 yards. The distance between infantry files was two feet. The standard marching speed for infantry at a walk was 60 yards per minute, at the double or quick step it was 80 yards per minute and at the run it was 160 yards per minute.

The Mexican army had used bugle calls to issue commands since 1825. When sounded, calls were taken up by all bugles for orders to March, Retreat, Assemble, Disperse, Halt, Open Fire, Cease Fire, Detach Skirmishers, Engage the Enemy, Pursue the

Enemy, Charge or Attack, Form Square and Form the Chain. When Retreat was sounded the line, reserves and skirmishers all turned to the left and retreated at the pace indicated. A Halt had the entire line stop and turn their front to the enemy. The Assembly was always executed at the double. The call to Disperse was used when traversing broken or wooded terrain. Open Fire had every man in a standing line select a target, while a marching line would form single ranks to fire alternately and battalions already in closed order would issue fire. A Cease Fire call stopped all firing and weapons that had been discharged were reloaded. Charge or Attack was with fixed bayonets to close with the enemy and no fire was to be issued. Against a cavalry attack the order was sounded to Form Square or a massed circle with the troops facing outwards toward the enemy with bayonets fixed. The front rank could be kneeling with weapons at a slant, the butt end of the musket supported against the ground and the knee. The call to Form the Chain had a line with groups of two to four sentries covering all open positions that were not fortified. In addition to bugle calls, officers could use their swords to transmit commands by holding them in various positions for signalling.

When in open encampments, guards with twelve to fifteen men each were to be sent out to 50 or 60 yards in front of every battalion. Sentries were sent out from these groups to a similar distance. The sentries would sound the alarm in case of attack and report back to the field guards so that all of them could fall back to their battalions that would be assembling into battle formations. Guards were also sent out to the flanks and rear. The officers of the guard would be responsible for dispatching lookouts, listening posts and small patrols to make continuous rounds to ensure that the unit was not the victim of a surprise attack.

Discipline was lenient for most minor infractions and military courtesy was ceremonial at best with salutes usually only being given by units presenting arms while in formation. Individuals were not required to salute until an order was issued, probably in an 1847 order that, according to Joseph Hefter, that said in part, "...in the presence of a superior, if he is not under arms or in formation, the soldier stands with his hand at the shako or his hat removed; in the street, he brings the right hand up to the shield of the shako..."

The outdated Light Infantry tactical manual of instruction from 1814 was replaced early in 1841 to make it "...more adaptable to the brave Mexican army...." The mission of the light infantry was to clear the way for the line infantry units and then follow after them. At the end of a battle they were to follow up a victory by pursuing the enemy or act as a rear guard to cover the retreat if the army was defeated. Light infantry soldiers were supposed to be able to learn the new rules in just four days with individual

instruction. Closed order, in depth, was the basic formation for the light infantry and they were supposed to be ready to deploy instantly into extended or mixed order by threes. Companies were deployed in alternate wings and were trained to go into formations from these positions. They could be formed two, three or four deep or deployed by halves to either the front or rear by right or left. Soldiers were trained to be able to issue fire at the command of Stand to Fire! and Open Fire! to the front or flanks while either gaining or losing ground. Individuals would try to find firing positions with cover while still keeping a semblance of order in the ranks. After the first man in the front rank fired he would begin reloading and the second man would fire as soon as the first man's weapon was primed again. Likewise the third man in the ranks would only fire after the second man was finished priming. In groups of three this procedure would guarantee that a continuous fire could be maintained. In addition any men in the second rank would hold fire until their front rank counterpart was reloaded so that there was always a loaded weapon for every pair of soldiers. This system sounded good in the instruction manual but it is doubtful that it lasted very long once actual combat began in the face of the enemy. Normally, after the first volley the troops would continue to fire at will.

In 1843 line infantry tactics were simplified by adopting a manual written by a Headquarters Staff attache, Captain Juan Ordonez. Although the Mexican military manuals were copied in detail from their Spanish, and later French sources, they were not always put into practice. There were some veteran line infantry regiments that were well drilled and disciplined. Many of these units performed very well on the field of battle. The four regiments of Light Infantry were probably the best troops in the army. They included a lot of veteran soldiers and were trained in the tactics of both line infantry and skirmishers. However, the system of conscription and impressment in order to fill the ranks, especially of the Active Militia units, undermined the quality of the soldiers and the training they got. According to the American minister Waddy Thompson they were drilled only occasionally and "...drilling consists mainly in teaching them to march in column through the streets." With units split into small contingents throughout the country they were never able to train in commands any larger than brigade strength. Thompson also states that only one soldier in ten had ever seen a gun, and probably only one in a hundred had actually ever fired one. The Mexican government did not allow its people to legally own firearms. The manual of arms was taught but there was no ammunition to spare for target practice and many recruits entered their first battle without ever having fired their weapons. Not surprisingly, marksmanship was very poor with an American combatant noting after the battle of Palo Alto that, "Though they loaded and fired very fast, they did not take good aim, or they would have killed every man of us." Texans had noticed, in their many encounters with Mexican infantry that, "...when in the act of firing their guns, ...[the Mexican soldiers] did not take aim, but pointed the guns towards [us] and just as they were about to fire turned their faces away, as if they were afraid to look in the direction they wished to shoot." After the battle of Resaca de la Palma American officers studied Mexican ammunition and found that the cartridges had twice as much powder as they should have had to compensate for its poor quality. This caused an excessive kick when fired and would bruise the shoulder of the soldier attempting to aim the weapon. The Mexican soldiers chose not to aim at all because of this and were even known to fire from the hip to avoid the severe recoil. Even at close range, their fire was usually high and accuracy in general was very poor.

The French system of bayonet drill developed by Pinette was adapted for tactical use in the Mexican army by Lieutenant Colonel Jose Lopez Uraga in 1844. This system had been approved by the French war ministry and tested in 1833 and 1836. Some new maneuvers were introduced by Uraga that were not in the originals. There were twenty-two basic positions to be learned. It was thought that bayonet drill would give the individual soldier more agility and confidence with his weapon. Despite this type of training for close combat, the continual revolutions that the army was involved in were rarely very bloody affairs. Long range artillery and musketry duels were preferable to closing in with the bayonet, for which there had never been much enthusiasm. Mathieu de Fossey, a French observer, wrote of this, "Mexicans dare not launch a bayonet assault on a fortified position, however weak it is; the smallest parapet looks to them like an impregnable bastion."

In practice the Mexican infantryman performed well despite the many drawbacks inherent in their system. The regulars could stand up to open field combat and often maneuvered with parade ground precision in the face of the enemy. The militia and other troops were really only of value on the defensive in some kind of field works or other prepared positions. When well led, which was the exception rather than the rule, the Mexican soldier could give as good as he got. Unfortunately, when it came to leadership, the odds were usually against him from the beginning.

CAVALRY

The Mexican cavalryman was recruited from the rancheros of mostly *mestizos* who considered themselves to be of a better class than the infantry. They were the most colorful and impressive corps of the army. The cavalry was the favorite with all of the Mexican officers due to the magnificent spectacle they presented in full battle array. The riders were skilled horsemen and excelled individually with lance and lasso. The regulars were trained but had little or no experience operating in units larger than a regiment. The Auxiliaries and Presidial cavalry were virtually worthless on the battlefield due to lack of discipline and morale. Most of these units were local rancheros who would decide whether to fight or not depending on how the battle was progressing at the time.

ORGANIZATION

The basic unit for the cavalry of the Mexican army was the regiment of four squadrons with two companies each. The cavalry, like the infantry, was deployed throughout the country in small detachments. Individual squadrons and companies were scattered and operated on their own most of the time with little opportunity to train together as complete regiments, much less any larger formations. In practice, whatever parts of units were present for a campaign were converged on the battlefield into regiment or brigade sized groups.

The headquarters staff for a cavalry regiment was made up of the Colonel, a Lieutenant Colonel, two Squadron Commandants, four Adjutant Lieutenants, four Guidonbearer Ensigns, a Chaplain, Surgeon, First Sergeant Marshall, one Cornet Major and a Cornet Corporal, three grooms, two Second Sergeants, saddler and armorer, two Corporals, tailor and carpenter, and three troopers as shoemaker, mason and baker, all mounted.

The eight companies that comprised a regiment each had a Captain, Lieutenant, two Ensigns, one First Sergeant and three Second Sergeants, nine Corporals, two trumpeters, fifty-two mounted troopers and eight dismounted troopers. Active Militia cavalry regiments adopted the same organization as the line units.

The law of July, 1839 had reorganized existing regular and active militia cavalry units into numbered regiments as in the infantry.

The First Line Cavalry Regiment was formed from the Regular Tampico and the Active Militia Cavalry of San Luis Potosi with a replacement cadre at San Luis Potosi.

The Second Line Cavalry Regiment was formed from the Regular Vera Cruz and the Active Militia Cavalry of Zacatecas with a replacement cadre at Zacatecas.

The Third Line Cavalry Regiment was formed from the Regular Delores (this unit had provided the majority of the cavalry present at the siege of the Alamo in 1836), and the Active Squadron of Durango with a replacement cadre at Durango.

The Fourth Line Cavalry Regiment was formed from the Regular Iguala and the Auxiliaries of Cold Country with a replacement cadre at Queretaro.

The Fifth Line Cavalry Regiment was formed from the Regular Palmar and the First and Second Active Militia Cavalry of Jalisco with a replacement cadre at Jalisco.

The Sixth Line Cavalry Regiment was formed from the Regular Cuautla and the Active Squadrons of Morelia with a replacement cadre at Guanajuato.

The Seventh Line Cavalry Regiment was formed from the Regular Mexico and Cuernavaca Squadron, the Auxiliaries of Ayotla, Chalco, Texcoco and Tulancingo with a replacement cadre at Mexico.

The Eighth Line Cavalry Regiment was formed from the Active Militia of Puebla and Active Squadron and the Auxiliaries of Tlaxcala with a replacement cadre in Yucatan.

There was a Ninth Line Cavalry Regiment in existence by 1841 but no other details are available about its creation.

In addition to the numbered line regiments there was also a Light Mounted Regiment of Mexico that had been raised in 1835, a Light Regiment of Vera Cruz, a Yucatan Squadron, a Light Puebla Squadron and a regular Tabasco Cavalry Company. A Light Cavalry unit that had been raised on June 12, 1840 was renamed on September 20, 1843 as the Mounted Rifles. On January 15, 1842 a heavy cavalry regiment was raised known as the Tulancingo Cuirassiers. An elite unit was designated on September 1, 1843 called the Hussars of the Guard of the Supreme Powers. This unit had been a light cavalry unit that was transformed on December 3, 1841 from a Public Security squadron. They were not officially referred to as Hussars until July 27, 1846, but they were to ride at the head of all cavalry formations and serve as the Presidential bodyguard. Another new cavalry unit was raised on July 19, 1843 that only had two squadrons and was known as the Jalisco Lancers. This unit, along with the Mounted Rifles, was classified as Active Militia and not incorporated into the organization of the regular army.

The Active Militia cavalry consisted of five regiments from Guanajuato, Morelia, Oaxaca, Queretaro and San Luis Potosi. There were also seventeen other detached squadrons from Bravos, California, Chalchicomula, Chiapas, Chinahuapan, Cuernavaca, First and Second Durango, Ixtlahuaca, Jalapa, New Mexico, Orizaba, First and Second Sierra Gorda, Teloloapan, Tlaxcala and Tula. In addition there were four squadrons and six companies of Active Militia Coast Guard Cavalry. There were also Presidial companies stationed on the frontiers with eight in Texas, three in New Mexico and six in California. New Presidial stations could also be created as the need arose as in January of 1842 when two new presidios were establish along the road from Mexico to Vera Cruz to watch over the prisoners that had been detailed to perform road construction tasks. The government had also experimented with allowing State governors to raise local Auxiliary Cavalry Companies that would be commanded by them in peacetime but were to be turned over to the jurisdiction of the military in time of war. However, the abuses of this system were so widespread that it had to be abolished.

WEAPONS

The horses used by the Mexican cavalry were small, being under eleven hands high, but they were hardy. They were described as being fiery and vicious but well trained and capable of enduring hunger, thirst and fatigue just as well as their riders. They could charge at full speed through an ordinary thicket for use in ambushes and irregular warfare. They were well controlled by their riders by the severe bridles that were used.

There is an account of the battle of Buena Vista that mentions that the horses "of a corps were alike in color." This probably refers to each regiment having all of its horses of the same color throughout, with every regiment trading different colored mounts with the other regiments, but no other confirmation of this has been found.

The standard Mexican cavalry saddle was made of a wooden frame with iron plates covered with leather and stuffed with horsehair in canvas cushions. There were iron stirrups and leather pistol holsters and a carbine boot was attached to the saddle as well. The pommel (front) and cantle (back) of the saddle were quite high and once mounted it was virtually impossible to unseat a well trained rider. The stirrups were hung directly under the rider so that he rode in a position almost as erect as when standing.

Mexican cavalry were armed with swords or sabers, *escopeta* or carbine, pistols and lances. The sword was hung on a sling from the waistbelt. The escopeta was a short, smooth-bore, light "blunderbuss" described as a bell-mouthed, bull-doggish looking musket. It fired a very heavy ball that was deadly when it hit, which was very seldom. Accuracy was so poor because the weapon was often held above the head and fired at random in order to avoid the tremendous 'kick' of the recoil. Carbines were carried in a leather boot at the right side of the saddle with the muzzle and ramrod pointed down. These were sometimes the Baker carbines with the same caliber as the infantry rifles. This weapon weighed six and one-half pounds with a twenty inch long barrel and an overall length of thirty-six inches. The sights were fixed, not adjustable. The muzzle had a deep funnel to allow the ball and patch to be held while the ramrod was being drawn for loading while the trooper was mounted. Cavalrymen would usually have one or two flintlock pistols as well. These were also wildly inaccurate weapons. Mexican cavalrymen also boasted about their abilities with the lasso, which was very common among them. Defensive weapons included brass or leather helmets with crests and brass cuirasses for some units.

The weapon that the Mexican cavalry were most

widely known for was the lance. In April of 1837 there had been some discussion about abolishing firearms altogether in the cavalry. Instead, a decree was issued that "...the First Company of all cavalry regiments shall be of lancers, made up of individuals with the aptitude and other requisites to perform this service..." Independent companies and squadrons were also to include a squad of eight lancers and a corporal in each. A Second Sergeant and an Ensign were to be in command of every lancer squad. The lances themselves were made from a one and one-half inch thick shaft of beech or nut wood approximately nine feet long including point and socket. The point was eight and one-quarter inches long with three or four cutting edges with bayonet-like concave gutters. There was a metal crosspiece at the lower end followed by a tube and two iron straps three feet long that were screwed onto the shaft as protection against saber cuts that could chop off the point. Under the metal crosspiece the lance pennon was hung. This was a two pointed pennant about a foot long in the regimental colors. Besides being ornamental it was meant to scare the enemy's horses by fluttering in front of their eyes. A leather sling was attached to the shaft of the lance to allow the rider to suspend the lance from the right arm or to support a thrust. The right stirrup had a leather tube for resting the lance and the cinch had a loop that could be used to make sure that the weapon was not lost while maneuvering the horse.

TACTICS

The Mexican cavalry used outdated Spanish tactics from manuals printed in Mexico in 1814 and 1824. In open terrain a mounted cavalryman would occupy three paces (about six feet) of frontage and nine paces (about eighteen feet) of depth. The distance between cavalry files was also three paces. Cavalry was to move at a speed of 120 yards per minute at a walk, 235 yards per minute at a trot and 385 yards per minute at a gallop. When in formation troopers counted off by fours going from right to left. The first, fifth and ninth men each responding to Number One and so on down the line. Mexican cavalry was trained to fight on foot and did so frequently in smaller actions or skirmishes. When large numbers of cavalry were present on either side, they rarely dismounted.

Cavalry were trained to respond to trumpet calls such as Saddle or General Call, the signal to saddle horses and for troopers to get ready for action. Then Croups, Assembly and the signal To Horse had officers and sergeants call out all troopers and after placing them in battle order, roll call was read and the troopers mounted. In the case of surprise attack or an alarm To Horse was sounded directly without a General Call. Other trumpet calls were March, Fall In, Honor Roll, Reveille or Prayer, Attention, Rest, Trot, Gallop, About Turn, To Order, Attack or Beheading, Halt, Retreat or Tattoo. When a charge was within 80 paces of the enemy the *Deguello*, meaning destruction, was sounded.

Sword or saber handling was also taught. The drawn saber was held point up and cutting edge forward. When the order Shoulder Saber was given the blade was slanted against the shoulder. In combat there were six standard cuts to be used. The first was from right to left diagonally through the enemy's left shoulder down to the right thigh. The second was the exact opposite of the first going from left to right. The third type of cut reversed the motion of the first one, going from the thigh on up to the shoulder, while the fourth cut was the reverse of the second one. Cut number five was a horizontal one from right to left while the sixth type of cut was from left to right across the neck of the enemy rider. There were also movements to Guard, Thrust and Cut to Rear as well as combinations of the standard cuts and orders to engage and protect against infantry.

The cavalry carbine drill was similar to the infantry rifle drill manual. The basic position of standing or marching had the weapon resting with the barrel close to the right shoulder, ramrod to front, arm extended vertically with the gun butt touching the trouser seam. On long marches the command, Arms at Ease! allowed the weapon to be carried slanted on either shoulder, muzzle upward, supported by one or both hands. The procedure to load the piece involved eleven main movements called out by numbers such as; Prepare to Load - one two! Open Pan - one! Draw Cartridge! Break Cartridge! Close Pan! Cartridge in Barrel! Draw Ramrod! Ramrod in Place! Shoulder Arms! To commence firing the command was: Prepare Arms - one - two - three! then Aim! and Fire! This could be sped up by ordering Rapid Fire - Load! which reduced the eleven loading and four firing commands to only four groups of motions. Volley and sustained fire were ordered by, Volley! First Rank! Prepare Arms! Open Fire! The command Halt Fire! caused all firing to stop and any unloaded weapons were immediately reloaded and everyone would shoulder arms. Some other commands were Present Arms!, Rest your Arms!, Brace Arms!, Review Arms!, Ground Arms!, Raise Arms! and Cover Arms! The cavalry also had commands to Hook Arms!, Release Arms!, Arms on Back! (with the butt of the weapon pointing upwards) and Unhook Arms! The loading and firing of pistols included the same basic movements as for the rifles or carbines.

The lancers had their own set of commands for wielding their deadly weapons. Rest Lances! meant to suspend the lance from the crook of the right arm by the use of the lance sling. Secure Lances! and Prepare Lances! meant to hold the lance vertically with the hand at neck level. Couch Lances! was for the attack and brought the lance to a horizontal position about two inches below the right breast and fixed between the arm and the body. Other commands brought the Lance Front! and Thrust to either Left or Right, Front or Rear and against Infantry or Cavalry! There were commands to Cover Back!, Guard Circumference of Horse!, Disengage! and Brandish! which had the rider stand up and lean forward while raising the lance to head height and move the lance point to form circles in the air in a threatening manner. Shoulder Lances! put the lance at rest across the right shoulder. Present Lances! brought the lance out straight up with the right arm extended from the body to the front. Lances may have only been carried during wartime and many troops that carried them were not always as proficient in their use as the drill manuals would indicate. Presidial troops, rancheros and guerrilla cavalry would almost always have lances with brightly colored pennants fluttering. In practice they would rarely use them except in the pursuit of a fleeing or already fallen foe.

Mexican cavalry were able to deal with infantry in square formation, it had been claimed, by lassoing men and pulling them out of the square to form a breach that would allow them to charge home. There are, however, no accounts of this actually happening during the war with the United States. The lasso was another weapon that was highly touted by Mexican cavalry officers but really only saw use in ambushes and skirmishes.

In the final analysis the Mexican cavalry did not live up to expectations in the test of combat. They were the most impressive and magnificent part of the army that also cost the most to maintain. Time and again they performed poorly or not at all in situations when they were need the most. They were not trained to operate in mass and they rarely charged home, especially against an enemy who was not already disorganized. The cavalry suffered from the same poor leadership problems as did their footbound companions with their commanders continually making excuses after the fact for substandard performance. Though at the outset they were the most feared part of the Mexican Army (especially the lancers) the American infantry eventually came to hold them in contempt.

ARTILLERY

The Mexican Artillery Corps was reorganized on September 14, 1838 to include three foot artillery brigades bearing flags and one mounted brigade with a guidon. There were also five standing companies for garrison duties. Mexico did not lack for artillery pieces with 635 cannon on hand and 104 more imported at the beginning of 1846. There were at least 140 field pieces included in these numbers and that gave Mexico at least four cannon for every 1000 men in the army. This was the amount recognized by the experts in the field as being adequate for a modern army. The problem was that many of these guns were honeycombed inside and otherwise old and useless. Most of the worst guns were at the various fortresses and coastal defenses and many dated back to the Spanish occupation before independence. The bronze cannon manufactured in Mexico in 1846-1847 were not at all satisfactory. The outdated Gribeauval pattern from the Napoleonic era was still in use for the guns and gun carriages. The gun barrels and their equipment were so heavy and clumsy that they were not very mobile at all. Ammunition was transported in carts drawn by mules or oxen and driven by civilian drivers hired by contract. These artillery teamsters were not at all familiar with proper artillery drill or tactics and would often look to their own safety as soon as the opportunity arose. As a result the Mexican artillery usually moved very slowly and once deployed on the battlefield it was difficult to get it moving again.

ORGANIZATION

The Artillery Corps Headquarters consisted of twenty-five senior officers with the insignia of squadron or battalion commanders. There was also a paymaster section and a company of arsenal workers.

The headquarters staff of a foot brigade had five senior and six junior officers, a Captain Paymaster, Chaplain, Surgeon, First Brigade Sergeant, a Drum and Bugle Major, an Armorer, eight pioneers with a Corporal, twelve musicians and two bandmasters. The foot artillery brigade consisted of eight companies which had sixty-six artillerists, twenty non-commissioned officers, two buglers and drummers and three officers in peacetime. Wartime organization was eighty-six gunners, twenty-two non-commissioned officers, two buglers and drummers and five officers.

The headquarters staff of the mounted brigade was the same as the foot brigades but with a Trumpet Major instead of a Drum Major and the addition of a Groom Marshal and two Saddlers. The mounted brigade had six companies with sixty-six gunners, twenty non-commissioned officers, two trumpeters and four officers with eighty-eight saddle horses and fifty draft horses. The horse artillery gunners were individually mounted. Most of the horses for artillery service were too light and frisky and there were only enough to equip four companies, not the six that were originally planned.

WEAPONS

The artillery used by Mexico, as mentioned previously, was generally substandard equipment. The guns were of all sizes and types ranging from 2 lb., 4 lb., 6 lb., 8 lb., 12 lb. and 16 lb. weights of shot with barrels made from iron or bronze. The forts usually had the larger weapons with the fortress of San Juan de Ulua, at Vera Cruz mounting 135 pieces of artillery ranging all the way up to 24 lb. guns and 84 lb. mortars. Mexican powder was inferior in quality and even their grapeshot was so poorly made as to have a much reduced range and a lessened effect.

TACTICS

The Mexican artillerymen were well trained. The artillery, being a technical branch, drew less from the politically minded officers and more from the better educated junior officers and some foreigners that had seen previous service in European armies. In December of 1843 there had been a decree to establish a special school for artillery and engineer officers but it was never accomplished due to a lack of funds. Many artillery officers had gone to the Military College at Chapultepec for instruction.

Despite the above mentioned organization, Mexican artillery was usually deployed piecemeal during the war. Typically a few guns were attached to various brigades if they were available. On the battlefield the Mexicans never had enough guns to be able to use effectively. In many actions the Mexicans had a variety of different weapons available but with rarely enough guns of the same type to form any kind of cohesive battery. The erratic supply situation combined with inferior powder and ammunition led to reduced combat effectiveness on the battlefield. The rate of fire was much slower and Mexican guns were simply not as deadly as the American artillery. The Mexican guns were best used in prepared defensive positions so that their limited maneuverability and uncertain supply capabilities were not as much of a factor in combat.

ENGINEERS

The Mexican Engineer Corps was established on September 14, 1838 with a Brigadier General as its Director. There were ten senior and forty junior officers with a *Zapadore* (Sapper) battalion of 600 men in six companies. The first and second companies were of Miner and Pontoniers and were equivalent to line grenadiers with three buglers per company. The other four companies each had three officers, five non-commissioned officers, two drummers, a fifer and 78 sappers each.

In battle, Engineer officers were at the side of the General in Chief to help lead columns, establish strongpoints, perform reconnaissance missions along rivers to discover fords and build bridges, repair or build new roads and direct attacks on or defenses of harbors or forts. They were useful in the planning and construction of many of the fortifications used by the Mexicans in several major battles. In practice the Zapadore companies were mainly used as elite infantry during the war.

The Mexican Military Academy, or *Colegio Militar*, had been formed in 1823. Legislation enacted on the 18th of November, 1833 called for the Academy to be moved to Chapultepec Castle. This was not accomplished until October of 1841 due to a lack of funds. Enrolment was increased from the original 100 cadets to 200, although actual attendance was only a fraction of that number. The three year curriculum was to include studies in mathematics, chemistry, physics, artillery, fortification, architecture, astronomy, and land surveying. Cadets were also expected to learn French and English and study tactics. The *Colegio Militar*, under the jurisdiction of the Engineer Corps, was to provide forty to fifty new junior officers every year to the army. There was a Cadet Company and a Sublieutenant Company headed by an infantry and a cavalry captain, respectively as first and second in command. The companies consisted of squads of eight under a Cadet Corporal with each group of two squads led by a Cadet Sergeant. Many officers of the Engineer Corps had graduated from here.

MEDICAL CORPS

The Medical Health Corps was enlarged and incorporated into the regular army on February 12, 1846. In peacetime the Inspector General held Brigadier General's rank with a Colonel as Hospital Director. There were eight Lieutenant Colonel Hospital Professors and forty Army Surgeons with the rank of Battalion Commandant. There were also forty Captain First Adjutants, forty Lieutenant Second Adjutants, thirty Sublieutenant Aspirants and an undetermined number of Meritorious Students.

Ambulance companies were formed with eight men per hundred combatants and had Sergeants and Corporals as first and second attendants. These men were trained by medical officers to handle the wounded and to carry stretchers. The bugle call "Hospital" had the men assemble towards the rear of the battleline near the main hospital tent usually located near the army headquarters tent. Medical officers were to attend the sick and wounded of both sides as the need arose. The Medical Corps was present and took part in all of the major actions of the war. Once again, as with the other branches of the military, in practice the Medical Corps was undermanned and poorly supplied. Unfortunately the wounded soldiers of the Mexican army often received little or no treatment on or near the battlefield from their own doctors.

LOGISTICS

The Mexican army was not very well supplied. There were continual scarcities of uniforms, equipment and armaments. Shortages of funds often delayed payments to contractors and the subsequent delivery of complete issues of dress or equipment. There were frequent requests from field commanders to the War Office about inadequate materials for uniforms being available or equipment that did not conform to regulations. Inventories listed more useless and outdated weapons available than serviceable or new ones. Soldiers slept dressed in uniform due to a lack of blankets or overcoats to keep them warm. This only served to wear out their uniforms even more quickly.

The Army was continually short of funds. Many citizens did make voluntary contributions of small amounts. However, the more affluent families were often forced to contribute by making "loans" of thousands of pesos to the government. There were also arbitrary seizures of private property and forcible appropriations taken from the States and even the Church. Santa Anna went so far as to use his own personal credit to help to raise the army that fought at Buena Vista. Soldiers were not issued regular rations. Instead they were to be paid daily through their officers and act as their own commissaries. Corrupt officers and a chronic lack of money meant that the troops were lucky to get enough money to pay for their basic rations. They often marched, fought and died on empty stomachs.

The gunpowder and ammunition made by Mexico was of inferior quality and in insufficient quantity for the needs of the army. The guns at the fortress of San Juan de Ulua, at Vera Cruz harbor, could scarcely reach hostile ships with their largest cannonballs because the powder was of such poor quality. The cannons at Tampico were useless due to a complete lack of ammunition. Many other harbor fortifications were defended by antiquated cannons with the forts at San Blas and Acapulco being among the few exceptions. The Mexican soldiers themselves also suffered from chronic shortages of ammunition. Recruits were routinely drilled and pronounced fit for service without ever having fired their weapons due to a lack of ammunition for practice purposes. At the defense of Churubusco it was reported that the garrison was overcome partly because their ammunition boxes contained the "ounce" ball for use in the larger bored muskets while they happened to be armed with rifles. The wooden stairway to the upper story of the convent showed large circular marks where the defenders tried to force the oversized lead balls down the barrels in despair by turning their rifles muzzle down and pounding the ramrods against the stair treads to no avail.

Summary

The Mexican Army looked formidable on paper. The colorful uniforms and veteran units made it look impressive in the field. The European military system that the Mexican army had adopted convinced most European observers that Mexico could win a war against the United States. Knowledgeable critics closer to the source could see that the army of Mexico was a hollow shell that would collapse under pressure. Its many weaknesses would become glaringly apparent once hostilities began. The Mexicans strived to become a first rate power with real military might and the potential for this did exist. However, the political turmoil, greed and corruption that continually plagued the central government and its leadership during this period led to the ultimate downfall of Mexico. When the Mexican army was finally committed to battle it came up far short of expectations. The bravery and endurance of the common soldier was without question, but poor leadership and inadequate supplies, and using outdated weapons and tactics led only to defeat.

The actual strength of the Mexican army at the beginning of hostilities is difficult to state with any certainty. Without a doubt it was nowhere near as large as what its organization on paper. Estimates by various writers range from a low figure of 23,550 to a maximum figure of 35,000 men under arms. Regardless of which figures are correct, it was certainly much larger than the American army sent against it at the beginning of the war.

Like the American army on the frontier, this force was spread out throughout all of Mexico. During the "Pastry War" of 1838 the French threat had prompted a call for an increase in the army to 60,000 men. It is very doubtful that this goal was ever reached due to the shortages of manpower and the inability to successfully enlist or recruit many soldiers.

THE MEXICAN ARMY AT THE OUTBREAK OF WAR IN APRIL 1846

REGULAR ARMY (EJERCITO PERMANENTE)

Infantry (11,501)
    12 Regiments of Line Infantry (numbered 1-12)
    4 Regiments of Light Infantry (numbered 1-4)
    Standing Battalion of Mexico
    Standing Battalion of the Californias
    2 Garrison Companies of Mexico
    Battalion of Invalids of Mexico
    Battalion of Invalids of Puebla
    Grenadiers of the Guard of the Supreme Powers

Cavalry (3,934)
    9 Regiments of Line Cavalry (numbered 1-9)
    Light Mounted Regiment of Mexico
    Light Mounted Regiment of Vera Cruz
    Light Cavalry Squadron of Puebla
    Cavalry Squadron of Yucatan
    Independent Company of Tabasco
    Mounted Rifles (Cazadores)
    Tulancingo Cuirassiers
    Hussars of the Guard of the Supreme Powers

Corps of Artillery (1,840)
    3 Brigades of Foot Artillery (8 companies in each)
    1 Brigade of Mounted Artillery (6 companies)
    5 Garrison Foot Artillery Companies
    Quartermaster Corps
    Artillery Artificiers Company

Corps of Engineers (442)
    1 Battalion of Sappers (Zapadores)
    Corps of Cadet of the Military Academy
    Detachment of Topographical Engineers

PRESIDIAL CAVALRY (1,209)
    8 Companies in Texas
    3 Companies in New Mexico
    6 Companies in California

TERRITORIAL MILITIA (MILICIA ACTIVA)

Infantry (6,470)
    5 Regiments — 1st Mexico, 2nd Mexico, 1st
        Guanajuato, 2nd Guanajuato, Puebla
    12 Battalions — Aguascalientes, Chihuahua,
        Guadalajara, Lagos, Michoacan, Oaxaca,
        Queretaro, San Luis Potosi, Sinaloa, Sonora,
        Sur, Zacatecas
    Coast Guard (3,624)
        13 Battalions
        3 Battalions in revolt in Yucatan

Cavalry (3,990)
    5 Regiments — Guanajuato, Morelia, Oaxaca,
        Queretaro, San Luis Potosi
    17 detached Squadrons - Bravos, California,
        Chalchicomula, Chiapas, Chinahuapan,
        Cuernavaca, 1st Durango, 2nd Durango,
        Ixtlahuaca, Jalapa, New Mexico, Orizaba, 1st
        Sierra Gorda, 2nd Sierra Gorda, Teloloapan,
        Tlaxcala, Tula
    Jalisco Lancers (2 squadrons)
    Coast Guard (531)
        4 Independent Squadrons
        6 Independent Companies

NATIONAL GUARD (GUARDIA NACIONAL)
    Various State units not individually accounted for
    here

TOTALS

Regular Army	17,717
Presidial Troops	1,209
Active Militia & Coast Guards	14,615
Grand Total	**33,541**

(Other Estimates: 14,770 Infantry, 7,050 Cavalry,
1,731 Artillery — Total of 23,551;
or, 32,000 men in the army plus 3,000 in Coast Guard
units — Total of 35,000)

UNIFORMS OF THE MEXICAN ARMY

The Mexican Army presented an impressive spectacle when in the field. The infantry formations displayed a brilliant spectrum of color and glittered with steel, silver, and gold. The cavalry showed off a rainbow of colorful uniforms, saddle blankets, and gayly fluttering lance pennons. The uniforms retained numerous details of the Spanish dress regulations from 1821, which were basically Napoleonic in style. New regulations for uniforms were issued in 1831, 1832, 1833, 1839, 1840 and 1841 (which re-established the regulations of 1839). These continual changes and a shortage of funds contributed to the problems that the Army had with contractors of getting regular supplies of complete uniforms that would conform to regulations.

Each soldier was supposed to be issued a barracks cap, three shirts, a cloth tailcoat, two canvas jackets, one pair each of gala (full dress) cloth and canvas pants, necktie, a pair of shoes, a shako complete with cords and ornaments, one overcoat, a blanket with carrier, a knapsack with straps, a tool set, canteen, crossbelt with cartridge box, crossbelt with frog, scabbard and bayonet, fusil and a satchel of trimmings, and a towel. This was seldom the case however, and there were frequent complaints and requests to the War Office for adequate supplies. General Ciriaco Vazquez wrote in February of 1842 that "...The greater part of the rank and file of the 2nd Active Battalion, 7th Regular Regiment are short of overcoats, blankets or any other heavier garment that could serve them as cover on rainy and cold nights or when asleep in their quarters, it being necessary for them to go to sleep dressed, with the result that the only uniform issue they possess is quickly destroyed. To avoid this damage and to provide them with an indispensable garment that will make their service more bearable ...have the kindness to inform His Excellency the President about the great necessity of providing them at least with one burlap blanket each". Three months later this same General submitted an estimate to the Departmental Treasury in Vera Cruz for complete canvas uniforms for each unit, explaining to them that, "...His Excellency desires that the units of his command shine not only by their discipline and training, but also by their equipment".

Mexican army uniforms while on campaign presented a myriad of contrasts and colors. The regular infantry units may or may not have had their regulation uniforms, depending upon how long ago they had last been supplied with new ones, and what the individual soldiers had been able to preserve from previous issues. Active Militia and National Guard units would have the best that their States could provide, which might have been similar to the regular army units that were stationed in their area, or it may have been no more than white canvas or linen cloth pants and jacket. The cavalry would most likely be the closest to having the current regulation dress, as they would be better off than their foot slogging counterparts financially and would normally see less wear and tear on their uniforms. The officer corps would most likely be magnificently attired in all of the gold and glory that they could muster. At a distance the army would present a colorful and impressive sight. Upon closer inspection, however, it would become evident that the army did not have the means to provide shoes (or sometimes even sandals) to all of its soldiers, must less intricate multi-colored uniforms in serviceable condition.

GENERAL STAFF, OFFICERS AND NCOS

Full dress uniform for generals was a turkish blue (dark blue) tailcoat with scarlet lining, lapels, turnbacks, collar, cuffs, and piping. The lapels, collar, and cuffs were edged with gold embroidery of interlaced palm, laurel, and olive leaves. Generals of a Division had two rows of embroidery on lapels and cuffs and one row on the collar while Generals of Brigade had a single row on all three areas. The coat had horizontal pocket flaps with three buttons, and gold epaulettes in raised leaf work with an embroidered metallic silver eagle and bullion fringe. Generals of Division had a sash of sky blue wound around the waist, while Generals of Brigade wore dark green sashes. Pants were white for gala (full dress) and dark blue or gray in the field. Black fore-and-aft bicorne hats edged with gold lace were worn topped with three plumes in the national colors above a tricolor cockade. All officers carried swords on waistbelts under the tailcoat when in the field.

The officers of the Headquarters Corps and serving as staff in the Quartermasters Office had deep red tailcoats with white lapels and gold embroidered buttonholes and lace. The turnbacks were white with eagle coattail clasps. The collar and cuffs were also white with wide gold lace. Piping was deep red and pants were dark blue with a gold stripe at the seam. Black bicorne hats were worn with gold lace edging and a tricolor cockade.

Officers with the rank of Colonel and below wore the same uniforms as their men but made of finer materials that would be less prone to shrink or fade. Colonels wore two epaulettes fringed with heavy bullion in gold with a single silver star on each one. Lieutenant Colonels used the same epaulettes but without the stars. Colonels and Lieutenant Colonels wore a red silk sash with tassels around the waist and a tricolor plume on the hat. First Adjutants also wore a red sash and had two epaulettes with smooth bullion straps and heavy fringe. Captains had two epaulettes of gold thread with cloth loops the same color as their coat. A single epaulette was worn by Lieutenants and Second Adjutants on the right shoulder. Sublieutenants, Subadjutants and Ensigns wore their single epaulette on the left shoulder. First Sergeants wore two crimson epaulettes made of silk while the Second Sergeants wore only one on the right shoulder. Corporals had a yellow diagonal stripe on each lower sleeve.

INFANTRY

The Mexican Army wore coats similar in style to the French 1815 pattern with a square cuff, sometimes having a cuff flap, with one, two or three buttons. All coats had epaulettes or shoulder straps, usually in crimson unless noted otherwise. The cuffs, collars, lapels and turnbacks were normally piped in the regimental colors. The turnbacks on the coats were shorter than the French style 'habit-veste'. Although the tailcoat was regulation dress for all infantry regiments there is evidence to suggest that frock coats may have been issued frequently for campaigns. These would be the same turkish blue color of the tailcoats, or possibly dark or medium gray. The frock coats would have a red collar and cuffs or simply red piping around the collar and cuffs, but without any specific regimental colors. The simple frock coat may have been easier to supply and more practical for use in the field than the official, more colorful and elaborate uniforms decreed for each unit.

The prevalent color for uniform coats and pants was designated as *turkish blue*, which is defined as the darkest blue in the spectrum. However, different interpretations by various government agencies and contractors could result in several distinct shades of blue from a blue-black to dark blue and even medium blue in some instances. Whenever considering shades of color found on uniforms it should be taken into account that all of the dyes in use at the time were subject to fading and becoming washed out with constant exposure to the elements and the hard use to which they were put.

Headgear for the infantry was the shako of either shiny or dull black leather ranging from seven to nine inches tall. There were a variety of patterns from 'stove-pipe' shakos with straight cylindrical sides to conical shapes that were round on top or even wider on top than at the base. The typical shako would have a black leather visor and a leather chinstrap held in place by a button on each side. There were a myriad of shako plates to be found bearing designs of Mexican eagles and snakes, bugles, cannon, laurel wreaths, ribbons and regimental names and numbers made from brass or other metal in oval, gorget or other badge shapes. The shakos were also decorated with tricolor cockades and cinch bands on top and bottom of yellow or reddish gold lace, copper, brass or black leather. Rifle companies and Light Infantry regiments wore a round green pompon while the fusilier companies and artillerists wore round deep red ones. The grenadier companies may have worn a round white pompon or, along with artillery officers, a cylindrical deep red pompon about six inches tall. Tricolor plumes were strictly reserved for senior combat officers. The Grenadiers of the Guard of the Supreme Powers wore black bearskin caps 20" high with a brass grenade shield on the front.

Soft forage caps or barracks caps that were widely used included a French-Spanish style *bonnet de police*, a smaller pointed and tasseled cap, a soft crown visored cap similar to the U.S. forage cap and a conventional French style kepi, although these were rare as the supply was cut off when the war began. The colors could be dark blue, sky blue, red, gray or possibly even green with distinctive color trim, piping and tassels.

Infantry wore white crossbelts to support the cartridge box and infantry sword that they carried, with an oval brass plate in the center of the 'X' formed on their chest. Light Infantry, the Standing Battalion of Mexico and the Grenadiers of the Guard wore black belts. Cartridge boxes and bayonet scabbards were of black leather. Leather or canvas knapsacks were carried along with a quart size wooden water bottle or hollowed out gourd as a canteen.

All infantry accessories such as buttons, letters, numerals and other insignia were to be in yellow or gold. The regimental number was to be stamped on all buttons and embroidered on the collar. Single vertical flashes on the cuffs were worn by grenadier and rifle companies while the elite companies in the light infantry or grenadier regiments wore a pair of flashes on each cuff to distinguish them. The infantry all wore plain white canvas pants during summer. White gaiters worn over the shoes are shown for some infantry in contemporary prints and paintings, however, uniform regulations, contracts or inventories do not list any such item. Other accessories sometimes shown for which there is no description or mention in regulations are bandsmens' chevrons, shako plumes, gorgets, kepis and colored field caps.

A decree was issued on July 10, 1839 that detailed distinctive uniforms for each regular infantry and cavalry regiment. On August 31, 1840 these were replaced with a new decree that attempted to standardize the uniform throughout the army. Then again on December 22, 1841 the July 10th decree was reinstated and confirmed. These are the uniforms

THE WAR IN MEXICO

called for in the official regulations that the Mexican Army used through at least 1847. There were several modifications and additions made to these in the years between 1841 and 1846 and they are included in the listings found below. The basic infantry uniform consisted of a turkish blue tailcoat and pants with a deep red stripe down the seams along with crimson epaulettes on both shoulders. The twelve numbered Regular Infantry Regiments as well as several special units each had varying colors of facings to distinguish them.

The First Infantry had yellow lapels with deep red turnbacks*, collar and cuffs and yellow piping. In addition a blue or white vest was also worn.

The Second Infantry had deep red lapels and turnbacks with a sky blue collar and deep red cuffs and piping.

The Third Infantry had crimson lapels and turnbacks with a sky blue collar, crimson cuffs and sky blue piping.

The Fourth Infantry had deep red lapels and turnbacks with a sky blue collar and cuffs and white piping.

The Fifth Infantry had deep red lapels and turnbacks, deep red collar, sky blue cuffs and piping.

The Sixth Infantry had white lapels with crimson turnbacks, collar and cuffs with piping in opposite colors. Piping in opposite colors would be white piping on all crimson areas and crimson piping on all white areas.

The Seventh Infantry had a single-breasted tailcoat without lapels but with gold embroidered

buttonholes instead, crimson turnbacks, and a green collar and cuffs with crimson piping.

The Eighth Infantry had sky blue lapels and turnbacks with deep red collar and cuffs, with piping in opposite colors.

The Ninth Infantry had purple lapels, with buff colored turnbacks and collar, purple cuffs, and piping in opposite colors.

The Tenth Infantry had purple lapels with deep red turnbacks and collar, purple cuffs, and buff piping.

The Eleventh Infantry was originally to have had green lapels and deep red turnbacks, collar and cuffs with piping in opposite colors. In 1841 the Eleventh Infantry was given a completely new uniform with a white tailcoat and crimson pants with a white stripe at the seam, sky blue lapels, deep red turnbacks, sky blue collar and cuffs, and piping in opposite colors.

The Twelfth Infantry had buff lapels, deep red turnbacks, buff collar and cuffs, and piping in opposite colors.

The First, Second and Third Light Infantry Regiments all had turkish blue single-breasted tailcoats and shoulder straps and gray pants with a crimson stripe at the seams. The coats had turkish blue turnbacks, collar and cuffs with deep red piping. The plain yellow embroidered initial "L" on the right and "P" on the left collar stood for "Ligero Permanente" or Regular Light Infantry. Shakos were black with brass bugle on the front and a tricolor cockade and the green pompon to designate light infantry. They may also have worn a gray roundabout or shell jacket piped in red for use in the field or as fatigues. A gray forage cap could be worn with the fatigues that had a red band around it with a yellow bugle device on the front.

The Fourth Light Infantry had its own distinctive uniform with a turkish blue tailcoat with crimson lapels, turnbacks and cuffs and emerald green epaulettes, collar and cuff patches. The collar had a yellow numeral "4" embroidered on each side in place of the usual "L" and "P" of the other Light Infantry regiments. All piping was white. The pants were turkish blue with a crimson stripe at the seams, in the summer months white pants were worn. The black shako had two black bands, a brass bugle device in place of a shako plate, a tricolor cockade and a green pompon.

The Fijo de Mexico (Fixed or Standing Battalion of Mexico, also known as the Mexico Garrison Battalion), wore a white single-breasted tailcoat with green epaulettes and sky blue pants with a red stripe at the seams. The coat had green turnbacks, collar and cuffs with deep red piping. This battalion had red pompons for the grenadier company, white pompons for the rifle company and green pompons for the fusilier companies.

The Fijo de California (Fixed or Standing Battalion of the Californias) wore a turkish blue single-breasted tailcoat and turkish blue pants with a deep red stripe at the seams. The coat had deep red turnbacks, collar

* The most invaluable source for detailed information about the Mexican Army is Nieto, Mrs. Angelina, Brown, Mrs. John Nicholas, and Hefter, Joseph. *The Mexican Soldier 1837-1847*. The work was illustrated and edited by Joseph Hefter and is generally referred to simply by his name alone. There is evidence that there was some confusion in the translation of some Spanish uniform terminology into English in the Hefter book. (Finke, Detmar H. "Reply to Terry D. Hooker's article 'Uniforms of the Mexican Army 1839-1846'." *El Dorado*. 3, no. 2 (July-August 1990): 2-4). The Hefter book lists the regulation colors for lapels and cuff bars in the translation but leaves out any mention of the turnbacks in the skirts of the tailcoat. Cuff bars, flaps or patches were not in general use in the Mexican army uniforms of this period and this term should have been translated as turnbacks instead. There is some corroboration of this in Knotel, Knotel & Sieg, *Uniforms of the World*. On page 322 there is mention of "skirt turnbacks" while there is no mention at all of cuff bars or flaps in describing Mexican uniforms. Joseph Hefter himself is supposed to have acknowledged the error in a letter to Mr. Finke cited in his article. Therefore the colors given in Hefter for cuff bars for the various regiments have been listed here as those for turnbacks instead. This is also supported by Katcher, Philip R.N. *The Mexican-American War 1846-1848*. p. 24-28. Although this is not new information as such, it is mentioned here because this may vary from other sources that have incorrectly assumed that the lapels and turnbacks on the tailcoat were always of the same color.

144

(with the initials "FC" embroidered on in yellow) and cuffs with all piping in opposite colors.

The remaining two Garrison Companies (sometimes known as the Standing Companies of Mexico, which may have been the last of the Coast Guard units) wore a turkish blue single-breasted tailcoat with red turnbacks and collar, with company initials embroidered on the collar, red cuffs and cuff patches, red piping and dark blue arabesques. The pants were white and all buttons were of plain brass. The Veteran Infantry Coast Guard Companies had the same uniform but the coat was different in that it had turkish blue lapels piped in red. They also wore blue three-pointed collar patches on the front of the collar.

The Battalion of Invalids of Mexico wore a turkish blue tailcoat with sky blue lapels, turnbacks, collar and cuffs with deep red piping and sky blue pants with a red stripe.

The Grenadier Guards of the Supreme Powers were originally to wear turkish blue tailcoats with sky blue collar trimmed with black arabesques and black cuffs with two vertical yellow grenadier flashes on them. The buttonholes were trimmed with yellow lace and there was yellow lace on the chest. The pants were dark blue and a 20" high bearskin cap and black (in place of white) leather belts and straps were worn. A brass shield with the unit designation was worn at the crossing of the shoulderbelts. This uniform was later changed to a deep red tailcoat with white lapels having eight buttonholes trimmed with yellow lace, sky blue turnbacks, collar and cuffs with white piping. The cuffs had double yellow flashes and the pocket flaps were vertical with three tassels. There was an embroidered grenade clasp on each coattail and the epaulettes were yellow and fringeless. The pants were sky blue with a yellow stripe at the seams and the fur cap had a brass grenade as a shield.

The Grenadiers of Toluca also wore a scarlet coat with white lapels and gold lace. The collar, cuffs and turnbacks were light blue with gold lace and there were four bars on the cuffs. Epaulettes were gold and black leather cross belts were worn. Trousers were light blue with a yellow stripe down the seams. A black bearskin with a gilt grenade plate and chinscales without cords or plume was also worn. This uniform is almost identical in description to that of the Grenadier Guards of the Supreme Powers, but no further information is available on this unit at this time to indicate why.

The Mexican Marines had a distinctive uniform of a dark green tailcoat with crimson lapels having nine buttonholes with pointed yellow lace trim. The turnbacks were yellow with two crimson silk anchors two inches high embroidered as coattail clasps. The collar was dark green with two inch high anchors embroidered in yellow silk. The cuffs were dark green with two rows of yellow lace and each sleeve had three diagonal yellow flashes. Piping was crimson and epaulettes were yellow, while the buttons were gilt anchors. The pants were crimson with a yellow stripe at the seams. The shako was covered with crimson cloth and had a tricolor cockade and a yellow pompon with a green streamer.

The uniforms of the Active Militia had been similar to those of the regulars up until April of 1842 when they were issued a standard uniform for all units. A good example of this uniform would be that of the Active Militia Companies of San Patricio. They were issued turkish blue tailcoats with crimson turnbacks, epaulettes, collar and cuffs with yellow piping on the collar. Fringeless epaulettes could also be worn or simple shoulder straps in turkish blue with yellow piping. There were yellow turnback ornaments consisting of two quivers containing three arrows each. The brass buttons were stamped with a company abbreviation and number. Pants were sky blue with a crimson stripe at the seams. Headgear was a black leather shako with a red band and pompon. The shako plate had the National Coat of Arms and company abbreviations and number. Dark blue barracks caps piped in crimson with a red tassel in front were also worn by the troops and the officers might wear a blue kepi in the field.

The original uniform of the Active Commerce Regiment of Mexico dates when the unit was raised it 1835 consisted of a turkish blue tailcoat with eight buttonholes trimmed with yellow lace instead of the usual lapels. The collar, cuffs and turnbacks were of black velvet with red arabesques and red piping. Dark blue or white pants were to be worn. This already showy uniform was further embellished by the unauthorized use of vertical flashes on the cuffs. This distinction was meant to be reserved for grenadier or rifle companies and the regiment was among those cited in 1836 for this abuse. It is not known whether this uniform survived the many changes in regulations over the years, or the disbandment and reformation of the unit in 1839.

The San Blas Battalion shows a uniform that is unique in that officers and men are clad differently. The officers wear a dark blue frock coat with dark blue collar, red cuffs and cuff flaps and yellow piping and epaulettes. The collars have red collar patches on the front. The pants are sky blue with a yellow stripe down the seam. Officers are shown wearing both shakos with red pompons and kepis of dark blue with a red band and yellow piping. The men are wearing gray frock coats with gray collars, red cuffs and cuff flaps with dark blue piping. The collar has red collar patches and there are no epaulettes visible. The men wear sky blue pants with a red stripe down the seam. Black shakos with red pompons and dark blue barracks caps with red band and piping are shown for headgear. All belts are in black for officers and men alike. These uniforms may have been according to regulations or they may have been improvised. The San Blas Battalion had at one time or another been an Active Militia unit, a Coast Guard Battalion and a regular Line Infantry unit which may in some way account for their unique uniforms.

The National Guard troops wore a medium to dark gray frock coat with red piping around the collar and cuffs, which were the same color as the coat. Epaulettes were yellow and pompons were red. The buttons and buckles were brass and all belts and straps were of black leather. Pants were sky blue with a yellow stripe at the seams and the headgear was still the standard black shako.

The uniform of the National Guard Buglers is given as a scarlet single-breasted coatee with dark blue collar, cuffs and turnbacks all piped in white. Three silver lace diagonal stripes, or half chevrons, were worn on the sleeve above the cuff and two more were placed on the upper arm. Epaulettes were silver and cartridge and sword belts were white. Trousers were light blue with a white stripe. A black shako was worn with a red band on top and a white band on the bottom and brass chinscales. It had a red pompon over the National tricolor cockade and a brass plate bearing the National coat of arms. It is not known if this was a unique dress uniform of some kind or if all musicians for the National Guard wore this to stand out from the rank and file. Uniforming musicians in either very bright or the reverse colors of a regiment was common practice among Napoleonic style armies but it is not known if that was the intent here.

CAVALRY

The Mexican Cavalry normally wore a waist length double-breasted jacket with lapels having short skirts with turnbacks in the rear. These tailcoats were more colorful and varied than the turkish blue of the infantry with each regiment having its own distinct combination of colors. The seat of the pants was lined with antelope skin for protection and the inside pant legs were lined with black leather and had black leather half-boots coming part way up from the bottom of the pant leg.

Cavalry headgear was similar to the infantry in its variety. The basic black shako was the norm with white metallic bands and a shako plate in one of several different styles. The pompons were red except for light cavalry regiments which had green. There were also Napoleonic era cuirassier or carabinier style helmets of black leather or brass with leopard skin turban, long black horsehair crests and tall tricolor pompons. Lancers might also wear a *tchapka* similar to the type worn by the Polish lancers of Napoleon's Army. This was a black leather cap with visor topped by a large flat square crown on a narrow square stem, usually brightly colored and highly decorated with silver lace and metallic ornaments. Black fur busbys were also worn by some of the Light Cavalry and Hussars. Another type of headgear common on the frontier was the broad brimmed black hat of the Presidial troops. It had a round crown and a white band. Guerillas and rancheros would usually be found wearing their native sombreros of whatever

color and style was to their liking.

A blanket and the riders' cape or overcoat were folded into a rectangle, rolled up and strapped underneath the cloth or leather saddle roll. The cylindrical roll would contain cloth, canvas or leather pants, a shirt, socks, brushes for cloth and shoes, a satchel with a comb, scissors, pins, accessories and boot grease. A canvas sack eighteen inches wide with two pockets contained an apron and sponge. Spare horseshoes were carried in a saddle pocket and the fatigue jacket and raincoat were folded and placed under the saddle roll.

All uniform accessories for cavalry were white or silver. The regimental number was stamped on all buttons and embroidered on the collar. Extra embroidery was prohibited except for coattail clasps of silver eagles two inches wide between the wingtips of the turnbacks. Cavalry epaulettes were usually dark green and pants would be turkish blue with a deep red stripe at the seams unless otherwise ordered.

The decree of July 10, 1839 spelled out the regulation uniform distinctions for each cavalry regiment and once confirmed this remained in effect with only minor changes until the end of the war.

The First Cavalry originally had a yellow tailcoat with deep red lapels, turnbacks, collar and cuffs with the piping in opposite colors. Pants were medium blue with a red stripe at the seams and the saddle blanket deep red with white trim. Later, on September 7, 1845 a new uniform was assigned to the First Cavalry consisting of a short dark green jacket with yellow lapels and turnbacks, dark green collar and cuffs and yellow piping. The epaulettes were dark green with deep red fringe, all buttons were of white metal and the pants were gray with red stripes at the seams. A black helmet with a horsehair crest and a deep red plume on the left side was worn along with a dark blue cape with a green collar. The saddle blanket and holster covers were deep red with white trim.

The Second Cavalry was originally given a yellow tailcoat with sky blue lapels, turnbacks, collar, cuffs and piping. Pants were turkish blue with a red stripe and the saddle blanket was turkish blue with white trim. However, a decree of March 30, 1846 renamed the Active Militia Cavalry Regiment of Queretaro as the Second Cavalry and the uniform was changed. The new Second Cavalry uniform was a yellow tailcoat with crimson lapels, turnbacks, collar and cuffs. The trousers were green with a white stripe and a red shako was worn. The saddle blanket was red with a white border.

The Third Cavalry wore a turkish blue tailcoat with white lapels and turnbacks. The collar and cuffs were green with piping in opposite colors. The saddle blanket was green with white trim.

The Fourth Cavalry wore a sky blue tailcoat with deep red lapels, turnbacks, collar and cuffs, and piping in opposite colors. The saddle blanket was green with white trim.

The Fifth Cavalry wore a turkish blue tailcoat with deep red lapels, turnbacks, collar and cuffs, and piping in opposite colors. Saddle blankets were deep red with white trim.

The Sixth Cavalry wore a green tailcoat with white lapels and deep red turnbacks. The collar, cuffs and piping were all white. Pants were green with a deep red stripe and the saddle blankets were red with white trim.

The Seventh Cavalry was originally issued a white tailcoat with sky blue lapels, turnbacks, collar and cuffs. Saddle blankets were green with white trim. Then on September 10, 1842 the uniform of the Seventh Cavalry was changed to a crimson tailcoat with green lapels having eight white lace trimmed buttonholes. The turnbacks, collar and cuffs were also green and piping was in opposite colors. Pants were green with a crimson stripe and saddle blankets were sky blue with white trim.

The Eighth Cavalry wore a turkish blue tailcoat with deep red lapels and white turnbacks. The collar was white and the cuffs were deep red with piping in opposite colors. The saddle blanket was green with white trim.

The Ninth Cavalry wore a green tailcoat with crimson lapels, turnbacks, collar and cuffs, and white piping. Saddle blankets were green with white trim.

The Light Mounted Regiment of Mexico had been raised in 1835 and was now given a uniform of a sky blue coatee without lapels. The turnbacks were scarlet as were the collar, cuffs, and epaulettes. The letters "LM" standing for "Ligero de Mexico", were embroidered on both sides of the collar in white. Pants were turkish blue with a deep red stripe at the seams. Regular cavalry shakos were worn with green pompons to designate light cavalry. The saddle blanket and a cloak were both sky blue with scarlet trim. This same uniform was also used by a Light Puebla squadron, a regular Tabasco Company, a Light Regiment of Vera Cruz, and a Yucatan squadron. It was also adopted as the uniform for all Active Militia Cavalry units with the exception of the Mounted Rifles and Jalisco Lancers (see below).

The regular Presidial Companies (with the exception of the California Companies) had a uniform of a medium blue coatee without lapels and with deep red turnbacks, low collar, and cuffs. The pants were also medium blue with a deep red stripe. A blue cloth cape was also worn. The headgear was a flat black broad-brimmed hat with a round crown and a white band around it. The name of the presidio was embroidered on the bandoleer worn with the leather cartridge box. The independent Presidial companies as well as those in New Mexico and Texas all wore this uniform. The California Presidial Companies had a garrison uniform of a turkish blue tailcoat with deep red lapels and turnbacks, green collar and cuffs and white piping. Pants were turkish blue with a deep red stripe and regular cavalry shakos were worn. The initial "AC" or "BC" were embroidered on the collar for Alta (upper) California and Baja (lower) California. The field uniform was a turkish blue round jacket with a deep red collar and cuffs. Gray side-buttoned chaparral pants were worn over boots and the familiar round black hat with a white band replaced the shako.

A light cavalry unit known as the Mounted Rifles had been raised in 1840, and in 1843 they were given new uniforms consisting of a dark green jacket with crimson lapels, turnbacks, collar and cuffs with white piping. The coat breast had twelve buttons trimmed with white lace (silver for officers) and the epaulettes were crimson. The trousers were green with a crimson stripe. Headgear was a black fur busby with yellow metal shield and a crimson bag and plume. They had a yellow cape and the saddle blanket and roll was green with crimson trim.

The Tulancingo Cuirassiers had a distinctive uniform of a sky blue jacket with crimson collar and cuffs and crimson pants with a sky blue stripe. A yellow metal cuirass and helmet was worn with white metal ornaments for troopers and silver for officers. The helmet had a horsetail crest on the comb and a tricolor pompon. Epaulettes were silver. Saddle blankets were sky blue trimmed in white for the troopers and silver for officers. Officers also had a silver belt and cartridge box as well as a bridle trimmed with silver. When off duty or dismounted the officers could wear a sky blue tailcoat with crimson turnbacks and a black bicorne hat. The pants for dismounted officers and troopers were in reverse colors of the mounted wear, being sky blue with a crimson stripe.

The Hussars of the Guard of the Supreme Powers was an elite unit with an elaborate uniform. They wore a deep red dolman without piping, but with white cord brandenbourgs and a white stripe down the center with spherical white metal buttons (possibly 4 rows of 12 each). The collar and pointed cuffs were ice blue edged with white lace. Slung over the left shoulder when not being worn was a pelisse of an ice blue color, without piping, with white cord brandenbourgs and black fur collar, cuffs and edging. The pelisse also had a white suspension cord with a slide button and two flounders at the left side. Pants were ice blue with a white stripe at the seams. Black leather half-boots, common for the Mexican cavalry, were worn. A black sabretache with one inch wide white lace on the side and bottom edges was suspended on two slings from a waistbelt. The headgear was a black fur busby with a red bag with white piping and tassel, a three yard long white safety cord, and a brass shield with the unit's name stamped on it. Saddle blanket and holster covers were deep red with white trim and the cloth saddle roll was ice blue with white piping. Lance pennons were red over blue.

The two squadrons of Jalisco Lancers wore a deep red single-breasted coatee with dark green turnbacks, collar and pointed cuffs. Piping was in opposite colors and yellow fringeless epaulettes were worn. Pants were turkish blue with a deep red stripe at the seams. They wore white leather straps, belt and swordknot. Headgear was a black leather tchapka with a deep red top, a central band of yellow with a brass plate, yellow cords, a tricolor cockade, and falling yellow plume in the front. Saddle blanket and holster covers were green with white trim and the saddle roll was green with a deep red cover.

ARTILLERY

The Foot Artillery dressed in a turkish blue tailcoat with black lapels and crimson turnbacks. The lapels had seven buttonholes trimmed with yellow angular pointed lace and the turnbacks had two inch long bomb coattail clasps. The collar, cuffs and piping were all crimson and epaulettes were yellow. The collar bore a flaming bomb embroidered in yellow silk along with the number of the Brigade (1 through 4) or Standing Company (1 through 5). Buttons were gilt with a bomb device on them. Pants were turkish blue with a crimson stripe and the black shako had a tricolor cockade and crimson pompon. Overcoats were turkish blue with crimson collar and embroidered bombs and unit numbers. Officers lapels were black velvet with gold lace and embroidery.

The Mounted Artillery wore the same dress as the Foot Artillery with the exception of a turkish blue coatee instead of a tailcoat with three half-inch diagonal white lace stripes on the forearm and a one and one-half inch band around the cuffs. Pants had antelope skin reinforcing on the inside leg and false boots. Horse equipment was similar to that for the cavalry with turkish blue saddle blanket and holster covers with a crimson border. Mounted gunners wore turkish blue capes.

ENGINEERS

The sapper battalion, as well as the rest of the Corps of Engineers, wore a turkish blue tailcoat with black lapels and crimson turnbacks. The collar was black, cuffs and piping were in crimson. There were special coattail clasps and buttons in yellow along with all accessories and epaulettes. Pants were medium blue with a crimson stripe at the seams. Black shakos were worn without cords and had crimson pompons. A gray frock coat was worn as an overcoat or as part of the undress uniform.

The Cadets of the Military Academy, under the jurisdiction of the Corps of Engineers, had worn a turkish blue tailcoat with sky blue collar and cuffs, yellow buttons and sky blue trousers. This uniform was changed in 1843 to a turkish blue tailcoat with crimson turnbacks, collar, cuffs, and piping and yellow buttons. Trousers were a somewhat lighter blue than the coats. Headgear was a black shako with a red band around the crown, a brass grenade insignia as shako plate and a red plume. Black leather belting was all of the infantry style with brass belt plates.

Cadets lower in rank than Second Lieutenant had a yellow lace border one-half inch wide on collar and cuffs. Cadet Sub-Lieutenants wore a single epaulette on the left shoulder. The undress uniform was a medium blue frock coat with red collar and cuffs. Trousers were dark blue in winter and white in summer. A blue visored cap or blue barracks cap with deep red lace and tassel was also worn. Shortly after the outbreak of war the cadets could be found in still another uniform, a service uniform consisting of a gray frock coat, trousers and barracks cap. The coat had a gray collar with three-pointed crimson collar patches, cuffs were gray with crimson cuff flaps with three gilt buttons at the points. The coat had a single row of gilt buttons stamped *Colegio Militar*. The belts were of black leather and gray spats were worn over the black shoes and under the trousers. The barracks cap was of medium height with golden yellow lace trim and tassels. Various paintings of the cadets killed while defending Chapultepec are shown in this uniform. Short, gray, round jackets were worn for drill or while on fatigue duty. These jackets had crimson facings and could be worn with plain gray or white duck trousers.

MEDICAL CORPS

Medical Officers wore a turkish blue tailcoat with turnbacks, collar and cuffs in the same color with crimson piping. Buttons were gilt eagles and coattail clasps were also eagles. Pants were turkish blue with a gold lace stripe at the seams. A black bicorne hat was worn along with a black leather sword scabbard and a sword with gold furnishings. In the field a turkish blue frock coat or a short military jacket was worn with crimson piping and yellow accessories. Pants were turkish blue with a crimson stripe. Rank insignia was the same pattern as the army but in crimson.

SUMMARY

The dizzying array of uniforms prescribed for the Mexican Army in the regulations of 1839 made it a truly impressive spectacle on the battlefield. The continual shortage of funds to pay contractors as well as chronic shortages of material made this magnificent assortment difficult, if not impossible, to maintain while the army was on campaign. The daily wear and tear, lack of proper replacements, and the improvisational skills of the common soldier made this army even more colorful than intended. The decree of 1840 to standardize uniforms throughout the army seems to have been an attempt to address this issue, but it was revoked only a year later in favor of the variations set forth in 1839. In retrospect, the funds probably would not have been available for standardized uniforms either, but this was the direction in which most modern armies were already headed.

148

From left to right in this picture by Hefter: a cadet in service uniform, an engineer officer instructor, cadet sublieutenant in dress uniform, a cadet in fatigue uniform and a bandsman. (Our thanks to the Company of Military Historians for this picture).

Author's Note: The main source for the material found in this chapter is *The Mexican Soldier 1837-1847* by Nieto-Brown-Hefter, edited and illustrated by Joseph Hefter. Most of the other sources derive much of their material from this small book.

THE U.S. ARMY

THE REGULARS

The United States Army appeared to be an insignificant force on the eve of hostilities with Mexico. The end of the War of 1812 had seen a drastic reduction in the size of the army due to the inherent distrust of a standing army exhibited by the American people. The popular image of the citizen-soldier coming to the aid of his country in time of war kept the regular army down to the size of a token force. There were thousands of miles of frontier and seacoast with unsettled borders with Great Britain and Mexico that needed watching and protecting. There were far flung posts in Indian country to patrol and seacoast forts to be manned. By comparison the army was indeed minuscule. In May of 1846 the army had only 637 officers and 5,925 enlisted men.

This small professional force was organized into eight regiments of infantry, four regiments of artillery and two regiments of dragoons. There were also 72 ships in the navy along with a single battalion of marines. The army was deployed, for the most part, in small detachments and isolated companies throughout the land. In addition to fighting Indians the soldiers sometimes protected them from the encroaching white settlers. Company level officers gained experience with small unit tactics but never had a chance to attempt the coordination required for fighting in formation with other units. Many long service officers had never seen their entire regiments together in one place to be able to drill or maneuver as a unit. Quite often, especially in the east, the only duty they performed was to assist in construction and engineering projects that could include bridges, roads, railroads and the improvement of harbors and inland waterways. Much of this was under the auspices of the Corps of Engineers which also lent officers to exploratory and map making expeditions. This dispersal was detrimental to army organization as a whole, although it was useful for the growing country that did not want to support a standing army. The size of the army, along with a miserly approach to its funding, forced the regulars to become a lean and tough group in order to survive.

The leadership of the army fell into two general categories. The older and more senior officers were mostly self-taught in the principles of the art of war. They had a wealth of experience, sometimes dating back to the War of 1812 and the Seminole War of the 1830s, but many should have been long retired. The prospects of retirement on a poverty level pension were recognized as being so bleak that the army kept them on at full pay in the service. Some of these men were no longer fit for command and many captains and colonels did not accompany their regiments when called to war citing various reasons for taking leave. Those with greater courage did go to war, like the elderly Colonel Josiah H. Vose of the Fourth Infantry who fainted and died while issuing orders during battalion drill on the parade ground when the regiment had gathered in New Orleans. Many of these veteran leaders did serve well in the war and Zachary Taylor and Winfield Scott, both self-taught, fall into this category. The lack of turnover resulting from this system of tenure led to a scarcity of promotions for the younger officers which caused many of the more educated to leave the army and seek opportunity in civilian life. In actuality many regiments were run by the more junior officers who accomplished the day to day tasks at the behest of their commanders. The junior officers were mostly better educated and trained in the history of the art of war at the U.S. Military Academy at West Point. While this establishment had been in existence almost 40 years its graduates had yet to prove themselves in a major war. Arguments had been made that the Academy was a waste of tax dollars and went against the idea of a volunteer militia as the answer to the military problems of the nation. The battlefields of Mexico offered a place for the professionals to show the skills they had learned in the fields of engineering, ordnance, topography, and leadership. In Mexico the former Cadets would prove themselves to be outstanding. Many of them would go on to lead the much greater armies of the North and South only fifteen years later.

THE VOLUNTEERS

The same day that President Polk sent a message to Congress announcing that a state of war existed because of the hostile acts of Mexico, May 11, 1846, a bill was passed by both the House of Representatives and the Senate authorizing the use of the militia and the calling up of 50,000 volunteers. These men would be enlisted as companies and larger formations of volunteer organized militia provided by the states. The volunteers were "to serve twelve months" or "to the end of the war" according to the wording of the bill. Unfortunately this allowed

The U.S. Army

each volunteer to decide for himself at the end of twelve months whether to remain in service or not. This would cause many problems later, in the midst of the campaign. The bill also extended the term of the militia in the service of the United States to six months. Due to the fact that the Mexican War was fought entirely on foreign soil, the militia, which was supposed to be only a home defence force, was not ever called into service.

The volunteers were to furnish their own uniforms and equipment with the United States providing the weapons. Volunteers were to receive compensation for clothing and the same rate of pay as the regulars. Officers were to be appointed according to the laws of their state. Field officers were sometimes quite good, with some being West Point graduates. Company level officers were often elected by the men and were very often incompetent.

General Zachary Taylor had called for Texas militia before hostilities had begun and received 1,390 men. General Edmund P. Gaines in New Orleans, who was Taylor's immediate superior had made an unauthorized call for six months militia from Alabama, Mississippi, and Missouri which brought in another 11,211 men. Gaines was reprimanded and relieved from command for this. Some of these men only served for three months, which was the term prescribed in peacetime, and then went home while others rejoined as twelve months men, or possibly for the duration of the war.

Infantry

The Regulars

The common soldier enlisted for five years at a rate of pay of about $7 a month. These were not the type of incentives that would induce men to sign up unless they had no other prospects to speak of in civilian life. As a result the army attracted the poor and uneducated, as well as many foreigners with no other options. As many as half of the foreign born soldiers were from Ireland and along with men from Germany, France, England, Italy, and elsewhere made up a total of about 42 percent of the army. The more industrialized northern states offered much more opportunity for civilian employment and so the southern states provided a much greater percentage of the manpower for the army. At this time enlistment in the army was closed to black Americans, even though they had served well in both the American Revolution and the War of 1812. Not until the Civil War would black soldiers be seen again in the Army of the United States.

Army regulations required that each recruit pass a physical exam given by a doctor. The men were told to disrobe so that obvious abnormalities and defects could be discovered as well as any brands that had been tattooed under the arm or on the hip

of undesirables by the authorities. The letter 'D' for deserter, or 'HD' for habitual drunkard would disqualify a man for enlistment. A recruit had to have front teeth strong enough to tear open a musket cartridge along with full flexibility of arms and legs. A guide for the medical examination of recruits at the time stated that, "Some recruits are so offensive in their breath ...as to be intolerable to their comrades; and, for these causes ...ought, unquestionably, to be rejected from any army." Recruits who passed the physical exam were given a complete bath and each had his "hair cut close to his head." Despite regulations, all of the rules were not always obeyed and there were several cases of women masquerading as men attempting to enlist. Sometimes these were the wives or girlfriends of soldiers, and sometimes they did it on their own. It is unlikely that any women actually served in combat, although Eliza Allen Billings from Maine did write a book after the war claiming that she fought and had been wounded at Cerro Gordo without revealing her secret.

The soldiers were quartered in billets that often had two men to a bunk about six feet long and four feet wide and padded with straw. Soldiers did not earn enough to support a family although some did take wives. These "marriages" were not always legal and many of the wives served as laundresses or cooks for the troops. In this official capacity they were issued rations and bedding and where possible, assigned to separate quarters. At times they were even provided with arms. Some of them would stay with the company even after their "husbands" had moved on or passed away, finding another soldier to "marry".

The lifestyle of these common soldiers was anything but free and easy, even in peacetime. Assignment to a unit posted in the east, nearer to the more civilized areas of the country was most desirable. All military posts shared the duties of working on civilian projects while still maintaining a high level of discipline among the soldiers. This was made more difficult by the soldiers' affinity for gambling and drinking, especially in the far flung posts where boredom was a factor. Fatigue from constant military drill and work on civilian projects also wore on the men. The result could be ill health and alcoholism among the poverty stricken soldiers.

Officers earned higher rates of pay but they were also expected to maintain a much higher standard of living. Often it was much more than they could afford unless they were from a wealthy family. Many officers ended up heavily in debt as a result. The more educated officers were able to find much better financial opportunities in civilian life, especially since advancement to higher ranks was so slow in the army.

The law passed by Congress on January 12, 1847

was an effort to entice more recruits into the army. A $12 bounty was offered for anyone who would enlist for five years or "during the war" with half of the money to be paid up front and the other half when the recruit actually joined his regiment. In addition, upon serving twelve months every soldier who had earned an honorable discharge was given 160 acres of land. Another act was passed on March 3, 1847 in which soldiers already in Mexico were offered the $12 bounty if they would re-enlist for the duration of the war. Privates who earned a certificate of merit for acts of bravery would earn a bonus of $2 per month extra pay. These measures helped to bring the new units from the "Ten Regiment Bill" up to strength for service in Mexico and encouraged many of the soldiers already there to stay on.

THE VOLUNTEERS

There was an overwhelming response to the call for volunteers. Men flocked to the colors eager for an opportunity to demonstrate their patriotism. Many had a desire for personal glory and foreign adventure. Others were out to avenge the dead heroes of the Texas Revolution of 1836 and the subsequent troubles with Mexico. A lot of people had actually had friends or relatives who had lost their lives fighting Mexico during the last ten years. Many men saw enlisting as a solution to their problems in civilian life. Some saw the army as a better job than what was available in the current weak economy. The majority were farmers or laborers from the largely rural population of the country at the time. There were fewer foreign born soldiers in the volunteers than in the regular army, but many recent immigrants saw military service as a way to learn the language and customs of their new country so that they would be better off when they got out to find employment in civilian life. A lot of the volunteers joined up simply to do something memorable and get away from their everyday lives. Some even used the service as a way to get free transportation to the frontier where they could desert and get a fresh start in a new place. The average age of the volunteers was around twenty-five or twenty-six years old, but there were soldiers of every age from thirteen to eighty.

ORGANIZATION

THE REGULARS

The U.S. Army at the beginning of hostilities with Mexico consisted of eight infantry regiments numbered one through eight. A regiment was commanded by a Colonel, with a Lieutenant Colonel as second in command and a Major as an additional field officer. The remainder of the regimental staff consisted of an Adjutant and Quartermaster (both Lieutenants drawn from the companies), a Quartermaster Sergeant, a Sergeant Major and two

Musicians. Each regiment was made up of ten companies. Eight of these companies were called battalion companies and the other two were called flank companies. One of the flank companies was designated as grenadiers, to be posted on the right side of the regiment and the other flank company was light infantry or rifles to be posted on the left side of the regiment while in line. The standard armament for the eight battalion companies was the smoothbore musket, while the flank companies were supposed to have rifles for skirmishing or sharpshooting. In actual practice there does not seem to be much distinction at all between any of the ten companies. (The term battalion was also used to refer to a unit five companies strong, or half of a regiment. Companies were usually grouped in battalions for special duties, it was not a commonly used unit either on or off the battlefield. A battalion could also contain more or less than five companies and they might even be from more than one regiment.) A company was commanded by a Captain and also had a Lieutenant and a second Lieutenant as commissioned officers. There were also four Sergeants, four Corporals and two Musicians in each company. The authorized strength of an infantry company was forty-two privates. This had been reduced from ninety privates by an act of Congress on August 23, 1842 that cut back on all branches of the military. Infantry companies seldom reached even the lower "paper" strength due to recruiting difficulties, desertion, sickness and men on various leaves of absence. Although the authorized strength of a full company should have been fifty-five men, at the beginning of hostilities the typical infantry company was anywhere from 15 to 25 percent lower than that. On May 13, 1846 an act of Congress was passed that raised the number of privates per company to a maximum of one hundred, although once again, this strength was only on paper.

Another act of Congress was passed on February 11, 1847 that authorized the establishment of nine additional infantry regiments. There were to be eight regular regiments numbered nine through sixteen and a regiment of Voltigeurs and Foot Riflemen. The act also authorized the appointment of an additional Major for each regiment. The organization of these eight regular regiments of the "new" army was identical to that of the "old" army with the addition of one more Second Lieutenant for each company.

The Regiment of Voltigeurs and Foot Riflemen was to be organized with an equal number of infantry and mounted men along with a battery of mountain howitzers and rockets all included in one regiment. It would constitute its own combined arms force on a regimental scale. When rapid movement was called for each rifleman on foot would climb up behind a mounted voltigeur. In practice, however, the unit never had the horses it was authorized and so it served as an additional infantry regiment armed with rifles and having the same organization as the other eight "new" army regiments.

THE VOLUNTEERS

All men between the ages of eighteen and forty-five were required by federal law since 1792 to enroll in the militia. The typical militia company was to have two officers, twelve non-commissioned officers and sixty-five privates. A militia regiment was to be made up of ten of these companies. In theory, the United States could call on almost two million militiamen in 1846. In practice, most of these units simply didn't exist. Technically, the militia was only supposed to serve for three months as a home defence force, not to be sent beyond the boundaries of the United States. That is why it was essential to rely on volunteers to carry the burden of the nations' manpower needs.

War fever was running high when the secretary of war issued the first call for about twenty thousand men from Alabama, Arkansas, Georgia, Illinois, Indiana. Kentucky, Mississippi, Missouri, Ohio, Tennessee, and Texas. The other states were to enlist another twenty-five thousand men for future use. Quotas were filled in a matter of hours in some places. In Tennessee ten times the number of volunteers came forward than had been called. Kentucky had four times as many as needed. Illinois had enough men for fourteen regiments when only four had been sought. Ohio took only two weeks to fill its three thousand man quota. Companies were usually accepted on a first come basis. Many companies that had been organized were also overstrength with more than 100 men each when authorized strength was only 64. Many volunteers were left behind and had to return home as they were simply not needed. This enthusiasm to serve would eventually fade as the war lasted longer than expected.

The actual organization of the volunteers was to be the same as for the regulars. Unlike the regulars, most volunteer regiments started out at full strength or very close to it. Unfortunately, desertion, disease and death thinned the ranks appreciably before most units ever saw action. The volunteer infantry units listed below served between May of 1846 and December of 1847, and the numbers in parenthesis are an estimate of the total number of men provided by each state.

Alabama	2 regiments, 2 battalions, 3 companies (2918)
Arkansas	3 companies (265)
California	1 company (47)
Florida	4 companies (323)
Georgia	1 regiment, 1 battalion (1390)
Illinois	6 regiments (5548)
Indiana	5 regiments (4470)

Iowa	1 company (73)
Kentucky	4 regiments (3962)
Louisiana	7 regiments, 1 battalion, 1 company (6698)
Maryland & DC	1 regiment, 1 battalion (1194)
Massachusetts	1 regiment (1047)
Michigan	1 regiment, 1 company (972)
Mississippi	2 regiments, 1 battalion (2319)
Missouri	2 regiments, 1 battalion, 4 companies (2429)
Mormons	1 battalion (585)
New Jersey	1 battalion (424)
New York	2 regiments (2665)
North Carolina	1 regiment (936)
Ohio	5 regiments (4694)
Pennsylvania	2 regiments, 1 company (2464)
South Carolina	1 regiment (1054)
Tennessee	5 regiments (4466)
Texas	1 regiment, 1 battalion, 2 companies (1103)
Virginia	1 regiment (1303)
Wisconsin	2 companies (146)

A total of fifty regiments, ten battalions and twenty-three Companies (53,495).

Some of these units had only short term enlistments and were replaced by other units from the same states at a later date.

WEAPONS

The United States had no lack of weapons available to arm its soldiers. The most common weapon issued to regulars and volunteers alike was the Model 1835 (sometimes referred to as the Model 1840) flintlock musket. This was a copy of the French Model 1822 musket which was also in use at the time. It was a smoothbore musket that was 0.69 caliber and was 57.75 inches long and weighed about ten pounds. The length of the barrel itself was 42 inches. The standard load was a cartridge that contained one round ball and three buckshot. A newer model musket was adopted by the army in 1842 that was identical in size and appearance to the Model 1835. This was also a smoothbore musket but it had a percussion cap system for firing. The percussion cap made the weapon easier to load and a bit more reliable. The average rate of fire for either of the smoothbore muskets was about two to three rounds per minute. American ordnance officers had encouraged the manufacture and use of the new system but very few companies went to Mexico equipped with percussion cap muskets. The ordnance department officials had reasoned that there was no time to properly train the troops in the use of the new weapon. Drill manuals did not exist that took these weapons into account. The older officers, including General Worth, were afraid that the troops would lose their percussion caps and thus render their weapons useless. They did not consider that the flints for the flintlocks could also be lost or adversely affected by wet weather, probably because these weapons had been in long use already. Therefore the majority of troops sent to Mexico used the smoothbore flintlock musket, of which there was a good supply.

The characteristics shared by both flintlock and percussion muskets alike were their abysmal accuracy beyond any distance except the shortest of ranges. Firing tests were done on these muskets in 1860 with the results showing only ten percent accuracy at a range of 100 yards under ideal conditions. Ulysses S. Grant, then a 2nd Lieutenant serving with the 4th Infantry, would later recall, "At the distance of a few hundred yards a man might fire at you all day without your finding it out." The tactics employed at the time had been adapted for these types of weapons. Infantry formations were supposed to deliver massed volleys of fire at short range into the enemy and follow with a bayonet charge in true Napoleonic style. At close ranges these weapons demonstrated a devastating effectiveness.

The Model 1841 U.S. Rifle adopted by the government would eventually make the smoothbore musket obsolete. This was sometimes called the 'Windsor', 'Whitney' or 'Jager' rifle but was generally known after the war as the 'Mississippi' rifle due to its use by the 1st Mississippi under the command of Colonel Jefferson Davis. The weapon weighed 9½ pounds and was 48 inches long with a 33 inch rifled barrel of 0.54 caliber. It fired a single spherical lead ball inserted in a greased patch. The paper cartridge contained 75 grains of powder and the rifle was fired using a percussion cap system. The rifle took longer to load than the smoothbore muskets and it usually could not accommodate a bayonet. However, it had an adjustable rear sight and was reasonably accurate up to 500 yards. This was the first mass-produced rifle with interchangeable parts to be authorized for use by the United States. Jefferson Davis insisted that his entire regiment be armed with this rifle and he even wrote his own manual for training his regiment. The U.S. Regiment of Voltigeurs and Foot Riflemen was also armed with this weapon.

Bayonets for the muskets were about eighteen inches long with a triangular shaped blade and could be fixed to the underlug at the end of the barrel. There were also sabre bayonets with brass hilts measuring 22 ½ inches long. Soldiers were also known to carry flintlock pistols, short artillery swords, Bowie knives and the new 5-shot Colt revolvers.

Officers and NCOs carried a straight-edged sword that was 38 ¾ inches long overall. The hilt was cast in brass and it was carried in a black leather scabbard with a brass throat and tip.

Tactics

The manual of instruction in use by the American army at the time of the Mexican War was General Winfield Scott's own "Infantry Tactics". This was a translation of the French *"Reglement concernant l'exercise et les manoeuvres d'infanterie du 1er aout 1791"* that Napoleon had used to train the Grande Armée. During the War of 1812 Winfield Scott, a Brigadier General at the time, had begun using the French drill manual in place of the existing "Hand Book for Infantry". Shortly after the war the new manual was officially adopted for the army and Scott added some of his own material resulting in the latest version, published in 1840, being used by the army that went to Mexico.

The regulations were used to drill the troops and train them in the basics of Napoleonic style formations and maneuvers. There were three phases explained in the manual. They were the School of the Soldier, the School of the Company and the School of the battalion. The infantry units would form in lines two ranks deep. The men were spaced in each rank in such a way that while facing forward and keeping shoulders square to the front the right elbow would just touch the elbow of the man adjacent without opening the arms. The distance from the back of the front rank to the front of the men in the back rank was only enough to allow the troops to execute facing movements such as "right face" or "about face", etc. On rough ground or when the troops were ordered to march at double time this distance was increased to thirty-two inches with the troops closing up again any time a halt was called. The men were trained to march using a "direct step" of twenty-eight inches in length taking ninety steps per minute. The "quick step" simply increased the number of steps taken to one-hundred and ten per minute. When ordered to advance at "double step" the length of the step was to be thirty-three inches and the cadence was increased to one-hundred and sixty-five steps per minute. A regiment was normally composed of ten companies. The regiment or any part of it that included two or more companies could also be known as a battalion. Two companies constituted a 'division' for purposes of performing evolutions. Regiments were trained in the use of columns for maneuvering into position before deploying into a line formation for firing. The interval between regiments could vary from as little as six yards up to twenty-four yards. The distances between regiments when formed in lines one behind the other could vary with the nature of the ground and the type of action being fought. Offensive actions usually called for the second line to be held close to be able to support the front line. Defensive situations called for the second line to provide a rallying point far enough in the rear to allow the first line to reform behind it in the event of being driven back. Forming square was still the best defense for infantry against enemy cavalry and the troops did it well.

The plan of action was spelled out in the drill books and regulations. Skirmishers were to screen the movements of friendly troops and engage the enemy while the infantry moved into position to fire. The thinly deployed skirmish lines could cause confusion and harass formed bodies of the enemy to buy time for their own formations to come up. Infantry columns would deploy into line formation and prepare for a close range firefight to be followed by a decisive bayonet charge on the disordered enemy troops. All the while the artillery would be lending its fire support from the front lines or on the flanks. Cavalry would then pursue a broken enemy to complete the victory. This was warfare by the book, but in Mexico the book was usually not practical to use.

The terrain that many battles were fought on made it impossible to deploy troops according to the formations that had been practiced. The army had to adapt to smaller and looser organizations to be able to deploy at all. At times the battles became man-to-man instead of regiment-to-regiment. The rough and varied terrain of Mexico offered defenders and attackers alike a challenge when it came to doing battle. American infantry were well trained in accurate fire at close range. Many soldiers were already familiar with firearms and did not need to be taught how to use them. The army encouraged marksmanship and even though the weapons provided were inaccurate at longer ranges they were put to deadly use when the troops closed with the enemy.

Visibility on the battlefield could also be a problem due to weather conditions, fires or clouds of gunsmoke from both sides. The American regular army units were well led by their junior officers and were able to adapt to many of these situations on the spot.

Many times the enemy was entrenched or in built up fortifications in cities. This called for an entirely different plan of attack. Small detachments called storming parties would be prepared for the assault. Artillery would attempt to prepare the way with bombardment followed by diversionary attacks in other locations. The attack would be carried out by these small groups of volunteers, often carrying scaling ladders or other tools to gain entry to their objectives. A great deal of faith was still placed in the bayonet charge which the Americans were often able to execute with great courage.

The American soldiers in Mexico were well armed and well trained and despite enduring great hardships they prevailed on their opponents. Many Americans saw these victories as being a part of their Manifest Destiny, but it had much more to do with planning and skill and the graduates of the military academy at West Point.

CAVALRY

THE REGULARS

The 1st and 2nd U.S. Dragoons, America's only cavalry in 1846, had been fighting Indians for ten years before the Mexican War. They were a tough bunch of hardened soldiers used to gruelling marches on the Plains and long odds in battle. The dragoons had a much lower percentage of recent immigrants in their ranks than there were in the infantry.

The Dragoons were well mounted on large horses and had been well trained for duty on the frontier. The regiments were spread out in company strength to small far reaching posts all over the West. Officers were not able to practice maneuvering forces larger than a company or two. The Dragoons acquired plenty of experience in light cavalry tactics while dealing with the Indians, though the traditional role of battle cavalry was not as familiar to them. Colonel Stephen Watts Kearny of the 1st Dragoons realized the difficulty of maintaining an effective cavalry arm under adverse conditions and attempted to remedy the situation. Kearny was able to rotate companies through his command and give them additional training in the fundamentals of field cavalry tactics. He was able to keep four companies at a time under his direct command and insured that all of the companies of the 1st Dragoons had been in direct contact with him and his ideas. The 1st Dragoons were probably the most efficient in their duties due to this extra effort and they were ready for the role they would be expected to play on the battlefields of Mexico.

As is often common in the mounted arm of any army the Dragoons considered themselves to be a cut above the average foot soldier. Typical was Samuel E. Chamberlain, a seventeen year old private in Company E of the 1st Dragoons who decided,

"...the Dragoons were far superior in materials to any other arm of the service. No man of any spirit and ambition would join the "Doughboys" and go afoot, when he could ride a fine horse and wear spurs like a gentleman. In our Squadron were broken down Lawyers, Actors and men of the world, Soldiers who had served under Napoleon, Polish Lancers, French Cuirassiers, Hungarian Hussars, Irishmen who had left the Queen's service to swear allegiance to Uncle Sam and wear the blue. Our officers were all graduates of West Point, and at the worst, were gentlemen of intelligence and education, often harsh and tyrannical, yet they took pride in having their men well clothed and fed, in making them contented and reconciled to their lot".

THE VOLUNTEERS

The Volunteer cavalry was truly a mixed force of variable quality. The most dangerous men were undoubtedly the Texas Mounted Volunteers under Colonel Jack Hays. These troops were a combination of several companies of Texas Rangers that already had a formidable reputation. They were excellent scouts and exhibited great skill at exterminating the guerrillas who had infested the army's lines of communication. Many had joined up to settle personal scores south of the border and they were responsible for numerous atrocities. The army found the volunteer units as a whole difficult to keep in check and Taylor was not sad to see most of them go when their short enlistment terms were up.

Although there were exceptions and some units acquitted themselves well, Sam Chamberlain gives as good an account as any when he says,

> "The material that these regiments were composed of was excellent… the men possessed fine physiques, and strength combined with activity, but they had no discipline, or confidence in their officers".

His comment on those officers was that,

> "The volunteer officers …would tie up a man one day, drink and play cards with him the next, and excuse their favorites from drill and guard duty; in short, most of them were totally incompetent, and a disgrace to their profession".

The lack of discipline and the unruliness of the volunteers made extra work for the Dragoons who were forced to patrol the countryside simply to keep the peaceful inhabitants safe from "these heroes" who were out to beat, rape, and rob them. The inexperience of the volunteers in campaigning also led to the deterioration of their combat worthiness. As described again by Chamberlain,

> "The really fine horses that they were mustered in with, they sold …and were now mounted on Mules or Mustangs that they had stolen. They took no care of their arms—not one Carbine in fifty would go off—and most of their Sabres were rusted in their scabbards".

ORGANIZATION

The two regiments of cavalry in regular service at the beginning of hostilities were the 1st and 2nd Regiments of U.S. Dragoons. Each regiment was organized with ten identical companies, similar to the infantry regiments. The regiment was commanded by a Colonel along with a Lieutenant Colonel, a Major and an Adjutant (with the rank of Lieutenant). There was also a Regimental Quartermaster, a Sergeant Major and a Quartermaster Sergeant. In addition each regiment had a Chief Musician and two Chief Buglers as well as a Principal Teamster who was usually a civilian contractor.

The ten companies each had a Captain, a Lieutenant and a 2nd Lieutenant for officers. Non-Commissioned Officers (NCO's) for each company were four Sergeants and four Corporals. There were also two buglers and a farrier and/or blacksmith. Two teamsters were also to be provided but they were normally under civilian contractors. The reduced strength companies at the beginning of the war were only authorized to have fifty privates. These figures would result in the "paper" strength of a company being three officers and sixty-one men. These numbers were rarely if ever achieved in the field with actual returns indicating shortages of up to 40% in some units.

The standard practice since the formation of the Dragoons in 1833 had always been to purchase horses of the same color for each company, and every company had different color horses than the next. This allowed for instant identification while in the field and it also enabled new horses to better assimilate with veteran horses that would adjust better to "recruits" of the same color.

Military legislation on May 13, 1846 authorized an increase in the number of privates to a hundred for each company of Dragoons. Once again these figures represent "paper" strength and were never actually achieved during the war.

On May 19, 1846 a new Regiment of Mounted Riflemen was added to the army. It had been organized for the purpose of guarding and patrolling the Oregon Trail but the decision was made to commit the unit to Mexico instead. This unit had the same table of organization as the two existing Dragoon regiments.

The "ten regiment bill" as it came to be known, was passed on February 11, 1847 and called for an additional regiment of cavalry that was to become the 3rd Dragoons. The new unit kept the same organization as the first two Dragoon regiments with the addition of a Surgeon and two Assistant Surgeons. An additional Major was also authorized for each mounted regiment.

Volunteer cavalry regiments were to be organized with only 64 men per company with ten companies per regiment. Due to the extreme enthusiasm at the beginning of hostilities many units exceeded this strength when originally formed. However, the journey to the theater of war along with the hardships of camp life thinned the ranks rapidly. Volunteer units fielded various numbers of companies with an ever changing total of men in each.

There were numerous formations of mounted volunteers that went to Mexico, though not all of them saw active service. Some arrived as reinforcements for General Taylor after the battles in northern Mexico had been fought and they ended up on patrol and garrison duty. The volunteer mounted units from the states listed below all served between May of 1846 and December of 1847. Numbers in parenthesis are an estimate of the total number of men provided.

Alabama	1 company (93)
Arkansas	1 regiment, 3 companies (1158)
California	1 battalion (470)
Georgia	1 battalion (657)
Illinois	1 regiment (425)
Iowa	2 companies (156)
Kentucky	1 regiment (838)
Louisiana	1 battalion (494)
Missouri	3 regiments, 2 battalions, 2 companies (3967)
Tennessee	1 regiment (944)
Texas	6 regiments, 1 battalion, 6 companies & a company of Indians (5569)

A total of 13 regiments, 6 battalions and 15 independent companies (14,771).

All of the above were to be organized as the U.S. Dragoons were but they mustered in at widely varying strengths and accurate numbers are difficult to come by.

Weapons

The primary weapon of the U.S. Dragoons was to be the Model 1840 Cavalry Sabre. The blade on this weapon was of polished steel about 1 ¼ inch wide at the hilt and a little less than 36 inches long with the overall length being about 38 ½ inches. The enlisted man's sabre hilt was of cast brass with wooden grips covered in leather and wrapped with brass wire. The officer's version was more ornate having a blade etched with designs and the letters "U.S." on both sides and with a hilt of gilded brass. This sabre was commonly known as the "old wristbreaker" and was patterned after the French light cavalry sabre of 1822. The Regiment of Mounted Riflemen also carried these weapons.

The Dragoons carried two different types of single-shot pistols into action in Mexico. The Johnson Model 1836 flintlock pistol was of 0.54 caliber with a round smoothbore barrel 8 ½ inches long. It had a brass front sight and pan and polished iron mountings with a swivel ramrod. The U.S. Model 1842 smoothbore percussion pistol began to be issued in 1845. It was also of 0.54 caliber and varied only slightly in size and shape from the Model 1836, having brass mountings instead of iron.

The Regiment of Mounted Riflemen were issued some of the new Whitneyville-Walker Colt revolvers in late 1847 to begin replacing their Model 1836 pistols. These were the largest Colt revolvers

produced weighing in at 4 ½ pounds with a 9 inch barrel. The "Walker" as it was known, was a five shot, 0.44 caliber pistol firing a conical or round bullet. This quickly became the preferred weapon of the Texas Rangers.

The Dragoons also had a carbine that had been designed for their use, the U.S. Model 1843 Hall breech-loader. This was a 0.54 caliber percussion weapon that was a direct descendant of the first percussion firearm in United States service. It had a 21 inch smoothbore barrel with case-hardened breech block, hammer, release plate and lever and trigger. The barrel and furniture were browned. (The chamber and lock of the Hall carbine could be removed by unscrewing a single screw. This allowed the dragoon to carry it as a concealed handgun on excursions into town. This was strictly against regulations, of course.) The Regiment of Mounted Riflemen carried the Model 1841 "Mississippi" Rifle described previously, slung over the left shoulder. This weapon was clumsy to handle while mounted and the Riflemen found it necessary to fire one round and then ride the enemy down with a sabre charge.

The Volunteer cavalry regiments were to be armed by the U.S. Government as well, but they also brought a wide variety of their own weapons along with their own horses.

The Quartermaster Department was responsible for supplying all horse equipments. The most common saddle in use by the Dragoons had been the U.S. Model 1841 which was manufactured by private contractors for the Army. This saddle was very similar in construction, design and shape to the British hussar saddle of 1805. It had a wooden pommel and cantle with a leather padded seat. There was a woolskin seat on the dress shabraque for parade and ceremonial exhibitions. Another type of saddle in use in 1846 was the Ringgold saddle designed by Major Samuel Ringgold. By the time the patent on this saddle was approved in 1844 the Army had already started to go to the greatly improved Grimsley saddle made by Thorton Grimsley. This saddle was less likely to make the horses back sore and it was popular with both dragoon and artillery officers. The saddle was better contoured to fit the horses back and it exerted equal pressure at all points of contact. The entire wooden tree was covered in rawhide that was sewed on while wet in a similar manner to the Mexican saddle, which gave it greater strength. It was the Grimsley pattern that the Regiment of Mounted Rifles was equipped with when it was formed, and this saddle continued to see use throughout the Civil War years.

Tactics

The War Department issued the first extensive manual of Cavalry Tactics in 1841. The manual provided for the training of troopers in every aspect of horsemanship and the evolutions of cavalry. The instructions were based on the French manual of the same period. This called for drilling the cavalry in two ranks. The regiment of ten companies was formed into five squadrons with a captain commanding each one.

The primary duty of the cavalry was scouting for the army to discover enemy positions and movements. Dragoons were also used to protect supply trains from attack by bandits and guerillas while on the march. On the battlefield the cavalry would guard the flanks of the infantry in line of battle as well as the rear areas. They were also called on to attack and defeat enemy cavalry directly to keep it from posing any kind of threat to the army. Cavalry was expected to threaten the enemy infantry and lines of supply as well as to follow up a defeated enemy. Unfortunately, the small numbers of Dragoons available for these numerous tasks made it impossible for them to achieve success in more than just a few areas. Although the Dragoons were trained to charge enemy cavalry as battle cavalry would, they were never deployed in enough strength to make this possible. Most of the time in Mexico the Dragoons had all they could do to simply secure the lines of communication of the army and perform basic scouting missions. On the battlefield itself the American cavalry was deployed to shield the army from enemy cavalry and was only rarely called on to charge into action. When they did engage enemy cavalry the Dragoons proved to be more than a match for their Mexican counterparts, who rode much lighter horses and were usually not willing to close into hand to hand combat. The Dragoons were most vulnerable in ambush and skirmish situations where the skilled Mexican riders usually had the advantages of terrain and the element of surprise.

The Dragoons and the Regiment of Mounted Rifles were trained to fight mounted and dismounted, which they did. Normally when dismounted, one out of every four men would be assigned as horse holders and sent to the rear with the horses until they were needed again. When dismounted the cavalry generally fought as skirmishers in an open formation and making use of cover if possible. The majority of the Mounted Rifles were actually forced to fight on foot throughout the campaign. Their horses were almost all lost at sea due to inadequate protection from the elements and the loss of ships in storms off the Texas coast. General Scott searched extensively for suitable replacements as the Mexican mustangs were too small to carry an American cavalryman and his equipment. In May of 1847 enough horses had been found to remount Company C, Captain Samuel H. Walker and Company I, Captain Charles F. Ruff, but the remainder of the regiment served as infantry throughout the war.

Volunteer cavalry units also fought mounted and dismounted, but they were the least trained of the volunteer units and often suffered from poor discipline. The volunteers added quite a bit to the minuscule amount of cavalry available to the army. However, they proved even more vulnerable to the ambush and surprise tactics of the Mexican cavalry and irregulars than the Dragoons.

ARTILLERY

Prior to the war the U.S. Artillery suffered from some of the same problems as the Infantry and Cavalry. The regiments were spread out at isolated posts all along the frontiers of the country. The ranks were filled with career soldiers and many of the officers were graduates of West Point. Scattered companies were responsible for garrisoning a multitude of coastal fortifications until Indian problems forced a frugal government to begin employing them as infantry units.

The U.S. Artillery was equipped with some of the best weapons in the world at the beginning of hostilities. The Artillery School, formed in 1824 at Fortress Monroe, Virginia was an advanced school for officers and served as a proving ground for artillery units to practice their professional skills. The high command had shown an early interest in the modernization and training of an effective artillery arm. Secretary of War Joel Roberts Poinsett ordered a board of officers to visit Europe in 1840 for the purpose of studying developments in artillery weapons. The board visited Austria, Belgium, England, France, Prussia, Russia and Sweden among others. They returned with samples of various types of cannon, alloys, ore and smelted metal used by the Europeans to manufacture weapons. Based on the findings of the board, which had been given permanent status, a complete artillery weapons system was designed and presented in the "Ordnance Manual for the Use of the Officers of the United States Army", which came to be known simply as the "Ordnance Manual of 1841." These efforts of the Ordnance Board resulted in an artillery arm for the U.S. Army that was second to none.

The War Department quickly realized that the best way to make the most of the modern equipment at hand was to give a high priority to an improved training doctrine for the men expected to employ it in the field. The Commanding General of the Army Winfield Scott reported in 1844 that updated systems of instruction were being provided for all branches of the service, including the artillery. This ultimately led to the publication of the "Instruction for Field Artillery, Horse and Foot" in 1845. This manual had originated with an edited version of an old French artillery manual that had been translated by Captain Robert Anderson, Third Artillery. The latest methods, based on a modified English system as developed by Company C, Third Artillery under Major Samuel Ringgold, were also incorporated into the instructions.

Artillerymen had usually fought as infantry against the Indians during the 1830's and they had become unaccustomed to the duties required for the artillery. In 1839 a training camp was established at Camp Washington, New Jersey, near Trenton, for the purpose of holding encampments to retrain artillerists in their craft. This was where the field artillery companies drew their guns and horses from. A light company from each regiment trained with Major Ringgold to learn the new skills and techniques required. Camp Washington was only open for a period of a few months after which each artillery regiment established its own training program using these light companies to train the remainder of the personnel in the unit. It was this training that allowed the U.S. Artillery arm to be prepared for the war in Mexico and to perform as well as they did.

ORGANIZATION

The U.S. Artillery was organized into four regiments numbered one through four. The chief of artillery was responsible only for supply while the batteries themselves were under the direct control of their brigade or division commanders. Each regiment was commanded by a Colonel, and his staff included a Lieutenant Colonel, a Major (a second Major was authorized after February 16, 1847), a Sergeant Major and a Quartermaster Sergeant. There were ten companies in each regiment lettered A through K (no Company J) and in theory each company would have been the equivalent of an artillery battery, but that was not the case. It had become standard practice to take the crews from coastal defense batteries and employ these artillery companies as infantry.

The artillery companies were never at full strength but they were authorized to have a Captain commanding along with two Lieutenants, a Second Lieutenant, four Sergeants, four Corporals, two Musicians, two Artificiers and fifty-four privates. A company of fifty men was typical even though on paper there should have been seventy. Legislation later authorized artillery companies of up to one hundred privates as in the Infantry and Dragoons, but these figures were never met. These artillery companies acting as infantry had campaigned against Indians in this manner and were as well trained as the regular infantry regiments. During the campaign in Mexico the companies were usually grouped as small regiments and often brigaded together along with the regular infantry establishment. These companies were capable of manning artillery batteries if called on to do so.

The artillery reorganization of 1821 had specified that one company in each regiment be equipped with horses and field pieces and designated as light artillery. It was not until 1838 that this procedure was begun with Company C, Third Artillery commanded by Major Samuel Ringgold. The level of training and

proficiency achieved by Ringgold was highly acclaimed. The success of this experiment encouraged the rapid expansion of the program. The new units even had to borrow some horses from the Dragoons to be able to practice. The other companies of light artillery were Company K, First Artillery under Captain Francis Taylor, Company A, Second Artillery led by Captain James Duncan and Company D, Fourth Artillery commanded by Captain John M. Washington. A fifth company was equipped in late 1845, prior to the beginning of hostilities, this was Company E, Third Artillery under Captain Braxton Bragg. These units served apart from the other companies and were often referred to simply by their commander's names instead of by their company and regimental designations. The batteries had been organized to have six guns apiece when each artillery company had been increased to seventy-one privates in 1838. The downsizing in 1842 by one artificier and sixteen privates would allow each company to crew only four guns apiece. The additional two guns per company were put into storage until they would be required for use.

Congress authorized the formation of a second light battery for each regiment on March 3, 1847. There were two companies that actually made the conversion during the war. The new light artillery companies were Company I, First Artillery commanded by Captain John B. Magruder and Company G, Fourth Artillery under Captain Simon H. Drum. In addition to these authorized additions to the light artillery batteries some companies were used to man batteries of heavy weapons or even captured equipment while on campaign. Company A, First Artillery under Captain Lucien B. Webster manned a battery of heavy artillery while serving under Zachary Taylor and Captain Edward J. Steptoe manned a field battery with men picked from various companies of the Third Artillery at the siege of Vera Cruz.

The field batteries of the artillery were attached to brigades by General Taylor in the campaign in northern Mexico. General Scott usually attached them to separate divisions during the march on Mexico City. Although there was a siege train present in each army mentioned above there was no actual artillery reserve established during the war.

There was also an experimental unit of artillery present with General Scott at the siege of Vera Cruz. This was the Howitzer and Rocket Company commanded by Major George H. Talcott and manned by personnel from the ordnance department. Originally non-combatants, the men of the ordnance department had been hired men performing the tasks of armorers, carriage-makers, blacksmiths and laborers. In June of 1846 this department was authorized to recruit and enlist enough volunteers to man a battery of mountain howitzers and a company of rocketeers. This company of rockets was later attached to the Regiment of Voltigeurs and Foot Riflemen.

There were also several volunteer artillery formations that went to Mexico. The numbers listed in parenthesis are an estimate of the number of men that served. There was one Company in California (41), one battalion from Louisiana (286), one Company from Maryland & the District of Columbia (136) and three Companies from Missouri (343). Total was one battalion and five companies of volunteer artillery (806). These units furnished their own equipment and elected their own officers as did the other volunteer units.

WEAPONS

The major weapons of the U.S. Artillery had been undergoing modernization during the decade preceding the war in Mexico. The old iron pieces were being phased out and replaced with new cannon made of bronze. The obsolete gun carriages leftover from the Revolution that had also seen service in the War of 1812 were being replaced with lighter, more mobile English style box trails. There were basically three types of cannon in use, guns, howitzers and mortars. Guns are long barreled and fire projectiles in a flat trajectory at high velocity. Howitzers are shorter barreled and usually of lighter weight but they can lob heavy projectiles in an arcing trajectory. Howitzers are sometimes more mobile than guns of a similar caliber but they have a shorter range. Mortars are short barreled and fire projectiles in a very steep trajectory. They are mainly useful in siege work, being able to fire at targets on the other side of walls or fortifications.

The guns provided for field service were 6 lb. and 12 lb. guns M1840 and the 12 lb. and 24 lb. howitzers, also M1840. (The weight given referring to the weight of the projectile being loaded into the piece, and M1840 being an abbreviation for Model 1840, the year of adoption.) There was also a 12 lb. mountain howitzer M1835 for specialized use in rough terrain. Guns available for siege work and garrison duty were the 12 lb., 18 lb. and 24 lb. M1840, 8-inch siege howitzer, an 8-inch and a 10-inch light mortar, a 16-inch stone mortar (firing a rounded stone) and a 24 lb. Coehorn mortar M1828. Seacoast artillery included a variety of types of cannon including, 32 lb. and 42 lb. guns M1840, 24 lb. guns M1819, 32 lb. guns M1829, 42 lb. guns M1831, 8-inch and 10-inch howitzers and 10-inch and 13-inch heavy mortars. In 1844 some of the 8-inch and 10-inch howitzers, the new Columbiads, had been added to the inventories available for field service, although they did not serve in Mexico.

The 6 lb. gun M1840 was the standard field piece of the army. This was a bronze weapon, with a smooth-bore diameter of 3.67 inches, weighing 880

pounds and having a tube length of 65. 6 inches. The maximum range was 1,500 yards but they were rarely used over 1,000 yards during the war. These guns were mounted on a standard two wheel carriage made of white ash with a box trail. (All carriages were similar in appearance and design with heavier construction to accommodate the weightier pieces.) They had excellent maneuverability and were capable of rapid fire. The woodwork on all equipment of the U.S. Artillery was painted "olive" which was a mustard green in color.

The 12 lb. howitzer M1840 was the primary field howitzer used by the army. Bronze, with a smooth-bore diameter of 4.62 inches and weighing 785 pounds with a tube length of 58.6 inches, it used the same carriage as the 6 lb. gun. The maximum range of this short barreled piece was approximately 1,000 yards.

The 12 lb. gun M1840 was the heaviest of the mobile field artillery. A bronze cannon, with a smooth-bore diameter of 4.62 inches, it weighed 1,800 pounds and had a tube length of 85 inches. The maximum range was just over 1,600 yards. The carriage was a heavier version of the one used by 6 lb. guns, but similar in appearance.

The 24 lb. howitzer M1840 weighed 1,320 pounds and had a tube length of 71.2 inches. It had a smooth-bore diameter of 5.82 inches.

The 12 lb. mountain howitzer M1835 was a bronze light field piece weighing only 210 pounds. The smooth-bore diameter was 4.62 inches and the overall barrel length was 37.21 inches. The mountain gun carriage was smaller than the standard field carriage and could be easily disassembled. The entire piece could be packed on three horses for transport.

The 12 lb. M1840, 18 lb, M1840 and 24 lb. M1840 siege guns were cast iron pieces that moved with the siege train following the army. The 12 lb. gun weighed 3,500 pounds and was 116 inches long, the 18 lb. gun weighed 4,750 pounds, and the 24 lb. gun weighed 5,600 pounds and was 124 inches long. The weight of these guns greatly limited their mobility and it was necessary to use draft oxen or mules with civilian drivers to haul them.

The small 24 lb. bronze Coehorn mortar M1828 weighed only 160 pounds without its bed. With the bed the total weight was almost 300 pounds but it could be manhandled into position when necessary. The overall length was 16.32 inches and it had a 5.82 inch smooth-bore barrel.

The 10-inch light mortar was only light when compared to the heavy mortars used for coastal defenses. It was short and squat measuring only 28 inches long but weighing 1,800 pounds.

Rockets were also used by the American Army. The antiquated British designed Congreve rockets were stabilized by a long stick at the end but remained very erratic in flight. The 9 lb. projectile was 16.25

inches long and 2.5 inches in diameter. The Hale's rockets used were developed by an American inventor, William Hale and remained under the control of the Ordnance Department. These were stabilized by three vents in the projectile which would cause it to rotate. The 6 lb. projectile was 2.25 inches in diameter while the 16 lb. version was 3.25 inches in diameter. Maximum ranges varied widely but the larger rockets could be fairly accurate (for rockets) at up to 2,200 yards. Rockets were fired from tubes, troughs, portable stands or simply propped up on the ground.

Ammunition supplies for these weapons were carried with the slow and unwieldy supply trains for the army. When going into action each cannon would have a limber and caisson attached and a six-horse team would pull them. Every limber carried a 600 pound ammunition chest made of black walnut and every caisson carried two. A covered battery wagon, carrying tools and spare parts for equipment and a travelling forge would also accompany each artillery company into the field.

There were several types of ammunition available to the gunners, each with its own uses. Solid Shot was a traditional solid cannon ball. Shells were hollow iron projectiles filled with a fused powder charge. Spherical Case Shot was a hollow ball filled with a load of scrap metal along with a powder charge. Canister was a tin cylinder filled with small shot and an exploding charge mainly used as an anti-personnel round. Grape Shot was also an anti-personnel weapon consisting of a cluster of solid balls between wooden blocks called sabots, held together by a cloth cover. When the shot was fired the cloth burned away and the shot would spray the area.

Artillery ammunition might be issued as 'fixed', 'semi-fixed' or 'separate loading' (also called 'unfixed') rounds. A complete round that was a single unit was called 'fixed'. A round that had two separate components of powder cartridge and projectile was called 'semi-fixed'. Ammunition that came in unfixed components so that the powder charge and projectile could be varied were called 'separate loading' or simply 'unfixed'.

TACTICS

The U.S. Artillery proved to be the most well trained and prepared for battle of all arms of the service. Each artillery company that had been equipped as a field battery was designated as a school for subalterns. Lieutenants from every other company in the regiment would rotate through these companies for the period of a year to acquire the knowledge and training to man a battery. Major Ringgold's Company C of the Third Artillery became known as the "flying artillery" due to its proficiency and speed in executing maneuvers in the field. This company was the only one to be given the

designation of Horse Artillery by the U.S. Army. In the horse artillery all crewmen were mounted on horses for the most rapid movement into action. The term "flying artillery" eventually came to be applied to the other light artillery companies as well. The difference between light artillery and horse artillery was that light artillery crewmen would normally walk beside the equipment so the horses would not become overworked and ride on the limbers and caissons when speed was important.

The training manual of field maneuvers for the artillery included the school of the piece, including the manual and mechanical maneuvers for preparing for battle; the school of the driver; the school of the cannoneer, mounted and the school of the battery. The text was basically for the foot artillery but with horse artillery variations being noted. Any artillerymen fighting as infantry were taught the "Infantry Tactics" manual. The cannoneers required for the service of a piece and its caisson were termed a platoon. There were eight men involved in firing the gun, they were referred to as numbers one through six and right and left gunners. The number one and two men worked together to handle the sponge; number 3 fired the piece using port-fire and linstock; numbers 4, 5 and 6 supplied number two with ammunition; the gunner of the right pointed the piece and the gunner of the left tended to the vent. The loading and firing procedure was divided into separate motions. The ability to move the piece, unlimbered, by hand was first introduced in this manual. The basic formations were column, line and in battery. While formed in battery the horses were to be facing the enemy. For movement purposes the double column of carriages was recommended at all times, but this normally proved impractical. The single column was used almost exclusively even though it was not authorized in the instructions. This manual allowed for much greater flexibility and made it possible to increase the mobility of the field artillery.

The artillery companies equipped as field artillery were allowed two hundred blank cartridges a year for practice firing and one-third that number of shot or shell. Commanders were to keep registers to record results of practices for range, accuracy, number of ricochets and bursting time for shells, among others. These reports were to be sent on to the War Department. The purpose of these exercises was to give the officers and men the knowledge necessary to allow them to be ready to make effective use of their weapons and to determine the condition of readiness of their guns and carriages. The maximum ranges for the various weapons in use varied but the actual effective range was usually no more than 1,000 yards in the field. This could be further limited by battlefield conditions and the need to actually sight the target from the guns. Guns were often deployed in relatively close proximity to the enemy for maximum effect. The gun commander or gunner, was in control of both the crew and the piece. The gunner was responsible for aiming the weapon by the direct sighting of the target using notches cut into the raised breech of the gun. The gunner could use an elevating screw to change the angle of elevation of the gun to achieve the ranges needed to hit the target. The gunner could also direct the crew to shift the angle of fire by moving the trail behind the gun to point in a different direction. Mortars and howitzers sometimes fired at such high trajectories as to make direct aiming impossible. A gunner's quadrant could be used to assist in calculating indirect firing. Mortars could also be aimed using aiming stakes set up between the weapon and the target. The range of the mortars could also be varied by changing the size of the powder charges used to launch the projectiles.

The U.S. Artillery acquitted itself well during the Mexican War. Many of its officers were graduates of the Military Academy at West Point and went on to become field officers in the Civil War thirteen years later. The American artillery was more than a match for its Mexican counterparts in mobility and firepower. Morale and esprit de corps were always high and the small and usually few American pieces achieved more than their commanders expected. In Mexico the U.S. Artillery was responsible for winning more than its fair share of the battles.

THE CORPS OF ENGINEERS

The U.S. Company of Sappers, Miners and Pontoniers were the enlisted soldiers of the Corps of Engineers, which had not had such an establishment until May of 1846. Sappers were engineer soldiers, miners were supposed to be elite engineers specialized in mining and countermining with tunnels for siege operations and pontoniers were supposed to handle and construct pontoon bridges. In practice this unit was used to build and improve roads for the army but they did take part in combat.

The authorized strength of the unit was that of a double size company of 100 men. The company became part of the Corps of Engineers based at and training at the Military Academy at West Point. Native born Americans were desired for this unit with naturalized citizens being accepted only if they had come recommended with extraordinary qualifications. Many were from New York City and other cities in the east.

The company was armed with the U.S. Sappers and Miners musketoon, Model 1847. This was a 0.69 caliber smoothbore musket measuring forty-one inches in length. It came equipped with a brass-handled, Roman-sword bayonet which was fixed on the right side of the barrel by a bayonet stud. It is probable that the bayonet was only for ceremonial use.

THE U.S. MARINES

The Marines served both aboard ship and with landing parties of sailors throughout the Mexican war. In addition, there were two units of Marines that saw service during General Scott's campaign. Marines from the Home Squadron under Captain Alvin Edson played a minor role in the landing and siege at Vera Cruz. A detachment of 180 men was available for shipboard and shore duties. They received praise from General Scott for their actions but Commodore Perry refused to let any Marine detachments march for the interior with the army. He insisted that their role in securing captured coastal areas and as ships guards was crucial to the success of his operations.

In May of 1847 the Commandant of the Marine Corps, Brigadier General Archibald Henderson, convinced President Polk that a Marine regiment could be raised and sent to fight with Scott's army more quickly and economically than a regiment of regulars. Henderson was actually looking for an opportunity for the Marines to win more recognition for the Corps by participating in the war's epic campaign to Mexico City. President Polk agreed to the plan, even though both the Home and Pacific Squadrons were asking for more Marines for shipboard duties.

The Marine regiment was authorized to add 12 commissioned officers, 50 petty officers, 50 musicians and 1,000 privates to the strength of the Corps. However, in the end, only a six company regiment could be formed and placed under the command of Brevet Lieutenant Colonel Samuel E. Watson. The recruiting had not been as successful as planned with most of the new Marines being as untrained and "green" as the rawest recruits gathered by the army. Experienced men simply could not be spared from other duties. The battalion that joined Scott on August 6, 1847 consisted of approximately 22 officers and 378 men. They were attached to General Quitman's Division and brigaded with the 2nd Pennsylvania Volunteers. The Marines saw action in the last battles for Mexico City but not as an intact unit. Separate detachments and storming parties had been formed using men from several regiments, including the Marines. It was in this manner that they distinguished themselves in the "Halls of the Montezumas."

THE MEXICAN SPY COMPANY

"Colonel" Manuel Dominguez was originally hired as a courier by General Worth after the capture of Puebla. On June 5, 1847 he was hired to work for General Scott's army carrying dispatches. Dominguez was a retired bandit leader who had numerous complaints against him from the Mexicans. By the end of June another 19 of his men had been released from prison and the Mexican Spy Company had been born.

The beginning of August saw General Scott officially authorize the formation of the Spy Company under the command of Dominguez. Eventually two complete companies were listed with each having a Captain, two Lieutenants, and the normal number of NCO's and men. They were armed with lances, carbines and sabres and wore a wide variety of dress. The two companies were under the direct control of General Scott and amounted to about 200 men who were being paid $20.00 a month for their services.

The Spy Company acted as couriers, escorts, guides, interpreters, scouts and spies for the American Army. They took some of the burden of these duties off of the American cavalry. There is no record of any lost dispatches, treachery or crimes committed against the Americans by the Spy Company. They were often in disguise as peasant farmers, merchants, guerillas, rancheros or beggars to obtain information about Mexican plans and operations. They engaged in battle against Mexican guerillas with some success and came to be despised by their enemies. Members of the Spy Company who were captured were shot on the spot.

The Mexican Spy Company was disbanded in June of 1848 and about half of the surviving members joined the Americans in leaving Mexico. Many of the contraguerillas of the Spy Company returned to their old ways on the Texas-Mexican border after the war. Manuel Dominguez and his family found it too dangerous to stay in Mexico and moved to New Orleans. Unfortunately the U.S. Government abandoned this faithful servant to his own devices to eke out a living, despite pleas from General Hitchcock that some sort of assistance was in order as repayment for a job well done.

SUMMARY

The United States began the war with an army of only 637 officers and 5,925 enlisted men in May of 1846. During the next two years the regular army added 1,016 officers and 35,009 enlisted men to the ranks for a grand total of 42,587 men. The men of the "old army" served an average of 26 months in the theater of war while the new regiments served only 15 months on average. The volunteers from the various states contributed a total of 73,532 men to the war effort. The volunteers had served an average of only 10 months in the field. The United States would once again cut back the peacetime army when the war ended with the argument of the value of the volunteer versus a standing army still unresolved.

One institution that did benefit was the Military Academy at West Point, whose place in the future of the nation was assured by the accomplishments of its graduates in Mexico. General Scott gave his tribute to the Senate when he said: "I give it as my fixed opinion that but for our graduated cadets the war between the United States and Mexico might, and probably would, have lasted some four or five years, with, in its first half, more defeats than victories falling to our share; whereas in less than two campaigns we conquered a great country and a peace without the loss of a single battle or skirmish." What none of the cadets (or anyone else) knew at the time was that the war they had just been through was but a dress rehearsal for the much greater conflict yet to come.

THE UNITED STATES ARMY AT THE BEGINNING OF HOSTILITIES

Infantry — 8 Regiments (numbered 1-8)
Cavalry — 2 Regiments of Dragoons (1st & 2nd)
Artillery — 4 Regiments (numbered 1-4)
  Most companies fought as infantry, only five companies were equipped as field artillery batteries with six 6 lb. bronze smoothbores each, they were:
  Company K, 1st Artillery, Capt. Francis Taylor
  Company A, 2nd Artillery, Capt. James Duncan
  Company C, 3rd Artillery, Maj. Samuel Ringgold
  Company E, 3rd Artillery, Capt. Braxton Bragg
  Company B, 4th Artillery, Capt. John M. Washington
Totals—637 officers & 5,925 men: other estimates—5,304 men, or 7,194 men in 37 Frontier Posts.

Units raised later:

May 1846
  The Regiment of Mounted Rifles (originally raised to patrol the Oregon Trail but diverted to Mexico when war was declared)
February 1847 (the "10 Regiment Bill")
  8 Regiments of Infantry (numbered 9-16)
  1 Regiment of Voltigeurs (riflemen)
  1 Regiment of Dragoons (the 3rd)
additional artillery companies equipped as field batteries:
  Company I, 1st Artillery, Capt. John Bankhead Magruder
  Company G, 4th Artillery, Capt. Simon Henry Drum
  Major George Henry Talcott's Howitzer and Rocket Company equipped with Hale's rockets

U.S. UNIFORMS

The uniforms of the U.S. Army during the Mexican War were supposed to be governed by the "Regulations for the Uniform and Dress of the Army of the United States" published on June 21, 1839 as General Order Number 36. This was a modification of the regulations that had first been issued in 1836. They would again be modified in 1841 and on June 4, 1846 they would be modified again by the addition of uniform details for the Regiment of Mounted Rifles and the Engineers. In 1847 the uniform for the Regiment of Voltigeurs and Foot Riflemen were added to the regulations. These regulations remained in force until the army replaced them with a new uniform in 1851. Evidently the uniform described in the regulations was very unpopular with a General Order from 1850 stating "A large number of the Officers of the Army, probably more than half, have applied since the war with Mexico, to have a uniform less expensive, less difficult to procure and better adapted to campaign and other service…" The best evidence of the unpopularity of these uniforms is that they were hardly ever worn by American troops in Mexico.

The regulations go into great detail to describe the dress uniform of all ranks and branches. There is mention of winter and summer undress or fatigue uniforms as well. The climate in many parts of Mexico would have made the summer fatigues of white jackets and pants very practical. However it is doubtful if they were ever issued, even though there is evidence that some were present in supply depots late in the campaign. The winter fatigue uniform was also eminently practical for the hot days and cold nights in the open countryside and this was the uniform that was prevalent throughout the campaign in Mexico. Officers could occasionally be found wearing the prescribed dress uniform, but usually they wore a combination of fatigue dress and non-regulation items. The enlisted men were much more prone to adopt articles of native dress including sombreros and ponchos in various styles and a rainbow of colors. The uniform supply situation was often very difficult and the fatigue uniforms, even though practical, did wear out under continuous use. Many uniforms were made locally out of materials purchased in Mexico when other supplies were lacking. These articles were manufactured as closely as possible to the original patterns but were of much lower quality.

A good example of the variety of clothing worn by the Regulars comes from Lt. Napoleon Jackson Tecumseh Dana, 7th Infantry who wrote to his wife on the march to Monterrey to tell her: "We wear all kinds of uniforms here, each one to his taste, some shirtsleeves, some white, some blue, some fancy jackets and all colors of cottonelle pants, some straw and some Quaker hats, and that is just the way, too, that our fellows went into battle. The Mexicans must have thought that we were real militia ragamuffins." A month later another letter relates: "I have on my old straw hat, those blue-checked pants made by your dear hands, which are torn in both legs and pretty well worn out, and that loose coat you made which you recollect washed white. I don't think there is much danger of a ranchero shooting at me for an officer of high rank. My trimmings don't show much. Both pairs of those check pants I have worn pretty well out".

The volunteers had even more problems with supplies than the regulars did upon reaching Mexico. The states that raised the volunteers were responsible for their uniforms and not all of them provided these for their troops. Some volunteer units had uniforms modelled on those of the regulars and were able to make do with using government issue items, when they were available. There were other regiments that had unique uniforms that deteriorated quickly and there were no replacements to be found. Finally, there were volunteers from some states that didn't have any uniforms at all when they reached Mexico. The shortage of uniforms for the regulars was already severe when these troops came and drew their own supplies. The quartermaster stores at Vera Cruz were looted by some of the newly arriving volunteers because they did not have their own uniforms. Eventually, many volunteers came to be wearing the same uniform as the regulars, which they seldom appreciated. There were a few units that were able to send officers back home to bring back newly made copies of their original uniforms. Other units followed the example of the regulars in acquiring local materials and talent to manufacture uniforms for them. The other popular source of clothing for the men was the native population itself. Volunteers acquired all manner of Mexican dress and could sometimes be mistaken for groups of locals rather than American troops. Serapes, ponchos, blankets, sombreros, straw hats, coats of various colors, jackets and trousers were all appropriated, bought or traded for to solve the clothing problems of the volunteers.

Regulars

The dress uniform of a U.S. Army Major General was a dark blue coat with two rows of eight gilt buttons each. The coat lining, collar, cuffs and skirt turnbacks were fine buff kersimere. The turnbacks were to have four buttons and a gold-embroidered star on them. A variation of this coat could be dark blue collar, cuffs and turnbacks with gold leaves embroidered on all of them. The buttons had a spread eagle and stars design on them and gold bullion epaulettes were worn with three silver stars on them. The undress coat was similar but without turnbacks or trim and it had nine buttons in two rows, grouped in threes. A buff silk net sash was worn with the silk bullion fringe hanging down on the left side. A black leather sword belt was worn over the coat and sash to hang the "General and Staff Officers Sword" Model 1832. The double-edged straight bladed sword was carried in a scabbard of black leather, steel or brass. Trousers were to be dark blue with a buff or gold stripe down the seam from October 1 through April 30 and plain white linen or cotton from May 1 through September 30. Black ankle boots or Jefferson boots were worn. A black cocked hat with black ribbons and cockade and gold loop and tassels was worn for full dress. The cockade and loop were decorated with a silver spread eagle with gold rays emanating from it with twenty-four silver stars. The plume was of yellow swan feathers eight inches long drooping down. Mounted officers also wore buff or white gloves and were authorized to wear a dark blue cloak with buff or dark blue lining.

The frock coat that all general officers were authorized to wear was dark blue with two rows of buttons that varied according to rank. Brigadier generals would have two rows of eight buttons each in pairs. The stand up collar and cuffs were dark blue and the coat lining was either blue or black. Shoulder straps of blue cloth were worn instead of epaulettes. A major general who was not the army commander wore two silver stars and a plume that had the top half black and the bottom half white. A brigadier general had a single silver star and wore a plume that had the top half white and the bottom half red. Sashes were also of buff silk net. Dark blue or white trousers, depending upon the season, without stripes were worn with ankle boots or Jefferson boots. All officers wore the Army Forage Cap Model 1839 which was dark blue with black patent leather visor and chinstrap. A button on each side of the cap held the chinstrap in place.

Staff officers wore a frock coat similar to that of the general officers except that it was single-breasted.

Sashes were of red silk net and the Model 1839 Forage Cap was worn. Different cap devices were authorized to be worn for the different branches of service but there is no evidence that this was done, with most examples of caps shown being unadorned. This officers' uniform was the same as that worn by Aides de Camp, the Quartermaster's, Pay and Subsistence Department, the Medical Department, the Corps of Engineers, and the Topographic Engineers with minor variations, usually in the type or arrangement of buttons.

All mounted officers had dark blue saddle cloths with gold lace and spread eagle designs for general officers. Mounted officers of the infantry had silver lace and white edging. All bridles and holsters were of black leather.

Infantry

The regimental infantry officers wore the dark blue frock coat with a single row of eight to ten buttons depending upon the length of the coat. The buttons were of white metal and the coat was lined in blue. The regulations had called for double-breasted coats as of February of 1847 but it is not known how common these were as the officers were already on campaign with the old style coat. The edges of the dark blue shoulder straps were also embroidered in silver. Rank distinctions were represented by a silver embroidered spread eagle for colonels; two silver embroidered leaves for a lieutenant colonel; two gold embroidered leaves for a major; two silver embroidered bars for a captain; one silver bar for a lieutenant and no bars for a second lieutenant. The trousers were to be sky blue with a one and one-half inch wide white stripe down the seam from October 1, through April 30. From May 1, through September 30 they were to be white. Crimson sashes were worn tied on the left side. Straps and belts were of black leather. Mounted officers carried the "Sabre for Mounted Artillery" Model 1840 while foot officers carried either the "Foot Officer's Sword" Model 1840 or the "Cavalry Sabre" Model 1840 in which case the waistbelt of the dragoons was worn. Regulation headgear for dress uniform was the black shako with a white metal bugle horn device below a brass eagle on the front topped off by a white plume for the infantry. If shakos were worn at all by the U.S. Army in Mexico they were probably not worn for long. The model 1839 forage caps were much more practical and popular. They were usually worn without any colored bands or other ornamentation. Officers could also have a blanket roll carried over the left shoulder and a haversack on the right side.

The winter fatigue uniform for the enlisted men was a jacket and trousers of sky blue kersey. The

Opposite: Artist H. Charles McBarron shows a Dragoon riding between an infantry officer and his men.

jacket was waist length and single-breasted with nine white metal buttons down the front. The collar and shoulder straps were trimmed with white worsted lace. The trousers did not have a stripe down the seam for privates. The same Model 1839 dark blue forage cap that the officers wore but with a white band around it was authorized for the enlisted men. The white band does not appear to have been worn at all but the cap did have a flap that came down over the collar to protect the back of the neck which was used by the men. The men all wore Jefferson boots. Sergeants had a white worsted stripe down the seams of each trouser leg and wore a red worsted sash around the waist tied on the left side. Sergeants wore three white upward pointing chevrons on each sleeve while corporals wore two. A sergeant major also had three arcs while a quartermaster sergeant had a lozenge. A dark blue upward pointing chevron worn near the cuff was awarded for five years of service. If it was edged in red then the service had been during wartime. The men also had sky blue or blue-gray overcoats with a shoulder cape for protection from the weather.

A black leather cartridge box having a brass oval plate with the letters "U.S." on the flap was worn. A whitened buff leather belt was worn over the left shoulder to which the cartridge box was attached and hung on the soldiers right side. The box held forty paper cartridges in tin dividers. Soldiers with flintlock muskets wore a brass brush and pick suspended from a button on the front of their jackets. Troops armed with percussion cap weapons would carry the caps in a special pocket on their jackets.

White leather waistbelts were used to carry the bayonet, in its scabbard of black leather, on the left side. The waistbelts also had a brass oval beltplate with the letters "U.S." on it. Sergeants also wore an infantry sword on the left side attached to a crossbelt over the right shoulder. Soldiers of all ranks carried a white cotton haversack under the left arm with a strap slung over the right shoulder. The haversack held the soldier's food and was to be marked in black with the regimental number, company letter and personal number of the soldier. A circular brass plate with an eagle design on it was worn at the center of the white crossbelts. The water bottle or canteen was carried on a strap and hung just above or next to the haversack. These were made out of thin sheet iron and painted light blue-gray. There were also wooden and rubber versions but the troops soon found that hollowed out gourds kept the water cooler than any of these. Knapsacks were made of black painted canvas mounted on wooden frames. The regimental numbers were painted on in white letters one and one-half inches tall. The straps were also black but the troops usually whitened them. The overcoat and other articles were stored inside while a blanket roll was strapped to the top. The blankets could be of many different colors including light blue, red, white or multi-colored.

Musicians wore the same uniform described above. The drums of the infantry had the arms of the United States painted on a blue field with the company letter and regimental number in a scroll underneath.

Voltigeurs and Foot Riflemen

This new unit was specified by the regulations of 1847 to only have fatigue uniforms issued. The uniform was to be the same as that of the infantry except for color. Officers were to have had dark gray frock coats and trousers and the men were also to be completely clad in dark gray. These uniforms were manufactured and sent to Mexico but they were lost at sea en route. As a result the Voltigeurs ended up with the standard issue fatigues in sky blue that the infantry wore. An attempt was made by the colonel of the regiment to get some type of distinctive uniform for his men by ordering black slouch hats and gray fringed hunting shirts but these were never issued.

Cavalry

The U.S. cavalry in Mexico dressed exclusively in their fatigue or undress uniform. The Dragoon officers wore a dark blue wool jacket that was single-breasted with nine buttons down the front. The collar had gilt lace trim with two loops on each side and small buttons at the back end of the loops. All buttons were gilt with a spread-eagle device with the letter D on the shield. The coat also had gilt lace trim on the pointed cuffs and the bottom and back seams of the jacket. Frock coats could also be worn by officers. The shoulder straps were shaped like epaulettes but fringeless and trimmed in gilt lace as well. Field grade officers wore dark blue trousers without stripes. Company officers would have the sky-blue or blue-gray trousers similar to the infantry, also without stripes. The trousers were reinforced in the seat and the inside of the legs with double layers of wool cloth. The waistbelt was black patent leather and the beltplate had the letter 'D' instead of 'U.S.' on it. Ankle boots of black leather with wrought iron spurs, also in black. Boots and shoes were all made to fit both the right and left feet at this time without any difference in size or shape. Officers wore the standard Model 1839 forage cap. Officers were also authorized to wear a deep orange color silk net sash tied on the right hip with both dress and fatigue uniforms.

All other ranks wore a dark blue single-breasted shell jacket with twelve buttons. The collar and jacket was trimmed as for officers but in yellow worsted lace. The trousers were the same sky-blue or blue-gray as for the infantry. Sergeants had two yellow stripes on each outer seam with a small space between them where the blue would show. Corporals and privates had a single yellow stripe down the seams. White buff leather waistbelts were worn with an oval beltplate bearing the letters 'U.S.' on it. Attached to the waistbelt were slings to hold the sabre and a shoulder belt that helped to support the weight of the sword and the cartridge boxes for pistols and carbines. Black ankle boots were worn with spurs. The standard Model 1839 forage cap was worn and although there was no authorization to wear a yellow band around the cap the 2nd Dragoons seem to have done so. The Dragoons all wore their Company initials, stamped in one inch high brass, on the front of the cap. Sergeants could also wear a yellow worsted sash tied on the right hip with their fatigue uniforms.

The Dragoons were authorized to wear white fatigue jackets and pants in summer weather but there is no evidence of these being issued in Mexico. In bad weather a double-breasted greatcoat with cape in blue-gray was worn by all ranks. These were normally carried rolled up and fastened over the pommel of the saddle in front of the holsters.

Each company of Dragoons was mounted on horses that were of the same color and different colors were to be used for every company. In March of 1837 Colonel Stephen Watts Kearny had redistributed the horses of the 1st Dragoon regiment according to color as follows: Companies A and K got black; Companies B, F and H got sorrels; Companies C, D, E, and I were given bays; and Company G had iron gray mounts.

The Regiment of Mounted Riflemen wore a uniform almost identical to that of the dragoons except for the trousers. These were to be dark blue with a black cloth stripe edged with yellow cord down the outer seam. This pattern was the same for both officers and men. The officer's sash was to be of crimson silk net tied on the right hip. The buttons and waist-belt plates bore the letter 'R' instead of the 'D' for dragoons. Finally the forage cap was ornamented with a gold embroidered spread-eagle with the letter 'R' in silver on the shield.

ARTILLERY

The artilleryman's uniform was the same as that for the infantry except that all lace and buttons were in yellow. Regulations did not allow for a red cap band around the bottom of the forage cap but it was often worn. A red stripe down the outer seams of the

U.S. Dragoon by Remington

168

trousers was authorized for officers and sergeants but there were several different types and all ranks seem to have worn them. Major Samuel Ringgold managed to get special uniforms for his own Company C of the 3rd U.S. Artillery as they were the only true "horse artillery" battery in the army. They had dark blue coats with the collar trimmed in red worsted wool tape instead of the normal yellow. The dark blue shoulder straps were also trimmed in red. The shako was black with a yellow metal crossed cannon device below an eagle and regimental number. The shako had red cords and a falling red horsehair plume. As with any of the specialized uniforms on campaign, when these wore out whatever was available would be substituted. Captain James Duncan's Company A of the 2nd U.S. Artillery had a reputation for ignoring uniform regulations and red flannel shirts were common wear in the field. The artillerymen were all issued with swords which were not of much practical use in the field.

The majority of artillery companies served in Mexico as light infantry and they were equipped as the infantry with muskets, cartridge boxes, haversacks, knapsacks and drums. The men wore a mixture of infantry and artillery uniform and were often referred to as the "red-legged infantry." The knapsacks had yellow letters instead of white on them and the drums had the arms of the United States painted on a red field instead of blue.

The men of the U.S. Ordnance Department used the same type of jackets and pants as the artillery but both were made of dark blue cloth with a scarlet welt (similar to piping) inserted in the collar seam and the outer seam of the pants. There is evidence that sky blue coats and pants were also worn, probably adopted in the field as regulation uniforms became scarce. They also had two crossed cannons in yellow paint as an emblem on their knapsacks.

The Corps of Engineers

The men of the Company of Sappers, Miners and Pontoniers had a dress uniform of a dark blue coat with black collar and cuffs. This was similar in style to the regulation dress uniform of the infantry and artillery that was rarely seen in Mexico. The cuffs had yellow trimmed buttonholes, the number corresponding to rank. The collar had a single yellow tape false buttonhole without any other trim. Privates had fringeless epaulettes, corporals had worsted epaulettes in the same style as subalterns and sergeants had the same style epaulettes of a captain in yellow silk. The coat had dark blue turnbacks and all buttons were brass. Pants were dark blue for officers with a wide black stripe down the seams. Non-commissioned officers and enlisted men had sky blue trousers with wide black stripes for the NCO's and narrow ones for privates. The black infantry style shako had a brass castle badge on it below the eagle emblem. A black pompon three inches in diameter

was worn on top of the shako. On campaign this company eventually adopted the fatigue uniform with the same forage cap, jacket and pants of the artillery but with dark blue or possibly white jackets instead of sky blue.

The Navy

The uniforms of the Navy were to be as described in the "Regulations for the Uniforms and Dress of the Navy of the United States, 1841." However, as in the army, full dress uniforms were rarely seen in Mexico. The only exceptions might be when high ranking Naval officers wanted to be conspicuous at ceremonies or formal meetings.

The undress uniform of a Naval officer consisted of a dark blue civilian style coat with dark blue lining and two rows of nine buttons each on the front. Senior commissioned officers could be distinguished by the number of buttons on cuffs, above pockets and skirt folds. Commanders, lieutenants and midshipmen wore similar coats but with fewer buttons. The shoulder straps were also made of blue cloth with gold embroidery. The devices on the shoulder straps designated rank with a Commodore having a silver star, a Captain having a silver eagle, an anchor for a Commander and no device at all for Lieutenants. Midshipmen had a gold embroidered anchor and star on both sides of the collar. All officers wore either blue or white trousers depending on the season. The dress uniform for a Commodore called for a black cocked hat with black silk cockade and gold bullion loops. Normal headgear for all officers was a visored cap of dark blue cloth with a gold lace band. Officers were also authorized to wear straw hats if they so desired.

Officers carried the Model 1841 saber which was a cut and thrust weapon at least twenty-six inches long. The grip was white and the scabbard was black leather with yellow gilt mountings. Swordbelts were of black glazed leather and were worn under the coat. The sword knot consisted of gold bullion and dark blue silk thread.

The enlisted men included petty officers, seamen, ordinary seamen and boys. There were several variations on the uniforms allowed depending upon the climate and the preference of their commander. When serving in cold weather they wore dark blue wool frocks or cloth jackets with linen or duck collars and cuffs. Trousers were dark blue. A blue vest was also to be worn with black hat, handkerchief and shoes. Warmer weather saw the men in white frocks with collars and breast lined with blue cotton cloth. White trousers with black or white hats and black handkerchiefs and shoes. Petty officers wore an eagle and anchor insignia on the sleeve in the reverse colors of their coats.

The men carried a two foot long Model 1841 Naval Cutlass with a straight double-edged blade. The grip was similar to that of the artillery swords and the scabbard was of black leather. When going ashore in landing parties the sailors were armed with carbines or muskets the same as those used by the army.

The Marines

The Marine uniforms in Mexico were very similar to those of the army and usually differed in only minor details. Field officers wore a dark blue double-breasted frock coat with a roll collar. There were eight brass buttons in each row and they each had the Marine insignia of an eagle grasping an anchor surrounded by stars on them. The field officers coat had four buttons on the sleeve, captains had three and the Lieutenants had two. Pants were sky blue and had a one and one-half inch red stripe down the seams. The Model 1839 Army Forage Cap was worn with Marine Corps buttons on it. Officers had a crimson sash of silk net wrapped twice around the waist. Marine officers were authorized to carry a "Mamluke" curved sword just over three feet long.

The Marines themselves wore a single-breasted shell jacket of sky blue kersey of the same type worn by the Army. These had nine buttons and did not have any of the white lace of the army jackets. Sky blue trousers were worn and sergeants were authorized the red stripes but may not have actually had them. Sergeants had two diagonal stripes of yellow worsted lace on each sleeve, below the elbow while corporals had only one stripe. All other weapons and equipment were patterned after those of the Army. The Marines were normally armed with flintlock muskets.

The Mexican Spy Company

The Mexican Spy Company wore a mixture of Mexican and American uniforms as well as native Mexican dress. The basic outfit might be the 'charro' dress of a Mexican ranchero with gray or brown jackets and pants made of leather and heavy cloth. A red scarf tied around the hat, possibly with the words "Spy Company" on it, was used as an identifying mark to friendly troops. Often the Spy Company was engaged in clandestine operations in open country and travelled in disguise as peons in traditional native dress. They wore many colored ponchos and large straw hats or sombreros with white cotton pants of varying lengths. The Company was later identified as having parrot green jackets with red collars, cuffs and turnbacks. These were undoubtedly captured Mexican cavalry uniforms that they put to good use. Insignia were the same as for the American army. Belts, straps and other weapons and equipment could be of Mexican or American origin. Late in 1848 members of the Spy Company were given the gray uniforms of the U.S. Voltigeur Regiment, but this would have been after they returned to the United States to seek refuge.

The Volunteers

Volunteer units were responsible for providing their own uniforms upon entering service. They were to apply for reimbursement from the government but the amount received was never enough to cover the cost of their goods. The variety of these different uniforms, or lack of uniform, worn in Mexico by the state troops almost defies description. There were quite a few formations that arrived in Mexico without uniforms at all. Some of these units remained this way while most of the others were issued the same fatigues as the regulars wore from the U.S. Quartermaster's Department. The sky-blue kersey was not at all popular among most volunteers, with them complaining about the army trying to make them $7 targets, but they had no other choice. Volunteer units even looted the Quartermaster's stores of uniforms and equipment in Vera Cruz, thus depriving the regulars of much needed resupply. Regiments that did arrive in Mexico with their own uniforms quickly saw most of them wear out and they were also given the U.S. Army fatigues as replacements. A few fortunate volunteers had uniforms sent or brought from home as replacements for their custom dress rather than being forced to switch to the army sky-blue. There were other units that came fairly well equipped and actually saw action dressed in their custom made, home grown uniforms. Some of these were variations of the uniforms the regulars wore while others were made in a number of different styles and colors. Many units also made use of captured clothing or uniforms made in Mexico, sometimes by the men themselves.

The following descriptions are not by any means a complete catalog of volunteer uniforms from the Mexican War. In many cases only brief or partial details are to be found about many units. There were not many examples of these uniforms preserved after the war since many had worn out or been replaced and quite a few were simply made from articles of civilian type clothing. Uniforms described may have varied from company to company within a unit and they were always subject to differences in colors due to the inexact nature of manufacturing at the time.

Alabama
There are reports of a company of Volunteers from this state wearing frock coats and trousers of green worsted.

Baltimore-Washington Battalion
This regiment wore the same uniform as the U.S. Army Regulars and by late 1847 had become quite a ragged looking bunch due to lack of supplies of fresh clothing.

District of Columbia and Maryland Volunteers
The rifle company that joined this unit in Mexico was described as having dark blue jackets and pants.

U.S. Uniforms

ILLINOIS VOLUNTEERS

The regiments from Illinois did not have a standard uniform even though the governor had recommended a blue jeans or roundabout jacket with a standing collar and brass buttons along with blue jeans pants and glazed caps. This was the basic uniform of the 4th Illinois as they left St. Louis for Mexico. Some officers had ordered customized versions of this outfit, including blue frock coats, buff stripes on the pants, and white caps if they could be obtained.

The manufacture of the uniforms was done by any independent source that wanted to get involved. The end result of this policy was that every company chose their own style and color of clothing and no two companies were the same. In general their uniforms are described as short jackets in various shades of blue or grey with either red or yellow facings. Sam Chamberlain was a Sergeant in Company A of the 2nd Illinois before joining the Dragoons later. He described their uniforms when they moved into camp: "We were uniformed as each company selected and strange grotesque costumes now filled the Camp". The company he was in, "...made choice of jacket and pants of blue mixed Kentucky jeans with yellow stripes across the breast like a Dragoon Bugler. By permission I had mine made with dark blue cloth, with only my Sergeant's chevrons, and it was quite a neat affair".

INDIANA VOLUNTEERS

Indiana decided to allow companies to chose their own uniforms with the stipulation that officers were asked to use the same style uniform as the Regulars. Dress uniforms were not used at all and the fatigues were to consist of a double-breasted hunter frock coat and pants of a gray mixed or sky blue jean material. The buttons were to be white metal with an eagle design stamped on. There were no stripes on the pants and the cap was the standard army forage cap or a cloth cap with a glazed leather top. The captain of each company was required to purchase two sets of uniform coat and pants, two pairs of shoes, a hat or cap in addition to the forage cap, two cotton and two flannel shirts, two pairs of drawers, stockings and a good blanket for every soldier in the company. A member of Company G of the 1st Indiana reported that they had blue coats and pants, both trimmed with silver lace. Company A of the 3rd Indiana reportedly left home with uniforms of "gray cashmere sack coats with black velvet stripes up the front, pants of the same material with black velvet stripes up the legs," and broad brim gray hats turned up at the side. It was reported of Company E of the 3rd Indiana that they had uniforms of "bright blue jeans" and they were to be called the "Brown County Blues". In practice many of these uniforms were actually dark blue as were those of the 5th Indiana.

KENTUCKY VOLUNTEERS

The official uniform was to be a deep blue roundabout coat and pants in the style of the Regulars. At least part of the 3rd Kentucky ended up with a butternut (Janes bark) color as they could not obtain material of the proper color. Marshall's Cavalry regiment was described as having picturesque dress with fanciful hats. The broad-brimmed drab beaver hats had several gold stars and it was formed into a three cornered shape with gold lace loops in the style of the American Revolution. Their boots reached above the knee and were equipped with huge spurs and faced with red morocco. The men went with beards unshorn.

1ST MASSACHUSETTS INFANTRY

This regiment requested that uniforms be issued consisting of a single-breasted gray coat with white collar, cuffs and turnbacks. Epaulettes and swords were to be of Army pattern. It is not known whether or not they actually received these uniforms.

MISSISSIPPI VOLUNTEERS

The colonel of the 1st Mississippi was Jefferson Davis and the uniforms of his men were described by Sam Chamberlain as he saw them at Buena Vista: "This gallant regiment passed by us with the light swinging step peculiar to Indians and hunters, their uniform a red shirt worn outside of their white duck pants, and black slouch hats, armed with Windsor Rifles, and eighteen-inch Bowie Knives". There are also accounts that mention straw hats being worn. Most likely their hats were a matter of personal preference.

Another Mississippi soldier, possibly from a different unit, had written home about the fact that Zachary Taylor had referred to his unit as "the striped tigers" because their uniform was all striped. This may be a reference to striped mattress ticking being used in place of woolen cloth.

The 2nd Mississippi is also known to have left home without sufficient clothing.

MISSOURI VOLUNTEERS

Battery A of the Missouri Light Artillery was dressed in the same style as the Regulars. They wore red bands and artillery emblems on their forage caps. Their jackets had red collars, and their trousers had a single red stripe for the men and a double stripe for officers. The officers also wore gold lace on the collar of their jackets. Doniphan's Missouri Mounted Riflemen were a complete contrast to the artillery with the men being described as ragged and dirty, and dressed as they pleased without uniforms. An eyewitness described these men: "If you can imagine a man about six feet two to four and a half inches high, and well proportioned, with a deer skin (hair on) hunting shirt and pantaloons, the seams fringed with the same material cut into strings, and a bear skin stretched over his face with nothing but eyeholes cut in it, you can see a large proportion of Doniphan's Regiment". This unit was also fond of carrying multiple weapons including the US M1841 Mississippi Rifle, flintlock pistols, original Colt revolvers (1836 model), and dragoon sabres or swords.

MORMON BATTALION

There was not a piece of uniform in the entire outfit. The "Saints" wore civilian clothing of dark blue, brown or gray trousers with blue, gray, red or white shirts. They did have U.S. Army weapons and equipment with crossbelts and packs.

NEW YORK VOLUNTEERS (STEVENSON'S REGIMENT)

Full uniform was a dark blue coatee made of wool with crimson facings along with gray-blue pants having a red stripe down the seams. Originally a dark blue or black shako with yellow piping was worn. When this unit reached California, they wore white pants and shell jackets with red collars and pointed cuffs. The shakos were replaced by the standard Army issue forage caps.

1ST NORTH CAROLINA INFANTRY

A major's uniform exists that has a dark blue, double-breasted coat and dark blue pants with a white stripe down the seams.

OHIO VOLUNTEERS

The uniforms of the Ohio Volunteers were basically the same as for the Regular Army with a few exceptions. The officers wore silver embroidered badges on the front of their forage caps. Officers of the rifle companies were to wear green stripes on the trousers instead of white and black shoulder belts to carry their sword instead of the usual white. The enlisted men wore single-breasted dark blue jackets with nine buttons and shoulder tabs. The cuffs had loops of worsted tape trim.

PENNSYLVANIA VOLUNTEERS

The Pennsylvania Regiments were to have the same uniform as that of the Regulars but it was made of a dark blue cloth. Each company had been responsible for having their own uniforms made. The elaborate dress uniforms of the militia companies that formed part of the two regiments had been left behind as being impractical when the men left for Mexico.

1ST SOUTH CAROLINA (THE PALMETTO REGIMENT)

The volunteers from South Carolina were supposed to have a blue or gray uniform in the same style as the Regulars except for wing-style shoulder straps and pointed white cuff lace. Jack Meyer in his *South Carolina in the Mexican War* says the uniforms "were lost in a shipwreck, recovered, sent to Charleston, shipped to New Orleans, sent on to Vera Cruz, then

put on Colonel McIntosh's wagon train for transport to Puebla. Unfortunately on 13 June, guerillas intercepted the train near the National Bridge. Thought McIntosh drove the guerillas off, he lost some of the wagons, including those with the uniforms."

In the meantime the regiment was forced to make do with blue, green, red, check or white shirts, Kilmarnock caps (among others), and every type of boot, shoe, and stocking imaginable. At Puebla General Scott had mercy on them and issued them with the regulation light blue Army uniform. The Palmettos had shiny metal replicas of a palmetto tree on their visored caps, which easily distinguished them from other regiments.

TENNESSEE

The Tennessee Mounted Volunteers were described as looking like a unit of Mexican irregular lancers with their serapes, ponchos and colored blankets, and oil cloth hats with broad brims.

TEXAS RANGERS

Once again Sam Chamberlain of the 2nd Dragoons gives a good description of these troops: "The Rangers were the Scouts of our Army and a more reckless, devil-may-care looking set, it would be impossible to find this side of the Infernal Regions. Some wore buckskin shirts, black with grease and blood, some wore red shirts, their trousers thrust into their high boots; all were armed with Revolvers and huge Bowie Knives. Take them altogether, with their uncouth costumes, bearded faces, lean and brawny forms, fierce wild eyes and swaggering manners, they were fit representatives of the outlaws which made up the population of the Lone Star State". The Texans were fond of firepower with many carrying a rifle, a couple of pistols and one or two Colt revolvers. Colonel Jack Hays was described as being dressed plainly with a blue roundabout jacket, black pants and a black cap and did not have any article of clothing to denote his rank or even that he was a part of the army.

VIRGINIA VOLUNTEERS

The original uniform contract called for a dark blue cap, shell jacket, and pants. The soldiers were also to receive two pairs of socks, two cotton shirts, two flannel shirts, a sky-blue overcoat, and a gray blanket. The caps varied slightly in shape from the standard U.S. Army forage cap. After six months of service their uniforms were worn to the point that they began to draw replacement clothing that was the same as the uniform of the Regulars.

SUMMARY

The U.S. Army, to its credit, did not attempt to force the wearing of regulation dress uniforms while on campaign in Mexico. These were Napoleonic in style, similar to the uniforms of the Mexican Army and would have been uncomfortable and unserviceable in the field. The winter fatigue uniforms used by the Americans in Mexico proved to be both popular and practical. The Regulars began the war fairly well supplied with uniforms and weapons. The United States did not suffer from the shortage of funds or raw materials with which to maintain its forces, as Mexico did. The main problem faced by the U.S. Army once hostilities began was keeping the lines of supply and communications open to the forces at the seat of the war. Shipments could be delayed or lost at sea en route. Once they reached Mexico, they might not be distributed due to the army being cut off from its base. The uniforms of the army on campaign eventually became ragged and were supplemented by many non-regulation items that were picked up locally.

The U.S. Army as portrayed in the lithographs of artists Carl Nebel and Henry Walke, who were eyewitnesses, was a smartly uniformed force with few, if any, articles of unauthorized clothing in evidence. While individual soldiers describe a variety of different items worn with or in place of the regulation uniform, the overall impression of the army in the field may have been fairly close to that shown by these lithographers. The Regulars were professional soldiers with enough discipline, drill and pride to give off the impression of being a sharper looking outfit than what a closer inspection would reveal. The sky-blue kersey uniforms were subject to fading into different shades of light blue, gray or almost white with long exposure to the elements. Uniform coats and pants would wear out and become shabby, so the troops patched them with red flannel. They might also be replaced by locally made goods or the regimental tailors could be called into service if raw materials were available. In a pinch, parts of Mexican uniforms or local civilian dress would suffice. Shoes were just one of the items of which the army was in dire need, both before and after the march to Mexico City. After the fall of Vera Cruz in March of 1847 the Quartermaster General reported several thousand troops as being barefoot. The soldiers' headgear on the march was often the straw hat or sombrero when the forage cap was lost, traded away or simply packed up awaiting the proper occasion for displaying it.

The volunteers were quite another story when it came to the supply of uniforms. The many different colors and types of uniforms they chose rivalled those of the Mexican Army itself. They were supposed to provide their own uniforms when the regiments had been formed, but this was not always the case. Many were forced to make do with government issue items or clothing obtained in Mexico. Soldiers proceeded to repair and customize their own uniforms with whatever materials were at hand. Due to this practice some volunteer units may have resembled Mexican troops more than American.

In the final analysis the American army was a colorfully and practically uniformed force. Individual soldiers adapted with whatever materials were at hand to make up for problems with the supply situation. As with any army on campaign in this period, there was no way to remain faithful to the uniform regulations. The uniforms that saw service in Mexico may not have been what the army had intended, but they did not hinder the soldiers in their activities while serving the purpose of clothing the army.

The quartermaster-general produced this lithograph in 1885 of how the U.S. Regulars were meant to look: a dragoon is shown passing two infantrymen and a voltigeur.

FLAGS, STANDARDS, MEDALS AND DECORATIONS

The flags and standards carried by both armies during the Mexican-American war were very important to the soldiers that carried them. They were much more than mere decorations or displays of patriotic fervor, they came to symbolize the regiment itself and its accomplishments in battle. Regulations specified colors and sizes of flags and standards for the regular army on both sides but volunteers and militia could have customized banners for every regiment or unit. Some representation of the national colors might be part of the regimental flag, or they might be carried as a separate flag altogether. This led to a great variety of different flags in use. The flag stood for the honor of the regiment. A regiment that had its flag captured by the enemy was disgraced. Besides the question of honor there were practical considerations to take into account.

The typical battlefield during the first half of the nineteenth century was a very noisy and confusing place to be. The booming of the cannon and the crash of muskets firing created a din that was almost impossible to penetrate. The normal sounds of large groups of men moving and equipment shifting combined with explosions and the cries of the wounded to distract the average soldier from hearing important orders and commands. Once a battle got underway clouds of gunsmoke and dust could obscure the view of the enemy and even friendly positions. Uniforms could become faded and covered with dust that could make them difficult to identify properly at a distance. In addition, even though the uniforms were often very distinctive the soldiers were in the habit of improvising whatever they could find to replace worn out items, including treasures from the enemy. This resulted in even more chances for confusion to reign on the battlefield. Victory might depend upon the timely movement of a regiment or the ability of a unit to stand fast. Without modern communications the commanding general faced the dilemma of relying on visual information and word of mouth transmittal of orders. The regimental flag was an answer to these problems of command and control of the troops.

The flag served as a marker for the location of the regiment on the battlefield. Couriers and senior officers could find the troops more easily to be able to issue their orders. The men could use the flag as a guide to determine what the regiment was supposed to be doing when orders were impossible to hear or difficult to understand. The flag acted as a rallying point for stragglers, detachments or skirmishers returning to the main body. The banner could also serve as an inspiration to the regiment or to the soldiers of other regiments. Upon reaching an objective a flag unfurled could beckon others to follow it to victory. When a standard would stand firm under terrible pressure from the enemy it appeared to demand the support of its friends to frustrate defeat. Carrying the flag into battle was a big responsibility and an honor that usually had to be earned. Casualty rates among standard bearers were always high, but there were always plenty of men to take their place and raise up the banner after it had fallen. Captured enemy flags were a real prize to exhibit as proof of victory. A regiment that had lost its flag in battle was akin to artillery crewmen that had lost their guns to the enemy. They must live with the disgrace and attempt to redeem themselves at every opportunity.

MEXICO

The basic flags and standards carried by many Mexican regiments prominently portray the national colors and coat of arms. A tri-color of equal size vertical stripes of green/white/red with green being closest to the pole was probably the most common. In the center of the flag, on the white background, would be the national coat of arms of a Mexican eagle in brown with a green serpent grasped in its talon and beak. Sometimes the eagle would be perched atop a cactus and have accoutrements at its feet or it might be partially circled in elaborate wreath designs. This design is often accompanied by lettering above and/or below to designate the regiment or unit that it belongs to. The coat of arms design has many variations with the eagle facing left or right, wings spread wide or close, and the amount of detail portrayed depending upon the skill of the flag maker. There are variations on the basic colors with a horizontally striped tricolor being used by some units. The colors could vary with evidence of both red/white/green, and also red/green/white from top to bottom. Once again the national coat of arms was displayed in the center of the flag. Many Mexican flags of all types had tricolor ribbons as streamers hanging from the top of the pike, sometimes with a tricolor cockade as well.

There were some Mexican flags that did not have the tricolor or coat of arms on them. They could be a solid color, such as red or green, with gold lettering to designate the unit they represented. These banners could also have other designs on them such as skull and crossbones in the case of a cavalry guidon. The San Patricio Company also had its own design featuring a portrait of Saint Patrick with a Harp of Erin and a shamrock.

Cavalry units often carried a swallowtail type guidon or large pennant. Lancers had lance pennons which were usually red. The Jalisco Lancers at Monterrey were described by an eyewitness as each man having a "Mexican flag waving from his lance". There are surviving examples of trumpet banners, some that were in use before independence with Spanish regiments.

There does not appear to have been much standardization involved in the manufacture or distribution of flags. There is every indication that most if not all units did have flags, but exactly how they acquired them is not clear. The flags and standards of the Mexican Army added to the spectrum of color already present in its uniforms made it a very impressive spectacle.

MEDALS AND DECORATIONS

The Mexican army did have medals that were cast to commemorate a particular battle, whether it had been a victory or a defeat. There were medals given for "Palo Alto", "Buena Vista", "Churubusco", "Molino del Rey" and "Chapultepec" among others. There was the "Angostura Cross" made of white enamel with gold edges, ornaments and eagle. There was also the "Chapultepec Cross" that had red enamel arms over a white disk. Crosses and wreaths were used quite a bit in the designs with ribbons that were multi-colored in the national colors of green-white-red, others were red and blue while some were

a solid color, such as red. There was also an embroidered round patch or emblem worn on the left sleeve that was issued to troops defending the Valley of Mexico. This was green with yellow circles inside and black lettering.

UNITED STATES

Regulars

The flags and standards carried by the Americans were mostly made according to the "General Regulations for the Army of the United States" from 1841. Regiments were to have two colors, the first was a variation of the national flag while the second color was a regimental flag. The flags were to be made of silk and measured six feet high by six feet, six inches long. They were mounted to a pike for a total length of nine feet, ten inches. The national colors were to have seven red and six white horizontal stripes of equal width. The upper corner nearest the pole was to contain a blue field with a star for each state in the union. During the war with Mexico, the national flags would have had twenty-eight stars. Iowa became the twenty-ninth state in December of 1846 but new flags were not issued to any of the units on campaign. There were no specifications as to how these stars should be arranged or even how many points they should have. Normally five-pointed stars were used and they were displayed in even horizontal rows. The name and number of the regiment was embroidered on the center stripe in silver for infantry, gold for artillery. The flags normally had yellow fringe all around them. All of the above pertains to regulations prescribed by the army. In actual practice there were many cases of non-conformity with some units using flags that were not government issue.

The second standard carried by each unit was the regimental flag. The infantry colors were to be the same size as the national flags with the same yellow

At left is the U.S. National Flag with 28 stars as used during the War. At right is the U.S. Marine variant.

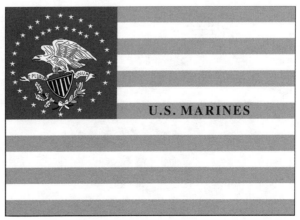

fringe and blue and white cords and tassels. The flag was blue with the "arms of the United States" embroidered in the center in silk. This was a depiction of an eagle in flight with a red scroll and the motto 'E Pluribus Unum' embroidered in gold letters in its beak. The eagle was also grasping a bundle of war arrows in one talon and an olive branch in the other. Above the eagle was a grouping of stars in rows or clusters corresponding as closely as possible to the number of states at the time. The name of the regiment was underneath the eagle in gold letters on a red scroll. These regimental flags had actually been used as the national colors up until 1841. Before that the regimental flags for the infantry were white or yellow. Some of these early regimental flags may have been used through the war in Mexico but they were not regulation by this period. Scrolls with battle honor inscriptions of the actions fought in Mexico were added after the war.

The U.S. Marine Corps battalion was issued its own flag that was a variation on the national colors with red and white stripes and a blue field. The blue field contained an eagle with a U.S. shield under it and the motto "E Pluribus Unum." The eagle and shield design are surrounded by a circular arrangement of twenty-nine stars five-pointed stars. (This flag was issued in 1847 and the star for Iowa was included.) The designation "U.S. Marines" was embroidered on the center red stripe in yellow.

The artillery flags were also the same size as the national colors in yellow silk with a design of two crossed cannons in gold in the center. The letters U.S. were in gold on a red scroll above and the regimental designation was similarly done below the cannons. Artillery flags were only displayed while the unit was on garrison duty or in other stationary posts and also when the unit was committed as infantry.

The dragoons carried only a single regimental flag into action. The mounted arm was less concerned with identification on the battlefield due to the small amount of friendly cavalry available in the first place and the sheer size of the profile that the units presented compared to the infantry. The flag was a smaller version of the regimental flag carried by the infantry regiments. It measured two feet, three inches tall by two feet, five inches wide and was also in dark blue silk with yellow fringe a bit longer than that of the infantry colors. The number and name of the regiment was in a scroll underneath the eagle.

The Regiment of Mounted Riflemen appear to have carried a standard similar in size but made of yellow silk with yellow silk fringe. The lances bearing all of the cavalry colors were to be a total of nine feet long. This non-regulation standard was carried throughout the Mexican war.

In addition to regimental colors each cavalry company carried a swallowtail guidon. These were two feet, three inches tall and three feet, five inches from the lance to the end of the fork. The top half was red with the letters 'U.S.' in white on it and a company designation while the bottom half was white with the word 'Dragoons' in red with the regimental number. This was later changed by the regulations of 1847 so that the top half only had 'U.S.' and the bottom half bore the letter of the company. These changes may not have affected units already participating in the campaign.

Garrison flags could be very large versions of the national flag measuring up to twenty feet tall by forty feet long. Often the troops did not have these flags with them so they had to be locally made out of materials at hand. There were also small camp colors to mark the location of regiments while assembling for parade or when encamped with other units. These were only about eighteen inches square and were white for infantry and red for artillery. They simply carried the number of the regiment painted on in reverse colors. They may have occasionally been carried into battle.

At left is the flag of the Mormon battalion, white with blue and red lettering.
A California flag is to the right: critics said the bear looked more like a pig.

VOLUNTEERS

There were no regulations regarding the sizes, designs or colors of the flags and standards carried by the volunteers. Many banners were very similar to U.S. regimental colors but with home made designs in the place of standard symbols. The flags were usually made at home and presented to the units upon their departure for the theater of war. Many flags were made after the unit had fought a battle and inscriptions were included on the flags mentioning its accomplishments. Some flags were made on the spot from materials at hand and did not conform to any existing designs. General Scott presented 31 flags to various units after the capture of Mexico City in a ceremony that celebrated the victory. The huge variety of colors carried by the volunteers makes it almost impossible to trace them all. Individual state archives may bear records of what some of these flags looked like, and occasionally they actually possess the original standard.

MEDALS AND DECORATIONS

The only medallions given out by the United States for the Mexican War were ordered by the Congress and awarded to General Taylor and General Scott. After the war several veterans organizations began to issue medals to their members to commemorate service in the war. The Aztec club issued more than one medal with ribbons to award their members, who were all officers during the war. The National Association of Mexican War Veterans awarded badges with ribbons to their members who were both officers and enlisted men. In addition other medals were cast and awarded to individuals by various groups which are too obscure to even be identified as this point. An example of this is a surviving medal for the "Conquest of the Californias" issued to a Lieutenant that saw service there.

The United States army had only one way to reward meritorious combat service at the beginning of the war with Mexico. This was the device known as brevet promotion. The officer that was awarded a brevet would assume the rank above the one that he presently held a commission for, (i.e.- A Captain would become a Brevet Major). Initially this was a way to reward officers for gallantry in the face of the enemy. The brevet rank carried no extra pay but in an army where normal promotion was painfully slow, it could be considered as the first step to achieving the next highest grade for the up and coming officer. It was often used as more of an honorific title to reward officers that had been prevented from normal promotion due to the lack of a retirement system. Officers could be given the responsibilities of their brevet rank to fill holes in the command structure or to accomplish specific tasks. Zachary Taylor was actually a Brevet Brigadier General at the beginning of the Mexican-American War. Brevets were given out quite frequently during the war with some officers earning two or three of them by the time it was all over.

On March 3, 1847 an Act of Congress was passed that established a Certificate of Merit for gallantry in action. The certificate entitled the recipient to additional pay of an extra two dollars per month. The award was only given out to privates and the first man to receive it was Private John R. Scott, B Company, 2nd Dragoons for his acts of heroism at the Battle of Cerro Gordo. The Certificate of Merit was awarded for conspicuous service to a total of 545 enlisted men during the course of the Mexican-American War.

Non-commissioned officers were not eligible for this award until 1854. This same award could also be given out to non-combatants and in peacetime for acts of heroism at the discretion of the President.

The Filson Club in Louisville, Kentucky has a reproduction of a variant commonly used of the National flag. The photograph has been taken from a ¾ view. (The Filson Club Historical Society)

Above is the Regimental Color of the 4th Illinois Infantry.
Below is the flank marker of the 4th Kentucky: this was used to show where the
regiment should form up in the field, and also probably to designate its spot in camp.
(Kentucky Historical Society/Military History Museum)

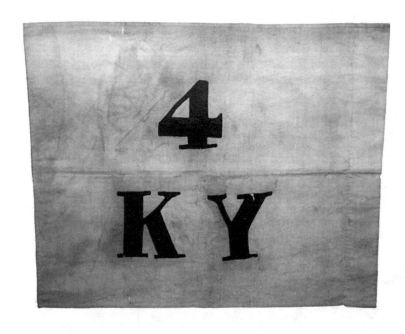

COMMENTARY ON THE COLOR PLATES

The study of military uniforms and their never ending variety of styles and colors is a fascinating subject that can sometimes be frustrating. Anyone who wishes to know what any armies actually looked like must realize that the answer to this question consists of two parts called theory and practice. The question presents many obstacles that must be overcome by careful study and some common sense to arrive at a reasonable answer. The best place to start is at the beginning with the regulations and decrees issued to describe the uniforms as they were, in theory, intended to look. The object is to end up by determining what the soldiers actually looked like, in practice, on the day of battle.

Regarding the style of the uniforms, it is safe to assume that the particulars as given in the orders were familiar to the contractors who were to manufacture these articles. Uniforms that have survived from the period show attention to most of the details listed in the regulations. There are some examples of non-regulation items appearing that may have been used in place of what was ordered or as a variation adopted by a particular unit or individual. When the uniforms were being made sometimes there could be shortages of particular materials and so substitutes were used. Soldiers were also known to customize their own uniforms for personal comfort or style. This could include extra lining or padding, the addition or removal of buttons and changes in pockets, collars, cuffs and trim. Although these alterations were not officially authorized they were usually overlooked, especially on fatigue uniforms.

When the armies took the field for a campaign the regulation uniforms began to wear out at a rapid rate. The soldiers would eventually be wearing tattered clothes and shoes that had to be replaced. A supply of new equipment was not always readily available and so the individual soldiers would be called upon to improvise. The first step was to patch up the uniform jacket or pants so that they would stay together a little longer in the hope that something better would come along. The simplest way to replace a worn or missing item was to simply "find" a new one that was suitable among friend or foe and acquire it through purchase, trade or theft. Alternatively the soldiers might make some of what they needed from materials obtained locally.

Materials might be acquired and turned into uniforms for an entire unit in this manner if necessary. There were instances of local seamstresses and tailors being employed to make uniforms where needed. The U.S. Army did set up shops for the manufacture of uniforms in Mexico when resupply had completely failed. The quality of materials was poor and the prices were inflated but they were manufactured to specifications that matched the uniform regulations as closely as possible.

On the day of battle itself the armies would attempt to look as impressive as possible. The Mexicans at Buena Vista had just been issued new uniforms and probably looked better there than at any other time during the war. Troops going into battle would ready their weapons and polish all of their metal accessories until they would shine. Uniforms would be cleaned up as much as possible. Hats, jackets or pants in good condition that the men had been saving for a special occasion were brought out. Any extra adornments that might not usually be worn were added to help dress up the uniform. It was good for the morale of the unit and the army to look its best and give the appearance, at least, of being ready for anything. During the course of a battle the state of the uniforms of units on both sides would quickly deteriorate as men lost or discarded weapons and equipment while fighting for their lives. By the end of the day the thirsty and exhausted, dust and blood covered soldiers would present a totally different appearance once again.

When attempting to describe the actual colors of uniforms there are various factors that must be considered in order to get the truest picture. The regulations specify the color just as well as they define the style for the uniforms being ordered. Contractors, once again would attempt to come as close as possible to the specifications decreed. In some cases substitute materials would be used that would not conform exactly to the colors being called for. Different dye lots of cloth could also vary in shades of the same color. If more than one manufacturer was involved there could be more than one interpretation of what the colors being requested actually looked like. The uniforms as completed might all be "dark blue" but they may not have all been the same shade of dark blue.

The dyes used in the early 19th century were not the same type of color-fast dyes used today. Many clothing manufacturers used darker shades than called for because they were aware that they would lighten with normal use. Every time the uniform was washed it would lose some of its color. The long exposure to sunlight and the elements would also fade the colors away. Before long the troops were in much lighter colored clothing than might be expected according to the regulations. Dark blue could fade to medium or light blue or gray, sky-blue might fade to light gray or even white, shades of red or green could be unrecognizable after long use. The uniforms of the troops would change colors under normal use even if they were kept in good shape. White uniforms or trousers came with the advantage of not changing colors at all.

The dilemma of determining true colors is sometimes compounded by surviving examples of uniforms in museums or private collections. Often it is not possible to tell exactly how different the colors are now from what they once were. The type of light that these articles are displayed in or photographed under may even contribute to changes in their appearance to the naked eye. When these items are portrayed in color prints or plates they are once again subjected to the interpretations of an artist and a printing process that may affect the exact shades of the colors being shown. These are the types of things that one must be aware of when making a judgement as to what the uniforms of the armies actually looked like more than a century ago.

The reconstructions of uniforms depicted in the color plates here have been done with these considerations in mind. The figures are based on the best evidence available at the time they were created. It should be obvious from the arguments put forth above that it is virtually impossible to say with certainty that this is exactly what these troops looked like. With this in mind it is reasonable to assert that this glimpse of the past is enlightening, even though other variations may also be valid. The reader is offered this view of the uniforms of the armies involved to aid in forming a better picture of how the participants might have appeared during the War in Mexico.

The figures shown in the plates are described from left to right.

PLATE 1—AMERICANS AT PALO ALTO

Company C, 3rd U.S. Artillery—Depicted here is part of the crew of a 6 lb. gun of the "flying artillery" commanded by Major Samuel Ringgold. They are wearing the special uniform and headgear that he devised of a dark blue coatee with red trim on the collar and shoulder knots instead of the usual yellow. The shakos also have the custom plumes and cords

that were not standard issue. These uniforms were probably not seen after Palo Alto and Resaca de la Palma as they began to wear out quickly and were replaced with standard issue. The artilleryman in the center wears the Foot Artillery Sword, Model 1832, while the other men carry the Sabre for Mounted Artillery, Model 1840.

PLATE 2—MEXICANS AT RESACA DE LA PALMA

2nd Light Infantry—This man wears the fatigue uniform that would also be common to the 1st and 3rd Light Infantry. This unit fought with great tenacity here giving credence to the assertion that the Light regiments were some of the best units in the army.

1st Line Infantry—This drummer wears the standard uniform of his regiment, not reverse colors as was common with Napoleonic era soldiers or even some Mexican National Guard units. The sandals worn were a cheap and easy replacement for boots that had worn out. The Indian conscripts recruited for the army were most likely comfortable in sandals, or even going bare-footed but these options were not necessarily the best footwear to have in adverse conditions on campaign.

6th Line Infantry—A fusileer showing the standard line infantry uniform. At Buena Vista and later battles the remnants of this unit were combined with the 7th and 8th Line Infantry to form the Mixed Santa Anna Regiment.

Light Mounted Regiment of Mexico—This figure is from one of the most famous light cavalry regiments in Mexico. Various other cavalry units adopted this same dress and it was also the regulation uniform for all of the Active Militia Cavalry. The troopers saddle blanket and rolled up cloak are on the ground in front of him.

Irregular Cavalry Lancer—This man typifies the Rancheros recruited by the "Chaparral Fox" all along the Texas-Mexican border. Many of these men were no more than brigands and ruffians who saw service as an opportunity for plunder. This man is in civilian clothing, as is normal for these units.

PLATE 3—AMERICANS AT MONTERREY

5th U.S. Infantry Officers, Sergeants and Privates—These men depict typical American infantry in their fatigue uniforms. It can be seen that officers uniforms were almost as plain as those of their men. The color variations in the blue of the jackets and pants are indicative of the results of wear while on campaign.

PLATE 4—MEXICANS AT BUENA VISTA

Tampico Coast Guards—This soldier is a member of the Veteran Infantry Coast Guard Company of Tampico as evidenced by his dark blue lapels and collar patches, which the single-breasted coats of the line companies did not have. These were the elite companies of the regiment. He wears a barracks cap instead of the normal shako.

11th Line Infantry—This unit was referred to as elite or veteran by Mexican chroniclers and foreign observers, which may be the reason behind the unique uniform it was issued.

Active Militia of Puebla (background)—This soldier wears what would have been the regulation uniform for all of the Active Militia infantry. Many Active Militia troops may have worn a simple frock coat with plain markings instead.

4th Light Infantry (falling backwards)—This unit was formed from the 3rd Line Infantry and given a unique uniform different from the other three Light Infantry units. This figure differs from the one shown by Hefter in the light of additional research by Detmar H. Finke. The trousers here are shown faded from their original dark 'turkish blue' color to a lighter shade of blue. During the summer months white pants would usually be worn.

Zapadores (falling forwards)—This soldier is from the Sappers, who were utilized as the elite infantry arm of the Mexican Engineers. These men rendered invaluable service later in the war by constructing many of the defenses and fortifications used by the army.

PLATE 5—AMERICANS AT BUENA VISTA

1st Illinois Volunteers—This soldier may have had a blue or gray uniform to start with, different companies made their own choices, but the color has faded as a result of being on campaign. Not all companies went in for the yellow lace trim on the chest, but comfortable headgear such as this straw hat was the norm.

2nd Indiana Volunteers—This volunteer shows another faded uniform that may have started out as "bright blue jeans" or even dark blue. Trousers could have been army issue sky-blue or something similar. He is wearing a glazed cap that was larger and more misshapen than the regular forage cap.

1st Mississippi Rifles—This man depicts the most common description of Colonel Jefferson Davis's volunteers. They had no bayonets for the rifles but 'bowie' knives were almost standard issue. Headgear was according to personal preference and straw hats and sombreros would not be uncommon.

Marshall's Kentucky Cavalry—The men turned up their hats into three cornered replicas of those worn during the American Revolution. There may not have anything else uniform about this unit although the trousers may have been army issue.

PLATE 6—MEXICAN CAVALRY AT BUENA VISTA

Tulancingo Cuirassiers (mounted)—This unit was given one of the most impressive uniforms in the Mexican army that brings to mind the heavy cavalry of Napoleon. Unfortunately for uniform enthusiasts there is evidence to suggest that the cuirass may not have actually been worn in the field. Another trooper of this colorful unit is seated on the ground at the far right.

1st Line Cavalry (sitting)—The uniform for this unit was changed from its original issue and it was the only Line Cavalry unit to actually be described as having a helmet for headgear instead of the normal shako.

8th Line Cavalry (mounted)—This man shows the more typical uniform of the line cavalry, including the shako, which could have pompon or plume as illustrated by the shakos visible in the background.

7th Line Cavalry (kneeling)—Here is another example of a distinctive uniform being issued for a veteran or elite unit, which the 7th was. The lacing on the lapels was unique among the uniforms of the Line Cavalry.

Jalisco Lancers (standing)—The headgear for this small unit was what distinguished it from all of the other lancers in the army. The style was reminiscent of the famous Polish Lancers of Napoleon. This 2 squadron unit was not regular army but of the Active Militia and no special status has ever been ascribed to them to justify their unique uniform.

PLATE 7—AMERICANS AT CERRO GORDO

Company of Sappers, Miners and Pontoniers—This unit was formed as the enlisted arm of the Corps of Engineers, which would have been equivalent to the Mexican Zapadores. They were not really meant to go into combat, but to assist in engineering tasks. However, it was not long before they were in the thick of things. The roman-sword bayonet shown here may have been issued more for dress parade at West Point than actual use in the field.

Artilleryman serving as Infantry—The majority of the artillery companies in Mexico served on foot as the "red-legged infantry" shown here. Infantry weapons and accoutrements were issued but the basic artillery uniform remains.

Pennsylvania Volunteers—There were two regiments from this state and their uniforms were of the same pattern as the regulars but both officers and men were known to customize their own dress somewhat as shown here with an unusual cap badge being worn by this officer.

4th Infantry—This man is wearing the overcoat that was standard issue and it was very useful for the cold nights in Mexico. In addition the protective neck flap is shown down on the forage cap. Some men cut these off entirely but others found them useful as a sun or rain shield.

PLATE 8—MEXICANS AT CHURUBUSCO

Mounted Artillerists (laying down and falling backwards)—The antelope skin lining and false boots on the trousers as well as the diagonal stripes on the sleeves identify these two figures as crew from the mounted artillery.

Foot Artillerists (falling forwards and on ground at far right)—The yellow uniform trim on the soldier falling closest to the cannon indicates that he is an enlisted man. The gold uniform trim worn by the man on the ground at the far right shows him to be an officer.

National Guard (on the ground in center—This man shows the basic uniform common for these troops. Many other variations would be possible including uniforms similar to regular units stationed in the area or even native peasant dress of white shirt and pants. It would all depend on how much time and money were available when the unit was activated.

San Patricio Regiment (marching group)—The men of the San Patricio unit could man guns or serve as foot soldiers when called upon to do so. They were Mexico's Foreign Legion. The flag is a reconstruction based on eyewitness accounts but it remains purely conjectural.

PLATE 9—AMERICANS AT CHAPULTEPEC

Regiment of Voltigeurs and Foot Riflemen—This unit was to have had a special gray uniform but were issued regular army clothing instead. This figure shows the white pants that were authorized for summer wear and yet another variant of a weathered blue jacket.

Regiment of Mounted Rifles (enlisted man)—The Mounted Rifles were forced to serve on foot although General Scott did manage to find enough horses to mount some of them during the campaign. At this battle horses would have been useless anyway.

Regiment of Mounted Rifles (officer)—Even though serving on foot this officer wears the sash hanging down on his right as the mounted arm required, foot officers wore it hanging to the left side. This unit was one of General Scott's favorites and they acquitted themselves well throughout the campaign.

1st South Carolina Volunteers (the Palmetto Regiment)—This picture shows a uniform similar to army issue but with variations in the trim on the shoulder straps and cuffs. The palm tree emblem distinguishes them from other volunteers or regulars. Just before this book went to press Jack Meyer, in his book *South Carolina in the Mexican War*, informs us that the Palmetto Regiment never received their own uniforms, but that General Scott had to get them issued the regulation light blue army uniform, distinguished only by a Palmetto badge on their caps.

PLATE 10—MEXICANS AT CHAPULTEPEC

10th Line Infantry—The green pompon indicates that this is soldier of the light company from this regiment. The color scheme of purple and buff is reconstructed here from the regulations but the exact shades of the colors used are not known. The turkish blue pants have clearly faded to a lighter shade after long use.

San Blas Battalion—This famous unit was another veteran unit that possessed uniforms that were somewhat unique. It is not known whether this occurred intentionally as with some other units or if it was due to the many different roles in which this unit was cast during the course of the war. Their flag is illustrated in the background.

Fijo de Mexico—This soldier is a fusileer as evidenced by the green pompon on his shako. The Fixed or Standing Battalion of Mexico did not use the same colors as the Line Infantry to designate elite companies. The other parts of the uniform were also non-standard for this special unit raised at the capital.

Military Academy Cadets—Only about 40 cadets were present at the defense of Chapultepec, which was their home during training and class. This cadet wears a blue fatigue jacket and older style blue and red barracks cap. Cadets who fought and died here also wore their service dress of gray frock coats and barracks caps.

PLATE 11—AMERICANS AT PUEBLA AND HUAMANTLA

Mexican Spy Company—The men of this unit would dress in whatever fashion was called for based on the mission that they were on. The red cloth tied on the hat was a convenient code for telling friend from foe. The words "Spy Co." were actually seen by witnesses but only when the unit was part of a larger group of American soldiers entering a city.

Texas Ranger—These were some of the most feared troops in the American army and they caused the most problems due to the vendettas they had against Mexicans in general, soldier or civilian. No uniform existed, even for the leaders, the only rule was just to have as much armament as could be carried.

4th Ohio Volunteer—This man shows a faded out version of the standard army issue worn by the regulars. Many volunteers were equipped with this outfit when they arrived in Mexico. Some units had even looted badly needed government stores in Mexico because no other uniforms were available for them.

9th Infantry—This soldier illustrates an extreme case of the unorthodox dress routinely worn by the regulars. The headgear is a native sombrero. The white pants might be army issue or looted from Mexican stores in Vera Cruz that had been captured. The shirt may have been brought from home or else it was acquired in Mexico. It is assumed that the regular army issue for this man has been worn out, discarded or is being saved for a special occasion. While the regulars may not have often gone to this extreme with unauthorized dress this example shows what was possible.

PLATE 12—MEXICAN GENERALS AND GUARD TROOPS

Grenadier Guard of the Supreme Powers—This larger than normal militia regiment was the parade unit of the Mexican army. This unit was considered elite mainly because of its status as a guard unit and its impressive special uniform, not because it had proven itself on the battlefield.

Hussars of the Guard of the Supreme Powers—This cavalry unit was the Presidential bodyguard for all military ceremonies and parades. The color of the pants and pelisse was supposed to be 'ice blue' which may have been even lighter than depicted here.

General of Division—The uniforms of the Mexican Generals were richly embroidered and ornate affairs. There was a great deal of leeway in what could be worn but the color of the sash (sky blue for Division Generals) and the pattern of gold embroidery were regulated as to rank. This rank would be equivalent to an American Major General.

General of Brigade—This Mexican Brigadier General is shown in full (gala) dress uniform. In the field Generals could wear simpler, less ornate uniforms or even civilian clothing. The sash (dark green) would be worn under a frock coat that was plain or had embroidered collar and cuffs with a single row of buttons.

PLATE 13—AMERICAN ARMY OF THE WEST AND IN CALIFORNIA

Missouri Mounted Volunteer—The descriptions given of these men include one with a man that wore a bearskin over his head, as shown here. This unit would more closely resemble a group of mountain men or trappers out on their own rather than soldiers in a military expedition.

LaClede Ranger—This is a reconstruction of a soldier from this unit recruited in Missouri in basically civilian dress. The Mormons on the trail feared these men marching with them more than they feared the Mexicans.

Mormon Battalion—These were the "Saints" that served as a battalion for the government mainly to make it easier for them to migrate west and make new homes there. Not counting the leaders appointed by the army to guide them, there was not a single item of uniform dress to be seen among them.

Navy Bluejacket—This sailor is typical of the men who manned the landing parties along the California coast and in the Gulf of Mexico. The hat could be black instead and the shirt could be white partly depending on the season of the year or the wishes of the captain of the ship. This man is off of the "CYANE" which saw much active duty.

1st Dragoons, Sergeant—This man shows the complete uniform of the Dragoons under General Kearny in California, although the difficulty of obtaining supplies made it virtually impossible to replace worn out uniforms. This man may have eventually ended up adopting civilian clothing or, not uncommonly, using articles of clothing provided by the navy. The letter on his forage cap indicates that he is from Company "C" of the 1st Dragoons which do not seem to have worn any cap bands on their hats as the 2nd Dragoons did.

PLATE 14—MORE MEXICAN UNITS

Mounted Rifles—This figure is a reconstruction from the descriptions given in Hefter but the exact color green of his uniform is conjectural. This may have been another case of a special uniform being created for a special unit, but not enough is known about this light cavalry regiment to justify this opinion.

Presidial Cavalry—The simple uniform of the Presidial soldiers shown here would have been a familiar sight all along the Mexican frontier. These small, far flung companies were responsible for the majority of the work involved in keeping order throughout the border settlements. There were rarely gathered as large groups and served mainly for scouting and patrol duty.

Volunteer Cavalry from the Southern Regions—This man illustrates civilian dress common among the irregular cavalry that joined the guerrilla bands raiding the supply lines of the American army. Serapes and capes were also commonly worn.

Californio or Ranchero—This is a typical example of the normal garb of the land owners in California and along the borders who fought against the American occupation. They were known for their colorful clothing and superb horsemanship. These irregulars had been conducting their own war against the Texans for years, while in California they had taken over and virtually ousted the Mexican government when the war began. There were no uniforms or formal military organization in existence among them.

Marine Infantry—The Mexican Marine uniform shown here was one of the most unusual among the foot troops. These men were used mainly for garrison duty in port facilities. There was virtually no chance to serve aboard ship as the Mexican Navy did not play any appreciable role in the war.

PLATE 15—AMERICAN FLAGS

It is probable that most units carried variants of the Stars and Stripes in the field. Certainly that is what the work of the war artist suggests. Such uniformity would have very useful for recognition purposes.

Regimental flags, if they were used, were of a fairly standard blue pattern, very similar to those used by

Union regiments in the Civil War. The flag of the 2nd Pennsylvania is an example. The flag of the Mounted Riflemen is interesting as it is an exception to the usual blue background. While many of the artillerymen served as infantry, it is not known if they ever carried their regimental flags in Mexico.

The Volunteer units probably carried the Stars and Stripes, or something similar. Substituting an eagle for the stars was often done. Most of the State flags were probably issued at the end of the campaign. Certainly the flag of the 2nd Pennsylvania was presented by General Scott in Mexico City.

The flag of the Menard Volunteers (4th Illinois), now in the Hall of Flags in the Capitol in Springfield, is intriguing as precursor to the battleflags common to the Confederate Army of Tennessee.

A New York Volunteer Flag is also shown.

PLATE 16—MEXICAN FLAGS

Most Mexican flags were variants of the tricolor, with the Eagle and Snake emblem. The example on top of the page is interesting because it uses a horizontal tricolor pattern and unorthodox colors, though it is hard to say what these were before they faded. It is attributed to no particular unit, but is said to have been captured in 1847.

More common variations of the usual tricolor are shown for the Artilleria de Mina, Battalion Fijo de Californios, and the Active Militia of Vera Cruz. The flag of the Artilleria de Mina was carried at Molino del Rey.

A soldier of the 3rd U.S. Artillery Regiment captured the flag of the Active Battalion of Lagos at Churubusco. The remnants of the Lagos and San Blas battalions were combined after the war to become the 15th Infantry.

A pennant used by a Mexican lancer at the Battle of Sacramento. On reverse was "Liberty or Death" in Spanish.

GLOSSARY

The words and phrases listed here are meant to assist the general reader with terms that may be difficult or foreign to them. Hopefully, these definitions will lead to a better understanding of what these technical or obscure words refer to in the text.

Active Militia (Activo Milicia)—Mexican territorial militia that was not part of the regular army but was a semi-permanent establishment.

arabesque—A complex and elaborate embroidered design of intertwined lines in geometric patterns or other shapes used as ornamentation on a uniform.

barracks cap—A fore-and-aft shaped soft undress cap also known as a garrison cap.

blouse—A short light coat. American volunteers sometimes wore unlined flannel shirts, which were roughly the equivalent. It was intended for use as a fatigue coat and was often known as a "sack coat."

brandenbourgs—Frogs and loops, usually of decorative braided cord.

brevet—A commission promoting an officer to an honorary rank higher than the one presently held. This was done to give an officer authority to command above his normal rank.

brig—A small two-masted ship with square-rigged sails.

Brown Bess—Nickname given to the British Long Land Pattern and Tower muskets of the late 18th and early 19th century.

bullion—A thick Gold or Silver cord made from thread and forming the fringe on an epaulette. The thinner cord was simply called fringe.

busby—A low-crowned fur cap, worn by hussars. It was named after the maker W. Busby of London.

cadre—A small group of key officers and men around which an expanded organization can be built or trained.

calendar—The calendar of days and dates for the year 1846 is the same as for the years 1987 and 1998. The year 1847 has the same calendar as the years 1993 and 1999. The year 1848 is the same as for the year 2000.

carbine—Cavalry version of the infantry musket made shorter for ease of use while mounted.

carronade—A short, light naval gun of relatively large bore that was a transition between the old long gun and the new shell gun. Carronades were cast in all calibers with the most common being 12 lb., 18 lb., 24 lb. and 32 lb. Carronades could be mounted in places where the heavier long guns could not be supported. Carronades were the principal armament in small frigates, brigs and sloops in this period.

cazadores—Rifle armed troops, usually light infantry, sometimes mounted.

chaparral—A close thorny thicket of shrubs and bushes, sometimes virtually impassable.

coatee—A close fitting coat cut across at the waist in front with short tails in the back.

cockade—A badge or rosette of ribbon or even leather worn on a soldier's headgear.

criollos (creole)—Caucasians (no Indian blood) born in Mexico. This was the aristocracy of Mexico.

cuff bars, cuff flaps, cuff patches—A vertical rectangular patch of cloth with buttons located on the cuff that was ornamental and often of contrasting color with the cuffs and other facings.

cuirass, cuirassier—A breastplate, usually of brass and the heavy cavalry troops that wore them.

dolman—A short, single-breasted jacket either waist length or with short skirts with loopings across the front, worn by hussars.

doughboy—Army slang for an infantryman or foot soldier. This term was first used during this period, but its origins are uncertain. Possibly referring to the doughy consistency of the pipeclay that had been traditionally used for the piping on uniforms. Another explanation is that the mud that the foot soldier would slog through would collect on his feet and would have a doughlike feel to it when walking. Alternatively the biscuits that were a staple part of the infantrymen's diet were made in the fire and would come out with a doughy middle. This term was popularized in referring to American soldiers in World War I.

dragoon—Originally referred to a mounted infantryman. Dragoons in Mexico, on both sides, were capable of fighting dismounted but mainly relied on the mounted charge with sabres or lances for combat.

duck—Cotton or linen cloth made finer or lighter in weight than canvas. Usually refers to white trousers or other material.

epaulette—An ornamental shoulder piece whose shape, size and color were used to indicate rank and branch of service.

facings—The colored distinctions on a uniform such as the collar, cuffs, lapels and turnbacks usually contrasting with the coat color.

false boots—see half-boots.

fatigue cap—see forage cap.

flintlock—A firearm using a gunlock that operates by a piece of flint striking steel when the trigger is pulled. The spark produced ignites the priming gunpowder and fires the weapon.

flounders—Oval or square braided cord usually with a heavy tassel.

flying artillery—Horse artillery that has its entire crew mounted. Especially refers to the U.S. 3rd Artillery, Company 'C' commanded by Major Samuel Ringgold.

foot artillery—A unit of artillery in which only officers and drivers are mounted on horses or gun carriages while the remainder of the crew must walk into battle.

forage cap—A low cloth or soft leather peaked cap with a broad crown all around. Normally worn with fatigue or undress uniform.

frigate—A fast, medium sized sailing warship mounting the main armament on a single gun deck.

frock coat—A long fairly snug fitting coat with stand-up collar and rear skirts (no turnbacks) falling anywhere in length from about one-third to three-fourths the distance from the hip to the knee. These could be single-breasted or double-breasted.

frog—An ornamental coat fastening or spindle-shaped button and loop. Also a sheath for attaching a bayonet or sword scabbard to the belt.

fusileer—A fusil was a light musket and the term for the soldiers who carried them was applied to all of the men in a unit who were not in specialized companies such as the Grenadiers or Rifles.

gachupines—Caucasians (no Indian blood) born in Spain. This was the ruling class in Mexico.

garita—A stone house that guarded the entrances to the city of Mexico along the various causeways. Normally used for customs officials and guards in peacetime, they were fortified with parapets and ditches and sometimes with artillery during the American assault.

gorget—Originally a crescent shaped piece of metal worn around the neck to designate rank. Used as the shape for some shako plates.

grapeshot—A cluster of small iron balls fired from a cannon that would disperse to inflict damage over a wider area than solid shot. It was used against men and horses at close range.

greaser—A derogatory slang word used by many Americans to refer to a Mexican. The Texans had been calling the Mexican rancheros "greasers" for quite some time because the leather coats and trousers they wore were shiny from "grease and long usage". Some soldiers even said that the term had been used as early as 1831. It may also have derived from a Mexican term, *los grisos* , used to refer to mixed white and Indian children of the early Spanish invaders, meaning a mixture of colors.

grenadier—Originally a soldier trained to carry and throw grenades. Typically larger and stronger men were chosen for this difficult task. Even though grenades were no longer employed the largest men in the regiment were still brought together to form an elite company of grenadiers armed with the same weapon as the other soldiers.

gringo—This was originally a Spanish term, *griego*, meaning 'greek' or some other foreigner who spoke with a pronounced accent. At the time of the Mexican War it was an insulting slang word referring to an American. It was also said to have come from a popular song in America at the time whose first words were "Green Grow the Lilacs", but this is probably just myth.

guidon—A cavalry flag or standard, often pennant shaped.

gunnades (gunades, insurance guns)—A naval gun that was a variation of the carronade but usually longer in caliber. Gunnades could be of any weight up to 32 lb. but the most common were the 6 lb. and smaller.

half-boots (false boots)—Leather cuffs and/or lining at the bottom of Mexican cavalry trousers.

haversack—A canvas or heavy linen bag used to carrying rations and miscellaneous items.

horse artillery—A unit of artillery in which all officers and crew are mounted on their own horses. This allows rapid movement so that the guns can keep up with cavalry units.

howitzer—A short cannon with a relatively large bore designed to launch projectiles at a higher angle than regular cannon. They can be used to fire explosive shells at infantry targets or behind fortifications.

hussar—Light cavalry, modelled after Hungarian light horse troops.

jacket—A short waist length single-breasted outer garment with stand up collar.

Jefferson boots—Shoes that came about two inches above the ankle joints of the wearer.

kepi—Originally a French designed military cap with a flat circular top and horizontal visor. The kepi became the standard issue headgear in the American Civil War.

kersey—A coarse woolen cloth, usually ribbed.

kersimere—A fine woolen cloth with a twill weave.

kilmarnock cap—A British style round cloth forage cap dating from the early 1830's. Named for the town in Scotland where it was manufactured, it was popular among some volunteers.

knapsack—A backpack, sometimes made of canvas or cowhide with the hair left on or covered with other fur.

lace—A flat braid used for trim on uniform lapels, collars, cuffs and elsewhere.

lapels—The turned back upper part of the front of a coat. The lapels were usually opened and worn buttoned back in warmer weather. This allowed the lining with the facing color to show clearly.

mestizos—Mexicans of mixed white and Indian blood.

Mexico—The Mexican union was made up of 19 states and 5 territories at the beginning of hostilities in 1846. The states were Chiapas, Chihuahua, Coahuila & Texas (as one), Durango, Guanajuato, Jalisco (or Xalisco), Mexico, Michoacan, Nuevo Leon, Oajaca (or Oaxaca), Puebla de los Angeles (later just Puebla), Queretaro, San Luis Potosì, Sonora & Sinaloa together as Estado de Occidente, Tabasco, Tamaulipas, Vera Cruz, Yucatan and Zacatecas. The territories were Alta (upper) California, Baja (lower) California, Colima, New Mexico and Tlascala. At this time Mexico City is also usually referred to simply as 'Mexico'.

musket—A smoothbore muzzle-loading shoulder arm that could be fired by a flintlock or percussion cap system.

National Guard (Guardia Nacional)—Local militia units

raised by states or cities in Mexico.

pelisse—Overgarment covered with loopings or braid usually edged with fur or imitation fur, carried by hussars, normally worn over the left shoulder held by a cord, basically to be worn over the hussars dolman instead of a greatcoat.

percussion cap—A system of firing a weapon using a gunlock that would strike a small metal cap containing fulminating powder to ignite the charge and fire the weapon.

piping—Ornamental trim originally of pipe-clay in the 18th century but made of narrow tubular strips of cloth in this period. This would be sewn on rounded edging for parts of a uniform that could include collars, cuffs, cuff bars, lapels and turnbacks, etc. Usually piping was of a contrasting color to highlight the part of the uniform it was on.

pompon—A tuft of worsted wool or other material worn on the top of the shako.

pronunciamento—A proclamation, usually issued by a general, promising reforms and the end of abuses in government designed to gain support for a rebellion.

ranchero—Spanish for rancher or farmer.

redan—A small defensive work usually with two sides coming together at an angle facing the enemy line of approach. Normally used to cover the front line or edge of camp, river, village or advanced post.

redoubt—A stronghold or breastwork constructed for defense, usually enclosed on all sides, sometimes provided with cannon.

rifle—A shoulder arm with grooves cut into the inside of the barrel with the purpose of giving the projectile being fired a spin to its motion. This gives the rifle much greater accuracy at longer range than for a comparable smoothbored weapon. Since the bullet must fit more snugly to take advantage of the grooves or rifling, the muzzle loading rifle is usually more difficult to load and results in a slower rate of fire.

roundabout—A sort and close fitting jacket with sleeves but without tails. Length was usually and inch or two below the waist.

round hat—Civilian style hat popular with some American volunteer units. Usually tall and high crowned with a narrow brim that could be rolled up or pinned up at the sides. Also known as a Beaver Hat, Plug Hat or Pot Hat.

sabretache—A decorated leather case hung from the sword belt of a cavalryman.

sapper (zapadore)—Mexican soldiers who were engineers as well.

see the elephant—To see the Elephant is to undergo any disappointment of high-raised expectations. Men who volunteered for the Mexican war, expecting to reap glory, but finding only sickness, fatigue, privations and suffering were said to have "seen the elephant." Often used to refer to the frightening experiences of the battlefield as well.

schooner—A ship with two or more masts, rigged fore and aft.

shabraque—Originally a saddle cloth that developed into an ornamental trapping.

shako—A cylindrical type of cap that could be of many different styles.

ship of the line—The largest class of sailing warship mounting the most guns.

shoulder knots—These were epaulettes without fringes.

sloop—A small fore-and-aft-rigged single masted sailing vessel.

sombrero—A broad-brimmed Mexican hat, usually with a tall crown, made of felt or straw. Sombreros could be a variety of colors and might be very decorative depending on the personal taste of the owner.

tete de pont—A field entrenchment, such as a redan, at the entrance to a bridge.

turnbacks—The front and rear edges of the coattails, turned back and fastened together at the bottom, usually revealing the contrasting color of the coat's inside lining. In the 18th century they were not only decorative, but practical as they gave the soldier's legs greater freedom of movement with the long coats being worn. Turnbacks on the shorter coats of the 19th century were purely ornamental.

United States—There were 28 states at the beginning of hostilities in 1846. They were Alabama, Arkansas, Connecticut, Delaware, Florida, Georgia, Illinois, Indiana, Kentucky, Louisiana, Maine, Maryland, Massachusetts, Michigan, Mississippi, Missouri, New Hampshire, New Jersey, New York, North Carolina, Ohio, Pennsylvania, Rhode Island, South Carolina, Tennessee, Texas (1845), Vermont, and Virginia. Iowa was admitted in 1846 and Wisconsin in 1848.

units of measure—One Mexican foot equals .926 English feet or about 11⅛ English inches.

voltigeur—A French term for light infantry. The U.S. Army regiment of Voltigeurs differed from regular infantry regiments in name only.

vómito—Yellow fever. This dreaded disease, for which there was no cure, was common along the low lying coastal areas of eastern Mexico during the rainy season from April to October.

welt—A strip of material folded over a cord and placed at the edge or seam of a uniform part to reinforce or trim it. Usually of a contrasting color. (see piping)

worsted—A fabric made of worsted thread which is smooth and hard-twisted made from long-staple wool.

BIOGRAPHIES

AMERICAN

The information listed below has been compiled from a variety of sources and is as complete as possible. The subjects' name includes the highest actual rank held during the Mexican War. An asterisk* after the name indicates a graduate of the Military Academy at West Point, which in a few cases occured after the Mexican War was over. The unit that he served in follows the name along with brevet rank promotions and the actions for which they were given. Any wounds or other remarks of interest are listed after this. The data following the dash is his later career; *background and highest rank achieved in the American Civil War are in italics.* Finally the date of birth (b.) and death (d.) are given where they are known.

Abercrombie, Major John J. *
5th Infantry; Bvt. Lt. Col. and wounded at Monterrey—*USV Brig. Gen.* b. 3/4/1798; d. 1/3/77

Adams, 2nd Lieutenant John *
1st Dragoons; Bvt. 1st Lt. at Santa Cruz de Rosales—*CSA Brig. Gen.* b. 7/1/25; *d. 11/30/64 at the battle of Franklin, TN.*

Allen, Major George W.
2nd Infantry; Bvt. Lt. Col., Palo Alto and Resaca de la Palma d. 3/15/48

Allen, Lieutenant Harvey *
2nd Artillery; Bvt. Capt., Molino del Rey—*USA Major* d. 9/20/82

Allen, Captain Robert *
Asst. Quartermaster; Bvt. Major, Cerro Gordo—*USV Brig. Gen.* b. 5/15/11; d. 8/5/86

Alvord, Captain Benjamin *
4th Infantry; Bvt. Capt. and Major, Palo Alto, Resaca de la Palma and Paso Ovejas—*USV Brig. Gen.* b. 8/18/13; d. 10/16/84

Anderson, Lieutenant George T. "Tige"
Georgia Mounted Volunteers—*CSA Brig. Gen.* b. 2/3/24; d. 4/4/1901

Anderson, Captain James W. *
2nd Infantry. died 8/22/47 of wounds received at the battle of Churubusco, Mexico.

Anderson, 2nd Lieutenant Richard H. *
2nd Dragoons; BVT. 1st Lt., San Augustin—*CSA Lt. Gen.* b. 10/7/21; d. 6/26/79

Anderson, Captain Robert *
3rd Artillery; Bvt. Major and severely wounded at Molino del Rey—*USA Brig. Gen., defended Fort Sumter in 1861,* b. 6/14/05; d. 10/26/71

Anderson, Lt. Colonel Samuel R.
1st Tennessee Volunteers—*CSA Brig. Gen.* b. 2/17/04; d. 1/2/83

Andrews, Colonel Timothy P.
Regiment of Voltigeurs & Foot Riflemen; Bvt. Brig. Gen., Chapultepec—d. 3/11/68

Archer, Captain James J.
Regiment of Voltigeurs & Foot Riflemen; Bvt. Major, Chapultepec—*CSA Brig. Gen.* b. 12/19/17; d. 10/24/64

Armistead, Lieutenant Lewis A. *
6th Infantry; Bvt. Capt. and Major, Contreras, Churubusco and Molino de Rey; wounded at Chapultepec—*CSA Brig. Gen.* b. 2/18/17; *killed 7/5/63 at the battle of Gettysburg, PA.*

Arnold, Lieutenant Lewis G. *
2nd Artillery; Bvt. Capt. and Major, Contreras, Churubusco and Chapultepec—*USV Brig. Gen.* b. 1/15/17; d. 9/22/71

Augur, 2nd Lieutenant Christopher C.*
4th Infantry—*USV Maj. Gen.* b. 7/10/21; d. 1/16/98

Bainbridge, Major Henry *
7th Infantry; Bvt. Lt. Col., Contreras and Churubusco, wounded at Monterrey. d. 5/31/57

Baker, Colonel Edward D.
4th Illinois Volunteers—*USV Maj. Gen.* b. 2/24/11; *killed 10/21/61 at the battle of Balls Bluff, VA.*

Bankhead, Colonel James
2nd Artillery; Bvt. Brig, Gen., Vera Cruz. d. 11/11/56

Barbour, Captain Philip N. *
3rd Infantry, Bvt. Major, Palo Alto and Resaca de la Palma; killed 9/21/46 at the battle for Monterrey, Mexico.

Barksdale, Captain William
2nd Mississippi Volunteers—*CSA Brig. Gen.,* b. 8/21/21; *killed 7/3/63 at the battle of Gettysburg, PA.*

Barnard, Captain John G.*
Engineers—*USV Brig. Gen.,* b. 5/19/15; d. 5/14/82

Barnes, Captain Joseph K.
Asst. Surgeon—*USA Surgeon General.* b. 7/21/17; d. 4/5/83

Barry, Lieutenant William F.*
2nd Artillery—*USV Brig. Gen.* b. 8/18/18; d. 7/18/79

Bate, Lieutenant William B.
3rd Tennessee Volunteers—*CSA Maj. Gen.* b. 10/7/26; d. 3/9/1905

Beall, Major Benjamin L. *
1st Dragoons, Bvt. Lt. Col. Santa Cruz de Rosales. d. 8/16/63

Beatty, Lieutenant Samuel
3rd Ohio Volunteers—*USV Brig. Gen.* b. 12/16/20; d. 5/26/85

Beauregard, Lieutenant Pierre G. T.*

Engineers, Bvt. Capt. and Major Contreras, Churubusco and Chapultepec; twice wounded at Chapultepec—*CSA General.* b. 5/28/18; d. 2/20/93

Bee, 2nd Lieutenant Barnard E. * 3rd Infantry, Bvt. 1st Lt. and Capt. Cerro Gordo and Chapultepec—*CSA Brig. Gen.* b. 2/8/24; *d. 7/22/61 of wounds received at the first battle of Bull Run, VA.*

Belknap, Lt. Colonel William G. * 5th Infantry, Bvt. Col. and Brig. Gen. Palo Alto and Resaca de la Palma, wounded at Resaca de la Palma. d. 11/10/51

Belton, Lt. Colonel Francis S. 3rd Artillery, Bvt. Col. Contreras and Churubusco. d. 9/10/61

Benham, Lieutenant Henry W. * Engineers, Bvt. Capt. and wounded at Buena Vista—*USV Brig. Gen.* b. 4/17/13; d. 6/1/84

Benton, Private William P. Regiment of Mounted Rifles—*USV Brig. Gen.* b. 12/25/28; d. 3/14/67

Blanchard, Major Albert G. * 12th Infantry—*CSA Brig. Gen.* b. 9/10/10; d. 6/21/91

Bliss, Bvt. Major William W. S. * Asst. Adjutants-General, Bvt. Major and Lt. Col. Palo Alto and Buena Vista.; future son-in-law to Zachary Taylor (nicknamed "Perfect Bliss") d. 8/5/53

Bonham, Colonel Milledge L. 12th Infantry—*CSA Brig. Gen.* b. 12/25/13; d. 8/27/90

Bonneville, Major Benjamin L. E.* 6th Infantry, Bvt. Lt. Col. Contreras and Churubusco, wounded at Churubusco. Explored the west in the 1830s and the Bonneville Flats were named for him. d. 6/12/78

Bragg, Captain Braxton * 3rd Artillery, Bvt. Major and Lt. Col. Monterrey and Buena Vista—*CSA Lt. Gen. and Army Commander* b. 3/22/17; d. 9/27/76

Brannan, Lieutenant John M. * 1st Artillery, Bvt. Capt. Contreras and Churubusco, severely wounded at

Chapultepec—*USV Brig. Gen.* b. 7/1/19; d. 12/16/92

Breckinridge, Major John C. 3rd Kentucky Volunteers—*CSA Maj. Gen.* b. 1/15/21; d. 5/17/75

Brooks, Lieutenant William T. H.* 3rd Infantry, Bvt. Capt. and Major Monterrey, Contreras and Churubusco—*USV Maj. Gen.* b. 1/28/21; d. 7/19/70

Brown, Major Jacob 7th Infantry. d. 5/9/46 of wounds received in defense of Fort Brown, TX.

Bryan, Major Goode * 1st Alabama Volunteers—*CSA Brig. Gen.* b. 8/31/11; d. 8/16/85

Buchanan, Commander Franklin, USN U.S.S. Germantown—*CSN Admiral. Captain of the C.S.S. Virginia (Merrimack) until wounded in action on 3/8/62 at the battle of Hampton Roads, VA the day before the ship encountered the U.S.S. Monitor. Fought against Rear Admiral Farragut at the battle of Mobile Bay, AL on 8/5/64.* b. 9/17/1800; d. 5/11/74

Buchanan, Captain Robert C. * 4th Infantry, Bvt. Major and Lt. Col. Palo Alto, Resaca de la Palma and Molino del Rey— *USV Brig. Gen.* b. 3/1/11; d. 11/29/78

Buckner, 2nd Lieutenant Simon B.* 6th Infantry, Bvt. 1st Lt. and Capt. Contreras, Churubusco and Molino del Rey—*CSA Lt. Gen.* b. 4/1/23; d. 1/8/1914

Buell, Lieutenant Don Carlos * 3rd Infantry, Bvt. Capt. and Major Monterrey, Contreras and Churubusco, severely wounded at Churubusco—*USV Maj. Gen.* b. 3/23/18; d. 11/19/98

Buford, Lieutenant Abraham * 1st Dragoons, Bvt. Capt. Buena Vista—*CSA Brig. Gen.* b. 1/18/20; d. 6/9/84

Burnside, 2nd Lieutenant Ambrose E.* 2nd Artillery—*USV Maj. Gen.and Army Commander, defeated at Fredericksburg* b. 5/23/24; d. 9/13/81

Butler, Colonel Edward G. W. *

3rd Dragoons. d. 9/6/88

Butler, Maj.-General William O. Volunteer Officer. d. 8/6/80

Cadwalader, Brig. General George Volunteer Officer, Bvt. Maj. Gen. Chapultepec—*USV Maj. Gen.* b. 5/16/06; d. 2/3/79

Caldwell, Major George A. Regiment of Voltigeurs & Foot Riflemen, Bvt. Lt. Col. Chapultepec.

Callender, Lieutenant Franklin D.* Ordnance, Bvt. Capt. Contreras and Churubusco, severely wounded at Contreras—*USA Lt. Col.* d.12/13/82

Campbell, Captain Charles T. 11th Infantry—*USV Brig. Gen.* b. 8/10/23; d. 4/15/95

Campbell, Colonel William B. 1st Tennessee Volunteers—*USV Brig. Gen.* b. 2/1/07; d. 8/19/67

Canby, Lieutenant Edward R. S. * 2nd Infantry; Bvt. Captain, Asst. Adjutants-General, Bvt. Major and Lt. Col. Contreras, Churubusco and Belen Garita— *USV Maj. Gen.* killed in action by Modoc Indians at Lava Beds, OR 4/11/73

Cantey, Adjutant James 1st South Carolina Volunteers, severely wounded at Churubusco—*CSA Brig. Gen.* b. 12/30/18; d. 6/30/74

Carleton, Captain James H. 1st Dragoons, Bvt. Major Buena Vista—*USV Brig. Gen.* b. 12/27/14; d. 1/7/73

Carson, Lieutenant Christopher "Kit Carson". Scout and Guide for Fremont and Kearny in California—*U.S. Colonel, 1st New Mexico Volunteers.* b. 12/24/09; d. 5/25/68

Casey, Captain Silas * 2nd Infantry, Bvt. Major and Lt. Col. Contreras, Churubusco and Chapultepec, severely wounded at Chapultepec—*USV Maj. Gen.* b. 7/12/07; d. 1/22/82

Cheatham, Captain Benjamin F. 1st Tennessee Volunteers—*CSA Maj. Gen.* b. 10/20/20; d. 9/4/86

Childs, Major Thomas * 1st Artillery, Bvt. Col. and Brig. Gen. Palo Alto, Resaca de la

Palma and Puebla. d. 10/8/53

Chilton, Captain Robert H. *
1st Dragoons, Bvt. Major Buena Vista—*CSA Brig. Gen.* b. 2/25/15; d. 2/18/79

Churchill, Lieutenant Thomas J.
1st Kentucky Rifles—*CSA Maj. Gen.* b. 3/10/24; d. 5/14/1905

Clanton, James H.
—*CSA Brig. Gen.* b. 1/8/27; d. 9/27/71

Clark, Colonel Charles
2nd Mississippi Volunteers—*CSA Brig. Gen.* b. 5/24/11; d. 12/18/77

Clark, Major John B.
1st Infantry. d. 8/23/47

Clark, Major Meriwether L. *
Lt. Artillery, Missouri Volunteers—*CSA Colonel.* d. 10/28/81

Clarke, Colonel Newman S.
6th Infantry, Bvt. Brig. Gen. Vera Cruz. d. 10/17/60

Clay, Captain Cassius M.
1st Kentucky Cavalry Volunteers—*USV Maj. Gen.* b. 10/19/10; d. 7/22/1903

Clemens, Lt. Colonel Jeremiah
9th Infantry. d. 5/21/65

Colquitt, Major Alfred H.
Paymaster Volunteer Officer—*CSA Brig. Gen.* b. 4/20/24; d. 3/26/94

Connor, Captain P. E.
Independent Company of Texas Rifles, wounded at Buena Vista—*USV Brig. Gen.* b. 3/17/20; d. 12/17/91

Cooke, Major Philip St. George *
2nd Dragoons, Bvt. Lt. Col. California; led the Mormon Battalion from Santa Fe to California—*USA Brig. Gen.* b. 6/13/09; d. 3/20/95

Cooper, Captain Douglas H.
1st Mississippi Rifles—*CSA Brig. Gen.* Superintendent of Indian Affairs. b. 11/1/15; d. 4/29/79

Cooper, Private Joseph A.
4th Tennessee Volunteers—*USV Brig. Gen.* b. 11/25/23; d. 5/20/1910

Corse, Captain Montgomery D.
Virginia Volunteers—*CSA Brig. Gen.* b. 3/14/16; d. 2/11/95

Couch, 2nd Lieutenant Darius N.*
4th Artillery, Bvt. 1st Lt. Buena Vista—*USV Maj. Gen.* b. 7/23/22; d. 2/12/97

Craig, Captain James
Battalion of Missouri Mounted Volunteers—*USV Brig. Gen.* b. 2/28/17; d. 10/21/88

Crittenden, Captain George B. *
Regiment of Mounted Rifles, Bvt. Major Contreras and Churubusco—*CSA Maj. Gen.* b. 3/20/12; d. 11/27/80

Crittenden, Lt. Colonel Thomas L.
3rd Kentucky Volunteers—*USV Maj. Gen.* b. 5/15/19; d. 10/23/93

Crittenden, 2nd Lieutenant Thomas T.
Battalion of Missouri Mounted Volunteers—*USV Brig. Gen.* b. 10/16/25; d. 9/5/1905

Crosman, Major George H.*
Quartermaster—*USA A.Q.M.G.* d. 5/28/82

Cross, Major Osborn *
Quartermaster—*USA A.Q.M.G.* d. 7/15/76

Cross, Colonel Trueman
Asst. Quartermaster General. Killed 4/21/46 by bandits on the Rio Grande.

Curtis, Colonel Samuel R. *
2nd Ohio Volunteers—*USV Maj. Gen.* b. 2/3/05; d. 12/26/66

Cushing, Brig. General Caleb
Volunteer Officer from Massachusetts. d. 1/2/79

Dana, Lieutenant Napoleon J. T. *
7th Infantry, Bvt. Capt. and severely wounded at Cerro Gordo—*USV Maj. Gen.* b. 4/15/22; d. 7/15/1905

Dashiel, Major Jeremiah Y.
Paymaster Volunteer Officer—*CSA Colonel.* d. 3/14/88

Davenport, Colonel William
1st Infantry. d. 4/12/58

Davidson, Sergeant Henry B. *
1st Tennessee Volunteers—*CSA Brig. Gen.* b. 1/28/31; d. 3/4/99

Davidson, 2nd Lieutenant John W.*
1st Dragoons—*USV Brig. Gen.* b. 8/18/24; d. 6/26/81

Davis, Colonel Jefferson *
1st Mississippi Rifles, severely wounded at Buena Vista; one time son-in-law to Zachary Taylor (his wife Sarah Knox Taylor died in 1835)—*CSA President 1861-1865.* b. 6/3/08; d. 12/6/89

Colonel Jefferson Davis

Davis, Sergeant Jefferson C.
3rd Indiana Volunteers—*USV Brig. Gen.* b. 3/2/28; d. 11/30/79

Deas, Zachariah C.
—*CSA Brig. Gen.* b. 10/25/19; d. 3/6/82

deLagnel, Lieutenant Julius A.
2nd Artillery—*CSA Brig. Gen.* b. 7/24/27; d. 6/3/1912

Dent, 2nd Lieutenant Frederick T.*
5th Infantry, Bvt. 1st Lt. and Capt. Contreras, Churubusco and Molino del Rey; severely wounded at Molino del Rey—*USV Brig. Gen.* b. 12/17/20; d. 12/23/92

Denver, Captain James W.
12th Infantry—*USV Brig. Gen.* b. 10/23/17; d. 8/9/92

DeRussy, 2nd Lt Gustavus A. *
4th Artillery, Bvt. 1st Lt. and Capt. Contreras, Churubusco and Chapultepec—*USV Brig. Gen.* b. 11/3/18; d. 5/29/91

Doniphan, Colonel Alexander W.
1st Missouri Mounted Volunteers. b. 7/9/08; d. 8/8/87

Doubleday, Lieutenant Abner *
1st Artillery—*USV Brig. Gen.* *Most famous as the supposed inventor of the game of baseball.* b. 6/26/19; d. 1/26/93

Drum, Captain Simon H. *
4th Artillery. killed in action 9/13/47 at the Belen Gate, Mexico City.

Dumont, Lt. Colonel Ebenezer
4th Indiana Volunteers—*USV Brig. Gen.* b. 11/23/14; d. 4/16/71

Duncan, Captain James *
2nd Artillery, Bvt. Major and Lt. Col. Palo Alto, Resaca de la Palma and Monterrey. d. 7/3/49

DuPont, Cmdr Samuel F., USN
U.S.S. Congress—*USN Rear Admiral in charge of South Atlantic Blockading Squadron.* b. 9/27/03; d. 6/23/65

Dunovant, Sergeant John
1st South Carolina Volunteers—*CSA Brig. Gen.* b. 3/5/25; *killed in action south of the James River on 10/1/64*

Dyer, Lieutenant Alexander B. *
Ordnance, Bvt. Captain, Santa Cruz de Rosales—*USA Brig. Gen.* b. 1/10/15; d. 5/20/74

Early, Major Jubal A. *
Virginia Volunteers—*CSA Lt. Gen.* b. 11/3/16; d. 3/2/94

Eaton, Captain Amos B. *
Chief Commisary of Subsistence (for Taylor), Bvt. Major, Buena Vista—*USA Brig. Gen. Sub.* b. 5/12/06; d. 2/21/77

Echols, Colonel Robert M.
13th Infantry. d. 12/3/47

Elliott, 2nd Lieutenant Washington L. *
Regiment of Mounted Rifles—*USV Brig. Gen.* b. 3/31/25; d. 6/29/88

Elzey, Lieutenant Arnold *
2nd Artillery, Bvt. Capt., Contreras and Churubusco—*CSA Maj. Gen.* b. 12/18/16; d. 2/21/71

Emory, Lieutenant William H. *
Topographical Engineers, Bvt. Capt. and Major, San Pascual, San Gabriel and Plains of La Mesa—*USA Maj. Gen.* b. 9/7/11; d. 12/1/87

Ewell, Lieutenant Richard S. *
1st Dragoons, Bvt. Capt., Contreras and Churubusco—*CSA Lt. Gen.* b. 2/8/17; d. 1/25/72

Fagan, Lieutenant James F.
Arkansas Mounted Volunteers—*CSA Maj. Gen.* b. 3/1/28; d. 9/1/93

Farragut, Commander David G., USN
U.S.S. Saratoga—*USN Rear Admiral. Captured New Orleans, LA, 4/62. Was the victor at the battle of Mobile Bay, AL on 8/5/64 where he uttered the famous quote "Damn the torpedoes! Full steam ahead!"* b. 7/5/01; d. 8/14/70

Forney, Lieutenant William H.
1st Alabama—*CSA Brig. Gen.* b. 11/9/23; d. 1/16/94

Foster, 2nd Lieutenant John G. *
Engineers, Bvt. 1st Lt. and Capt., Contreras, Churubusco and Molino del Rey; severely wounded at Molino del Rey—*USA Maj. Gen.* b. 5/27/23; d. 9/2/74

Franklin, 2nd Lt William B.*
Topographical Engineers, Bvt. 1st Lt. at Buena Vista—*USA Brig. Gen.* b. 2/27/23; d. 3/8/1903

Fremont, 2nd Lieutenant John C. "the Pathfinder"; Topographical Engineers; California Volunteers; Lt. Col. Regiment of Mounted Rifles—*USA Maj. Gen.* b. 1/21/13; d. 7/13/90

French, 2nd Lieutenant Samuel G.*
3rd Artillery, Bvt. 1st Lt. and Capt. Monterrey and Buena Vista; wounded at Buena Vista—*CSA Maj. Gen.* b. 11/22/18; d. 4/20/1910

French, Lieutenant William H. *
1st Artillery, Bvt. Capt. and Major, Cerro Gordo, Contreras and Churubusco—*USV Maj. Gen.* b. 1/13/15; d. 5/20/81

Frost, 2nd Lieutenant Daniel M. *
Regiment of Mounted Rifles, Bvt. 1st Lt., Cerro Gordo—*CSA Brig. Gen.* b. 8/9/23; d. 10/29/1900

Fry, Lieutenant Birkett D.
Regiment of Voltigeurs & Foot Riflemen—*CSA Brig. Gen.* b. 6/24/22; d. 1/21/91

Fry, Captain Speed S.
2nd Kentucky Volunteers—*USV Brig. Gen.* b. 9/9/17; d. 8/1/92

Galt, Major Patrick H.
2nd Artillery, Bvt. Lt. Col., Contreras and Churubusco. d. 1/9/51

Gardner, 2nd Lt Franklin *
7th Infantry, Bvt. 1st Lt. and Capt., Monterrey and Cerro Gordo—*CSA Maj. Gen.* b. 1/29/23; d. 4/29/73

Gardner, Major John L.
4th Artillery, Bvt. Lt. Col. and Col., Cerro Gordo and Contreras. d. 2/19/69

Gardner, 2nd Lt William M.*
2nd Infantry, Bvt. 1st Lt. and wounded at Contreras and Churubusco—*CSA Brig. Gen.* b. 6/8/24; d. 6/16/1901

Garland, Lt. Colonel John
4th Infantry, Bvt. Col. and Brig. Gen., Palo Alto, Resaca de la Palma, Contreras and Churubusco. d. 6/5/61

Garnett, Lieutenant Robert S. *
4th Artillery, Bvt. Capt. and Major, Monterrey and Buena Vista—*CSA Brig. Gen.*, Cousin to Richard B. Garnett who died at Gettysburg. b. 12/16/19; *killed 7/13/61 at the battle of Corrick's Ford, VA.*

Garrard, Captain Theophilus T.
16th Infantry—*USV Brig. Gen.* b. 6/7/12; d. 3/15/1902

Gates, Colonel William *
3rd Artillery. d. 10/7/68

Gatlin, Captain Richard C. *
7th Infantry, Bvt. Major and wounded at Monterrey—*CSA Brig. Gen.* b. 1/18/09; d. 9/8/96

Geary, Colonel John W.
2nd Pennsylvania Volunteers, wounded at Chapultepec—*USV Brig. Gen.* b. 12/30/19; d. 2/8/73

Getty, Lieutenant George W. *
4th Artillery, Bvt. Capt., Contreras and Churubusco—*USV Brig. Gen.* b. 10/2/19; d. 10/1/1901

Gibbon, 2nd Lieutenant John *
4th Artillery—*USV Maj. Gen.* b. 4/20/27; d. 2/6/96

Gibbs, 2nd Lieutenant Alfred *
Regiment of Mounted Rifles, Bvt. 1st Lt. and Capt.Cerro Gordo and Belen Gate;

wounded before Cerro Gordo—
USV Brig. Gen. b. 4/22/23; d.
12/26/68

Gilbert, Lieutenant Charles C. *
1st Infantry—*USV Brig. Gen.* b.
3/1/22; d. 1/17/1903

Gillespie, Major Archibald H.
USMC. California Volunteers.

Gilmer, Lieutenant Jeremy F. *
Engineers—*CSA Maj. Gen.* b. 2/
23/18; d. 12/1/83

Gladden, Lt. Colonel Adley H.
South Carolina Volunteers,
wounded at Belen Gate—*CSA
Brig. Gen.* b. 10/28/10; d. 4/12/62
*of wounds received at the battle of
Shiloh.*

Glenn, Captain Thomas
14th Infantry, Bvt. Major,
Chapultepec.

Goldsborough, Lieutenant Louis
M., USN
U.S.S. Ohio—*USN Captain.
Commander of the North Atlantic
Blockading Squadron.* b. 2/18/05;
d. 2/20/73

Gordon, 2nd Lieutenant George H.*
Regiment of Mounted Rifles,
Bvt. 1st Lt. and wounded at
Cerro Gordo—*USV Brig. Gen.* b.
7/19/23; d. 8/30/86

Gorgas, Lieutenant Josiah *
Ordnance—*CSA Brig. Gen.* b. 7/
1/18; d. 5/15/83

Gorman, Colonel Willis A.
4th Indiana Volunteers,
wounded at Buena Vista—*USV
Brig. Gen.* b. 1/12/16; d. 5/20/76

Graham, Captain Lawrence P.
2nd Dragoons, Bvt. Major, Palo
Alto and Resaca de la Palma—
USV Brig. Gen. b. 1/8/15; d. 9/
12/1905

Graham, Lt. Colonel William M.*
11th Infantry. killed 9/8/47 at
the battle of Molino del Rey,
Mexico.

Granger, 2nd Lieutenant Gordon *
Regiment of Mounted Rifles,
Bvt. 1st Lt. and Capt.,
Contreras, Churubusco and
Chapultepec—*USV Maj. Gen.* b.
11/6/22; d. 1/10/76

Granger, Captain Robert S. *
1st Infantry—*USV Brig. Gen.* b.
5/24/16; d. 4/25/94

Grant, 2nd Lieutenant Ulysses S.*

4th Infantry, Bvt. 1st Lt. and
Capt., Molino del Rey and
Chapultepec—*USA Lt. General
& Army Commander.* 18th
President of the United States,
1869-1877. b. 4/27/22; d. 7/23/85

Grayson, Captain John B. *
Commisary of Subsistence, Bvt.
Major and Lt. Col., Contreras,
Churubusco and Chapultepec—
CSA Brig. Gen. b. 10/18/06; d.
10/21/61

Green, Captain Thomas
1st Texas Mounted Volunteers
(fought at San Jacinto in the
Texas Revolution, 1836)—*CSA
Brig. Gen.* b. 1/8/14; *killed 4/12/
64 at the battle of Blair's Landing,
LA.*

Greer, Sergeant Elkanah B.
1st Mississippi Rifles—*CSA
Brig. Gen.* b. 10/11/25; d. 3/25/77

Gregg, Major Maxcy
12th Infantry—*CSA Brig. Gen.* b.
8/1/14; *killed 12/15/62 at the
battle of Fredericksburg.*

Griffin, 2nd Lieutenant Charles *
Artillery—*USV Maj. Gen.* b. 12/
18/25; d. 9/15/67

Griffith, 2nd Lieutenant Richard
1st Mississippi Rifles—*CSA
Brig. Gen.* b. 1/11/14; *killed 6/29/
62 at the battle of Savage's Station,
VA.*

Gwynne, Major Thomas P.
6th Infantry. died 2/26/61

Hagner, Lieutenant Peter V. *
Ordnance, Bvt. Capt. and Major,
Cerro Gordo and Chapultepec,
wounded at Chapultepec—
USA Lt. Col.

Halleck, Lieutenant Henry W. *
Engineers, Bvt. Capt., Califor-
nia—*USA Major General & Army
Commander.* b. 1/16/15; d. 1/9/72

Hamer, Brig. General Thomas L.
Volunteer Officer, 1st Ohio. died
12/2/46

Hamilton, Lieutenant Charles S.*
5th Infantry, Bvt. Capt.,
Contreras and Churubusco;
severely wounded at Molino del
Rey—*USV Maj. Gen.* b. 11/16/
22; d. 4/17/91

Hamilton, 2nd Lieutenant Schuyler*
1st Infantry, Bvt. 1st Lt. and
Capt., Monterrey and Mill

Flores—*USV Maj. Gen.* b. 7/25/
22; d. 3/8/1903

Hancock, 2nd Lieutenant
Winfield S. *
6th Infantry, Bvt. 1st Lt., Contreras
and Churubusco—*USA Brig. Gen.*
b. 2/14/24; d. 2/9/86

Hanson, Lieutenant Roger W.
Kentucky Volunteers—*CSA
Brig. Gen.* b. 8/27/27; d. 1/2/63

Hardee, Captain William J. *
2nd Dragoons, Bvt. Major and
Lt. Col., Medelin and San
Augustin—*CSA Lt. Gen.* b. 10/
12/15; d. 11/6/73

Hardeman, William P. "Gotch"
Texas Volunteers—*CSA Brig.
Gen.* b. 11/4/16; d. 4/8/98

Hardie, Major James A. *
1st New York Volunteers—*USA
Brig. Gen.* b. 5/5/23; d. 12/14/76

Hardin, Colonel John J.
1st Illinois Volunteers. killed 2/
23/47 at the battle of Buena
Vista, Mexico.

Harney, Colonel William S.
2nd Dragoons, Bvt. Brig. Gen.,
Cerro Gordo—*USA Brig. Gen.* b.
8/27/1800; d. 5/9/89

Harrison, Private Thomas
1st Mississippi Rifles, discharged for disability 10/9/
46—*CSA Brig. Gen.* b. 5/1/23; d.
7/14/91

Haskin, Lieutenant Joseph A. *
1st Artillery, Bvt. Capt. and
Major, Cerro Gordo and
Chapultepec; lost his left arm at
Chapultepec—*USA Brig. Gen.* b.
6/21/18; d. 8/3/74

Hatch, 2nd Lieutenant John P. *
Regiment of Mounted Rifles,
Bvt. 1st Lt. and Capt.,
Contreras, Churubusco and
Chapultepec—*USV Brig. Gen.* b.
1/9/22; d. 4/12/1901

Hawes, 2nd Lieutenant James M.*
2nd Dragoons, Bvt. 1st Lt., San
Juan de los Llanos—*CSA Brig.
Gen.* b. 1/7/24; d. 11/22/89

Hawkins, Major Edgar S *
1st Infantry, Bvt. Major, Fort
Brown. d. 11/5/65

Haynie, Lieutenant Isham N.
6th Illinois Volunteers—*USV
Brig. Gen.* b. 11/18/24; d. 5/22/68

Hays, 2nd Lieutenant Alexander*

4th Infantry, Bvt. 1st Lt., Palo Alto and Resaca de la Palma—*USV Brig. Gen. b. 7/8/19; killed 5/5/64 at the battle of the Wilderness.*

Hays, Harry T.
—*CSA Maj. Gen. b. 4/14/20; d. 8/21/76*

Hays, Lieutenant William *
2nd Artillery, Bvt. Capt. and Major, Contreras, Churubusco and Chapultepec; wounded at Molino del Rey—*USV Brig. Gen. b. 5/9/19; d. 2/7/75*

Hebert, Lt. Colonel Paul O. *
14th Infantry, Bvt. Col., Molino del Rey—*CSA Brig. Gen. b. 12/12/18; d. 8/29/80*

Heckman, Sergeant Charles A.
Regiment of Voltigeurs & Foot Riflemen—*USV Brig. Gen. b.12/3/22; d. 1/14/96*

Heintzelman, Captain Samuel P.*
2nd Infantry, Bvt. Major, Huamantla—*USV Maj. Gen. b. 9/30/05; d. 5/1/80*

Henry, Captain William S.*
3rd Infantry, Bvt. Major, Monterrey. d. 3/5/51

Hill, 2nd Lieutenant Ambrose P. *
1st Artillery—*CSA Lt. Gen. b. 11/9/25; killed in action 4/2/65 at the battle of Petersburg.*

Hill, Lieutenant Daniel H. *
4th Artillery, Bvt. Capt. and Major, Contreras, Churubusco and Chapultepec—*CSA Lt. Gen. b. 7/12/21; d. 9/24/89*

Hindman, 2nd Lieutenant Thomas C.
2nd Mississippi Infantry—*CSA Brig. Gen. b. 1/28/28; d. 9/28/68*

Hitchcock, Lt. Colonel Ethan A.*
3rd Infantry, Bvt. Col. and Brig. Gen., Contreras, Churubusco and Molino del Rey—*USV Maj. Gen. b. 5/18/1798; d. 8/5/70*

Hobson, Lieutenant Edward H.
2nd Kentucky Volunteers—*USV Brig. Gen. b. 7/11/25; d. 9/14/1901*

Hogg, Private Joseph L.
—*CSA Brig. Gen. b. 9/13/06; d. 5/16/62*

Holmes, Major Theophilus H. *
8th Infantry—*CSA Lt. Gen. b. 11/13/04; d. 6/21/80*

Lieutenant Thomas Jackson

Hooker, Lieutenant Joseph *
1st Artillery; Bvt. Capt. Asst. Adjutants-General, Bvt. Major and Lt. Col., Monterrey, National Bridge, Chapultepec—*USA Brig. General & Army Commander. b. 11/13/14; d. 10/31/79*

Howe, Lieutenant Albion P. *
4th Artillery, Bvt. Capt., Contreras and Churubusco—*USV Brig. Gen. b. 3/13/18; d. 1/25/97*

Huger, Captain Benjamin*
Ordnance, Bvt. Major, Lt. Col. and Col., Vera Cruz, Molino del Rey, Chapultepec—*CSA Maj. Gen. b. 11/22/05; d. 12/7/77*

Hunt, Lieutenant Henry J.*
2nd Artillery, Bvt. Capt. and Major, Contreras, Churubusco and Chapultepec; wounded at Molino del Rey—*USV Brig. Gen. b. 9/14/19; d. 2/11/89*

Hunter, Major David*
Paymaster—*USV Maj. Gen. b. 7/21/02; d. 2/2/86*

Ingalls, 2nd Lieutenant Rufus *
1st Dragoons, Bvt. 1st Lt., Embudo and Taos, NM—*USV Brig. Gen. b. 8/23/18; d. 1/15/93*

Iverson, 2nd Lieutenant Alfred, Jr.
Georgia Volunteers—*CSA Brig. Gen. b. 2/14/29; d. 3/31/1911*

Jackson, Colonel Henry R.
Georgia Volunteers—*CSA Brig. Gen. b. 6/24/20; d. 5/23/98*

Jackson, Private James S.
1st Kentucky Cavalry—*USV Brig. Gen. b. 9/27/23; killed 10/8/62 at the battle of Perryville.*

Jackson, Lieutenant Thomas J. *
1st Artillery, Bvt. Capt. and Major, Contreras, Churubusco and Chapultepec—*CSA Lt. Gen. "Stonewall Jackson" b. 1/21/24; d. 5/10/63 of wounds received at the battle of Chancellorsville.*

Jesup, Brigadier General Thomas S.
Quartermaster General for Taylor. b. 12/16/1788; d. 6/10/60

Johnson, Lieutenant Bushrod R. *
3rd Infantry—*CSA Maj. Gen. b. 10/7/17; d. 9/12/80*

Johnson, Lieutenant Edward *
6th Infantry, Bvt. Capt. and Major, Molino del Rey and Chapultepec—*CSA Maj. Gen. b. 4/16/16; d. 3/2/73*

Johnston, Colonel Albert Sidney*
Texas Rifle Volunteers—*CSA General. b. 2/2/03; killed 4/6/62 at the battle of Shiloh, TN.*

Johnston, Lt. Colonel Joseph E. *
Regiment of Voltigeurs & Foot Riflemen; Captain, Topographical Engineers, Bvt. Major and Lt. Col., Cerro Gordo and Chapultepec; wounded near Cerro Gordo and at City of Mexico—*CSA General. b. 2/3/07; d. 3/21/91*

Jones, 2nd Lieutenant David R. *
2nd Infantry, Bvt. 1st Lt., Contreras and Churubusco—*CSA Maj. Gen. b. 4/5/25; d. 1/15/63*

Jordan, Lieutenant Thomas *
3rd Infantry; Captain, Asst. Quartermaster—*CSA Brig. Gen. b. 9/30/19; d. 11/27/95*

Judah, 2nd Lieutenant Henry M.*
4th Infantry, Bvt. 1st Lt. and Capt., Molino del Rey and Chapultepec—*USV Brig. Gen. b. 6/12/21; d. 1/14/66*

Kautz, Private August V. *
1st Ohio Volunteers—*USV Brig. Gen. b. 1/5/28; d. 9/4/95*

Kearny, Captain Philip
1st Dragoons. A nephew of Brig. General Stephen W. Kearny, Bvt. Major, Contreras and Churubusco; wounded and lost

his left arm at Churubusco—*USV Maj. Gen. b. 6/2/15; d. 9/1/62 at the battle of Chantilly, VA.*

Kearny, Brigadier General Stephen W.
Commander of the Army of the West, twice wounded at San Pascual, CA, Bvt. Major Gen. b. 8/30/1794; d. 10/31/48

Kemper, Captain James L.
Virginia Volunteers—*CSA Maj. Gen. b. 6/11/23; d. 4/7/95*

Kenly, Major John R.
Maryland & District of Columbia Volunteers—*USV Brig. Gen. b. 1/11/18; d. 12/20/91*

Ker, Captain Croghan
2nd Dragoons; severely wounded at Molino del Rey

Kershaw, Lieutenant Joseph B.
1st South Carolina Volunteers—*CSA Brig. Gen. b. 1/5/22; d. 4/13/94*

Kimball, Captain Nathan
2nd Indiana Volunteers—*USV Brig. Gen. b. 11/22/22; d. 1/21/98*

King, Captain John H.
1st Infantry—*USA Brig. Gen. b. 2/19/20; d. 4/7/88*

Knipe, Joseph F.
—*USV Brig. Gen. b. 3/30/23; d. 8/18/1901*

Lally, Major Folliot T.
9th Infantry, Bvt. Lt. Col. Paso Ovejas, National Bridge and Cerro Gordo

Lane, Colonel James H.
3rd Indiana Volunteers—US Senator from Kansas. *Played a major role in creating the Kansas Jayhawkers and Redlegs,* b. 6/22/14; d. 7/11/66

Lane, Brig. General Joseph
Volunteer Officer, Bvt. Maj. Gen., Huamantla. b. 1814; d. 4/19/81

Lane, Captain Walter P.
Texas Rangers, fought at San Jacinto in Texas Revolution, 1836—*CSA Brig. Gen. b. 2/18/17; d. 1/28/92*

Lawler, Captain Michael K.
3rd Illinois Volunteers—*USV Brig. Gen. b. 11/16/14; d. 7/26/82*

Lear, Major William W.
3rd Infantry. d. 10/31/46 of wounds received at the battle of Monterrey, Mexico.

Lee, Major Francis *
4th Infantry, Bvt. Lt. Col. and Col., Contreras, Churubusco and Molino del Rey d. 1/19/59

Lee, Captain Robert E. *
Engineers, Bvt. Major, Lt. Col. and Col., Cerro Gordo, Contreras, Churubusco and Chapultepec; wounded at Chapultepec—*CSA General in Chief. b. 1/19/07; d. 10/12/70*

Captain Robert E. Lee

Little, Lieutenant Lewis H.
7th Infantry, Bvt. Capt., Monterrey—*CSA Brig. Gen. b. 3/19/17; killed 9/19/62 at the battle of Iuka, MS.*

Lockwood, Midshipman Henry H.*
USS United States—*USV Brig. Gen. b. 8/17/14; d. 12/7/99*

Logan, 2nd Lieutenant John A.
6th Illinois Volunteers—*USV Maj. Gen. b. 2/9/26; d. 12/26/86*

Longstreet, Lieutenant James *
8th Infantry, Bvt. Capt. and Major, Contreras, Churubusco and Molino del Rey; severely wounded at Chapultepec—*CSA Lt. Gen. b. 1/8/21; d. 1/2/1904*

Loring, Major William W.
Regiment of Mounted Rifles, Bvt. Lt. Col. and Col., Contreras, Churubusco and Chapultepec; lost his left arm at

Chapultepec—*CSA Maj. Gen. b. 12/4/18; d. 12/30/86*

Lovell, Lieutenant Mansfield *
4th Artillery, Bvt. Capt., Chapultepec; wounded at the Belen Gate—*CSA Maj. Gen. b. 10/20/22; d. 6/1/84*

Lowd, Captain Allen
2nd Artillery, Bvt. Major, Fort Brown. d. 11/25/54

Lowrey, Private Mark P.
2nd Mississippi Volunteers—*CSA Brig. Gen. b. 12/30/28; d. 2/27/85*

Lucas, 2nd Lieutenant Thomas J.
4th Indiana Volunteers—*USV Brig. Gen. b. 9/9/26; d. 11/16/1908*

Lyon, Lieutenant Nathaniel *
2nd Infantry, Bvt. Capt., Contreras and Churubusco; wounded at the Belen Gate—*USV Brig. Gen. b. 7/14/18; killed 8/10/61 at the battle of Wilson's Creek.*

Lytle, Captain William H.
Independent Company of Ohio Volunteers (attached to 2nd Ohio)—*USV Brig Gen. b. 11/2/26; d. 9/20/63 of wounds received at the battle of Chickamauga.*

Mackall, Lieutenant William W. *
1st Artillery; Bvt. Capt. Asst. Adjutants- General, Bvt. Major, Monterrey, Contreras and Churubusco—*CSA Brig. Gen. b. 1/18/17; d. 8/12/91*

Maclay, Lieutenant Robert P. *
8th Infantry; wounded at Resaca de la Palma—*CSA Brig. Gen. b. -/-/20; d. -/-/1903*

Magruder, Captain John B. *
1st Artillery, Bvt. Major and Lt. Col., Cerro Gordo and Chapultepec; wounded at Chapultepec—*CSA Maj. Gen. b. 5/1/07; d. 2/18/71*

Maltby, Private Jasper A.
15th Infantry; severely wounded at Chapultepec—*USV Brig. Gen. b. 11/3/26; d. 12/12/67*

Maney, Lieutenant George E.
3rd Dragoons—*CSA Brig. Gen. b. 8/24/26; d. 2/9/1901*

Manigault, Lieutenant Arthur M.
1st South Carolina Volunteers—

CSA Brig. Gen. b. 10/26/24; d. 8/17/86

Mansfield, Captain Joseph K. F. *
Engineers, Bvt. Major, Lt. Col. and Col., Fort Brown, Monterrey and Buena Vista; severely wounded at Monterrey—*USA Brig. Gen.* b. 12/22/03; *d. 9/18/62 of wounds received at the battle of Sharpsburg, MD.*

Manson, Captain Mahlon D.
5th Indiana Volunteers—*USV Brig. Gen.* b. 2/20/20; d. 2/4/95

Marcy, Captain Randolph B. *
5th Infantry—*USV Brig. Gen.* b. 4/9/12; d. 11/2/87

Marshall, Colonel Humphrey *
1st Kentucky Cavalry Volunteers—*CSA Brig. Gen.* b. 1/13/12; d. 3/28/72

Marshall, Brig. General Thomas
Volunteer Officer. d. 3/28/53

Martin, Lieutenant James G. *
1st Artillery; Capt. Asst. Quartermaster, Bvt. Major, Contreras and Churubusco; lost his right arm at Churubusco—*CSA Brig. Gen.* b. 2/14/19; d. 10/4/78

Mason, 2nd Lieutenant John S. *
3rd Artillery—*USV Brig. Gen.* b. 8/21/24; d. 11/29/97

Mason, Colonel Richard B.
1st Dragoons, Bvt. Brig. Gen., California. d. 7/25/50

Maury, 2nd Lieutenant Dabney H.*
Regiment of Mounted Rifles, Bvt. 1st Lt. and severely wounded before Cerro Gordo—*CSA Maj. Gen.* b. 5/21/22; d. 1/11/1900

Maxey, 2nd Lieutenant Samuel B.*
7th Infantry, Bvt. 1st Lt., Contreras and Churubusco—*CSA Maj. Gen.* b. 3/30/25; d. 8/16/95

May, Captain Charles A.
2nd Dragoons, Bvt. Major, Lt. Col. and Col., Palo Alto, Resaca de la Palma and Buena Vista. d. 12/24/64

McCall, Captain George A. *
4th Infantry; Bvt. Major, Asst. Adjutants-General, Bvt. Lt. Col., Palo Alto and Resaca de la Palma—*USV Brig. Gen.* b. 3/16/02; d. 2/26/68

McCarty, Major Justus I.
10th Infantry. d. 6/8/81

McClellan, 2nd Lieutenant George B. *
Engineers, Bvt. 1st Lt. and Capt., Contreras, Churubusco and Chapultepec—*USA Major General & Army Commander.* b. 12/3/26; d. 10/29/85

Lieutenant George McClellan

McCown, Lieutenant John P. *
4th Artillery, Bvt. Capt. Cerro Gordo—*CSA Maj. Gen.* b. 8/19/15; d. 1/22/79

McCulloch, Colonel Benjamin
Independent Company of Texas Volunteers—*CSA Brig. Gen.* b. 11/11/11; *killed 3/7/62 at the battle of Pea Ridge.*

McCulloch, Captain Henry E.
Texas Rangers. Younger brother of Ben McCulloch—*CSA Brig. Gen.* b. 12/6/16; d. 3/12/95

McDowell, Lieutenant Irvin W. *
1st Artillery; Bvt. Capt. Asst. Adjutants-General, Bvt. Capt., Buena Vista—*USV Maj. Gen.* b. 10/15/18; d. 5/4/85

McGinnis, Captain George F.
5th Ohio Volunteers—*USV Brig. Gen.* b. 3/19/26; d. 5/29/1910

McGowan, Captain Samuel
South Carolina Volunteers, Quartermaster—*CSA Brig. Gen.* b. 10/9/19; d. 8/9/97

McIntosh, Lt. Colonel James
5th Infantry, Bvt. Col., Palo Alto and Resaca de la Palma; wounded at Resaca de la Palma. d. 9/26/47 of wounds received at the battle of Molino del Rey,

Mexico.

McKean, Sergeant Major Thomas J.*
15th Infantry, declined Bvt. to 2nd Lt.; severely wounded at Churubusco—*USV Brig. Gen.* b. 8/21/10; d. 4/19/70

McKinstry, Lieutenant Justus *
2nd Infantry; Captain, Asst. Quartermaster, Bvt. Major, Contreras and Churubusco—*USV Brig. Gen.* b. 7/6/14; d. 12/11/97

McLaws, Lieutenant Lafayette *
7th Infantry—*CSA Maj. Gen.* b. 1/15/21; d. 7/24/97

McMillan, Sergeant James W.
4th Illinois Volunteers—*USV Brig. Gen.* b. 4/28/25; d. 3/9/1903

McNair, Sergeant Evander
1st Mississippi Rifles—*CSA Brig. Gen.* b. 4/15/20; d. 11/13/1902

Meade, 2nd Lieutenant George G. *
Topographical Engineers, Bvt. 1st Lt., Monterrey—*USA Brig. General & Army Commander.* b. 12/31/15; d. 11/6/72

Lieutenant George Meade

Miller, William
—*CSA Brig. Gen.* b. 8/3/20; d. 8/8/1909

Mills, Major Frederick D.
15th Infantry. killed 8/20/47 in action at San Antonio, Mexico.

Milroy, Captain Robert H.
1st Indiana Volunteers—*USV Maj. Gen.* b. 6/11/16; d. 3/29/90

Mitchell, Lieutenant Robert B.
5th Ohio Volunteers—*USV Brig. Gen.* b. 4/4/23; d. 1/26/82

Montgomery, Captain William R.*
8th Infantry, Bvt. Major and Lt. Col., Palo Alto, Resaca de la Palma and Molino del Rey; wounded at Resaca de la Palma and Molino del Rey—*USV Brig. Gen.* b. 7/10/01; d. 5/31/71

Moore, Captain Samuel P.
Asst. Surgeon—*CSA Surgeon General.* d. 5/31/89

Moore, Lt. Colonel Thomas P.
3rd Dragoons. d. 7/21/53

Morgan, Major Edwin W. *
11th Infantry. d. 4/16/69

Morgan, Colonel George W. *
15th Infantry, Bvt. Brig. Gen. and wounded at Contreras and Churubusco—*USV Brig. Gen.* b. 9/20/20; d. 7/26/93

Morgan, Captain James D.
1st Illinois Volunteers—*USV Brig. Gen.* b. 8/1/10; d. 9/12/96

Morgan, Lieutenant John H.
Kentucky Cavalry Volunteers—*CSA Brig. Gen.* b. 6/1/25; *killed 9/4/64 by Union cavalry patrol.*

Mott, 2nd Lieutenant Gershom
10th Infantry, did not actually serve in Mexico—*USV Maj. Gen.* b. 4/7/22; d. 11/29/84

Mower, Private Joseph A.
Engineers—*USA Maj. Gen.* b. 8/22/27; d. 1/6/70

Myers, Captain Abraham C. *
Asst. Quartermaster, Bvt. Major and Lt. Col., Palo Alto, Resaca de la Palma and Churubusco—*CSA Q.M.G.* b. 5/?/11; d. 6/20/89

Nagle, Captain James
1st Pennsylvania Volunteers—*USV Brig. Gen.* b. 4/5/22; d. 8/22/66

Naglee, Captain Henry M. *
1st New York Volunteers—*USV Brig. Gen.* b. 1/15/15; d. 3/5/86

Negley, Private James S.
1st Pennsylvania Volunteers—*USV Brig. Gen.* b. 12/22/26; d. 8/7/1901

Nelson, Midshipman William "Bull"
—*USV Maj. Gen.* b. 9/27/24; d. 9/29/62

Norvel, Lt. Colonel Ralph G.
10th Infantry.

Oglesby, Lieutenant Richard J.
4th Illinois Volunteers—*USV Maj. Gen.* b. 7/25/24; d. 4/24/99

Ord, Lieutenant Edward O. C.*
3rd Artillery—*USV Maj. Gen.* b. 10/18/18; d. 7/22/83

Palmer, Major Andrew T.
14th Infantry. d. 6/20/58

Palmer, 2nd Lieutenant Innis N.*
Regiment of Mounted Rifles, Bvt. 1st Lt. and Capt., Contreras, Churubusco and Chapultepec; wounded at Chapultepec—*USV Brig. Gen.* b. 3/30/24; d. 9/9/1900

Parsons, Captain Mosby M.
1st Missouri Mounted Volunteers—*CSA Brig. Gen.* b. 5/21/22; d. 8/15/65 in Mexico fighting guerillas for the Emperor Maximillian

Patrick, Captain Marsena R. *
2nd Infantry, Bvt. Major, Mexico—*USV Brig. Gen.* b. 3/11/11; d. 7/27/88

Patterson, 2nd Lieutenant Francis E.
1st Artillery—*USV Brig. Gen.* Son of Maj. General Robert Patterson. b. 5/7/21; d. 11/22/62

Patterson, Maj.-General Robert
Volunteer Officer—*USV Bvt. Maj. Gen.* b. 1/12/1792; d. 8/7/81

Paul, Captain Gabriel R. *
7th Infantry, Bvt. Major, Chapultepec—*USV Brig. Gen.* b. 3/22/13; d. 5/5/86

Payne, Lt. Colonel Matthew M.
4th Artillery, Bvt. Col., Palo Alto and Resaca de la Palma; severely wounded at Resaca de la Palma. d. 8/1/62

Peck, Lieutenant John J.*
2nd Artillery, Bvt. Capt. and Major, Contreras, Churubusco and Molino del Rey—*USV Maj. Gen.* b. 1/4/21; d. 4/21/78

Pemberton, Lieutenant John C.*
4th Artillery, Bvt. Capt. and Major, Monterrey and Molino del Rey; wounded at City of Mexico—*CSA Lt. Gen.* b. 8/10/

14; d. 7/13/81

Perrin, Lieutenant Abner M.
12th Infantry—*CSA Brig. Gen.* b. 2/2/27; *killed 5/12/64 at the battle of Spottsylvania.*

Phelps, Lieutenant John W. *
4th Artillery, declined Bvt. Capt—*USV Brig. Gen.* b. 11/13/13; d. 2/2/85

Pickett, 2nd Lieutenant George E.*
8th Infantry, Bvt. 1st Lt. and Capt., Contreras, Churubusco and Chapultepec—*CSA Maj. Gen.* b. 1/28/25; d. 7/30/75

Pierce, Lt. Colonel Benjamin K.
1st Artillery. d. 4/1/50

Pierce, Brig. General Franklin
Volunteer Officer. 14th President of the United States, 1853-1857. b. 11/23/04; d. 10/8/69

Pike, Captain Albert
Arkansas Mounted Volunteers—*CSA Brig. Gen.* b. 12/29/09; d. 4/3/91

Pillow, Brig. General Gideon J.
Volunteer Officer, wounded at Cerro Gordo and Chapultepec—*CSA Brig. Gen.* b. 6/8/06; d. 10/8/78

Pitcher, 2nd Lieutenant Thomas G.*
8th Infantry, Bvt. 1st Lt., Contreras and Churubusco—*USV Brig. Gen.* b. 10/23/24; d. 10/21/95

Pleasanton, 2nd Lieutenant Alfred*
2nd Dragoons, Bvt. 1st Lt., Palo Alto and Resaca de la Palma—*USV Maj. Gen.* b. 7/7/24; d. 2/17/97

Plummer, 2nd Lieutenant Joseph B.*
1st Infantry—*USV Brig. Gen.* b. 11/15/16; d. 8/9/62

Plympton, Lt. Colonel Joseph
7th Infantry, Bvt. Col., Cerro Gordo. d. 6/5/60

Pope, 2nd Lieutenant John *
Topographical Engineers, Bvt. 1st Lt. and Capt., Monterrey and Buena Vista— *USA Maj. Gen.* b. 3/16/22; d. 9/23/92

Porter, Captain Andrew *
Regiment of Mounted Rifles, Bvt. Major and Lt. Col., Contreras, Churubusco and Chapultepec—*USV Brig. Gen.* b. 7/10/20; d. 1/3/72

BIOGRAPHIES

Porter, Lieutenant David D., USN
U.S.S. Spitfire—*USN Rear Admiral in charge of Mississippi Squadron and present at the capture of Vicksburg in 7/63.* b. 6/8/13; d. 2/13/91

Porter, Lieutenant Fitz-John *
4th Artillery, Bvt. Capt., Molino del Rey; wounded at Belen Gate—*USV Maj. Gen.* b. 8/31/22; d. 5/21/1901

Porter, Major Giles *
4th Artillery. d. 5/31/78

Porter, Lieutenant Theodric H. *
4th Infantry. killed 4/19/46 near the Rio Grande.

Posey, Lieutenant Carnot
1st Mississippi Rifles; wounded at Buena Vista—*CSA Brig. Gen.* b. 8/5/18; *d. 11/13/63 from a wound received at the battle of Bristoe Station.*

Potter, 2nd Lieutenant Joseph H.*
7th Infantry, Bvt. 1st Lt. and severely wounded at Monterrey—*USV Brig. Gen.* b. 10/12/22; d. 12/1/92

Prentiss, Captain Benjamin M.
1st Illinois Volunteers, Adjutant—*USV Maj. Gen.* b. 11/23/19; d. 2/8/1901

Preston, Lt. Colonel William
4th Kentucky Volunteers—*CSA Maj. Gen.* b. 10/16/16; d. 9/21/87

Price, Brig. General Sterling
Volunteer Officer from Missouri—*CSA Maj. Gen., commanded at Iuka,* b. 9/20/09; d. 9/29/67

Prince, Lieutenant Henry *
4th Infantry, Bvt. Capt. and Major, Contreras, Churubusco and Molino del Rey; severely wounded at Molino del Rey—*USV Brig. Gen.* b. 6/19/11; d. 8/19/92

Quitman, Brig. General John A.
Volunteer Officer, Bvt. Maj. Gen., Puebla b. 9/1/1798; d. 7/17/58

Rains, Captain Gabriel J. *
7th Infantry—*CSA Brig. Gen.* b. 6/4/03; d. 8/6/81

Ramsay, Captain George D. *
Ordnance, Bvt. Major, Monterrey—*USA Brig. Gen.* b. 2/21/02; d. 5/23/82

Ramsey, Colonel Albert C.
11th Infantry. d. 3/9/69

Ransom, Colonel Trueman B.
9th Infantry. killed 9/13/47 during the assault on Chapultepec Castle, Mexico.

Reno, 2nd Lieutenant Jesse L. *
Ordnance, Bvt. 1st Lt. and Capt., Cerro Gordo and Chapultepec; severely wounded at Chapultepec—*USV Maj. Gen.* b. 6/20/23; *d. 9/14/62 at battle of South Mountain, MD.*

Reynolds, Lieutenant John F. *
3rd Artillery, Bvt. Capt. and Major, Monterrey and Buena Vista—*USV Maj. Gen.* b. 9/20/20; *killed 7/1/63 at the battle of Gettysburg.*

Richardson, Lieutenant Israel B. *
3rd Infantry, Bvt. Capt. and Major, Contreras, Churubusco and Chapultepec—*USV Maj. Gen.* b. 12/26/15; *d. 11/3/62 of wounds received at the battle of Antietam.*

Ricketts, Lieutenant James B. *
1st Artillery—*USV Brig. Gen.* b. 6/21/17; d. 9/22/87

Ridgely, Bvt. Captain Randolph *
3rd Artillery; Asst. Adjutant General, Bvt. Capt., Palo Alto and Resaca de la Palma. d. 10/27/46

Riley, Lt. Colonel Bennet
2nd Infantry, Bvt. Brig. Gen. and Maj. Gen., Cerro Gordo and Contreras. Fort Riley, Kansas was completed in the year of his death and named in his honor. d. 6/9/53

Ringgold, Captain Samuel *
3rd Artillery. died 5/11/46 of wounds received at the battle of Palo Alto, TX.

Ripley, Lieutenant Roswell S. *
2nd Artillery, Bvt. Capt. and Major, Cerro Gordo and Chapultepec—*CSA Brig. Gen.* b. 3/14/23; d. 3/29/87

Roane, Colonel John Selden
Arkansas Mounted Volunteers—*CSA Brig. Gen.* b. 1/8/17; d. 4/8/67

Roberts, Captain Benjamin S. *
Regiment of Mounted Rifles, Bvt. Major and Lt. Col.,

Chapultepec and Pass Guadalajara—*USV Brig. Gen.* b. 11/18/10; d. 1/29/75

Robinson, Lieutenant John C.
5th Infantry—*USV Brig. Gen.* b. 4/10/17; d. 2/18/97

Ross, Lieutenant Leonard F.
4th Illinois Volunteers—*USV Brig. Gen.* b. 7/18/23; d. 1/17/1901

Rousseau, Captain Lovell H.
2nd Indiana Volunteers—*USV Maj. Gen.* b. 8/4/18; d. 1/7/69

Rowley, Captain Thomas A.
Pittsburg, PA Volunteer Company (attached to MD & DC Volunteers)—*USV Brig. Gen.* b. 10/5/08; d. 5/14/92

Rucker, Captain Daniel H. *
1st Dragoons, Bvt. Major, Buena Vista—*USV Brig. Gen.* b. 4/28/12; d. 1/6/1910

Ruggles, Captain Daniel *
5th Infantry, Bvt. Major and Lt. Col., Contreras, Churubusco and Chapultepec—*CSA Brig. Gen.* b. 1/31/10; d. 6/1/97

Rush, 2nd Lieutenant Richard H.*
2nd Artillery—*USV Colonel of the 6th Pennsylvania Cavalry (Rush's Lancers).*

Russell, 2nd Lieutenant David A.*
4th Infantry, Bvt. 1st Lt., National Bridge and Cerro Gordo—*USV Brig. Gen.* b. 12/10/20; *killed 9/19/64 at the battle of Winchester, VA.*

Savage, Lt. Colonel John H.
11th Infantry—*CSA Colonel, 16th Tennessee Volunteer Infantry.*

Scammon, Lieutenant Eliakim P.*
Topographical Engineers—*USA Brig. Gen.* b. 12/27/16; d. 12/7/94

Scantland, Captain James M.
14th Infantry, Bvt. Major, Chapultepec. d. 7/22/49

Scott, Captain Robert K.
1st Pennsylvania Volunteers—*USV Brig. Gen.* b. 7/8/26; d. 8/12/1900

Scott, Major Martin
5th Infantry, Bvt. Lt. Col., Monterrey. killed 9/8/47 at the battle of Molino del Rey, Mexico.

Scott, Maj. General Winfield

197

General in Chief—*USA Commander in Chief.* b. 6/13/1786; d. 5/29/66

Scurry, Major William R.
2nd Texas Mounted Volunteers—*CSA Brig. Gen.* b. 2/10/21; *killed 4/30/64 at the battle of Jenkins' Ferry, AR.*

Sedgwick, Lieutenant John *
2nd Artillery, Bvt. Capt. and Major, Churubusco and Chapultepec—*USV Maj. Gen.* b. 9/13/13; *killed 5/9/64 at the battle of Spottsylvania.*

Semmes, Lieutenant Raphael, USN
U.S.S. Somers—*CSN Captain of the C.S.S. Alabama, commerce raider.* b. 9/27/09; d. 8/30/77

Seymour, Lt. Colonel Thomas H.
12th Infantry, Bvt. Col., Chapultepec. d. 9/3/68

Seymour, 2nd Lieutenant Truman *
1st Artillery, Bvt. 1st Lt. and Capt., Cerro Gordo, Contreras and Churubusco—*USV Brig. Gen.* b. 9/24/24; d. 10/30/91

Shackelford, Lieutenant James M.
4th Kentucky Volunteers—*USV Brig. Gen.* b. 7/7/27; d. 9/7/1909

Sherman, Captain Thomas W.*
3rd Artillery, Bvt. Major, Buena Vista—*USV Brig. Gen.* b. 3/26/13; d. 3/16/79

Sherman, Lieutenant William T.*
3rd Artillery, Bvt. Capt., California—*USA Major General & Army Commander.* b. 2/8/20; d. 2/14/91

Shields, Brig. General James
Illinois Volunteer Officer, Bvt. Maj. Gen. and severely wounded at Cerro Gordo—*USV Brig. Gen.* b. 5/10/10; d. 6/1/79

Shover, Captain William H. *
3rd Artillery, Bvt. Capt. and Major, Monterrey and Buena Vista. d. 9/7/50

Sibley, Captain Henry H. *
2nd Dragoons, Bvt. Major, Medelin—*CSA Brig. Gen.* b. 5/25/16; d. 8/23/86

Slack, Captain William Y.
2nd Missouri Volunteers—*CSA Brig. Gen.* b. 8/1/16; *killed 3/21/62 from wounds received at the*

battle of Pea Ridge.

Slaughter, 2nd Lieutenant James E.
Regiment of Voltigeurs & Foot Riflemen—*CSA Brig. Gen.* b. 6/?/27; d. 1/1/1901

Smith, Captain Andrew J. *
1st Dragoons—*USV Maj. Gen.* b. 4/28/15; d. 1/30/97

Smith, Captain Charles F. *
2nd Artillery, Bvt. Major, Lt. Col. and Col., Palo Alto, Resaca de la Palma, Monterrey, Contreras and Churubusco—*USV Maj. Gen.* b. 4/24/07; d. 4/25/62

Smith, 2nd Lieutenant Edmund Kirby *
7th Infantry, Bvt. 1st Lt. and Capt., Cerro Gordo and Contreras—*CSA General.* b. 5/16/24; d. 3/28/93

Smith, Captain Ephraim Kirby *
5th Infantry. d. 9/11/47 of wounds received at the battle of Molino del Rey, Mexico.

Smith, 2nd Lieutenant Green Clay
Kentucky Volunteers—*USV Brig. Gen.* b. 4/4/26; d. 6/29/95

Smith, 2nd Lieutenant Gustavus W.*
Engineers, Bvt. 1st Lt. and Capt., Cerro Gordo and Contreras—*CSA Maj. Gen.* b. 12/1/21; d. 6/24/96

Smith, 2nd Lieutenant Martin L.*
Topographical Engineers, Bvt. 1st Lt., Mexico—*CSA Maj. Gen.* b. 9/9/19; d. 7/29/66

Smith, Brig. General Persifor F.
Col. Regiment of Mounted Rifles, Bvt. Maj. Gen., Monterrey, Contreras and Churubusco d. 5/17/58

Smith, 2nd Lieutenant William D.*
2nd Dragoons; severely wounded at Molino del Rey—*CSA Brig. Gen.* b. 7/28/25; d. 10/4/62

Stafford, Private Leroy A.
Louisiana Volunteers—*CSA Brig. Gen.* b. 4/13/22; *died 5/8/64 from wounds received at the battle of the Wilderness.*

Staniford, Lt. Colonel Thomas
8th Infantry, Bvt. Col., Palo Alto, Resaca de la Palma and Monterrey. d. 2/3/55

Steele, 2nd Lieutenant Frederick*

2nd Infantry, Bvt. 1st Lt. and Capt., Contreras and Chapultepec—*USV Maj. Gen.* b. 1/14/19; d. 1/12/68

Steele, Lieutenant William*
2nd Dragoons, Bvt. Capt., Contreras and Churubusco—*CSA Brig. Gen.* b. 5/1/19; d. 1/12/85

Steen, 2nd Lieutenant Alexander E.
12th Infantry, Bvt. 1st Lt., Contreras and Churubusco—*CSA Brig. Gen. killed 11/27/62 at the battle of Kane Hill, AR.*

Steen, Captain Enoch *
1st Dragoons, Bvt. Major and wounded at Buena Vista—*USA Lt. Col.* d. 1/22/80

Steptoe, Captain Edward J.*
3rd Artillery, Bvt. Major and Lt. Col., Cerro Gordo and Chapultepec d. 4/1/65

Stevens, Lieutenant Isaac I. *
Engineers, Bvt. Capt. and Major, Contreras, Churubusco and Chapultepec; severely wounded at San Cosme Gate—*USA Maj. Gen.* b. 3/25/18; *killed 9/1/62 at the battle of Chantilly, VA.*

Stevenson, Captain Carter L.*
5th Infantry—*CSA Maj. Gen.* b. 9/21/17; d. 8/15/88

Stevenson, Captain John D.
1st Missouri Mounted Volunteers—*USV Brig. Gen.* b. 6/8/21; d. 1/22/97

Stone, 2nd Lieutenant Charles P.*
Ordnance, Bvt. 1st Lt. and Capt., Molino del Rey and Chapultepec—*USV Brig. Gen.* b. 9/30/24; d. 1/24/87

Stoneman, 2nd Lieutenant George*
1st Dragoons, served as Quartermaster of the Mormon Battalion—*USV Maj. Gen.* b. 8/22/22; d. 9/5/94

Sturgis, 2nd Lieutenant Samuel D.*
1st Dragoons—*USV Brig. Gen.* b. 6/11/22; d. 9/28/89

Sully, Lieutenant Alfred *
Infantry—*USV Brig. Gen.* b. 5/22/20; d. 4/27/79

Sumner, Major Edwin V.
2nd Dragoons, Bvt. Lt. Col. and Col., Cerro Gordo and Molino del Rey; severely wounded at

BIOGRAPHIES

Cerro Gordo—*USV Maj. Gen.* b. 1/30/1797; d. 3/21/63

Swartwout, Captain Henry *
2nd Artillery. d. 7/1/52

Sweeney, Lieutenant Thomas W.
2nd Infantry; lost his right arm at Churubusco—*USV Brig. Gen.* b. 1/25/20; d. 4/10/92

Swords, Major Thomas *
Quartermaster, Bvt. Lt. Col., Mexico—*USA A.Q.M.G.* b. ?/ ?/ 07; d. 3/2/86

Sykes, Lieutenant George *
3rd Infantry, Bvt. Capt., Cerro Gordo—*USV Maj. Gen.* b. 10/ 9/22; d. 2/8/80

Taliaferro, Major William B.
9th Infantry—*CSA Maj. Gen.* b. 12/28/22; d. 2/27/98

Tattnall, Commander Josiah, USN U.S.S. Spitfire—*CSN Captain of the C.S.S. Virginia (Merrimack), ironclad after the battle of Hampton Roads, VA on 3/9/62.* b. 11/9/ 1795; d. 6/14/71

Taylor, Captain Francis *
1st Artillery, Bvt. Major and Lt. Col. d. 10/12/58

Taylor, Captain George W.
10th Infantry—*USV Brig. Gen.* b. 11/22/08; *d. 9/1/62 from wounds received at the battle of Cub Run, VA.*

Taylor, Captain Nelson
1st New York Volunteers—*USV Brig. Gen.* b. 6/8/21; d. 1/16/94

Taylor, Lt. Colonel Joseph P.
Chief Commissary for Northern Forces, Bvt. Col—*USA Brig. Gen.* Brother of Zachary Taylor. b. 5/ 4/1796; d. 6/29/64

Taylor, Richard
Secretary to Zachary Taylor, his father—*CSA Maj. Gen.* b. 1/27/ 26; d. 4/12/79

Taylor, Lieutenant Thomas H.
3rd Kentucky Volunteers—*CSA Brig. Gen.* b. 7/31/25; d. 4/12/ 1901

Taylor, Maj. Gen. Zachary
Commander of the "Army of Occupation"—12th President of the United States from 1849-1850. b. 11/24/1784; d. 7/9/50

Temple, Colonel Robert E. *
10th Infantry. d. 7/20/54

Thomas, Major Charles
Quartermaster, Bvt. Lt. Col., Mexico—*USA A.Q.M.G.* d. 2/1/ 78

Thomas, 2nd Lieutenant Edward L.
Georgia Mounted Volunteers—*CSA Brig. Gen.* b. 3/23/25; d. 3/ 8/98

Thomas, Lieutenant George H. *
3rd Artillery, Bvt. Capt. and Major, Monterrey and Buena Vista—*USA Maj. Gen.* b. 7/31/ 16; d. 3/28/70

Thomas, Bvt. Major Lorenzo *
Asst. Adjutants-General, Bvt. Lt. Col., Monterrey—*USV Brig. Gen.* b. 10/26/04; d. 3/2/75

Thornton, Captain Seth B.
2nd Dragoons; wounded at Carricitos Ranch. b. ?/?/14; d. 8/18/47 at San Antonio in the Valley of Mexico.

Tibbatts, Colonel John W.
16th Infantry. d. 7/5/52

Tilghman, Captain Lloyd *
Maryland & District of Columbia Volunteers—*CSA Brig. Gen.* b. 1/18/16; *killed 5/16/63 at the battle of Baker's Creek, MS.*

Todd, Captain John B. S. *
6th Infantry—*USV Brig. Gen.* b. 4/4/14; d. 1/5/72

Totten, Colonel Joseph G. *
Chief of Engineers, Bvt. Brig. Gen., Vera Cruz—*USA Brig. General & Chief of Engineers.* b. 4/17/1788; d. 4/22/64

Tower, Lieutenant Zealous B. *
Engineers, Bvt. Capt., Cerro Gordo, Contreras, Churubusco and Chapultepec; wounded at Chapultepec—*USA Brig. Gen.* b. 1/12/19; d. 3/20/1900

Towson, Brigadier General Nathan
Paymaster General, Bvt. Maj. Gen., Mexico. d. 7/20/54

Tripler, Major Charles S.
Surgeon, Medical Director for Twigg's Division—*USA Bvt. Brig. Gen.* d. 10/20/66

Trousdale, Colonel William
14th Infantry, Bvt. Brig. Gen., Chapultepec d. 3/27/72

Twiggs, Brig. Gen. David E.
2nd Dragoons, Bvt. Maj. Gen., Monterrey—*CSA Major General.* b. ?/?/1790; d. 7/15/62

Van Derveer, Captain Ferdinand
1st Ohio Volunteers—*USV Brig. Gen.* b. 2/27/23; d. 11/5/92

Van Dorn, Lieutenant Earl *
7th Infantry, Bvt. Capt. and Major, Cerro Gordo, Contreras and Churubusco; wounded at Churubusco—*CSA Maj. Gen.* b. 9/17/20; *defeated at Pea Ridge and Corinth, assassinated by a jealous husband 5/7/63*

Van Vleit, Lieutenant Stewart *
3rd Artillery—*USV Brig. Gen.* b. 7/21/15; d. 3/28/1901

Vaughn, Captain John C.
5th Tennessee Volunteers—*CSA Brig. Gen.* b. 2/24/24; d. 9/10/75

Viele, 2nd Lieutenant Egbert L. *
1st Infantry—*USV Brig. Gen.* b. 6/17/25; d. 4/22/1902

Vinton, Captain John R. *
3rd Artillery, Bvt. Major, Monterrey. killed 3/22/47 at the siege of Veracruz, Mexico.

Waite, Major Carlos A.
8th Infantry, Bvt. Lt. Col. and Col., Contreras, Churubusco and Molino del Rey—*USA Colonel.* d. 5/7/66

Walker, Lieutenant John G.
Regiment of Mounted Rifles, Bvt. Capt., San Juan de los Llanos; severely wounded at Molino del Rey—*CSA Maj. Gen.* b. 7/22/22; d. 7/20/93

Walker, Captain Samuel H.
Regiment of Mounted Rifles. Killed in action 10/9/47 at Huamantla, Mexico.

Walker, Captain William H. T. *
6th Infantry, Bvt. Major and Lt. Col., Contreras, Churubusco and Molino del Rey; severely wounded at Molino del Rey—*CSA Maj. Gen.* b. 11/26/16; *killed 7/22/64 at the battle of Atlanta.*

Walker, Lieutenant William S.
Regiment of Voltigeurs & Foot Riflemen, Bvt. Capt., Chapultepec—*CSA Brig. Gen.* b. 4/13/22; d. 6/7/99

Wallace, Lieutenant Lewis "Lew"
1st Indiana Volunteers—*USV Maj. Gen.* Author of the book "Ben Hur: A Tale of the Christ". b. 4/10/27; d. 2/15/1905

Wallace, Lieutenant William H. L.
1st Illinois Volunteers, Adjutant—*USV Brig. Gen.* b. 7/8/21; *d. 4/10/62 of wounds received at the battle of Shiloh.*

Ward, Sergeant Major John H. H.
7th Infantry; wounded at Monterrey—*USV Brig. Gen.* b. 6/17/23; d. 7/24/1903

Ward, Major William T.
4th Kentucky Volunteers—*USV Brig. Gen.* b. 8/9/08; d. 10/12/78

Washington, Major John M. *
3rd Artillery, Bvt. Lt. Col., Buena Vista. d. 12/24/53

Wayne, Captain Henry C. *
Asst. Quartermaster, Bvt. Major, Contreras and Churubusco—*CSA Brig. Gen.* b. 9/18/15; d. 3/15/83

Webster, 2nd Lieutenant Joseph D.
Topographical Engineers—*USV Brig. Gen.* b. 8/25/11; d. 3/12/76

Webster, Captain Lucian B. *
1st Artillery, Bvt. Major and Lt. Col., Monterrey and Buena Vista. d. 11/4/53

Weightman, Captain Richard H.
Light Artillery, Battalion of Missouri Volunteers—*CSA Colonel. killed 8/10/61 at the battle of Wilson's Creek.*

Weisiger, 2nd Lieutenant David A.
1st Virginia Volunteers—*CSA Brig. Gen.* b. 12/23/18; d. 2/23/99

Welsh, Sergeant Thomas
2nd Kentucky Volunteers; severely wounded at Buena Vista—*USV Brig. Gen.* b. 5/5/24; d. 8/14/63

Wessells, Captain Henry W. *
2nd Infantry, Bvt. Major, Contreras and Churubusco; severely wounded at Contreras—*USV Brig. Gen.* b. 2/20/09; d. 1/12/89

West, Captain Joseph R.
Independent Volunteer Company (attached to the MD & DC Volunteers)—*USV Brig. Gen.* b. 9/19/22; d. 10/31/98

Wheat, Captain Chatham Roberdeau
Tennessee Mounted Volunteers—*CSA Colonel of the 1st Louisiana Special Battalion (Wheat's Tigers.)* b. 4/9/26;

killed 6/27/62 at the battle of Gaines' Mill, VA.

Whitaker, 2nd Lieutenant Walter C.
3rd Kentucky Volunteers—*USV Brig. Gen.* b. 8/8/23; d. 7/9/87

Whitfield, Lt. Colonel John W.
2nd Tennessee Volunteers—*CSA Brig. Gen.* b. 3/11/18; d. 10/27/79

Whiting, Major Levi
1st Artillery. d. 8/3/52

Wilcox, 2nd Lieutenant Cadmus M.*
7th Infantry, Bvt. 1st Lt., Chapultepec—*CSA Maj. Gen.* b. 5/29/24; d. 12/2/90

Williams, Lt. Colonel Alpheus S.
Michigan Volunteers—*USV Brig. Gen.* b. 9/20/10; d. 12/21/78

Williams, David H.
—*USV Brig. Gen.* b. 3/19/19; d. 6/1/91

Williams, Colonel John S.
4th Kentucky Volunteers, earned the nickname "Cerro Gordo"—*CSA Brig. Gen.* b. 7/10/18; d. 7/17/98

Williams, Lieutenant Seth *
1st Artillery, Bvt. Capt., Cerro Gordo—*USV Brig. Gen.* b. 3/22/22; d. 3/23/66

Williams, Lieutenant Thomas *
4th Artillery, Bvt. Capt. and Major, Contreras, Churubusco and Chapultepec—*USV Brig. Gen.* b. 1/10/15; *killed 8/5/62 at the battle of Baton Rouge.*

Wilson, Lt. Colonel Henry
1st Infantry, Bvt. Col., Monterrey d. 2/21/72

Winder, Captain John H. *
1st Artillery, Bvt. Major and Lt. Col., Contreras, Churubusco and City of Mexico—*CSA Brig. Gen.* b. 2/21/1800; d. 2/7/65

Withers, Colonel Jones M. *
9th Infantry—*CSA Maj. Gen.* b. 1/12/14; d. 3/13/90

Wofford, Captain William T.
Georgia Mounted Volunteers—*CSA Brig. Gen.* b. 6/28/24; d. 5/22/84

Wood, Major Robert C.
Surgeon; son-in-law of Zachary Taylor—*USA Asst. Surgeon General.* d. 3/28/69

Wood, 2nd Lieutenant Thomas J.*
Topographical Engineers, Bvt.

1st Lt., Buena Vista—*USV Maj. Gen.* b. 9/25/23; d. 2/25/1906

Wool, Brigadier General John E.
formerly 6th Infantry, Bvt. Major Gen., Buena Vista—*USA Major General.* b. 2/29/1784; d. 11/10/69

Worth, Brigadier General William J.
formerly 8th Infantry, Bvt. Maj. Gen., Monterrey b. 3/1/1794; d. 5/7/49

Wright, Captain George *
8th Infantry, Bvt. Major, Lt. Col. and Col., Contreras, Churubusco and Molino del Rey; wounded at Molino del Rey—*USV Brig. Gen.* b. 10/21/01; d. 7/30/65

Wright, Major Joseph J. B.
Surgeon—*USA Bvt. Brig. Gen.* d. 5/14/78

Yell, Colonel Archibald
Arkansas Mounted Volunteers. Killed 2/23/47 at the battle of Buena Vista, Mexico.

MEXICAN BIOGRAPHIES

Complete biographical information on the Mexican leaders is difficult to come by in English. The details listed below are combed from a myriad of sources and are meant to give a picture, even though incomplete, of the men opposing the American army in Mexico. There were many Mexicans that served during the war as enlisted men or junior officers who, like the Americans, went on to greater fame and fortune later in life. A few of the more well known men in this category are also listed here.

Alcorta, Brig. General Lino Jose
fought in the Texas Revolution; he was Minister of War and Marine under Santa Anna in 1846

Almonte, General Juan Nepumoceno
b. 1803. educated in the United States; he was captured at San Jacinto in 1836 with Santa Anna; Foreign Minister to the United States when diplomatic rela-

tions were broken off; declared himself President in 1862 and supported the French in the War of the Intervention. d. 1869.

Alvarez, Major General Juan born 1/27/1780. Military service began in 1810; In command of the cavalry defending Mexico City; he became President of Mexico in 1855; he fought for the Juarez government as a division commander during the War of the French Intervention; died 8/21/67.

Ampudia, Major General Pedro de b. 1803. Cuban. He had a reputation for cruelty originating when he put down a revolt in Tabasco in 1844 and upon receiving the surrender of the rebels on terms, had them all shot instead. He then proceeded to have the head of their leader fried in oil to make it last longer on display in the town square. This well known episode is what led him to be called the "Culinary Knight" by the American General Worth. He was the Commander of the Division of the North at the beginning of hostilities; commanded the army at Monterrey; commanded the brigade of light troops at Buena Vista.

Anaya, General Pedro Maria born in 1795. Military sevice began in 1811. He acted as the interim President of Mexico for Santa Anna from 4/2/47 until June of that year; second in command in defense of Churubusco and was captured; elected interim President again on 11/11/47 by the peace party and served until 1/8/48.

Arista, Major General Mariano born 7/1802. Military service began in 1813 as a cadet. He had red hair, was a native of San Luis Potosi and had lived in Cincinnati at one time. Took over command of the Division of the North from Ampudia in 4/46. Commanding officer at Palo Alto, Resaca de Guerrero (Resaca de la Palma) and Matamoros; went on to become

President of Mexico from 1/15/51 to 1/5/53. died 8/7/55.

Berriozabal, Felipe
b. 1829. Served as an enlisted man in 1846 and later became a general fighting for Juarez, commanding a brigade at Puebla in 1862. d. 1900

Bravo, General Nicolas
Military service dating back to 1811; Acting President of Mexico from 7/28/46 to 8/6/46; commanded the defense of Chapultepec

Arista

Canales, Brig. General Antonio a highly educated lawyer-politician and self-styled general originally from Monterrey; continually tried to establish Tamaulipas or some other part of the northern Mexican states as his own independent state apart from Mexico; harbored a long standing hatred for Texans even though he had frequently allied with them and recruited them for his schemes, he was viewed by them as a cowardly conspirator and border ruffian who could not be trusted; he was known as the "Chaparral Fox" ("the Fox" in Spanish is "el Zorro") and some of the men who would later become the Texas Rangers had scores to settle with him and his band, they tried to hunt him down many times but he survived the

war; he was in command of irregular cavalry at Palo Alto and Buena Vista; a believer in divination who would govern many of his actions by having his horoscope read, he was about 41 years old in 1846.

Canalizo, Major General Valentin born about 1797 at Monterrey. Military service from 1811; He was in command of the cavalry of the Army of the East in defense of the position at Cerro Gordo.

Castro, Brig. General Jose Maria Commandante in California in the Los Angeles area

Corona, General Antonio Chief of Artillery at Buena Vista

Cos, Brig. General Martin Perfecto de
Santa Anna's brother-in-law. He fought in the Texas Revolution. Commanded a brigade in the Tampico area.

Diaz, Porfirio
b. 9/15/30. Served as an enlisted man in the National Guard (from his home state of Oaxaca?) during the war. He went on to become a General for Juarez during the French Intervention, commanding a brigade at Puebla in 1862, and eventually became President and Dictator of Mexico from 1877 until 1911. d. 7/2/1915

Gaona, Brig. General Antonio He surrendered the Fortress of San Juan de Ulloa to the French in the "Pastry War" of 1838; he was in charge of a brigade defending Mexico City.

Garcia, Brig. General Jose Maria 1st Infantry Brigade commander at Palo Alto in place of Mejia who was ill. Later served under Maximilian until 1866.

Garcia Conde, Brig. General Jose Maria
cavalry brigade commander at Monterrey and commanded a brigade in Buena Vista campaign.

Garcia Conde, Brig. General Pedro cavalry commander at the Battle of the Sacramento in the defense of Chihuahua.

Guzman, Major General Luis
commander of a division in the
Buena Vista campaign.

Heredia, Brig. General Jose A.
Commandante at Chihuahua in
February of 1847

Herrera, General Jose Joaquin de
b. 1792. Entered military service
as a cadet in the Spanish Army
in 1809. President of Mexico
from 9/14/45 to 12/31/45 and
again from 5/30/48 until 1/15/
51. He commanded a part of the
army under Santa Anna after
the fall of Mexico City. d. 2/
1854.

Jararo, Brig. General Jose Maria
Brigade commander at Cerro
Gordo

Juarez, Benito
b. 3/21/06. Governor of Oaxaca
in 1847; President of Mexico
from 1858-1872 he is looked
upon as a combination of the
George Washington and
Abraham Lincoln of Mexico. He
fought and won the war to keep
Mexico free from the Emperor
Maximilian during the French
Intervention from 1861-1867. d.
7/18/72

Juvera, Brig. General Julian
In command of a cavalry
brigade at Buena Vista

Landero, Brig. General Jose Juan
Took over the command at Vera
Cruz to negotiate a surrender.

La Vega, Brig. General Romulo
Diaz de
Infantry brigade commander at
Palo Alto and Resaca de
Guerrero where he was cap-
tured; Artillery and infantry
brigade commander at Cerro
Gordo where he was once again
captured.

Lombardini, Major General
Manuel Maria
b. 1802 in Mexico City; Military
service dating from 1821;
Infantry division commander at
Buena Vista. Later President of
Mexico from 2/8/53 until 4/
20/53; d. 12/22/53.

Mejia, Brig. General Francisco
Commander of garrison at

Matamoros in April of 1846 and
then commanded garrison of
Monterrey; Brigade commander
at Buena Vista; Justin Smith
gives a description of a small,
pockmarked man with blue
glasses, who looked like a
drunk and was known for his
bad health and pompous
vocabulary.

Micheltorena, Brig. General Manuel
Governor of California from late
1842 until early 1845; Santa
Anna's Chief of Staff at Buena
Vista.

Minon, Brig. General Jose Vincente
Cavalry brigade commander at
Buena Vista

Paredes

Mora y Villamil, Brig. General
Ignacio
Chief of Engineers at Buena
Vista. Acted as a peace commis-
sioner in 1848.

Morales, Brig. General Juan
Commander at Vera Cruz until
the surrender.

Negrete, Miguel
b. 1824. He fought in the
Mexican-American War and
later became a general under
Juarez. He commanded the forts
at Puebla in 1862. d. 1897.

Ortega, Major General Jose
Maria
Commander of the Third
Infantry Division at Buena Vista

Pacheco, Major General Francisco
Division commander at Buena
Vista; Foreign Minister in
summer of 1847

Paredes y Arrillaga, Major
General Mariano
b. 1/6/1797; He entered military service in 1812. Commander of the Army of the
North in 1845. He was President
of Mexico from 1/4/46 until 7/
28/46. He took over the supreme command of the army in
June of 1846. d. 9/49

Pena y Barragan, Brig. General
Matias
led counterattacks at Molino del
Rey and defended San Cosme
Gate at Mexico City

Perez, Brig. General Francisco
Brigade commander at Buena
Vista, Churubusco, Molino del
Rey and Chapultepec

Pinzon, Brig. General Luis
Brigade commander at Cerro
Gordo

Ramirez, Brig. General Simeon
Brigade commander at
Monterrey and again at Molino
del Rey and Mexico City.

Rangel, Brig. General Joaquin
Brigade commander at Cerro
Gordo, in support at Contreras,
Molino del Rey and
Chapultepec and saw action at
the San Cosme Gate.

Rea, Brig. General Joaquin
Guerrilla leader in the Puebla
area in the summer of 1847

Requena, General Tomas
Second in command of the
Army of the North in the
summer of 1846.

Rincon, Major General Manuel
In charge of the defense of
Churubusco.

Romero, General Manuel
Commander of a cavalry
brigade at Monterrey.

Salas, Brig. General Jose Mariano
Commander of the garrison of
Mexico City until he was
decreed President on 8/6/46, he
was overthrown on 12/23/46.
He was later second in com-
mand after Valencia at
Contreras.

BIOGRAPHIES

Santa Anna, General Antonio Lopez de
b. 2/21/1795. He entered the army on July 10, 1810 at the age of 15 as a cadet in the Fijo de Vera Cruz regiment. In 1812 he was wounded by an arrow in the left arm at the action of Amoladeras and promoted to sub-lieutenant. He fought in Texas on August 18, 1813 at the Battle of Medina against revolutionaries. He was breveted to Captain in 1820 and to Lieutenant Colonel in 1821. Iturbide promoted him to a full Brigadier General and after fighting the Spanish at Tampico in 1829 he was made a General of Division. He became President of Mexico for the first time in 1833 and was to repeatedly hold the office a total of 10 more times over the next 22 years. Santa Anna was in command at the Alamo and San Jacinto (where he was captured) during the Texas Revolution.

After this Santa Anna went to Washington to see President Andrew Jackson. While he was there a secretary and interpreter named James Adams noticed his habit of chewing "chicle" which he cut from a tropical vegetable of some kind. He persuaded Santa Anna to leave him his supply, to which he added sweeteners and a sugar coating. Chiclets Gum was born and Adams made a fortune.

Santa Anna fought against the French at Vera Cruz in the so called "Pastry War" of 1838 where he lost his left leg to grapeshot. During the war with the United States he was in direct command at Buena Vista against Taylor and at Cerro Gordo, and in the defense of Mexico City against Scott. d. 6/21/76

Seguin, Colonel Juan N.
b. 10/27/06; He served at the Alamo in 1836 as a courier for Travis; commanded Tejano (Mexican settlers living in Texas) cavalry at San Jacinto. He changed sides to Mexico in 1842 when he and other hispanic settlers were poorly treated after the Texas revolution. He led a small band of forty irregular cavalry that operated in the Monterrey area; fought at the battle of Buena Vista. Eventually he reconciled with the state of Texas. The city of Seguin, Texas, northeast of San Antonio, was named for him. d. 8/27/90

Terres, Brig. General Andres
In command at the defense of the Belen Gate, he was captured there.

Tornel y Mendivil, General Jose Maria
Minister of War and Marine in early 1846.

Torrejon, Brig. General Anastasio
Brigade commander (mostly cavalry) at Carricitos Ranch, Palo Alto, Monterrey and Buena Vista, also at Contreras and the San Cosme Gate.

Urrea, Brig. General Jose
He fought in the Texas Revolution and was the victor over Fannin at Goliad, at which he carried out the order issued by Santa Anna to massacre the prisoners there. He was a cavalry brigade and Guerrilla commander in the Northern Theater of Operations during the war with the United States.

Valencia, Major General Gabriel
Commander of the Army of the North in defense of Mexico City and at Contreras.

Vasquez, Brig. General Ciriaco
Infantry Brigade commander at Cerro Gordo, where he was killed in action.

Zaragoza, Ignacio
b. 1829. He was enlisted as a cadet in 1846. He became the hero of the Battle of Puebla in 1862 where he defeated the French on the glorious 5th of May, a victory celebrated today as Cinco de Mayo. d. 9/8/62

LOS NINOS HEROES (THE HEROIC CHILDREN)

There were six brave young cadets who died defending their school at Chapultepec Castle on September 13, 1847. Their battle cry was reported as, *"Viva Mexico! Viva el Colegio Militar!"* (loosely translated as "Long live Mexico! Long live the military academy!"). Their heroic last stand is one of the few events of the Mexican-American War still remembered in Mexico and the cadets are honored on the anniversary of the battle every year.

Juan de la Barrera, Lieutenant - Zapadores; b. 1827
Juan Escutia, Cadet - 1st Company; b. 2/22/27; He fell to his death from the heights of Chapultepec while clutching the flag of the garrison to keep it from falling into enemy hands.
Francisco Marquez, Cadet - 1st Company; b. 1833
Agustin Melgar, Cadet - 2nd Company; b. 8/28/29
Fernando Montes de Oca, Cadet - 1st Company; b. 1832?
Vicente Suarez, Cadet - 2nd Company; b. 1827

NOTES ON THE ORDERS OF BATTLE

Primary source material has been used as much as possible in compiling the Orders of Battle. Often sketchy or incomplete information is all that was available for a particular action, especially for the Mexican side. Information on the Mexican army is hard to come by, let alone confirm, simply because so little actually exists. Many of the Mexican sources do not contain much hard data because none was available at the time, or possibly it was lost later. Books written over the years draw mostly on the same source material because there is so little available. Information on the American army is more complete and easier to confirm. The primary sources contain more complete documentation including after action reports and official returns. However, with many independent observers present there are some conflicting figures and I have tried to reconcile them where possible.

The listings are a gathering together of the best information available for each army. No assumptions have been made about which units were present, names of commanders or numbers of men involved. Every effort has been made to cross check all of the facts with at least two sources. The figures given in parentheses after a unit name are the number of men present at that time. The sources often give different estimates of numbers available in particular units or present for a battle. Where this occurs the various totals have all been given with the most reliable or exact sources listed first and the wider ranging or less substantiated estimates placed last. There is

really no way of determining at this point in time which figures are exactly correct.

The Mexican listings will often name units of Active Militia or National Guard troops that are never mentioned again or do not appear to be included within the normal organization of the Mexican army. Sometimes a uniform picture is all that suggests the existence of such ephemeral units. These may have been local units of hastily raised militia that ceased to exist after a battle or simply never left the area in which they were raised once the armies and the war moved on. This type of information has long since melted into obscurity. The Mexican army often converged small units or detachments into larger groups and this has been noted wherever possible.

The rank of commanders listed is as of the dates indicated. The Americans did not often list 'brevet' before a rank when referring to an officer. The Mexicans used both ranks together such as *General graduado Colonel* (Colonel acting as General), and where this is known it has been given.

In addition to the primary sources "The War with Mexico" by Justin H. Smith has been very valuable in actually listing many units. Almost all of the information for the Mexican and American navies comes from "Surfboats and Horse Marines" by K. Jack Bauer which includes more detailed information about individual ships and their captains

BIBLIOGRAPHY

The sources listed here are by no means the only ones available concerning the Mexican American War, although they do include some of the best and most complete on the subject. A more extensive bibliography is given by Tutorow (see below). The most highly recommended reading from the list below would have to be K. Jack Bauer's *Mexican War* for military history, Bernard DeVoto's *Year of Decision* for historical perspective and Justin Smith's two volume *War with Mexico* for the best and most complete treatment of the conflict. Many of the titles listed here are available at new and used book stores or through the local library system.

Allsop, David. *The Texan War of Independence and the U.S.-Mexican War 1846-48.* Northern Ireland: Frei Korps, 1983. A basic reference guide for wargamers containing some uniform and order of battle information.

Anderson, Robert. *An Artillery Officer in the Mexican War.* Freeport, NY: Books for Libraries Press, 1971.

Angle, Paul M. "The Mexican War" *Chicago History,* 1, no. 8 (Summer 1947): 215-220.

Athearn, Robert G. *War with Mexico.* American Heritage, New York: Dell Publishing Co. Inc., 1963.

Baker, B. Kimball. "The St. Patricks fought for their skins, and Mexico" *Smithsonian,* (March 1978): 95-101. A basic account of the San Patricios with some excellent illustrations by Don Troiani.

Ballentine, George. *Autobiography of an English Soldier in the United States Army.* Edited by William H. Goetzmann. Chicago, IL: R.R. Donnelley & Sons Co., 1986.

Bancroft, Hubert Howe. *History of Mexico, Vol. 5, 1824-1861.* San Francisco: A.L. Bancroft & Co., 1885. This entire set is very good for information about the Mexican side of affairs.

Barcena, Jose Maria Roa. *Recuerdos De La Invasion Norte Americana 1846-1848,* 3 Volumes. S.A. Mexico: Editorial Porrua, S. A., 1947.

Barrante, William T. "Kentucky in the Mexican War" *Military Collector & Historian,* 36, no. 3 (Fall 1984): 112-113.

Bauer, K. Jack. *The Mexican War 1846-1848.* New York: Macmillan Publishing Co., Inc., 1974. This is probably the best book for the military history of the war.

Bauer, K. Jack. *Surfboats and Horse Marines: U.S. Naval Operations in the Mexican War, 1846-1848.* Annapolis, MD: U.S. Naval Institute Press, 1969. This is the definitive book on the history of the naval war against Mexico complete with ship listings.

Bauer, K. Jack. *Zachary Taylor: Soldier, Planter; Statesman of the Old Southwest.* Baton Rouge, LA: Louisiana State University Press, 1985.

Baylies, Francis. *A Narrative of Major General Wool's Campaign in Mexico in the Years 1846, 1847 & 1848.* Albany, NY: Little & Co., 1851.

Berg, Richard & Balkoski, Joe. "Veracruz: U.S. Invasion of Mexico 1847" *Strategy & Tactics.* 63 (July-August 1977): 4-18.

Biggs, Donald C. *Conquer and Colonize: Stevenson's Regiment and California.* San Rafael, CA: Presidio Press, 1977.

Bill, Alfred Hoyt. *Rehearsal for Conflict: The war with Mexico 1846-1848.* New York: Cooper Square Publishing, Inc., 1969.

Birkhimer, William E. *Historical Sketch of the Organization,* *Administration, Materiel and Tactics of the Artillery, United States Army.* New York: Greenwood Press, Publishers, 1968. Originally published: 1884 by James J. Chapman.

Brooks, Nathan Covington. *A Complete History of the Mexican War 1846-1848.* Chicago, IL: Rio Grande Press, Inc., 1965. First Published, 1849.

Callcott, Wilfred Hardy. *Santa Anna: The Story of an Enigma Who once was Mexico.* Hamden, CT: Archon Books, 1964.

Caraza, Leopoldo Martinez. *La Intervencion Norte Americana en Mexico 1846-1848.* Mexico: Panorama Editorial, 1981.

Caruso, A. Brooke. *The Mexican Spy Company: United States Covert Operations in Mexico, 1845-1848.* Jefferson, NC: McFarland and Company, Inc., 1991. Some interesting facts about many different uses of intelligence gathering services used by the Americans in Mexico.

Casey, Brig. General Silas. *Infantry Tactics.* Dayton, Ohio: Morningside House, Inc., 1985. Originally published in 1862.

Chalfant, William Y. *Dangerous Passage: The Santa Fe Trail and the Mexican War.* Norman and London: University of Oklahoma Press, 1994. This deals mainly with Indian troubles along the trail.

Chamberlain, Samuel E. *My Confession.* New York: Harper and Brothers, Publishers, 1956. One of the best books to read for a personal account of the war and the many adventures of a dragoon written in a down to earth style.

Chambers, William. *Sketch of the Life of General T.J. Chambers of Texas.* Galveston, TX: Galveston News, 1853.

Chance, Joseph E. *Jefferson Davis's Mexican War Regiment.* Jackson and London: University Press of Mississippi, 1991. A good look at one of the most famous units in the war and its commander.

Chidsey, Donald Barr. *The War with Mexico.* New York: Crown Publishers, Inc., 1968.

Clark, Francis and Lynch, James. *The New York Volunteers in California.* Glorieta, New Mexico: The Rio Grande Press, Inc., 1970.

Connor, Seymour V. and Faulk, Odie B. *North America Divided: The Mexican War 1846-1848,* New York: Oxford University Press, 1971. This book has an extensive annotated bibliography at the end of the text to recommend it.

Conrad, Robert T. *General Scott and His Staff.* Freeport, New York: Books for Libraries Press, 1970. First Published, 1848.

Cutrer, Thomas W. *Ben McCullough and the Frontier Military Tradition.* Chapel Hill: University of North Carolina Press, 1993.

Daniels, George G. ed. *The Spanish West.* The Old West Series, New York: Time, Inc., 1976. As always the Time-Life books provide a great background and general coverage of the subject.

DePalo, William A., Jr. *The Mexican National Army, 1822-1852.* College Station: Texas A&M University Press, 1997.

DeVoto, Bernard. *The Year of Decision 1846.* Boston: Little, Brown & Co., 1943. An excellent book to read for pleasure that tells what else was going on concurrently with the war in Mexico, such as the tragedy of the Donner party for one.

Dillon, Lester R. Jr. *American Artillery in the Mexican War 1846-1847.* Austin: Presidial Press, 1975. The best book to learn about the American artillery and the role it played in winning the war.

Downey, Fairfax. *Texas and the War with Mexico*. New York: American Heritage Publishing Co., Inc., 1961. Despite being aimed at younger readers, the color photographs make this worth looking at.

DuFour, Charles L. *The Mexican War: A Compact History 1846-1848*. New York: Hawthorn Books, Inc., 1968.

Eisenhower, John S.D. *So Far From God: The U.S. War with Mexico 1846-1848*. New York: Random House, 1989. One of the more recent works this book covers quite a bit in very readable style. The military aspect is still covered more thoroughly by Bauer or Smith.

Elliot, Charles Winslow. *Winfield Scott: The Soldier and the Man*. New York: Macmillan Co., 1937. A good biography of Scott but not as detailed as one would like concerning the war.

Elting, John R. ed. *Military Uniforms in America, Vol.II: Years of Growth 1796-1851*. 114-135. San Rafael, CA: Presidio Press, 1977. Excellent color plates and descriptions but only of American units.

Fehrenbach, T.R. *Fire and Blood: A History of Mexico*. New York: Bonanza Books, 1985. A classic work that is a must read for anyone interested in Mexican history.

Fehrenbach, T.R. *Lone Star: A History of Texas and the Texans*. New York: Collier Books, 1985. A very good book that covers the history of Texas and its relationship to Mexico.

Ferrell, Robert H. ed. *Monterrey is Ours! The Mexican War Letters of Lieutenant Dana 1845-1847*. Lexington, KY: The University Press of Kentucky, 1990.

Field, Ron. *Mexican American War 1846-48*. London: Brassey's (UK) Ltd., 1997.

Finke, Detmar H. "Reply to Terry D. Hooker's article 'Uniforms of the Mexican Army 1839-1846'" *El Dorado*. 3, no.2 (July-August, 1990): 2-4.

Freeman, Douglas Southall. *R.E. Lee: A Biography*. New York: Charles Scribner's Sons, 1936.

Frost, J., L.L.D. *The Mexican War and its Warriors*. Maryland: Heritage Books, Inc., 1989.

Fuller, Maj. Gen. J.F.C. *Decisive Battles of the U.S.A.* 147-170. New York: Thomas Yoseloff, Inc., 1942.

Funcken, Liliane et Fred. *L'Uniforme et les Armes des Soldats des Etats-Unis*. Casterman, 1-1979, 2-1980.

George, Isaac. *Heroes and Incidents of the Mexican War*. Hollywood, CA: Sun Dance Press, 1971.

Gibson, George Rutledge. *Journal of a soldier under Kearny and Doniphan 1846-1847*. Philadelphia: Porcupine Press, 1974.

Greenwald, William. "The March of the Mormon Battalion" *The Courier* 9, no. 4: 57, 1990.

Greer, James K. *Buck Barry—Texas Ranger and Frontiersman*. Lincoln: University of Nebraska Press, 1978.

Gruber, Robert H. "The Cross, Porter and Thornton episodes: America's inauspicious entry into the Mexican War" *Military History of Texas and the Southwest* 12, no. 3: 185-201, 1975.

Hackenburg, Randy W. *Pennsylvania in the War with Mexico, the Volunteer Regiments*. Shippensburg, PA: White Mane Publishing Co., Inc., 1992.

Hanighen, Frank C. *Santa Anna: the Napoleon of the West*. New York: Coward-McCann, Inc., 1934.

Hardin, Dr. Stephen. *The Texas Rangers*. London: Osprey Publishing, Ltd., 1991.

Harlow, Neal. *California Conquered: War and Peace on the Pacific 1846-1850*. Berkeley & Los Angeles: University of California Press, 1982.

Haythornthwaite, Philip. *Weapons & Equipment of the Napoleonic Wars*. Poole, Dorset: Blandford Press, 1979.

Heller, Charles E. & Stofft, William A., eds. *America's First Battles 1776-1965*. (Chapter 3- K. Jack Bauer, "The Battles on the Rio Grande: Palo Alto and Resaca de la Palma, 8-9 May 1846.) University Press of Kansas, 1986.

Heitman, Francis B. *Historical Register and Dictionary of the United States Army, From Its Organization, September 29, 1789, to March 2, 1903*. 2 vols., Urbana: University of Illinois Press, 1965.

Henry, Robert Selph. *The Story of the Mexican War*. New York: Frederick Ungar Publishing Co., 1961. A very good book that covers the war and politics without getting bogged down.

Henry, William S. *Campaign Sketches of the War with Mexico*. New York: Arno Press, 1973. This is an excellent reprint of a personal account of the campaign.

Hitchcock, Ethan Allen. *Fifty Years in Camp and Field*. Edited by W.A. Croffut., Freeport, New York: Books for Libraries Press, 1909. Often quoted in other works, this book reveals much about the personality of its author while serving up fascinating facts.

Hitchman, Richard. "Rush to Glory: The U.S.-Mexican War 1846-1848" *Strategy & Tactics*. 127 (June-July 1989): 14-26, 60.

Hoffman, William S. *North Carolina in the Mexican War, 1846-1848*. Raleigh, N.C.: State Department of Archives and History, 1969.

Holland, Cecelia. "The Old Woman's Gun" *MHQ: The Quarterly Journal of Military History*. 3, no. 4 (Summer, 1991): 58-67.

Holt, Thaddeus. "Checkmate at Mexico City" *MHQ: The Quarterly Journal of Military History*. 2, no. 3 (Spring, 1990): 82-93.

Hooker, T. "Uniforms of the Mexican Army 1839-1847", Part I. *Tradition*. 64: 29-32; Part II. *Tradition*. 66: 22-25. These two articles are derived from the information in the Hefter book but are much better organized and explained.

Horgan, Paul. *Great River: The Rio Grande in North American History, 2 Vols*. New York: Rinehart & Co., Inc., 1954. This is another good read covering the history of the area from earliest times.

Hughes, Maj.Gen. B.P. *Firepower*. London: Arms and Armour Press, 1974.

Hughes, John T. *Doniphan's Expedition*. Chicago: Rio Grande Press, 1962.

Hughes, Nathaniel Cheairs, Jr. *General William J. Hardee, Old Reliable*. Baton Rouge & London: Louisiana State University Press, 1965.

Jacobsen, Jacques Noel, Jr. *Regulations and Notes for the Uniform of the Army of the United States, 1847*. New York: Manor Publishing, Staten Island, 1977.

Johannsen, Robert W. *To the Halls of the Montezumas: The Mexican War in the American Imagination*. New York: Oxford University Press, 1985. An excellent book that reveals a wealth of information about what American culture was like in the 1840's and how it was influenced by the War in Mexico.

Johnston, Abraham Robinson & Edwards, Marcellus Ball & Ferguson, Philip Gooch. *Marching with the Army of the West 1846-1848*. Philadelphia: Porcupine Press, 1974.

Jones, Oakah L., Jr. *Santa Anna*. New York: Twayne Publishers, Inc., 1968.

Katcher, Philip R.N. *The Mexican-American War 1846-1848*. London: Osprey Publishing, Ltd., 1976. This book is part of the Osprey Men-At-Arms Series #56. It has eight pages of color plates and good uniform descriptions.

Katcher, Philip R.N. "Some Volunteer Uniforms of the Mexican War" *Campaigns* 42 (1982): 12-15.

Kerrigan, Evans E. *American War Medals and Decorations*. New York: The Viking Press, 1964: 18.

Kimmel, Ross M. "American Forces in the War with Mexico, 1846-1848", *Military Illustrated Past & Present*. part 1, 40 (Sept. 1991) 27-36; part 2, 42 (Nov. 1991) 34-41; part 3, 44 (Jan. 1992) 9-14; part 4, 45 (Feb. 1992) 11-15; part 5, 47 (April 1992) 8-14; part 6, 48 (May 1992) 28-31. This six part series is a must see for anyone interested in American uniforms of the period. Many

206

reconstructions and photographs of surviving uniforms in color along with explanations make this set of articles well worthwhile.

Knotel, Richard & Knotel, Herbert & Sieg, Herbert. *Uniforms of the World.* New York: Charles Scribner's Sons, 1980.

Lamego, Miguel A. Sanchez. *El Battalion de San Blas 1825-1855: brief chronicle of an heroic outfit.* Mexico, 1964. This booklet is a companion to the Hefter book but only deals with one regiment. Some color plates and interesting facts about the organization of the Mexican forces after independence.

Lamego, Miguel A. Sanchez. *El Colegio Militar y la Defensa de Chapultepec en Septiembre de 1847.* Mexico, 1947.

Lamego, Miguel A. Sanchez. *The Second Mexican-Texas war 1841-1843.* Hillsboro, TX: Hill Junior College, 1972. A good book about the little known conflicts between Texas and Mexico after the Texas Revolution and before the Mexican War.

Langellier, John. *US Dragoons 1833-55.* London: Reed International Books, Ltd., 1995. This book is in the Osprey Men-At-Arms Series #281. It contains eight pages of color plates, three of which pertain directly to the War in Mexico.

Lavender, David. *Climax at Buena Vista.* Philadelphia & New York: J.B. Lippincott Co., 1966. A good book covering the campaign in the north by Zachary Taylor.

Lewis, Lloyd. *Captain Sam Grant.* Boston: Little, Brown and Co., 1950. A very good book about Grant and some of his ideas and opinions regarding the war.

Mansfield, Edward D. *The Mexican War: A History of its Origin.* New York, NY: A.S. Barnes & Co., 1873. Often quoted, this firsthand source has quite a bit in the way of statistics and information on orders of battle for the Americans.

Marshall, Bob. "Ho, for the Halls of the Montezuma" *The Courier.* 9, no. 1 (1989): 5-6.

Marshall, Bob. "A brief view of the Mexican-American War" *The Courier.* 9, no. 1 (1989): 9-10.

Marshall, Bob. "The Battles of Palo Alto and Resaca de la Palma" *The Courier.* 9, no. 1 (1989): 13-19.

Marshall, Bob. "The United States Army during the Mexican-American War" *The Courier.* 9, no. 2 (1989): 19-25.

McCaffrey, James M. *Army of Manifest Destiny: The American Soldier in the Mexican War, 1846-1848.* New York: New York University Press, 1992. This was a good compilation of data about the army that fought in Mexico.

McClellan, Geirge Brinton. *The Mexican War Diary of George B. McClellan.* Edited by William Starr Myers. New York: DaCapo Press, 1972. Original edition, Princeton University Press, 1917.

McCutchan, Joseph D. *Mier Expedition Diary: A Texan Prisoner's Account.* Austin, TX: University of Texas Press, 1978.

McHenry, Robert. *Webster's American Military Biographies.* New York: Dover Publications, inc., 1978.

McWhiney, Grady. *Braxton Bragg and Confederate Defeat, Vol. I.* Tuscaloosa and London: The University of Alabama Press, 1991.

McWhiney, Grady & Jamieson, Perry D. *Attack and Die: Civil War Military Tactics and the Southern Heritage.* Alabama: University of Alabama Press, 1982.

McWhiney, Grady & McWhiney, Sue. eds. *To Mexico with Taylor and Scott 1845-1847.* Waltham, MA: Blaisdell Publishing Co., 1969.

Meltzer, Milton. *Bound for the Rio Grande: The Mexican Struggle 1845-1850.* New York: Alfred A. Knopf, 1974.

Meyer, Jack Allen. *South Carolina in the Mexican War: A History of the Palmetto Regiment of Volunteers, 1846-1917.* This book had not been published when we went to press, but the author kindly gave us some useful details from the manuscript.

Miller, Robert Ryal. *Shamrock and Sword: The St. Patrick's Battalion in the U.S.-Mexican War.* Norman, OK: University of Oklahoma Press, 1989. A complete history of this famous unit during the war.

Miller, Robert Ryal. ed. *The Mexican War Journal & Letters of Ralph W. Kirkham.* College Station, TX: Texas A&M University Press, 1991.

Mills, Bronwyn. *The Mexican War.* New York & Oxford: Facts on File, 1992.

Nance, Joseph Milton. *After San Jacinto: The Texas-Mexican Frontier 1836-1841.* Austin, TX: University of Texas Press, 1963. This and its companion volume (see below) provide a detailed look at the troubles between Texas and Mexico before the war. Mainly from the Texan point of view.

Nance, Joseph Milton. *Attack and Counterattack: The Texas-Mexican Frontier, 1842.* Austin, TX: University of Texas Press, 1964.

Nardo, Don. *The Mexican-American War.* San Diego, CA: Lucent Books, 1991.

Nevin, David. *The Mexican War.* New York: Time-Life Books, Inc., 1978. Once again an excellent book just for the pictures if nothing else.

Nevin, David. *The Texans.* New York: Time-Life Books, Inc., 1975.

Nichols, Edward J. *Zach Taylor's Little Army.* Garden City, NY: Doubleday & Company, Inc., 1963.

Nieto, Mrs. Angelina & Brown, Mrs. John Nicholas, & Hefter, Joseph. *The Mexican Soldier 1837-1847.* Mexico: Nieto-Brown-Hefter, 1958. This is the 'bible' on the Mexican army of this time. The amount of research done by Hefter has not been equalled to this day. Every attempt has been made to include as much pertinent information from this book as possible into the book you are now reading, but if you can get a look at the Hefter book itself it is still worthwhile.

Norman, C.A. "Mexico 1845-7 (Some notes on Campaign Dress during the U.S./Mexican War). *El Dorado.* 3, no. 5 (January-February 1991): 1-2.

Nunis, Doyce B., Jr. *The Mexican War in Baja California.* Los Angeles, CA: Dawson's Book Shop, 1977. Fairly complete book on the subject incorporating Henry Halleck's memoirs of the campaign.

Olivera, Ruth R. & Crete, Liliane. *Life in Mexico under Santa Anna 1822-1855.* Norman, OK and London: University of Oklahoma Press, 1991. A good background guide to what Mexico was like during this period.

Peskin, Allan. ed. *Volunteers: The Mexican War Journals of Private Richard Coulter and Sergeant Thomas Barclay, Company E, Second Pennsylvania Infantry.* Kent, OH: Kent State University Press, 1991. These personal accounts contain much amusing and informative material. Interesting look at how two different soldiers view the same events.

Pivka, Otto von. *Armies of the Napoleonic Era.* Newton Abbot, Devon: David & Charles Ltd., 1979.

Ramirez, Jose Fernando. *Mexico During the War with the United States.* Edited by Walter V. Scholes, Translated by Elliot B. Scherr. Columbia, MO: University of Missouri, 1950.

Ramsey, Albert C. ed. & trans. *The Other Side: or Notes for the History of the War between Mexico and the United States.* New York: Burt Franklin Press, 1970. One of the best books in English that tells about the Mexican side of the conflict. Some questions have been raised by other historians (see Bancroft) about the accuracy of the translation from the original Spanish so there may be errors present. There is much useful information about orders of battle and it is used as the main source for many who try to detail this information.

Reed, Nelson. *The Caste War of Yucatan.* Stanford, CA: Stanford University Press, 1964.

Reid, Samuel C., Jr. *The Scouting Expeditions of McCulloch's Texas Ranger.* Freeport, NY: Books for Libraries Press, 1970.

Ripley, R.S. *The War with Mexico (2 Volumes).* New York: Burt Franklin Press, 1970. A very readable account by a participant but with a definite American bias.

Robinson, Fayette *Mexico and her Military Chieftains* Glorieta, NM:

Rio Grande Press, Inc., 1970. Not as helpful as might be hoped. It was written while the war was still in progress and came out originally in 1847. Much of what is in here is general knowledge of the Mexican leaders at the time, some of it unsubstantiated.

Sandweiss, Martha A. & Stewart, Rick & Huseman, Ben W. *Eyewitness to War: Prints and Daguerreotypes of the Mexican War, 1846-1848.* Fort Worth, TX: Amon Carter Museum, 1989. Absolutely the best source available showing the war through the visual means available at the time.

Santa Anna, Antonio Lopez de. *The Eagle: The Autobiography of Santa Anna.* Edited by Ann Fears Crawford. Austin, TX: State House Press, 1988. An interesting book to read once the events have been learned of elsewhere, as this account leaves out quite a bit and does not begin to explain many of the authors' actions.

Scott, Colonel H.L. *Military Dictionary.* New York: Greenwood Press, 1968. Originally published by D. Van Nostrand in 1861.

Scribner, Benjamin Franklin. *Camp Life of a Volunteer: A Campaign in Mexico.* Austin, TX: Jenkins Publishing Co., 1975.

Selby, John. *The Eagle and the Serpent: The Invasions of Mexico 1519 and 1846.* London: Hamish Hamilton, 1978.

Semmes, Raphael. *Service Afloat and Ashore during the Mexican War.* Cincinnati: Wm. H. Moore & Co., 1851.

Sigsworth, Grant. "The Campaign for California in the Mexican-American War" *The Courier.* 9, no. 3 (1989): 5-10.

Singletary, Otis A. *The Mexican War.* Chicago and London: University of Chicago Press, 1965.

Smith, George Winston & Judah, Charles. *Chronicles of the Gringos: The U.S. Army in the Mexican War, 1846-1848, Accounts of Eyewitnesses and Combatants.* Albuquerque, NM: University of New Mexico Press, 1968. This book should be required reading for anyone interested in firsthand accounts of the war by regulars and volunteers alike. An excellent collection of far flung materials that are often hard to come by on their own.

Smith, Justin H. *The War with Mexico (2 Volumes).* Gloucester, MA: Peter Smith, 1963. Despite many criticisms of bias, many of which are deserved, there is no doubt that this is still the premier book to read concerning all aspects of the Mexican-American War. The amount of research and documentation evident here is unsurpassed. The footnotes alone could make a good book. Don't miss this is you have any interest in the period at all.

Stapp, William Preston. *The Prisoners of Perote: A Firsthand Account of the Mier Expedition.* Austin, TX: University of Texas Press, 1977.

Steffen, Randy. *The Horse Soldier 1776-1943. Volume I, The Revolution, the War of 1812, the Early Frontier, 1776-1850.* Norman, Oklahoma: University of Oklahoma Press, 1980: 88-188. The most complete source for the U.S. Cavalry available. Includes all uniform and accoutrement information currently available.

Sweet, David. "A Few Mexican Standards of the Mexican War" *The Courier.* 9, no. 3 (1989): 55.

Traas, Adrian George. *From the Golden Gate to Mexico City, the U.S. Army Topographical Engineers in the Mexican War, 1846-1848.* Washington, D.C.: U.S. Government Printing Office, 1992. A very interesting book that offers a look at some of the excellent maps in the National Archives.

Tutorow, Norman E. *The Mexican-American War: An Annotated Bibliography.* Westport, CT: Greenwood Press, 1981. The most extensive bibiliography on the Mexican War yet published, it has become somewhat outdated due to the quantity of recently published materials but it is still the best starting place for discovering source materials.

Tyler, Sgt. Daniel. *A Concise History of the Mormon Battalion in the Mexican War 1846-1847.* Glorieta, NM: The Rio Grande Press, 1969.

Tyler, Ronnie C. *The Mexican War: A Lithographic Record.* Austin, TX: Texas State Historical Association, 1973. A very well done little book that shows how the lithographic record of the war can be used by historians. Many full color prints of period paintings.

Upton, Emory. *The Military Policy of the United States.* New York: Greenwood Press, 1968: 195-222. Originally published in 1904.

Urwin, Gregory J. W. *The United States Cavalry: An Illustrated History.* Poole, Dorset: Blandford Press, 1983. This book and its companion (see below) have general accounts of the war and two color plates each to illustrate American uniforms.

Urwin, Gregory J. W. *The United States Infantry: An Illustrated History 1775-1918.* London, New York, Sydney: Blandford Press, 1988.

Vaughan, Ron. "The Buena Vista Campaign" *The Courier.* 9, no. 4 (1990): 27-33.

Vaughan, Ron. "The Mexican Army" *The Courier.* 9, no. 6 (1991): 5-13.

Vaughan, Ron. "The Vera Cruz & Cerro Gordo Campaign-1847" *The Courier.* 55 (1991): 55-60.

Wallace, Edward S. *Destiny and Glory.* New York: Coward-McCann, 1957.

Warner, Ezra J. *Generals in Gray; Lives of the Confederate Commanders.* Baton Rouge & London: Louisiana State University Press, 1959.

Warner, Ezra J. *Generals in Blue; Lives of the Union Commanders.* Baton Rouge & London: Louisiana State University Press, 1964.

Waugh, John C. *The Class of 1846.* New York, NY: Warner Books, Inc., 1994. A well written account of the careers of the West Point graduates of 1846 during the Mexican war and beyond.

Webb, Walter Prescott. *The Texas Rangers: A Century of Frontier Defense.* Austin, TX: University of Texas Press, 1987.

Weber, David J. *The Mexican Frontier 1821-1846: The American Southwest under Mexico.* Albuquerque, NM: University of New Mexico Press, 1982.

Weems, John Edward. *To Conquer A Peace: The War between the United States and Mexico.* Garden City, NY: Doubleday & Co., Inc., 1974. An extensive account of the causes of the war and political as well as military events that resulted. This book concentrates on a central cast of characters and does a good job of telling their story.

Weigley, Russell F. *The American Way of War: A History of Unites States Military Strategy and Policy.* New York, NY: Macmillan Publishing Co., Inc., 1973.

Weigley, Russell F. *History of the United States Army.* enlarged edition. Bloomington, IN: Indiana University Press, 1984.

Wilcox, Cadmus M. *History of the Mexican War.* Washington, D.C.: The Church News Publishing Company, 1892. A very extensive account by one of the participants that includes many personal anecdotes and adventures along with a complete account of the war. Never re-printed but it deserves to be. Well worth a look.

Williams, T. Harry. *With Beauregard in Mexico; The Mexican War Reminiscences of P.G.T. Beauregard.* New York: Da Capo Press, 1969.

Wynn, Dennis J. *The San Patricio Soldiers: Mexico's Foreign Legion.* Texas Western Press, University of Texas at El Paso, 1984.